FIRE ON THE WATER

The USS Kearsarge *and the CSS* Alabama

By

James Gindlesperger

BURD STREET PRESS

SHIPPENSBURG, PENNSYLVANIA

This Burd Street Press publication
was printed by
Beidel Printing House, Inc.
63 West Burd Street
Shippensburg, PA 17257-0708 USA

The acid-free paper used in this book meets the guidelines for permanence and durability of the Committee on Production Guidelines for Book Longevity of the Council on Library Resources.

For a complete list of available publications
please write
Burd Street Press
Division of White Mane Publishing Company, Inc.
P.O. Box 708
Shippensburg, PA 17257-0708 USA

Library of Congress Cataloging-in-Publication Data

Gindlesperger, James, 1941-
    Fire on the water : the USS Kearsarge and the CSS Alabama / by James Gindlesperger.
    p. cm.
Includes bibliographical references and index.
ISBN 1-57249-378-X (alk. paper)
    1. Kearsarge (Sloop) 2. Alabama (Screw sloop) 3. United States--History--Civil War, 1861-1865--Naval operations. 4. Naval battles--France--Atlantic Coast--History--19th century. 5. Merchant ships--United States--Registers. 6. Sailors--Confederate States of America--Registers. 7. Sailors--United States--Registers. I. Title.

E595.K2G56 2004
973.7'5--dc21

                                                              2003048173

To those who go to sea in defense of their country

"Eternal Father, Strong to Save" (The Navy Hymn)

Eternal Father, strong to save,
Whose arm hath bound the restless wave,
Who bidd'st the mighty ocean deep
Its own appointed limits keep;
Oh, hear us when we cry to Thee,
For those in peril on the sea!

CONTENTS

List of Illustrations and Maps vii

Acknowledgments ix

Introduction xi

Chapter 1: The *Alabama* (June 1861–January 1862) 1

Chapter 2: The *Kearsarge* (June 1861–January 1862) 8

Chapter 3: The *Alabama* Sets Sail (January–June 1862) 21

Chapter 4: The Early Cruise of the *Kearsarge* (February–
August 1862); The Outfitting of the *Alabama* (July–
August 1862) 35

Chapter 5: September 1862
The *Alabama* 48
The *Kearsarge* 58

Chapter 6: October 1862
The *Alabama* 67
The *Kearsarge* 80

Chapter 7: November–December 1862
The *Alabama* 84
The *Kearsarge* 97

Chapter 8: January–February 1863
The *Alabama* 101
The *Kearsarge* 111

Chapter 9: March–April 1863
The *Alabama* 114
The *Kearsarge* 120

Chapter 10: May–June 1863
The *Alabama* 133
The *Kearsarge* 141
Chapter 11: July–August 1863
The *Alabama* 144
The *Kearsarge* 154
Chapter 12: September–October 1863
The *Alabama* 159
The *Kearsarge* 166
Chapter 13: November–December 1863
The *Alabama* 170
The *Kearsarge* 179
Chapter 14: January–February 1864
The *Alabama* 185
The *Kearsarge* 189
Chapter 15: March–April 1864
The *Alabama* 196
The *Kearsarge* 202
Chapter 16: May 1–June 18, 1864
Preparation for Battle 208
Chapter 17: The Battle 223
Chapter 18: The Rescue 238
Epilogue 254
Appendix A: Ships Captured or Detained by the *Alabama* 273
Appendix B: Officers and Crew of the *Alabama* 281
Appendix C: Officers and Crew of the *Kearsarge* 287
Notes 294
Bibliography 310
Index 316

ILLUSTRATIONS & MAPS

Photos, following page 126:

Raphael Semmes and John Winslow 127

Stephen Mallory and Gideon Welles 128

The *Alabama* 129

The *Kearsarge* 130

The *Alabama* sinks the *Hatteras* 131

The *Alabama* captures the *Ariel* 131

Kearsarge inspection of crew 132

Sunday services on the deck of the *Kearsarge* 132

Photos, following page 245:

The officers of the *Kearsarge* 246

Plate rescued from wreck of *Kearsarge*, engraved
with date of battle 246

Two interpretations of the battle 247

CSN buttons worn by Raphael Semmes 248

A piece of an oar from an *Alabama* lifeboat 248

The *Deerhound* 249

The *Alabama* burning the *Brilliant* 249

Semmes and his officers from the *Sumter* 250

Winslow and his officers after the battle 250

The engine room gong from the *Kearsarge* 251

Engine register from the *Kearsarge* 251

The gun that sank the *Alabama* 252

Kearsarge ship's company 252

Unexploded shell in sternpost of the *Kearsarge* 253

Maps:

The Cruise of the *Alabama* xvi

The Battle 231

Acknowledgments

Anyone who has done any research or writing will agree that having a supportive family and circle of friends lightens the burden beyond imagination. I have been encouraged and supported in my efforts throughout the process of bringing this work to fruition, and I must publicly thank my wife, my children, other relatives, and those friends who have offered words of encouragement from the very beginning. A special thank you goes to my son, Mike, who located many of the sources at the United States Naval Academy which I used to create this story. He saved me countless hours of work.

Employees at the Naval Academy must be acknowledged, for they too made my job much easier than it could have been. The personnel at the Nimitz Library never failed to cheerfully assist when asked, and even though it seemed as if I encountered a different person every time I visited, every one of them was pleasant, helpful, and eager to please. Archivist Gary LaValley and his staff in Special Collections were especially helpful.

Jim Cheevers and the staff in the Naval Academy's Preble Museum were extremely accommodating, and they provided much insight into the artifacts on display. I would be remiss if I did not let them know of my appreciation.

I must also thank my employer, Carnegie Mellon University, for allowing me the flexibility to travel and perform the necessary research. Also, Carnegie Mellon's outstanding interlibrary loan department, and especially Geri Kruglak, never failed to be helpful and supportive. Time after time I thought I had given Geri an impossible source to locate, only to have her prove me wrong. The slightest bit of information was all she needed, and within a few days I would receive word from her that my information was ready.

As always, the staffs at the National Archives and the Library of Congress went out of their ways to accommodate my requests for information. I'm sure that dealing with the public on a daily basis has to be frustrating at times, but they never let it show.

To the Navy Office of Information, the United States Army Military History Institute, the Washington Navy Yard, the Naval Historical Center's Ships History Branch, and Westminster John Knox Press go special words of appreciation. Their invaluable assistance must be publicly recognized. Likewise, I must thank Maurice Rigby for his assistance with verifying the names of certain CSS *Alabama* crew members.

Without the help of the University of Alabama and, more specifically, the William Stanley Hoole Special Collections Library, many of the sources used in putting this story together would never have been located. The university's generosity in placing much of their collection online was immensely helpful, and I am indebted to them for that effort. Such rare and valuable documents could never have been accessed otherwise.

To my publisher, Harold Collier, and my editors, Alexis Handerahan and Marianne Zinn, go my heartfelt thanks and appreciation for their guidance and patience throughout this project.

Finally, to those friends and loyal readers of my previous books who kept tabs on the progress of this work, your words of support and encouragement meant more than you'll ever know. Thank you so much. At last I can tell you: here it is! I hope you find it was worth the wait.

INTRODUCTION

When the average American thinks of the Civil War, if he thinks about it at all, he usually thinks of land battles. Gettysburg, Antietam, and Shiloh come to mind. If pressed to talk about the role of the navies in the war, most will shrug their shoulders, mumble something about the blockade, and try to change the subject.

While the roles of the navies may not be well known to the casual observer of the Civil War, those roles were important, nonetheless. Many significant advances in naval warfare were developed during the Civil War, including the use of steam power, armor plating for protection, and the first submarine. Such advances were not lost on observers of the day, as revealed by this comment that appeared in the *New York Times*: "It is evident that the world is at the commencement of a new era in naval warfare, in consequence of the introduction of steam as a propelling power for ships, and its application by the chief maritime nations to vessels of war."[1]

As war clouds gathered, the rhetoric also became more heated. Newspapers became propaganda tools on both sides of the ocean. Shortly after Fort Sumter was fired on, the *New York Times* reluctantly agreed that many English newspapers showed support for the Union but railed against the British press nonetheless: "There is no evidence, from the latest advice, which we give elsewhere, that they have been touched with any effectual saving grace; their spirit is just as contemptible, their morality just as low as ever . . ."[2]

It became apparent that the war would not end soon. It would spread from land battles to those fought on the rivers and oceans. In the early stages of the war, the Confederate States of America could fight on the rivers, but she had virtually no seagoing navy, nor did she have the industrial base to build one. There were no shipyards in the Southern states to speak of, or machine shops. Raw materials, except for timber, were in short supply. If the Confederacy was to be able to fight effectively on the seas, it quickly became apparent that it would be necessary to devise a naval strategy that would neutralize the superiority of the Union's navy.

The Confederacy turned to a time-honored system that had proven effective in the past for nations with little or no naval power who found themselves fighting against an established navy: commerce raiding. The United States had used such a tactic against Britain during the Revolutionary War, and the Confederacy reasoned that a similar strategy would work again, this time for the fledgling government.

The commerce-raiding strategy eventually expanded to a three-phased plan. The first phase concentrated on creating so many problems for Union shipping that President Abraham Lincoln would be forced by popular opinion to negotiate a peaceful end to the war or risk economic chaos in the North. The second part sought to inflict havoc on the high seas and force the Union navy to take ships away from the blockade in order to chase down the offending Confederate vessels and open Southern ports for commerce. Finally, the South hoped to prevent, or at least curtail, the ability of the North to import goods that could aid or prolong the war effort.

To raid enemy commerce, however, required ships, and the Confederacy owned none that could be counted on to be effective against Northern shipping. Privateers could be employed, but most had already deduced that there was far more money to be made by running the Union blockade. Commerce raiding was secondary, leading the Confederacy to seek a more reliable tactic.

The chosen method involved commissioned warships that were built elsewhere and purchased by the Confederacy. The commissioned ships would have to be among the world's fastest if they were to be expected to overhaul the speedy Union clippers. They would also have to be highly maneuverable for the inevitable encounters with Union gunboats.

Confederate Secretary of War Stephen R. Mallory believed that only one country could build ships that met such stringent requirements: England. However, the Foreign Enlistment Act contained a multitude of clauses that had been included to prevent England from doing anything that would show partiality to either belligerent. British subjects were not allowed to enlist on any belligerent vessels, removing, at least in the legal sense, any possibility of obtaining a crew in England. Also, neither the Union nor the Confederacy could bring any captured ships, or prizes, into a neutral port. The clause that appeared to be most prohibitive to Mallory's plan forbade the fitting out of any armed ships for either side. The penalty for noncompliance was a hefty fine, imprisonment, and seizure of the offending vessel.

British shipbuilders quickly spotted a loophole in this portion of the act, which said nothing about building and fitting out an unarmed vessel for a neutral country, or even an individual. The argument defending this action was that the crime was the actual equipping of warships, not their construction.[3] Confederate agents quickly used this flaw in the act to their advantage.

In April 1861, Mallory sent James D. Bulloch to Europe with the singular mission of directing the organization and operations of the fledgling navy. His directive was to procure the ships that would eventually comprise the heart of the Confederate navy. His options were to purchase existing ships or construct new ones, but whichever approach he used he had to disguise or omit any apparatus that could be used in warfare. To divert any suspicion Bulloch was further instructed to obtain guns from one source, gun carriages from another, small arms from still another, and shot and shell from a fourth. Purchases of clothing, hammocks, and provisions were to be spread among several suppliers.[4]

Over the course of the war, the Confederate cruisers procured by Bulloch and others would capture or destroy more than 250 Union merchant vessels. The CSS *Alabama* alone accounted for approximately one of every four Union merchant ships lost.

When the *Alabama* struck out on her maiden voyage, her captain was Raphael Semmes, who by then had already taken 18 Union prizes as skipper of the *Sumter*. The *Alabama*'s cruise lasted about two years, during which time she created havoc for Union shipping. Her success caused a rapid escalation of maritime insurance rates, making it financially difficult for many Union shippers to continue operating. Others had little success in finding dependable ships after their owners grew reluctant to risk their destruction at the hands of Semmes and his crew. On those increasingly rare occasions when ships were to be found, the shippers were often unable to sign up a full crew, either because most of the able-bodied men had already gone off to war or because those who remained available were less than anxious to go off to fight others who were now being referred to as pirates in the Northern press. Hundreds of Union ships changed their registries, reasoning (incorrectly) that they would not be taken as prizes if they sailed under another country's flag.

Destruction of the *Alabama* became a top priority for Union officials, and at one point in the war, some two dozen Union ships were committed to tracking down and sinking the *Alabama*.

The USS *Kearsarge*, captained first by Charles Pickering and later by John Winslow, chased the *Alabama* around the world. The two finally met in an epic battle off the coast of France.

The following pages represent the chase and the ultimate struggle. The problems each ship encountered along the way are also chronicled, as are the daily routines of the men who comprised the crews. The events are presented exactly as they were recorded by the men who lived them. As often as possible, conversations were taken verbatim from personal accounts. No attempt is made to depict one crew or the other as the hero or villain. No judgments are made. That is left to the reader, if he so desires.

A writing style has been chosen that will best bring these men and their ships back to life one more time. They may only live in the imagination of you, the reader, but for the few hours it takes to read this work, their lives and exploits will become real once more.

Now, as you prepare to read this exciting story, allow your mind to drift back to the 1860s. Become a part of the scene. Sign on with a crew and feel the salt spray in your face, smell the pungent odor of gunpowder, and hear the sails ripple in the wind. Experience the exhilaration of the *Alabama*'s crew as another prize is burned, and the frustration of the men of the *Kearsarge* as they learn they have missed crossing the *Alabama*'s wake by less than a day.

Whichever ship you find yourself identifying with, remember that both crews were filled with brave men. Remember, and while you read, become one of them.

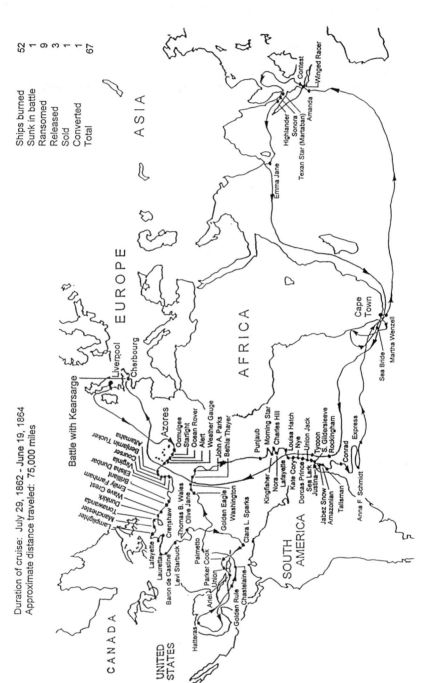

Duration of cruise: July 29, 1862 – June 19, 1864
Approximate distance traveled: 75,000 miles

Ships burned	52
Sunk in battle	1
Ransomed	9
Released	3
Sold	1
Converted	1
Total	67

The Cruise of the *Alabama*
(not to scale)

CHAPTER ONE

THE *ALABAMA* (JUNE 1861–JANUARY 1862)

James Dunwoody Bulloch carried the weight of a new nation on his shoulders. The success or failure of the Confederate navy, and perhaps the entire Confederacy, rested solely on his ability to build and equip a navy that was capable of destroying the enemy's commercial shipping fleet while avoiding destruction itself. That alone was not an easy task. Doing it within the restrictive edicts of the Foreign Enlistment Act made it a formidable task indeed.

To add to his challenge, the enemy knew what he was up to. Unfriendly eyes followed his every move throughout the streets of Liverpool. He was sure he was being followed on many of his visits to Liverpool's docks along the Mersey River, and since his arrival in England a few months earlier his mail had been rifled, strange messages had been sent to him, and his life had been threatened.

He trusted none and suspected all. From the fishmongers plying their trade on the dock to the street urchins who would steal from the devil himself, given the opportunity, he truly believed that any of these could be Yankee spies, each one waiting for him to make just one crucial mistake.

Confederate Secretary of War Stephen Russell Mallory had given him the heady responsibility of building the navy, and Bulloch was determined to show Mallory that he had chosen the right man. As the official agent for the Confederate States of America he had been charged with a singular mission by Secretary of War Mallory: "Get us some ships. Buy them, build them, or whatever you find necessary, but get us some ships!" Specifically, Mallory wanted six steam propeller ships, and the Confederate Congress had appropriated $1 million for that purpose.[1]

He was not the only agent in England; there were also many representing the Union, and Bulloch was sure they had been responsible for his missing mail and the death threats. He had been known as an agent before he even arrived in England, with Union newspapers detailing his departure, his mission, even the amount of money he had at his disposal.[2] It hadn't taken him long to realize that the Union spies were just as good at their jobs as he hoped he was at his, and he had vowed never to underestimate them. While the Confederacy had many sympathizers in Liverpool, he had quickly learned to assume nothing.

Bulloch had already been successful in arranging for ships to be built, and he had purchased others. The Confederate navy, however, was still far too small to have much effect on the Union. More ships would be needed, many more, and it was in that capacity that he had begun to spend his days at the Liverpool docks.

Bulloch had served in the United States Navy from the time he was a lad of 16, serving under two of the greatest naval commanders ever, David Glasgow Farragut and David Dixon Porter. He had even been a commander of a merchant ship himself. Bulloch had been selected for his job for a singular reason: he knew ships!

And well he should. Serving in the navy until he was 30 years old, he had resigned to become a captain with the Mail Steamship Company. In this role he had, of necessity, learned the world's shipping lanes, the ins and outs of maritime commerce in general, and the details of naval armament in particular.[3]

A native of Georgia, his sympathies had remained with his native state when the war began. After careful consideration he had offered his services to the fledgling Confederate government, which quickly accepted.

At the time, Bulloch was in command of the SS *Bienville*, a United States mail steamer, and many Confederate officials had badgered him to seize the ship. After all, they argued persuasively, it could be converted into one more badly needed ship of war. Bulloch, however, felt that it was only right to return her to New York, her home port. Fortunately for Bulloch, Jefferson Davis had agreed and the pressure had subsided as quickly as it had begun.

He had cruised around the world, survived a shipwreck, and had proven to be an able scholar, finishing second in his class at the naval school in Philadelphia in 1845. He had agreed to this assignment in Europe on the condition that he be awarded the command of one of the ships that he would ultimately have built. Mallory had agreed.[4]

His trip to Europe had been less than direct, having taken the train from Montgomery to Louisville and Detroit, where he crossed into Canada. Once in Canada he had taken the Grand Trunk Railway to Montreal, where he had boarded the Allen Line steamer *North American*, bound for Liverpool.[5] By the time he had arrived, Queen Victoria had made his job all the more difficult by issuing a proclamation of neutrality. A neutral country would never knowingly build a fighting ship for a belligerent party.

Back in the United States, newspapers in the North had protested the queen's proclamation. The *New York Times* took the position that by publicly stating her country's neutrality, Queen Victoria was actually implying that England was recognizing two separate governments in the United States.[6] When France's Secretary of Foreign Affairs, M. Edouard Antoine Thouvenel, issued orders to French officials in the insurgent states to remain neutral, the *Times* blasted the French as well, saying that "We submit that international discourtesy could take no more offensive form." The *Times* went on to complain that the French government had ". . . official knowledge of only one power within the territorial bounds of the Union, and that is the Government of the United States."[7]

While the Union's newspapers railed against the European powers, Bulloch had been able to skirt the neutrality proclamation by acting on his own behalf, rather than as an agent for a belligerent. The British had no laws prohibiting the sale of a ship to an individual, no matter what country he came from, and Bulloch was learning to use that loophole to his advantage. His first contract had been with William C. Miller and Sons of Liverpool, and the ship they supplied him would be registered as the *Oreto*, an Italian vessel, to avoid any suspicion. She was to be re-christened the *Florida* once in international waters.[8] Now nearing completion, it would not be long before she would be searching the world's trade routes for Union merchant ships. Bulloch was determined that she would soon have company.

Once in England, Bulloch had gone out of his way to avoid violating the British Foreign Enlistment Act, which forbade British citizens from equipping, arming, or recruiting ships of war for either the Union or the Confederacy. He had even gone to the trouble of enlisting the aid of F. S. Hull, a prominent attorney in Liverpool, to keep him abreast of any changes in the act. All finances had been set up through Fraser, Trenholm and Company, a local business house.[9] If by chance he did slip up, the trail back to the Confederacy would not be an easy one to follow.

Bulloch was fully aware that England's sympathies varied from person to person, town to town, and newspaper to newspaper. He was not even sure if certain newspapers believed the same way two days in a row. For the most part, however, it seemed apparent to him that trusted friends in England would be few. Within the space of two weeks he had read such unfriendly remarks as "We cannot recognize the South"[10] and "The American President, when he heard that a collision had occurred between the Southerners and the forces of the Union, could not possibly have remained quiescent."[11] Still another had written, "The Government of Washington acts completely within the bounds of prudence as well as right, in making the military preparations, which it announces. We are glad it has taken this course."[12] If he expected to find only friends in England, he quickly changed his mind.

Bulloch spent much of his time around the docks observing and listening. Asking questions in a casual manner that would not lead anyone to suspect his real motives, he quickly learned that one shipbuilder stood above all others in the city. John Laird and Sons had gained the well-earned reputation of constructing some of the finest ships built anywhere in the world, and Bulloch turned to them to build the first of many ships they would furnish the Confederate navy.

Bulloch had met the elder John Laird before, although Laird was retired and no longer an active part of the business. Now a member of the British Parliament,[13] John still checked in with his sons, William and John, Jr., on a regular basis, just to ensure that they were not cutting corners. Bulloch also casually knew the two younger men, although certainly not as well as he knew John, Sr. He would come to know them much better over the ensuing months.

The Lairds had been in business since 1829. It is unlikely they had ever had a customer who placed demands and restrictions on them such as those imposed by Bulloch. Ever mindful of the Foreign Enlistment Act, Bulloch insisted on secrecy from the start. He told the Lairds that he was to be the sole owner of the new vessel, and if they suspected that their ships were being build for a belligerent nation, there is no record of their giving voice to those suspicions. Those who knew not only quality workmanship, but also the ability to maintain discretion, had recommended the Lairds to Bulloch. Both would be vitally important on this project.

Although the Lairds, as well as other shipbuilders, were beginning to build their ships of iron, Bulloch insisted that his first ship be constructed solely of wood. When the Laird brothers questioned the wisdom of building a ship of wood, Bulloch gave them his prepared answer, telling them that he intended to use his new vessel on a cruise around the world, and that he would, no doubt, be entering ports where they may not have the knowledge or means of making repairs to iron. He reasoned that anyone could repair a wooden ship, and his story convinced the Lairds.

The real reason for Bulloch's insistence on wooden construction lay in his belief that wood decks would be of sufficient strength and better able to accommodate the weight of large guns without adding any unnecessary weight. With the vessel's speed one of the most important factors to be considered, he didn't wish to do anything that could impair it even by a fraction of a knot. Of course, to even discuss that with the Lairds could be construed as violating the Foreign Enlistment Act and jeopardize the entire project.

When Bulloch first visited the Laird dock he already had the preliminary design prepared. The ship would be a bark-rigged steamer with two engines and the capacity to carry 350 tons of coal. The keel was to be two hundred eleven feet, six inches and her overall length two hundred twenty feet, with a beam of thirty-one feet, eight inches.

Bulloch also had a plan for a lifting apparatus for the screw, a mechanism capable of lifting the screw out of the water when the ship was under sail. The screw wouldn't be needed while the ship was sailing, and when left in place it would do nothing but provide drag and reduce the sailing speed. The final design for this mechanism was left to Fawcett, Preston and Company.

Most sailing steamers cruised under sail as much as possible to conserve coal. However, the ability of the Confederacy's ships to minimize the use of coal was even more important than it normally would be, for a reason that Bulloch could not reveal. One of the provisions of the neutrality laws was that belligerent vessels could only replenish their coal bunkers in a neutral port every three months, and with the possibility of more nations declaring neutrality, the number of available ports could be reduced drastically. Entering ports to recoal could also reveal the ship's location to enemy cruisers.

Bulloch also asked for a double suit of sails and the usual equipment for an East Indian voyage, requesting sufficient spare blocks, hawsers, and running gear for a full year. A condenser with a cooling tank would supply fresh water. The ship's bridge was placed in the center of the vessel, just before the funnel, and there were to be five boats: a cutter and a launch situated amidships, a gig and a whaleboat between the main and the mizzenmasts, and a dinghy astern.

There would be port steerage for the engineers, starboard for the midshipmen. A berth deck, sized for 120 men, completed the living arrangements.[14]

No mention was made of equipping the new ship with guns. Bulloch intended to do that later, after the ship had departed from England's waters. At this stage he simply wanted to establish the basic design. He and his government believed they were within the intent of the neutrality laws as long as the ships were not outfitted while in a neutral port.[15]

The agreed upon price was £47,500, to be paid in five equal payments of £9,500.* The first payment was due when Bulloch and the Lairds

---

* At the 1861 exchange rate, about $229,900 in equal payments of $45,980.[16]

signed the contract. The second payment was scheduled to be paid when the frame was up; the next payment when the upper- and lower-deck shelves were in place and the beams were in. The fourth payment came due when the ship was launched, with the final payment due when the vessel was successfully tried.[17]

The contract also called for shot racks to be fitted around the hatches and decks, as may be needed, and three shell rooms and a magazine.[18] Despite this, the Lairds never commented on such unusual accommodations for a merchant ship. Perhaps they really chose not to know any more than would be necessary to build the vessel. The elder John Laird already suspected Bulloch's ship was to become a ship of war but he never asked for confirmation, and Bulloch never offered any. Years after the war was over, Laird told Bulloch that he appreciated the Confederate agent's secrecy. Laird only knew what the general public knew, and he never had to fear being caught in an embarrassing lie on the floor of Parliament.[19]

The ship was to be known as the *290*, a name selected by the Lairds. The name *290* would eventually give rise to much speculation in the Northern states. One of the most popular theories offered would be that 290 wealthy Englishmen had raised the cash to finance her construction.[20] This, of course, would have been a violation of neutrality laws, and, although untrue, the story provided fodder for outcries against the British government for not doing more to stop the construction of what the Northern press would refer to as "pirate ships."

The real reason for the name was far less sinister. The ship that Bulloch had signed for simply happened to be the 290th ship built by John Laird and Sons, and the numerical name was the standard designation given to every Laird ship as it was being built. It would be up to Bulloch to give the ship a more permanent name.

CHAPTER TWO

THE *KEARSARGE* (JUNE 1861–JANUARY 1862)

While the Union held a marked superiority over the Confederacy in naval power at the war's beginning, the Federal navy was still of no size to carry on a war on the world's oceans. To enlarge the navy, Union Secretary of the Navy Gideon Welles had ordered the construction of several dozen gunboats. Welles, along with many other Union officials, believed that a successful blockade could quickly end the war and bring the rebellious states back into the fold. Most of the new ships ordered by Welles were destined to become part of the Union blockade.

Several of these vessels were under construction even as Bulloch was supervising the construction of the *290*. In the summer of 1861 one such ship was taking shape at the Portsmouth Navy Yard. Situated on an island in the Piscataqua River on the border of New Hampshire and Maine, Portsmouth was alive with activity. Not only were new ships being built, but old ships of all sizes and shapes were being refitted to be pressed into service as naval vessels.

One of those new ships, under the supervision of Isaiah Hanscom, was already behind schedule. With two main boilers plus an auxiliary, she was to be remarkably similar to the *290* in size and speed.[1] She was to be christened the USS *Kearsarge*.

By the fall of 1861, the *Kearsarge* had her bottom sheathed in copper. Although much of her work above the water line remained to be completed, she was floated, nonetheless, freeing up badly needed dry dock space. Once out of dry dock, the work on the *Kearsarge* resumed, with hundreds of shipfitters, carpenters, and assorted other craftsmen swarming over her every day.

To command this new vessel, Welles selected Charles W. Pickering, who had been a sailing man all his life. In fact, Pickering's experience extended back 39 years, when he had entered the navy as a midshipman at the age of six![2] Pickering had reported to Captain George F. Pearson, the commandant, who had given Pickering his crew quotas. With the *Kearsarge* still under construction, Pickering began handpicking his officers. He wanted them to become familiar with their new ship as quickly as possible. William H. Cushman would be his chief engineer, James Whittaker the first assistant engineer. William H. Badlam signed on as second assistant engineer. An initial crew size of 31 was approved. To fill the crew, advertisements were placed in area newspapers.[3] The response was less than overwhelming.

The navy of 1861 offered little in the way of excitement or glory. The army was another story. With patriotism at a fever pitch, a young man joining the army could be almost certain to have an opportunity to fight the rebels. On the other hand, joining the navy was looked down upon by many young men of service age, with the attitude that joining the navy would offer them little chance for adventure. Even if they were lucky, the most they could reasonably hope for was to guard a port and maybe chase some blockade runner back out to sea. As a result, the early months of the war found army recruiting stations overflowing, while those responsible for filling naval crews found themselves forced to resort to tactics which, to be kind, could often best be referred to as somewhat less than ethical. Further, many of those who might be tempted to sign on with a Federal gunboat had already signed on with the crews of merchant ships, cutting into the available supply of potential crew members still further.

By early December 1861 the *Kearsarge*'s engines had been received from their manufacturer, the Hartford foundry of Woodruff and

Beach,[4] and had been installed and tested. Cushman, as chief engineer, had supervised their installation and initial operation. The tests were generally successful.

A few weeks later, armed with a fresh authorization from Welles to expand the size of the crew,[5] Cushman had taken to the streets in an attempt to sign on some new recruits. The earlier advertisements had seen limited success, and he still needed about twice as many men as he had. Late in the afternoon of January 24, 1862, he returned leading a ragtag band of some 81 new crew members.

He had found them in and around the Charlestown Navy Yard, and their general appearance told Pickering that many of them might not be so eager to sign on once they sobered up.

Pickering knew that little good would be gained by challenging his chief engineer's selections. Without a crew, even the best ship in the world would be forced to sit in port. Nothing else had worked, and Cushman had brought back an adequate number of warm bodies to give him a crew of sufficient size to set sail. After all, they would probably never be called on to fire a gun in anger, so how good would they have to be to sit in a harbor and look menacing to would-be blockade runners?

The *Kearsarge* was certainly in no condition to put to sea yet, with her decks littered with construction debris, builders working their ways through the new recruits even as Pickering was still looking them over, and supplies still lying in nondescript piles on the dock. Perhaps he could whip them into some semblance of a crew by the time the *Kearsarge* was ready to weigh anchor. Probably overflowing with reservations, Pickering decided to make the most of it.

He took a position on top of a nearby barrel and gave a brief speech. After introducing himself as the ship's commander, he mentioned that the crew may not begin to receive any pay until the ship was actually under sail, although that was still an uncertainty. Word was still awaited from Washington, and Pickering made a point of emphasizing that so there would be no questions later.

Pickering then ordered the colors hoisted, and as the bleary-eyed recruits watched the Stars and Stripes unfurl in the biting January wind, Pickering said, "I hereby commission this ship the USS *Kearsarge*!"[6]

For the next several days the crew busied themselves by stowing supplies and shoveling coal into the bunkers. One of their number, however, was no longer present to render his assistance. On January 28, 1862, Landsman John Coalter had the dubious distinction of becoming the first member of the *Kearsarge*'s crew to desert. There would be more to come over the next few years, many more. The crew would be depleted still further over the next few days, as Peter Mulhall, a marine, and Seaman Andrew Tupic were sent to the hospital, and Coal Handler Richard Vincent deserted.[7]

Most of the armament was now in position, with two huge 11-inch Dahlgren guns, a 28-pounder rifle, and four 32-pound smoothbores garnering a great deal of attention from the men in their spare time.

On February 5, 1862, the ship was deemed seaworthy. A pilot came on board to guide her out of the harbor, and with a crowd of several thousand cheering onlookers, the *Kearsarge* slowly got under way.[8] As she passed Fort Constitution, the fort's gunners fired a cannon salute.[9] Within a few hours, she was on the open seas. A sleek beauty, she had cost her government the grand sum of $272,514.99 to build.[10]

Pickering's original orders had been to take the *Kearsarge* to the Gulf of Mexico for blockade duty. However, Gideon Welles had received word that the *Sumter*, a Confederate cruiser which had been responsible for the sinking of several United States merchant ships, may be in the Azores. Hoping that the *Kearsarge* may be able to find her, he had revised Pickering's orders accordingly.[11]

Within the first 48 hours of the cruise, the barometer dropped precipitously from 31.70 inches to 29.44 inches.[12] The storm hit them the second day out, and the new vessel tossed from side to side, often listing so badly that it seemed as if the waves were above the yardarms. The roar of the storm discouraged any attempt on the part of the officers to shout orders. Many of the crew cursed their luck as loudly as they could, perhaps hoping that their anger would calm the violent winds. Others, however, were unable to give voice to their complaints. In the sailors' vernacular of the time, they were busy paying tribute to Neptune. In less colorful terms, they were losing their lunch.

Fighting feverishly, those crew members who were not too seasick rushed headlong to lash down everything they could grasp. Instinctively ducking their heads as each new wave crashed into them, they vowed to fight the elements with every ounce of strength they could muster. The *Kearsarge* rose to the crest of a wave, only to quickly descend into a trough where a crewman, looking in any direction, saw nothing but water around and above him. The helpless ship rolled and tossed wherever the storm chose to throw her.

Someone shouted that the launch was about to be lost. Several men worked their ways hand over hand along the ice-encrusted rail to the tiny boat, which by now was being slammed violently against the rail with each rolling motion of the ship. It was only a matter of time before it would go the way of the already lost dinghy and cutter unless the brave souls, struggling to bring her onto the deck, could somehow be success-ful. A seaman lost his grip as the launch swung away from the ship once again, and only the quick reaction of a fellow crew member, who grabbed his leg as he slid past on the icy deck, prevented him from being lost overboard.

With the ship tossing completely out of control, the desperate men lashed themselves to anything that looked like it wouldn't float away. The howl of the storm drowned out the prayers of those who called upon a higher source of help. By now only a few had not succumbed to seasickness.

For nearly seven days the *Kearsarge* fought the stormy sea. With nearly every crew member seasick, including Captain Pickering, nobody had the luxury of skipping his turn at watch. One after another, seasick crewmen stumbled to their stations, counting the minutes until their four-hour turn was complete. The main topic of conversation was not where they were headed, but whether the ship would sink or not. Few believed it wouldn't.

Several days into the storm the head was blown away. Water found its way into the powder magazine, and even the captain's cabin did not escape the wrath of the storm's fury. Pickering had to don boots to move around his quarters.

Chief Engineer Cushman reported that the waves washing over the side were putting the fires out. Finally, in a fit of desperation, he ordered the hatches battened down to keep the water out, eliminating all air circulation in the engine room. Those working in that part of the ship suffered from the extreme heat while their shipmates on deck tried everything they could think of to keep warm in their constantly soaked clothing. The lack of air took a toll on the engines as well, and Cushman was forced to shut down the engines to allow them to cool. With no engines, the ship had no power at all with which to fight the storm. They were restarted as soon as they had cooled enough, and the deck officer headed the ship into the storm.

Finally, after several days, the winds calmed ever so slightly, and the seas didn't toss quite as much. Pickering, seeing the ebbing of the storm, ordered the call that nearly all seamen of the time loved to hear: "All hands, splice the main brace!" This call signaled the permission to have a drink, and instantly, all crew members lined up at the grog tub, including those who still were fighting the ravages of seasickness.[13]

As if to test the resolve of the men of the *Kearsarge*, the storm picked up once again less than a day later. Unbelievably, this storm proved to be worse than the first, and the crew was ordered aft to avoid being washed overboard.[14]

Then, one of the seamen reported an even more serious problem to the deck officer: two of the fresh-water tanks had begun to leak. Fresh water was flowing freely into the bilge, and he noted that even with the bilge being pumped they were having trouble staying ahead of it. The decision was made to pump what was left in the leaking tanks into the good tanks, hoping they could at least salvage what was left until the leaks were patched. The leaking tanks were seen as a bad omen. A new ship, and already she was developing leaks, and the news was about to get worse.

What the deck officer did not know was that the water in the leaking tanks had already been contaminated with seawater from the bilge, and by pumping the contents into the remaining tanks, all the water was now contaminated. There were now less than two gallons of fresh water for each man on board the *Kearsarge*; two gallons each for drinking, bathing, and cooking. This new crisis was even more serious than the seemingly constant battering from the storms of the past several days.[15]

Pickering gathered his officers to discuss the situation. The storm had pushed them so far off course that it would be folly to sail for the Azores to look for the *Sumter* without fresh water. The decision was made to head for the nearest landfall, the island of Madeira, off the coast of Africa. En route, the elements took one last punch at the luckless crew, with a third storm hitting them just a few days later. This one, however, lasted only a day, and the crew paid it little heed after all they had been through.

As if to make up for all the rain that had fallen on the *Kearsarge* over the past two weeks, the sun now came out and drew the water from the decks. Small wisps of steam rose as the sun did its work. As the ship reached more tropical latitudes, the sun grew hotter, the decks became steamier, and the crew's thirst grew greater.

Finally, on February 22, 1862, the cry came down from the lookout, "Land, ho! Just off the starboard bow!"

Those on deck rushed to the rail, straining to catch sight of the first signs of land. Soon, those on the forecastle confirmed the lookout's report, and the crew members congratulated themselves for having survived the first leg of the journey.

* * *

The *Kearsarge* had only been anchored for a short time before the American consul came aboard. After the proper greetings had taken place the consul revealed his true reason for meeting with Pickering: the *Sumter* was anchored at Gibraltar. The *Kearsarge* was the closest ship to Gibraltar, and with the Confederate ship sitting at anchor it would be relatively easy to slip in and sink her.

The storms had taken their toll, however, and the *Kearsarge* was in no shape to engage in even a one-sided battle. An assessment had indicated that it would require at least five days to make even the most basic repairs. Pickering expressed his regrets, but he and his ship had been through too much in the past few weeks to take the risk.

For the next five days the crew busied themselves making repairs. Some caulked leaks, others worked on the engines, still others made the necessary repairs to the fresh-water tanks. The tanks were refilled, and coal bunkers were replenished. All the while, natives circled the *Kearsarge* in small bumboats, selling trinkets, fruits, brightly colored cloth, and anything else the crew seemed to have a fancy for. With none of the crew members having much money, tobacco and old clothing became the currency of choice.[16]

The anchor was hoisted, and within hours of putting to sea the *Kearsarge* was struck by another gale. This time, however, damage was minimal. Most of the crew became seasick again, and many of them must have wondered whether they would ever feel normal again.

Early the next morning, the first sail of the cruise was spotted. Excitement replaced the logy feeling that had been dogging those with seasickness. There would finally be some activity other than fighting the weather. This is what they had signed on for! The excitement was short-lived, however, as the sail belonged to an English merchant ship bound for Brazil. Another disappointment was in store the next day, as a promising sail turned out to belong to a Spanish bark.

That evening, following their meal and end-of-day chores, the crew gathered on deck for the evening's entertainment. Most evenings, George "Ham Fat" Williams, Pickering's personal cook, and his brother, Edward, were part of the program. The brothers were two of the 14 black crew members, and George particularly was well liked by the crew. Always humming, he also served as the ship's drummer. In his time on the *Kearsarge* he had gained a well-earned reputation as an excellent singer and dancer.

Another black crew member, Joachim Pease, was more introverted and rarely participated in the evening's entertainment. When he did, it was usually as a spectator. Because of his quiet nature he was not as well known to the other crew members as the Williams brothers, but before the cruise was over, every crew member would know who Joachim Pease was and how well he could fight.[17]

On March 4, 1862, the *Kearsarge*'s lookout spotted land. It wasn't long before the walled city of Cadiz, Spain, was visible off the bow. A pilot came out to meet them and escort them into the harbor, and within a short time the *Kearsarge* was at anchor.

Within an hour of anchoring, American Consul Ebenezer Eggleston boarded the *Kearsarge* to meet with Pickering. In full dress regalia, Eggleston informed Pickering that the *Sumter* had been in Cadiz, but was now in Gibraltar.

Pickering advised Eggleston that he was only planning to remain in port long enough to take on some coal, after which he would resume his search for the *Sumter*. In the course of the conversation Eggleston expressed his hope that Pickering could bring the *Sumter*'s captain back in irons. That captain was none other than Raphael Semmes, a name that was becoming synonymous with piracy in the North.

Not only would Pickering never fulfill Eggleston's wish, that "pirate" would continue to be a thorn in the side of Union shipping for some time to come.

While waiting for coal, Pickering set up the first gun drills for the crew. Since none of the men knew enough about the guns on the *Kearsarge* to fire them, the drill was a walk-through. The crew grumbled and complained as they were forced to repeat the maneuvers several times.

Pickering, recognizing the possibility of encountering the more experienced crew of the *Sumter* at any time, grew impatient with the repeated mistakes. A fight with the *Sumter* right now would prove disastrous to the Union ship.

As Franklin Graham and the other gunners gave instructions to their respective crews, the officers looked on with thinly disguised amusement. The gun crews were every bit as inept as the first impressions they had given.

On March 7, only partially recoaled, the *Kearsarge* set sail once more. There had been little coal available in Cadiz, but while Pickering would have preferred to take on a full load, he felt comfortable in the knowledge that he had been able to replenish at least a portion of what he needed.

The trip to Gibraltar was a short one, and as the *Kearsarge* entered the straits Pickering ordered another gun drill with live ammunition. The gunners patiently reviewed the procedure with their crews, reminding them of the proper sequence. Each crew had the opportunity to fire a few shots. For most, the roar was a new experience, and many of them spent the next several hours trying to clear the ringing from their ears. There was no target, and hence no need for aiming, but by the time the last round had been fired the crews were beginning to look like they might be able to hold their own if the chips were down.

By evening, the *Kearsarge* entered the harbor. The men gazed in awe at the Rock of Gibraltar off the port bow. Pickering ordered a signal rocket fired, to alert the *Tuscarora*, another Union ship that was believed to be in the harbor to blockade the *Sumter* and ensure that she didn't escape. The *Tuscarora* soon answered with rockets of her own, and the *Kearsarge* turned in the direction from which the rockets had been fired, eventually anchoring near the Union vessel. The arrival of the *Kearsarge* brought a visit from the port officer, who informed Pickering that the *Kearsarge* could only remain in port for 24 hours.[18]

The crew of the *Kearsarge* was on deck early the next morning, eager to get the day's chores done so they could go to where the *Sumter* was believed to be anchored. As soon as the morning cleaning was completed, the *Kearsarge* made way for the *Sumter*, anchored only a short distance away. Eager faces crowded the rails, straining for their first glimpse of the infamous "pirate" ship. Before long a battered-looking vessel flying the Confederate ensign appeared. The *Kearsarge* anchored some one hundred yards off her stern.

The crew gazed in amazement at the sight of the rebel ship, obviously in a bad state of repair and looking as if she could sink at any moment. Nearly two months in port had not improved her appearance any, and by now a large portion of her crew had deserted.

Inquisitive faces peered back from the *Sumter*, each crew seemingly intent on intimidating the other. As the *Kearsarge* watched, several members of the *Sumter*'s crew launched one of her boats and defiantly passed back and forth under the *Kearsarge*'s bow. It was as close as the two crews would get to a real encounter.

That evening the American consul from Tangier, James DeLong, who was visiting Gibraltar, came aboard the *Kearsarge* to dine with Pickering. As they ate, the conversation inevitably turned to the *Sumter* and her captain, Raphael Semmes. DeLong gleefully related a story to Pickering.

As the wine glasses were refilled, DeLong told how Semmes had sent two men, Henry Myers and Thomas Tunstall, to Cadiz to buy some coal for the *Sumter*. Myers was the *Sumter*'s paymaster and Tunstall had once been the American consul in Cadiz. They had traveled to Cadiz on a French ship, and DeLong had had both men arrested as soon as they stepped ashore. Morocco, the United States, and several other countries had signed a treaty allowing foreign consuls total jurisdiction over their own citizens, and DeLong took full advantage. Even though he had very little legal ground to stand on, he had them imprisoned at Fort Warren in Boston Harbor.[19]

A furious Semmes had insisted that both men were citizens of the Confederacy, not the United States, and that they should have been granted protection under the French flag since they were on a French ship.[20] The unimpressed DeLong had ignored every point Semmes had made, and Myers and Tunstall remained in prison.[*]

The next day the *Kearsarge* departed for Tangier. To show his support for DeLong in his diplomatic battle over Myers and Tunstall, Pickering ordered a nine-gun salute to the consul as the *Kearsarge* entered the harbor. Then, as a salute to Morocco, he offered up a 21-gun salute. On shore, the forts responded with a salute to the *Kearsarge* from their own guns.

As usual, the *Kearsarge* was quickly surrounded by native boats nearly as soon as she anchored, and the bartering soon was on in earnest. The following day, March 11, 1862, the *Kearsarge* departed for Algeciras, Spain.

Sadly, within hours the *Kearsarge* recorded her first death among the crew. Sabine DeSanto, a Portuguese who served as a steward for the ship's steerage officers, died of pneumonia even as his crew mates enjoyed their usual evening singing and dancing on deck. This strange juxtaposition of death amidst merriment was not unusual considering the medical techniques of the day. Crew members knew that even the slightest injury or illness could be exacerbated by the poor medical

---

[*] Although both men were still in prison at Fort Warren at the time, Myers would eventually be exchanged after a great deal of legal maneuvering. Tunstall, however, would remain in prison for 16 months, paroled only after promising to live outside the United States for the duration of the war.

attention they would receive, and DeSanto's death, although unexpected, was not particularly unique.

Surgeon John Browne was still thinking of DeSanto the next day when his steward, George Tittle, reported for duty. Tittle and Browne discussed DeSanto's death briefly, both knowing more would follow. The ship had been hit with a rash of ailments, and several of the crew were seriously ill with respiratory problems. Raspy coughs emanated from every part of the ship, no matter what the hour, and Browne felt helpless to do anything to relieve the suffering of those afflicted. Tittle himself was about to become a casualty of the crude medical procedures of the day.

As Browne and Tittle talked, the surgeon casually took Tittle's hand and turned it over to examine it. Several weeks earlier, Browne had performed a tonsillectomy on one of the crew. After the operation, Tittle was cleaning up when he had accidentally cut his forefinger on one of the scalpels that had been used in the surgery. An infection had set in, and Browne had been treating Tittle with little success. Tittle's entire hand had swollen badly, and Browne had already lanced it several times to drain fluid.

As Tittle gingerly held out his hand for the surgeon to examine, he kept his eyes on Browne, wondering what he was thinking. Browne obviously did not like the appearance of the hand. The injured finger had turned black, indicating that gangrene had set in.

Browne looked up at Tittle without saying anything, then returned his gaze back to the blackened flesh. Finally, he reluctantly reached the conclusion that the finger would have to be amputated.

Realizing he needed help that was beyond anything available on board the *Kearsarge*, Browne had the surgeon from the *Tuscarora* summoned. The two discussed Tittle's hand briefly, with the *Tuscarora*'s doctor agreeing with Browne's assessment. The operation was soon under way, with Tittle given chloroform to anesthetize him. At the first touch of the scalpel, however, Tittle withdrew his hand. A second dose of chloroform was administered, with similar results.

The two surgeons had never seen a man still able to react after two full doses of chloroform, and they feared a third dose could have fatal results. They made the decision to continue the operation, using several crew members to hold Tittle in place. With crew members holding each arm and leg, and several others draped across Tittle's torso, Browne and the *Tuscarora*'s doctor began the surgery. At the touch of the scalpel the partially sedated patient began to writhe in pain, and it took the full strength of every man in attendance to hold him down. Despite his attempts to struggle free, he was no match for those who were holding him, and within minutes the injured finger was removed.[21] None of those present saw anything unusual about the procedure.

CHAPTER THREE

THE *ALABAMA* SETS SAIL (JANUARY–JUNE 1862)

In early winter of 1861, at about the same time that the *Kearsarge* was trying to assemble a crew, Bulloch returned to Savannah by way of Bermuda. He booked passage on the *Fingal*, a blockade runner whose mission was to take on a load of Southern cotton and transport it to England. Bulloch was accompanied by Colonel Edward C. Anderson of the Confederate army, who had been in Europe arranging for the purchase of munitions. The second officer of the *Fingal* was John Low, an associate of Bulloch's. The cotton was to be used as partial payment for the ships which Bulloch and his compatriots were having built for the Confederacy. In Bulloch's absence, Lieutenant James H. North was the acting Confederate naval agent in England.

Unfortunately for Bulloch, not to mention the Confederate States of America, the blockade effectively prevented the *Fingal* from returning to England. What was originally intended to be a short trip for Bulloch turned into one of much longer duration, and Christmas found him still in Savannah.

Finally, his patience exhausted, Secretary of the Navy Stephen Mallory sent a message to Bulloch telling him to get to England any way that he could. The same message contained Bulloch's commission as a

21

commander, along with orders to take command of one of the cruisers being built in England when he arrived. At the same time Mallory appointed Low to the rank of master.

Mallory's plan called for Bulloch to assume command of a new ship nearing completion in England, a vessel named the *Oreto*. Bulloch had been instrumental in her construction and seemed a logical choice. North was scheduled to take the *290*.

Northern officials were rapidly growing suspicious of the *Oreto*, and several letters of protest had already been filed with the English government. Even though the English said they had investigated and found no violations of the British Foreign Enlistment Act, the Confederacy was anxious to get her to sea, fearing that she could be impounded at any time.[1] There could be no delays, and Bulloch, recognizing that his difficulty in getting back to England may cause him to miss the *Oreto*'s departure, worried that he may not get a second opportunity to command a Confederate ship of war. He asked Mallory if he could command the *290* instead, knowing that she would not be departing for several more months. Mallory agreed.[2]

To comply with Mallory's order to get to England any way he could, Bulloch gained passage on the *Annie Childs*, which was scheduled to soon leave Wilmington, North Carolina, for England. Loaded with cotton and tobacco, the *Annie Childs* was ready for her run at the blockade. For nearly a week her crew closely watched the three Union ships blocking the harbor out of Wilmington. Finally, on February 5, 1862, the *Annie Childs* took advantage of foggy and rainy conditions and stealthily crept out of port, unmolested.[3]

Upon his arrival in England, Bulloch was surprised to note that the *Oreto* was still in port. Knowing he had been given command of the *290*, he therefore offered the *Oreto* to North. North, however, still had designs on the *290* and allowed the *Oreto* to sail without him on March 22, 1862. The successful departure of the *Oreto* allowed the Confederacy to pass her first true test of the Foreign Enlistment Act.

Once the *Oreto* was under way, North dashed off a missive to Mallory, complaining that Bulloch had unfairly received a promotion over him, and that Bulloch had taken command of the *290*, which North believed was rightfully his. Mallory, unaware that the *Oreto* had already sailed, sent a message back to North telling him to command " . . . the ship built by Captain Bulloch . . . ," meaning the *Oreto.*

North, capitalizing on the confusion, conveniently decided that Mallory must have meant the *290*, even though he knew that Bulloch had arranged for the construction of both vessels. Taking no chance that Mallory would correct him, North did not respond to the secretary's message. Armed with the message from Mallory, albeit with his own interpretation, he confronted Bulloch. Not realizing the confusion, whether real or fabricated, Bulloch assumed Mallory had changed his mind, and he relinquished the command of the *290* to North.

* * *

While the *Annie Childs* was attempting to leave port, Raphael Semmes was aboard his own ship, the *Sumter*. In need of repairs after a successful voyage in which he had taken 18 Union prizes, eight of which had been burned, he had put in at Gibraltar. Quickly however, almost as if on cue, the United States gunboat *Tuscarora* had entered the harbor, trapping the *Sumter*. Semmes was effectively cornered.

Semmes had been born in Charles County, Maryland, on September 27, 1809. His ancestors had come from England in the 1600s and, proud of his heritage, he had been a loyal citizen of the United States since his birth. In 1826, President John Quincy Adams had appointed him a midshipman in the United States Navy. However, he did not enter active service for six years, allowing time to study law. The practical Semmes had concentrated on maritime law, an area that had already served him well in his role as commander of the *Sumter*. He had been promoted to lieutenant in 1837, moved to Alabama in 1842, and served in the war with Mexico. While commanding the brig *Somers* in a blockade of the Mexican coast, his ship had been lost in a fierce gale. Semmes was one of the few who had been rescued. The experience had left him shaken, and he told friends that he never again would lose a ship or crew.

---

* The use of ship names was routinely avoided so that no connection could be made to the Confederacy if the mail was intercepted. While this may have been prudent from a political standpoint, it would cause no end of confusion to those receiving the messages.

After the war he had served as an inspector of lighthouses, eventually advancing to the position of secretary of the Lighthouse Board. Then, on February 15, 1861, the state of Alabama had seceded from the Union. Although a loyal citizen of the United States, Semmes felt closer to his adopted home state. After much deliberation, he resigned his commission and offered his services to his new country, the Confederate States of America.

He had received his first assignment from President Jefferson Davis, who had sent him north to recruit mechanics who might be willing to assist in the manufacture of ordnance and rifle machinery. Semmes had proven to be a worthy representative of the new government, obtaining machinery for rifling cannon, along with the skilled workers needed to operate it.

As a reward for his efforts, and recognizing his skills, Confederate officials had placed him in charge of the Confederate Lighthouse Bureau, but within two weeks he had been reassigned. His new assignment: proceed to New Orleans and prepare a ship for sea duty. That ship was to become known as the CSS *Sumter*.[4]

Now, unable to take the *Sumter* out of Gibraltar, he proceeded to London with one of his officers, John McIntosh Kell. While in London he met with Bulloch, who still harbored hopes of commanding the *290*. Magnanimously, Bulloch offered to step aside in favor of Semmes, an offer that Semmes refused.

It was not long before Semmes and Kell were presented with the opportunity to return home on the *Melita*, a blockade runner. Although anxious to see his family once again, Semmes had misgivings about returning on a blockade runner. Fearing recognition and probable capture if the *Melita* was unsuccessful in her attempt to run the blockade, Semmes visualized severe punishment for having been captain of the *Sumter*. His fears were not without merit. His wife was already under surveillance.[5]

The captain of the *Melita* reassured Semmes that he would be stopping first at Nassau, where Semmes could debark while the *Melita*'s cargo was being transferred. His fears assuaged, Semmes boarded the blockade runner, which set sail May 19, 1862.

On his arrival in Nassau, Semmes found a letter waiting for him. The letter, dated May 2, 1862, was from Mallory, ordering him to take command of a new ship being constructed in Liverpool. The letter identified the ship only as the *290*.[6] While the ship had previously been promised to Bulloch, the fate of the *Sumter* had made Semmes and his officers available immediately. Mallory could not afford to allow experienced officers to languish around the decks of a ship that would probably never sail again, and he gave Bulloch the news in a similar letter.

Stressing secrecy, Semmes immediately wrote to North, telling him of the change in plans.[7] Meanwhile, a disappointed Bulloch read the secretary's message: "Your services in England are so important at this time, that I trust you will cheerfully support any disappointment you may experience in not getting to sea . . ."[8] For his part, North complained so vehemently that he received a stern reprimand from Mallory, shortly after which he resigned his commission and retired from the navy.[9]

* * *

On May 15, 1862, the Lairds held the customary launching ceremony for the *290*. To fail to do so would have added to the already mounting suspicion on the part of the Union.

Prior to the launching the Laird brothers suggested that Bulloch select a better name than the *290* for the ceremony. Bulloch knew he couldn't give the new ship a name that would tie her to the Confederacy, and he asked the Lairds for suggestions. The brothers quickly suggested naming the ship in honor of a woman friend. The woman's name was Henrietta, and to protect her privacy, the Lairds suggested using the name Enrica, a Spanish derivative. Bulloch agreed and the launching took place as scheduled. It was not long before rumors spread that the *290*, now the *Enrica*, was being built for the Spanish government. This didn't bother Bulloch. If people thought she was Spanish, so much the better.[10]

On each visit to the dock Bulloch never failed to be impressed with the quality of the Lairds' work and their attention to detail. Even minor defects did not escape the watchful eyes of the Lairds.[11] However, the visits were not without the occasional inevitable disagreements. Bulloch, feeling the stress of his job, was becoming sensitive to the growing international disapproval of the Confederacy's burning of Union ships. He feared that world opinion was turning against the South, and he had argued that this practice should be stopped.[12] His arguments had fallen on deaf ears.

One disagreement with the Lairds centered on the bolts for the broadside guns. The Lairds saw no need for them on a merchant ship. Bulloch, of course, knew the ultimate purpose of the ship and insisted on having the bolts installed.

Finally, the exasperated Lairds confessed their fears that Bulloch's merchant ship was looking more and more like a ship of war. The Confederate agent had already insisted that openings be cut into the bulwarks, openings that looked suspiciously like gun ports. He also had insisted on swivel sockets on the deck, and the Lairds complained that every time they had installed swivel sockets for other customers they had been used for pivot guns.

Bulloch didn't want to lie to the brothers. On the other hand, he didn't want to place them in a position that could be construed to be a violation of the Foreign Enlistment Act. If they were put into prison, or if the *Enrica* were to be confiscated, his entire project would be jeopardized. Plans for a Confederate navy would be seriously in danger. Putting the Lairds at ease became more important right now than the actual construction itself. Weighing his words carefully, he offered the explanation that he was simply looking to the future. Even though he planned to use her as a merchant ship, he said, hoping he sounded convincing, there may be an opportunity to sell her some day. If she already had the provisions for conversion to a ship of war, it would be much easier.

The explanation seemed plausible enough. Even if it wasn't entirely true, it sounded true enough to convince any outsider who may be questioning the purpose of the ship, and there were many. (Bulloch's journal revealed his concerns: "I soon learned that spies were lurking about, and tampering with the workmen at Messrs. Lairds, and that a private detective named Maguire was taking a deep and abiding interest in my personal movements.")[13] To Bulloch's relief the Lairds accepted his explanation and made the modifications he requested.

The Lairds made the completion of the *Enrica* a high priority, and by mid-June she was deemed ready for a trial voyage. To take the vessel out required a captain with a Board of Trade Certificate, and Bulloch selected Captain Matthew J. Butcher.[14] Bulloch had met Butcher a few years earlier when Butcher was chief officer of the Cunard steamship *Karnak*. The two had become friends, and Bulloch had complete confidence in Butcher's abilities.[15] More importantly, he trusted him to remain silent. This was important because the wrong man could betray Bulloch, or even turn the ship over to the Union. Bulloch knew that Butcher would not say anything without Bulloch's approval. Despite this trust, however, the need for secrecy was even greater, and Bulloch took no chances, telling Butcher that the ship would be sailing for the West Indies.*

The initial trial completed, the *Enrica* returned to the Lairds' docks, where minor problems were corrected and final construction details were completed. However, problems were brewing. The United States consul to Liverpool, Thomas H. Dudley, was gathering information on the *Enrica*. Dudley was a zealous patriot and had been furious when the *Oreto* had successfully put to sea. He had vowed that it would not happen again. Depending heavily on his top spy, British detective Matthew Maguire, Dudley was acquiring extensive information about the *Enrica* on a regular basis. Maguire employed a vast network of agents, and as early as May he had identified the *Enrica* as a sister ship to the *Oreto*.[16] Despite the confidence the Laird brothers had expressed in their workers, Maguire had been able to ingratiate himself with several of them, who in turn passed along information which proved to be unerringly accurate.

By the time the *Enrica* returned from her trial voyage, Maguire had learned that Bulloch was to be her commander, he knew the number of guns she was to eventually carry, and he had determined that several officers from the *Sumter* would be serving on her.[17] A week later he passed along information to Dudley that debunked the rumor that the *Enrica* was a Spanish ship. The Lairds' gateman had told him that she was being built for the Confederacy.[18]

Now, Dudley had something he could sink his teeth into. He conferred with Charles Francis Adams, United States minister to London, who authored a letter to Lord Russell, a member of the British Parliament.

---

* Eventually Bulloch would tell Butcher of the *Enrica*'s true mission. Butcher is believed to be the only outsider to whom Bulloch ever confided this information.

In the letter, Adams charged that the construction of the *Enrica* was a "manifest violation" of the Foreign Enlistment Act, and that the ship should be detained. Russell had customs officials scour the ship, but nothing was found that proved the contention.[19]

On July 12, 1862, the *Enrica* moved to a public wharf. There, the coal bunkers were filled and provisions were brought aboard. At about that same time, Semmes and several of his officers were setting sail for Liverpool aboard the *Bermuda*. It would not be long until the *Enrica* and her new captain would be united in history, if all went according to plan.[20]

However, all did not go according to plan. Three days before the *Enrica* moved, Dudley thought he had all the evidence he needed. He sent a letter to the collector of customs at Liverpool which outlined why the United States believed the *Enrica* was actually a Confederate warship. Dudley's letter had included information gleaned from statements made by anonymous informers. This anonymity rendered the information suspect, at least in the eyes of the Customs Board, and consequently, no action was taken.[21]

The Customs Board's refusal to take action had infuriated Dudley, and he had summoned Maguire to his office. Dudley had told Maguire that he wanted names and affidavits. If the British wouldn't accept anonymous information, Dudley planned to make it impossible for them to ignore him! He authorized Maguire to pay as much as was necessary to get the information. In a relatively short time the ever efficient Maguire returned with the information the consul had wanted. The detective presented Dudley with sworn affidavits from two seamen, William Passmore and Richard Broderick.*

Dudley, always cautious, queried Maguire as to whether the men had the necessary experience to make them believable. Maguire assured him that both were experienced, offering as proof the fact that Passmore had served in the Crimean War on Her Majesty's Ship *Terrible*, and that Broderick was a shipwright. They knew ships, and more importantly to Dudley, they knew the *290*, in particular.†

---

* Richard Broderick is identified in some sources as Richard Brogan.

† The United States government and her spies referred to the ship as the *290* long after she had set sail and had been renamed the *Alabama*. Northern officials rarely used the name *Enrica* in either conversation or letter.

Passmore's testimony was especially helpful to Dudley's cause, stating that Captain Butcher had told him personally that the ship would be fighting for the Confederacy and that Butcher had signed on Passmore as an able seaman. Passmore's affidavit went on to incriminate Bulloch as well, stating that the Confederate agent was at the dock regularly and was to be the ship's fighting captain. Passmore also described the vessel's accommodations for weaponry.[22]

Broderick's testimony was equally helpful, confirming Passmore's contention that the ship was being built for the Confederate government. He identified Bulloch as a "Southern Commissioner" and said that Butcher had recruited him to sail on the *290* as a carpenter's mate. Broderick had refused because he thought the wages were too low. He also said that John Laird was present when the wages were discussed, although he did not charge that Laird was aware that the *290* would be a fighting ship.[23]

Armed with this new and incriminating intelligence, including construction materials and paint colors,[24] Dudley forwarded the affidavits to the Port Collector, who gave them to the Customs Board. Amazingly, at least in the eyes of the government of the United States, the Board again refused to take action.

His patience exhausted, Ambassador Adams dropped hints to Lord Russell that he would return to the United States if Russell didn't soon do something about the *290*. This would be tantamount to breaking off diplomatic relations, something that could draw England into the war. Russell, who up to this point had been merely sympathetic, now saw the potential ramifications, and it was only then that he recommended the *290* be seized.[25]

The affidavits were forwarded to the Queen's Advocate Sir John Harding for evaluation. Before he could act, however, Harding took ill, causing a delay of several days. Other British officials stepped in and, under pressure from Dudley, finally agreed that at least some of the affidavits had merit. Based on this information, the order was given to impound the *290*.

The order, however, came too late. Bulloch had already received an anonymous message that it would not be safe for the *Enrica* to remain in port another 48 hours.* It would not be possible for Semmes to arrive in time to take the *Enrica* to sea, forcing Bulloch to quickly make alternate plans.[26]

Bulloch immediately went to the Lairds and requested a second trial run, which was approved by the builders. Captain Butcher was told to be ready to sail the next day. On July 28 the *Enrica* was moved further down the Mersey River.

To avoid conflicts with the Foreign Enlistment Act, she would be unarmed. Bulloch had already hired Sinclair, Hamilton and Company, a London firm that was sympathetic to the Confederate cause, to locate a tender that would transport the *Enrica*'s armament to a rendezvous point. They had found the *Agrippina*, a 350-ton bark, which they purchased for £1400.† The *Agrippina*'s captain, a Scotchman named Alexander McQueen, was a heavy-drinking braggart whose personal shortcomings would eventually cause many problems for the Confederacy.[27] The *Agrippina* quickly took on guns, powder, and other provisions that were to be transported to the still unknown rendezvous.

Bulloch, Butcher, and Paymaster Clarence Yonge then proceeded to the office of their financiers, Fraser, Trenholm and Company, where arrangements were made for final payment to the Lairds. Upon leaving their office, Bulloch wrote out instructions for Captain McQueen to proceed to the Azores and meet an unnamed steamer (the *Enrica*), taking special precaution to refer to the *Agrippina*'s "cargo" without specifying war materiel:

> You will proceed at once to sea with the brig *Agrippina*, now under your command, and make the best of your way to the bay of Praya, in the island of Terceira, one of the Azores. Praya is on the east side of the island, and is the best and safest anchorage in the entire group, except Fayal, and being less frequented than this latter place, all supplies are cheaper and you will have less difficulty in

---

* Mr. S. Price Edwards was collector of the Port of Liverpool at the time, and many accused him of being the informant. Some went so far as to accuse Edwards of accepting a bribe from Bulloch to look the other way when it came time for the *Enrica* to depart. Both Edwards and Bulloch denied this, even after the war, and Edwards told friends that the accusations and attacks on his integrity deeply pained him. He never fully recovered from the furor, and the true identity of the informant has never been proven.[28]

† About $6,800.

transferring the coals and other portions of your cargo to the steamer which will soon follow you . . . You will be visited, soon after anchoring, by the health officer, to whom you will simply report that you have put in for supplies . . . It is hoped that the steamer will not be far behind you; indeed you may find her already in the bay. The name of the commander of the steamer is Butcher. He will have a letter to you with authority to take whatever quantity of coal and other articles of your cargo he may require . . . You are to consider all orders from the commander of the steamer as authorized by us, with or without any letter of advice. If any vessel is at anchor in Praya when you arrive, hoist your number, and should it be your consort, she will stop a white English ensign to the after shroud of the main rigging. If the steamer arrives after you, she will, upon anchoring, make this same signal of the white English ensign in the main rigging, which you will answer with your number, after which you can communicate freely.

Then, perhaps in deference to McQueen's character flaws, he added some incentive:

. . . upon your safe return to England, which we confidently anticipate, we shall be happy to make you a tangible acknowledgment for any extra exertions you may make for the satisfactory accomplishment of the voyage.[29]

Following his written instructions to McQueen, Bulloch next penned a note to Yonge, referring to the *Alabama* by name for the first time: "You will join the C.S.S. *Alabama*, temporarily under the orders of Captain M. J. Butcher." Bulloch continued his instructions to Yonge, telling him to familiarize himself with the invoices for the *Alabama* so that he know exactly what will be placed on board, and to mingle with the crew and officers and try to interest them in sailing for the Confederacy.[30]

Early the next morning a small ferry, piloted by George Bond, sailed down the Mersey to the dock where the *Enrica* was berthed. Among those on board were Bulloch, Yonge, and the Lairds and their daughters. Within a few hours they had transferred to the *Enrica*, and by midmorning the *Enrica*, accompanied by the tug *Hercules*, left port for what those on board believed to be another trial cruise. Bulloch had the *Enrica* festooned with flags and banners, and he made a great show of hosting what appeared to be a gala party. Anyone watching would, with any luck, assume the *Enrica* was on a pleasure cruise, hardly the type of trial one would associate with a ship of war. Once under way, Bulloch announced that the *Enrica* would stay out all night, but the passengers could return to Liverpool on the *Hercules*.

That night Bulloch wrote out instructions for Butcher, placing on paper for the first time any intimation that the new vessel would truly be a ship of war:

> . . . Get the gun carriages out of their cases and place them in their proper places, the carriage for 8-inch gun [*sic*] on the quarter deck, and the one for the 7-inch gun immediately forward of the bridge. The carriages for the broadside guns place opposite the side ports. The cases containing the guns, being filled with small fixtures and equipment's, had better be left as you find them until the Confederate States officer who is to command the ship arrives. The cases containing the shot can be opened and the shot put in the racks on deck, each rack being so fitted as to receive its proper shot. The shells you will place in the shell room, each in its proper box, the spherical shells in the starboard and the elongated shells in the port shell rooms. The pistols are in four small cases made so that two of them will fit into each of the arm chests on the quarter deck. Put these in the chests as soon as you get them on board . . .[31]

At 7:00 A.M. the next day, Bulloch met Bond and the *Hercules*. Also present were the potential crew members who had been recruited by the agent. However, the men were not alone. A woman accompanied each, most claiming to be the wife of the man she clung to, although it was apparent that few real wives were in attendance. Most were denizens of Liverpool's waterfront brothels who insisted on accompanying their "husbands" to their ship since they would not be seeing them for some time. It was no coincidence that the paymaster happened to be on that ship, and the ladies were familiar enough with shipboard procedures to realize that the crew members were likely to receive their advance pay as soon as they signed on. Nearly every man who signed on was destined to begin his cruise with empty pockets. Their female friends returned to Liverpool on the *Hercules*, most with more money in their purse than they had taken with them on their visit to the *Enrica*.[32]

With the USS *Tuscarora* believed to be in the area, Bulloch had ordered Butcher to take the *Enrica* through the more demanding North Channel. The weather was stormy as the *Enrica* followed the Irish coast. Although it made for a less-than-pleasant introduction to the new crew members, the weather was perfect for eluding enemy cruisers, and the *Tuscarora* was never seen. This prompted the commander of the *Tuscarora*, T. A. Craven, to complain to his superiors that as long as the "order in council" prohibits United States ships of war from lying in British ports it will be impossible to keep "these piratical vessels" from being fitted and getting to sea.[33]

At dusk, a fishing boat was hailed, and Bulloch and Bond were taken ashore. They would return to Liverpool in the morning, where Bulloch would learn that his anonymous informer had been correct. The *Enrica* had scarcely set sail before the British government had decided that she should be seized. The decision had come too late, however, and the *Enrica* was safely under way.[34]

In early August, Semmes and his officers arrived in Liverpool on the *Bahama*, only to learn of the *Enrica*'s departure. Joined by several additional officers from the *Sumter,* they met with Bulloch, who brought them up to date on the *Enrica*'s destination. Five days later, accompanied by Bulloch, they all reboarded the *Bahama*, bound for the Azores and their new ship. The Azores had been selected because the islands were part of Portugal's territory, and Portugal had minimal power. Even if detected, Bulloch knew the Portuguese would do little more than protest. The relatively remote location, removed from the main shipping lanes, was also attractive.

The *Enrica*'s voyage to the Azores was not without incident. Heavy seas had battered the new vessel almost continuously, and she arrived at the rendezvous with her port bow post missing and the foremast stays ripped from their mountings.

Anchored in the harbor at Praya Bay in Terceira, repairs were made as she awaited the arrival of the *Agrippina*.[35] A passing Union whaling vessel, identifying herself as the *Rising Sun*, asked the *Enrica*'s identity. Butcher responded, "We're the *Barcelona*, bound for Mexico!" Butcher's reply gave the new ship her fourth name in her brief history.

On August 18, 1862, the *Agrippina* arrived. The planned process of identification was followed, and the *Agrippina* docked as close to the *Enrica* as was practical. The carpenter and carpenter's mates immediately scribed large circles on the decks for the pivot guns while other crew members fit the side tackles to the broadside guns. Shot and shell were stowed into the appropriate magazines, and spare sails were brought aboard. A block and tackle arrangement was set up and the transfer of guns and equipment began. The difficult task of moving large guns from one ship to another was made even more dangerous by heavy swells, and several times the two vessels nearly collided. Finally, McQueen deemed it prudent to move his ship farther away until morning, when visibility was better. Their tasks done for the day, the crews of both ships spliced the main brace.

The work resumed the next morning, and the crews labored throughout the day. Slowly, the *Enrica* was taking on the appearance of a ship that could hold her own against any foe.

CHAPTER FOUR

THE EARLY CRUISE OF THE *KEARSARGE* (FEBRUARY–AUGUST 1862); THE OUTFITTING OF THE *ALABAMA* (JULY–AUGUST 1862)

It was early April 1862, shortly after Semmes had paid off the crew members of the *Sumter*. The *Kearsarge,* in need of repairs, had made her way to Cadiz. Entering the busy harbor, the *Kearsarge* picked her way through ships of all sizes and in every imaginable condition. The crew shook their heads in wonder as they speculated, with only a slight degree of sarcasm, as to which ones would still be afloat the next day.

Once anchored, Pickering and Lieutenant Thomas Harris had gone ashore, placing Acting Master James Wheeler in charge. After the evening chores had been completed, Wheeler had directed Boatswain James Walton to pipe the crew to the main deck for the evening dance. Soon fiddles, banjos, and sundry other instruments appeared and it wasn't long before the band was playing in earnest, if slightly out of tune.

At some point in the evening Wheeler motioned for Walton to pipe the tune to splice the main brace. The more observant crew members saw the signal and began forming the line at the grog tub even before Walton was able to raise his pipe. Each eagerly consumed his ration. Many then reentered the line for a second serving.

Predictably, a protest erupted. One of the offenders was shoved out of line, but he immediately tried to reclaim his position. The shoving

35

became more violent, and in a matter of seconds the shoving escalated into a minibrawl. Wheeler rushed into the melee where bloody noses were already apparent, shouting to several officers to place the men who were taking part in irons.

The officers immediately grabbed the guilty parties and ushered them away, as those who remained behind gave three rousing cheers for Wheeler, who mounted a capstan and thanked the men. The music resumed, but within only a few minutes Seaman Robert Strahan, who had consumed several rations of grog, tried to strike Wheeler. Strahan found himself joining the earlier miscreants. They all would soon have company in the person of Ordinary Seaman George Andrew, who decided his hammock should be tossed overboard. When Wheeler ordered him to jump overboard and retrieve it, Andrew responded with an oath. Wheeler then had Andrew taken to join the others in the brig, as the band continued to play.[1] Wheeler was, no doubt, quite happy to see Pickering return to take back his command.

The morning of April 6, 1862, Pickering observed a neighboring ship, the Union merchant steamer *Oraville*, preparing to weigh anchor. Pickering hailed the ship and asked where she was bound for, hoping he could send along a sack of mail. The *Oraville*'s captain was willing to comply, and Surgeon Browne suggested to Pickering that several sick men also be sent back to the United States. Four crew members had been seriously ill and their conditions were worsening. Browne, knowing there was little more he could do to help them, feared that they may not survive if they remained on board.

Pickering nodded in agreement and shouted his request that they be taken onto the *Oraville* for transport home. The *Oraville*'s captain agreed, and within minutes Ordinary Seamen James Burns, Manuel Lewis, Jacob Pike, and Henry Van Dyke were assisted into the launch, bound for the *Oraville* and home. The remainder of the crew gathered around the ill men to say their good-byes amid much handshaking. The mail sack quickly followed them into the boat, and the crew of the *Kearsarge* was reduced by four members.[2]

To properly make all the repairs the *Kearsarge* needed would require the skills of some of the local craftsmen, so Pickering had a pilot come aboard and direct the *Kearsarge* upriver to La Carraca. There, several Spanish craftsmen boarded. Pickering had no way of knowing that the craftsmen would not work swiftly, and the *Kearsarge* would not be ready to sail for two full months.

During this time the crew of the *Kearsarge* began to dwindle. On April 29, P. E. Stevens transferred to the USS *Ino*, and on May 13 another crew member, First Class Fireman John Chase, was sent home because of illness. Before he boarded the *Speedwell,* his friends presented him with some money they had collected to help his family while he recovered.[3]

Two weeks later two more members of the crew left, although under conditions less honorable. First Class Fireman Charles Maguire approached Pickering and asked for an advance in his pay to send his needy mother. The sympathetic Pickering was immediately taken in by Maguire's sad story and offered to give the young man a two-month pay advance. The paymaster would be the last man on the *Kearsarge* to see Maguire for nearly a week. His friend, John Griffin (also known as John Taylor), was also missing, and Pickering offered a reward for their return. Six days later a local policeman brought the two back to the *Kearsarge*, both wearing civilian clothes and looking much the worse for wear. Pickering, obviously angered at having been duped, had them both placed in double irons and thrown into the brig. Somehow, even though guarded closely, the two managed to escape and were never seen again. How they were able to make their exit was never determined.[4]

Finally, on June 7, the Spanish workers finished their job and the *Kearsarge* weighed anchor. Shortly after getting under way, a Spanish steamer appeared on the *Kearsarge*'s stern. She appeared anxious to pass, but Pickering would have none of that. He demanded more steam, and the engine room obliged. In only a few minutes the impromptu race was over, with the Spanish vessel falling far behind. Although the crew viewed the event as a lark and cheered mightily when it became apparent that their opponent could not keep up with them, Pickering was actually testing his ship. If he could pull away from this vessel, he could also reasonably expect to be able to overhaul any Confederate ships he may happen to see on his cruise.[5]

The *Kearsarge*'s destination was Algeciras and the *Sumter*, and as the Union ship approached the harbor, Pickering ordered small arms drills and several practice broadsides from his guns. This would keep his gunners sharp, but more importantly it would send a message to onlookers, especially the crew of the *Sumter*, of just what his ship was capable of doing.[6]

Entering the harbor, the *Kearsarge* anchored near the *Tuscarora*, whose captain gave them the news that the *Sumter* had been abandoned. The broadside had gone for naught!

To counter the disappointment felt by the crew, Pickering sent Officers' Cook Charles Fisher and Ordinary Seamen William Gowin and Martin Simpson ashore to purchase some new instruments for the band. By the time they returned, the *Kearsarge*'s rigging had been decorated with flags, and the crews of the *Tuscarora* and another Union ship, the *Release*, had come aboard. Several civilian spectators joined them all on the quarterdeck, and soon the air was filled with the sounds of a minstrel concert. Morale on the *Kearsarge* soared even higher when they learned that a bag of mail had been left in port for them.[7]

On June 15, Pickering allowed several of the crew to go ashore. It was their first liberty in several months, and they acted predictably. Many got drunk and began fighting, first among themselves, then with some of the local citizens. Those who were unfortunate enough to be fighting when the police arrived found themselves spending the night in jail. When released the next morning, they returned to the *Kearsarge* only to find an unsympathetic Pickering waiting for them, and they were put in irons for getting back late. The furious Pickering swore he would grant no more liberty.[8]

Eight days later, however, he relented. The results were the same as before, with four crew members being jailed. One of them would stay behind bars for nearly two weeks.

Five days after that episode, several more crew members got in fights with crews from other ships. By now the Spanish governor had had enough. He told Pickering that his men were no longer permitted to come ashore. A few brave souls who tried to sneak ashore the next night were met by local vigilantes, who forced them back to the ship.[9]

The cruise of the *Kearsarge* was only five months old, but it was already proving to be an eventful one!

* * *

Outfitting the *Enrica* was a hectic process. Speed was important, because an enemy cruiser could enter the harbor at any time. Without a trained crew, the *Enrica* would be at the enemy's mercy. There was also the ever present danger that local authorities would get suspicious of the two ships and their activities, notifying the mainland. Thus it was that every man on board both the *Agrippina* and the *Enrica* worked with one eye cast toward the harbor entrance, warily watching for a sail in the distance.

On the morning of August 20, 1862, their fear became a reality. The lookout called for Butcher with an urgency in his voice that brought Butcher to the deck immediately. Seeing Butcher approach, the lookout pointed out to sea where a steamer was just appearing on the horizon. As it loomed larger, Butcher was joined at the rails by several crew members anxiously waiting for their orders. Butcher, recognizing that his inexperienced men would never be able to fight off boarders who intended to take his ship, decided to do nothing. He knew that there was no hiding the guns that were already in the process of being mounted on the deck. He wasn't sure what he would tell the boarding party, if there was to be one, but he would have to come up with a story very quickly.

The approaching ship made no effort to turn. There was no doubt that she was coming directly to the harbor. Had the *Rising Sun* betrayed their position? As the tension mounted, the men agreed that the Union whaler had departed very suspiciously, with no farewell and in an apparent hurry. The question on every man's lips now was what would become of them if they were captured.

Raising his spyglass, Butcher searched for a flag. Finally, the stranger was close enough that he could make it out. It was British! The approaching ship was neutral! When he learned the ship was the *Bahama*, Butcher's breath escaped in a loud sigh of relief. The *Bahama*. Bulloch's ship. Searching the faces along the *Bahama*'s rail, he at last spied his old friend. Even as the two waved greetings to one another, the *Bahama* dropped a small boat. Bulloch and several others climbed over the side and into the craft, rowing toward the *Enrica*.

Boarding the *Enrica*, Bulloch strode directly toward Butcher, extending his hand in greeting. The two exchanged pleasantries, whereupon Bulloch turned and motioned toward the group who had accompanied him from the *Bahama*. A small-framed man of medium height stepped forward confidently. Erect and exhibiting a military bearing, he took Butcher's extended hand and pumped it vigorously, introducing himself as Raphael Semmes and telling Butcher that he would be the captain of the ship once she got to sea.

Butcher had heard of Semmes but had expected him to be a larger man. Butcher returned the greeting, his eyes transfixed by the piercing gaze of the man who would be taking over the *Enrica*. Off to the side, curious crew members may have fixed their attention on another characteristic of Semmes's appearance: his mustache. Heavily waxed, he had twirled it until it formed a sharp uplifted point on either side of his mouth. Someone observed that such a mustache must require a lot of beeswax to maintain, unintentionally giving rise to a nickname that would accompany Semmes throughout his entire cruise: Old Beeswax.

The formalities of introduction completed, the job of outfitting the *Enrica* quickly resumed. The work continued throughout the day until, by midafternoon, the swells made it too dangerous to continue. Bulloch ordered the ships to Angra Bay, on the other side of the island, where the waters would be calmer. The *Bahama* would tow the *Enrica* to save her coal.

A towline was hastily rigged between the two vessels, and shortly the three ships made their way to the leeward side of the island. Reaching the bay, they were signaled by a port customs official to proceed around the point of the island and anchor with the rest of the ships in the harbor. Bulloch ignored the signal and ordered the anchors dropped and the transfer of guns to resume.

In the calmer waters the transfer of guns and other necessities of war proceeded uneventfully. The only tense moment had come when a suspicious Portuguese official had arrived to question the purpose of the three ships. Bulloch had explained that the *Enrica* needed repairs and the other two ships were merely assisting. The ruse was successful, but it underscored the need for completing the work rapidly.[10]

By nightfall, all weaponry had been moved onto the *Enrica*. All that remained was the loading of coal and she would be ready to move out to sea. The three ships moved to Angra de Heroismo for the task of coaling. Sailing around the island's point, they were challenged from shore. The challenge was followed by the unmistakable roar of a shore cannon. For some reason, the small armada was being fired on!

The *Bahama*'s Captain Tessier, who was commanding the lead boat, ordered his engines to full speed. The *Agrippina* followed suit. The *Enrica*, still being towed by the *Bahama*, could do nothing to help. No further aggression came from the shore battery, however.

The following morning, as coal was being loaded into the *Enrica*'s bunkers, several small boats approached. From the *Enrica* it was apparent that some of the boats contained armed soldiers, and Bulloch refused to allow them to board with their weapons. Only two unarmed officials were allowed on the ship, and they quickly became agitated when they spied the guns on deck. Gesturing animatedly and shouting in Portuguese, there was no mistaking their ire, despite the fact that nobody on the *Enrica* had the slightest idea what they were saying. Through gestures of their own, Semmes and Bulloch were able to calm the men, after which they offered them a tour of the vessel as a show of goodwill.

As the tour concluded, the English consul arrived. Conferring with the Portuguese officials, he then translated for Semmes and Bulloch, explaining that they would have to register at the customs office before taking on any more coal. Semmes and Bulloch agreed and then asked why they had been fired on the previous evening. After a short exchange between the consul and the officials, the consul interpreted for Semmes. Unaccustomed to seeing three ships coming into the harbor in convoy, the shore battery had been concerned the *Enrica*, *Agrippina*, and *Bahama* were going to invade them. They denied firing on the small armada, however, insisting that the shot had come from a departing mail packet, rather than from them.[11]

Once registered with the customs office, the coaling of the *Enrica* resumed. On August 24, 1862, the outfitting and coaling was completed. The *Enrica* was no longer dependent on the *Agrippina* or the *Bahama*. She was now in fighting trim. All that remained to be done was to clean up the coal dust, set her rigging, and she would be ready for the open sea.[12]

Now in international waters, Semmes gave the signal for the *Enrica* to fire her first shot, and one of the 32-pounders responded with a resounding roar. Semmes gave a rare smile of approval at the sound and summoned the men of all three ships to the afterdeck of the *Enrica*. As the assemblage watched, the British flag flapped from the top of the mizzenmast, a gentle breeze keeping the banner in graceful motion.

William Breedlove Smith, the captain's clerk, took a position on a gun carriage and pulled a document from inside his coat. The ship drew uncharacteristically silent as Smith read Mallory's orders for Semmes to take over the vessel. Finishing, he turned to Semmes.

Semmes strode to the gun carriage, then paused slightly before christening the ship the *Alabama*. At his signal the Union Jack was replaced by a flag that none of the men had ever seen. Watching the ensign rise to the top of the mast, some speculated they were to be sailing under a French flag, while others were sure it was Norwegian. The answer soon came when Semmes informed them that the flag was that of the Confederate States of America.

Confused murmurs broke out in the crowd. Most had never heard of the Confederate States of America. The men drew silent as Semmes announced that the men from the *Enrica* were now relieved of their contracts and were free to return home. However, he urged them to consider staying on. "The ship you are standing on will take prizes all over the world," he told them, emphasizing that the Confederate Congress would vote her crew one-half of the value of those prizes, to be divided among every man who agreed to sign on. When he told them that they would be paid double their English wages, in gold, Semmes now had their undivided attention.

He promised the men fair treatment, generous rations, rations of grog twice daily, and the chance to lie alongside the enemy's cruisers. A low hum rose from the crowd, as many had already stopped listening at the promise of a double grog ration daily.

They were brought back to reality as Semmes went on to explain that the *Alabama* was not a privateer but was a ship of war. She would not be roaming solely for the purpose of plundering. Rules and regulations would govern her crew, and anyone who disobeyed those rules would be subject to punishment. Wanting them to know the whole story before they signed on, he promised they would work hard in all climates and weather, at times with little or no rest, and they would be boarding prizes at any hour of the day or night. Then, he told them that any man who signed on would be forfeiting the protection of the British flag, and if captured, or if the cruise was not successful, they all may hang. None would be able to say they weren't forewarned.[13]

Semmes signaled the boatswain to pipe the men down, and they quickly gathered in small groups to discuss the offer. As the officers meandered through the crowd, Paymaster Clarence Yonge carried his shipping papers amidships and took a position on a capstan. Bulloch and Smith joined him. Slowly, prospective crew members were directed to them and, as Yonge signed them on, Bulloch and Smith paid each signee.[14] The process took several hours, and it was nearly midnight when the last man had signed. Semmes looked over the list. More than 80 crew members! Not a full complement, but certainly enough to set sail.

With the signing on of a crew completed, Bulloch and Semmes walked toward the gangway, joining those who had decided against signing on. Bulloch shook hands with each of the new crew members who had signed on, before bidding Semmes a cordial farewell. He then made his way to the *Bahama*.

When all had boarded the *Bahama*, the crew of that ship prepared to make way. Within minutes the engines were fired and the *Bahama* slowly began to move away. Spontaneously, the *Bahama*'s crew gave out three cheers, which were answered by the crew of the *Alabama*.[15]

Semmes watched the *Bahama*'s lanterns grow smaller in the distance. From the stern of the *Bahama*, Bulloch may have swallowed hard to rid himself of the lump in his throat. He undoubtedly watched as long as the *Alabama*, the ship he had labored so hard to bring alive, remained visible. He could not have known that he would never see her again.

At dawn a refreshed Semmes arose and explored his new ship. Already his crew stood respectfully when he entered their area. An intangible air of authority surrounded his presence, even before he spoke. He visited the machine shop, then inspected the condenser, where seawater could be made into fresh water for cooking, drinking, and bathing. Reaching the deck, he looked up at the cloudless sky and took a deep breath. There was nothing like breathing the sea air on a clear day.

As he watched his helmsman he saw for the first time the inscription on the wheel. *"Aide toi et Dieu t'aidera,"* he read to himself. "Help yourself and God will help you."[16] Although he had had nothing to do with selecting the inscription, it fit nicely with his own beliefs.

Semmes was accompanied on the tour of the new ship by his first lieutenant, or first luff in the parlance of the sea, John Kell. Kell was a native of Georgia who had entered the navy 20 years earlier. He was proud to say that he had been present when the United States flag was hoisted over Monterey. Now, however, he served in a different navy.

He and Semmes had a relationship that went back many years. When Kell had been in the United States Navy only a few years, he had refused to light candles for the wardroom officers on the sloop of war *Albany*. For this disobedience, he had been dismissed from the navy, his career seemingly over. However, his attorney had pressed for a retrial that had resulted in an acquittal. Kell was restored to his former rank and his naval career was back on track. His attorney had been Raphael Semmes.[17]

When war broke out, Kell followed the path so many Confederate naval officers had followed, and he resigned his commission. He offered his services to the Confederacy, was commissioned as a lieutenant, and was sent to New Orleans, where he reported to Semmes on the *Sumter*.[18] Some have offered the opinion that Kell, still carrying a grudge against the navy for putting him through a court-martial, was more than eager to serve against the Union. Clean-shaven then, he had since grown a full beard which he vowed to keep until the Confederacy gained her independence.

At the age of 39 he was still in prime physical condition, and his sturdy stature gained immediate respect from the crew. On the *Sumter* he had been considered a firm taskmaster, but benevolent. Even those who had suffered punishment under his hand were grudgingly forced to admit that he was a fair man. Everyone on that ill-fated vessel, from the cabin boys up to Semmes himself, had nothing but respect for Kell's judgment.[19]

Crates still lined the deck, a condition that Semmes would tolerate only for the length of time it would take to get things stowed away. He instructed Kell to have Jack move the powder and shot down to the magazines, then get into the newly issued uniforms. That done, he intended to take stock and see what the crew had in the way of seamanship.

Kell knew that Jack was not an individual, but rather the collective term for the crew. Semmes rarely referred to the men as anything but Jack. Kell was not sure that Jack knew a whole lot about sailing, from what he had observed, but he would let his captain find that out for himself. He knew that it would ultimately be his job to bring the crew around, anyway.

Teaching a crew was not an unfamiliar task for Kell. It had taken some time to get the *Sumter*'s crew into shape, but once trained, things had gone reasonably well. If the crew of the *Alabama* duplicated the *Sumter*'s cruise, Kell knew that Semmes would be happy.

Next morning, the crew was ordered to the quarterdeck. Overnight, an amazing transformation had taken place. Where stood grimy, poorly dressed and offensive-appearing drifters less than 24 hours earlier, now stood sharply attired sailors of the Confederate navy! Each man had been issued a new white frock and pants, with the uniform topped off by a sennett hat. The men gaped at one another, and probably at themselves, with many wearing new clothing for the first time in their lives.

The crew was called to attention to hear the Articles of War.[20] As the articles were enumerated, the crew could not help but focus on the one phrase that seemed to jump out at them with frightening regularity, the death penalty. As reference to the ultimate punishment was repeated several times for various offenses, Jack grew increasingly nervous, each man restlessly shuffling his feet and stealing a glance out of the corner of his eye to see if that phrase was having the same effect on anyone else. A man could die just for having signed his name to the crew list, and for a country and cause that he had never heard of until the evening before. Some must have had second thoughts about the adventure that lay before them.

For the first week, the days were devoted to preparing the guns for firing and teaching the crew what to do at their battle stations. Kell worked tirelessly, noting that maybe 30 of the men were good seamen. The remaining 50, however, ". . . looked as if they need some man-of-war discipline to make anything of them."[21]

Finally, on August 30, 1862, the *Alabama* gave chase for the first time. Hearts pounding with excitement, the crew lowered the propeller and fired the boilers. Within 15 minutes the *Alabama* was under steam power, the crew's efficiency astonishing even Semmes. Their quarry was no match for the sleek newcomer to the seas. In only a short time the *Alabama* drew close to the brig, which sent up her colors. To Jack's disappointment, the vessel was French. There would be no prize taken on this chase.

Less than 24 hours later, the *Alabama* got a second opportunity, with similar results. This time they found that the ship they had been chasing was Portuguese.

On September 2, the frustration continued as the French bark *La Foi* became the hunted.[22] The *Alabama* quickly overtook the French vessel, which hove to when she saw that it would be futile to try to outrun the rebel ship.

John Low and George Townley Fullam were ordered to board the *La Foi* to check her papers. If she showed any sign of having American owners or of carrying Union goods, she would be sunk.

Semmes chose Low and Fullam as heads of the boarding party for two reasons: both had given Semmes a favorable impression as to their dependability and, perhaps more importantly, Low and Fullam were both British. Semmes hoped to convince captured prizes that he was piloting a British vessel, and the British accents of the boarding party would do much to carry off that charade. If boarded prizes believed their captor was British, they would not be reporting that there was a Confederate ship in the area. They may file a complaint with the British government, but that was no concern of Semmes.

Although countrymen, Low and Fullam were diametrical opposites in personality. Low was quiet and went about his business methodically and professionally. Fullam, while professional in his own way, was more outgoing and fun-loving, and he had become an ardent supporter of the Confederate cause in the short time he had been on board. Only 21 years of age, he was muscular and exhibited great skill at handling small boats. This skill would serve him well as he directed the small boarding dinghy toward the captured vessel.[23] Fullam could hardly contain his enthusiasm when chosen to board the *La Foi* and was more than a little disappointed when it became apparent that she was, indeed, French and would have to be released.

As the *La Foi* proceeded on her way, the *Alabama*'s crew grumbled and cursed their luck. Kell admonished them, telling them that there were plenty of Union ships in the area. It would just be a matter of time until they ran across one of them. Then, every member of the crew would be glad he signed on. The men agreed that Kell was probably right, but for now, three consecutive chases had come up empty and the effect was disheartening. Anxious for some action himself, Kell knew that the next chase had better bear fruit or he may have a problem on his hands with his impatient crew.

CHAPTER FIVE
SEPTEMBER 1862

Captain's Steward A. G. Bartelli pounded on the door to Raphael Semmes's cabin, as he often did. Sails had been sighted and the captain had given standing orders to be called when sails appeared, no matter what he was doing.

Semmes leaped to his feet. He had been writing a letter to his wife, Anne Elizabeth. He had no idea when he would find a ship to take it back to a Southern port to be mailed, but it helped him feel closer to her. He had just finished inquiring about their children when Bartelli had pounded on his door. He and Anne Elizabeth had six children, three sons and three daughters, and Semmes missed them terribly. Young Samuel Spencer, Oliver John, Electra Louisa, Catherine Middleton, Ann Elizabeth, and Raphael, Jr., were never far from his thoughts. Although he loved being in charge of a warship, he sometimes thought that he was shirking his duties as a father, and he wrote as often as he could.[1] Racing as fast as his 53-year-old legs would carry him, Semmes reached the deck to see several sails to his port. Kell had already decided which one he wanted to go after, and the chase was on. Those crew members who did not have specific duties to perform while in pursuit had gathered along the rail to observe.

It was not long before it became apparent that the *Alabama* was chasing a fast ship. The *Alabama* gained little, and Semmes feared that he may outrun the other ships and end up with nothing. However, the spirit of the chase was a difficult one to overcome, and the Confederate ship pressed on. As the space between the two grew slightly narrower, Kell lowered his glass and reported that the quarry was Portuguese. The *Alabama* had been chasing a neutral!

Undaunted, Semmes ordered Kell to have the *Alabama* turned around. He would go back and check on one of the others. The frustrated Kell did as he was told, and before long another of the original sails was seen in the distance. She did not appear to be moving. As the *Alabama* drew closer it was apparent that their prey was unconcerned about the approaching stranger. A large sperm whale had been killed and the crew was working feverishly to cut it up and take on the blubber and oil. Semmes ordered the British flag run up, which was quickly answered by the flag of the whaler. She flew the Stars and Stripes! The *Alabama* would have her first prize, if nothing went wrong. The indifferent crew continued their work as Semmes and his ship drew alongside.

The whaler's captain appeared at the rail. Spying him, Semmes shouted, "I'm sending a boat!" There was no answer.

The *Alabama*'s crew dropped the cutter into the water, which was swiftly boarded by 19-year-old Lieutenant Richard Armstrong, 21-year-old Master's Mate George Fullam, and several crew members. Reaching the American ship, the *Alabama*'s men scrambled up her side. An indignant captain, who demanded to know the purpose of the boarding, met them.

Fullam drew himself up to his full height and informed the captain that his ship was now the prize of the Confederate States Steamer *Alabama*, Captain Semmes commanding. He then ordered the captain to fetch his papers and come with the boarding crew.

The confused captain went to his cabin and soon returned with his papers. He followed Armstrong's direction into the cutter and was taken to the *Alabama*. As the little boat approached, Semmes ordered the Confederate flag run up the mast.

The captain introduced himself as Abraham Osborn, his ship the *Ocmulgee*, a whaler out of Martha's Vineyard, Massachusetts. Osborn handed over his papers and watched as Semmes read them carefully. There was no doubt in Semmes's mind that the *Ocmulgee* was Union. Not only had Osborn told him directly, the papers confirmed it.

An uneasy Osborn was beginning to realize that this was more than a simple misunderstanding. He asked Semmes what was to become of his ship. When told that his ship was going to be burned, Osborn's face went pale and he found it difficult to breathe. He had been captured by pirates, he thought.

Semmes explained that his orders from his government were quite clear, and that his only option was to take Osborn and his men prisoners and destroy their ship. He told Osborn that he and his crew could pack their boats with provisions and anything else they thought they may need. Their flag and chronometer, however, were to be brought to Semmes.[2]

Dismissed, Osborn returned to his ship to give the news to his crew. As they gathered personal belongings and provisions, the *Alabama*'s boarding party transferred pork, beef, and sundry items from the *Ocmulgee*'s hold. She had only been at sea some two months, and her supplies were still largely untouched, having been provided for a four-year tour.[3]

Back on the *Alabama*, Semmes watched the activity with no emotion. When Master's Mate James Evans asked if they were actually going to burn the *Ocmulgee*, Semmes replied in the affirmative, explaining that when he was captain of the *Sumter* he had stopped many Union ships that were carrying what were claimed to be neutral cargoes. When taken to Cuba for adjudication, however, Semmes had lost nearly every one of them. They were returned to their owners, and Semmes had promised himself that he would never go through that again. From that point on, unless they could absolutely prove to him that they were neutral, they would meet the torch.[4]

Semmes looked up at the darkening sky and recognized that there was no hurry. It would soon be dark, and there was no reason his men had to carry out his edict that night. If there were any other ships nearby, he feared the blaze may frighten them away. No, he could wait for dawn.

By now the officers and crew of the *Ocmulgee* were being escorted back to the *Alabama*. Semmes ordered the officers placed in irons and the crew to be taken below and placed under guard.

The flag and the chronometer were taken to Semmes's cabin, where Semmes gave Sailing Master Arthur Sinclair the job of winding the chronometer, as well as any future chronometers the *Alabama* may take. Chronometers were nice and portable, and they made good souvenirs. Semmes vowed to himself that there would be more. Many more.

At dawn's first light the officers and crew of the *Alabama* gathered on deck. Semmes directed Sinclair to take some men and go burn the *Ocmulgee*. All others gathered at the rail to watch the spectacle, which Semmes justified by saying that they were only doing at sea what the Yankees were doing back home.[5]

On the *Ocmulgee*, Sinclair gathered his crew and asked them if any of them had ever fired a ship before. Each man looked around him, wondering if he was the only one who had never done it. As it turned out, none had ever been a part of burning a prize.

"Well, then," said Sinclair. "Listen close. Here's what I want you to do. First, cut up with your broadax the cabin and forecastle bunks. These are generally made of white pine. You will, no doubt, find the mattresses stuffed with straw, and in the cabin pantry there will be at least a keg of butter and lard. Make a foundation of the splinters and straw, then pour the lard and butter on top. Make one pile in the cabin, the other in the forecastle. Get your men in the boats, all but the incendiaries, and at the given word 'Fire!' you may shove off. And you can take it as truth, before you have reached your own ship, the blaze will be licking the topsails of this ship!"[6]

At the first sight of flames the crew on board the *Alabama* let out a cheer. Only the dignity of their ranks kept the officers from joining in. All watched as the flames leaped from spar to spar, the *Ocmulgee*'s sails unfurling in the heat. Occasionally, a piece of canvas sail would burn away and drift off aimlessly in the breeze. Then, the mainmast swayed, finally toppling in a shower of sparks, prompting another cheer from the throng crowding the rail. Below deck, Captain Osborn must have cringed with every cheer.

Finally, the hull of the *Ocmulgee* lurched to the side, and within minutes the sea claimed her. As she settled beneath the waves the black smoke of burning whale oil was replaced by a snowy white cloud of steam as the ocean extinguished the flames. In only minutes, there was little evidence that the *Ocmulgee* had ever existed.

Next morning, September 6, the crew was mustered on deck in their dress uniforms. Again, Semmes had the Articles of War read, reinforcing what the men had already heard several times. No crew member of the *Alabama* would ever be able to say he did not know his duties as spelled out by the Articles, if Semmes had his way.

After muster the *Alabama* drew close to shore, where the officers and crew of the *Ocmulgee* were paroled. They rowed to shore in their own whaleboats, which Semmes had graciously spared from the conflagration. They would not remain silent on their arrival, and the story of their ordeal made the rounds of the bars and brothels of Flores, eventually reaching the ears of the captain of the English ship *Cairngorm*. The Englishman would carry the story to the editors of *Harper's Weekly*, which would trumpet in its headline six weeks later: Another Pirate at Work! The story would tell not only of the burning of the *Ocmulgee*, but also of four others, one of which had supposedly been captured within sight of the *Cairngorm*. Had Semmes seen a copy of the newspaper, he would have been pleased to note that his ship had been properly identified, albeit by her old name of *290*.[7]

Within minutes of sending the men of the *Ocmulgee* ashore, another sail was spotted. The *Alabama* gave chase, only to have the ship's captain identify her as the French bark *Senegambia*.[8]

That disappointment was soon forgotten, however, with the sighting of still another sail. This one looked as though it may be a United States whaler, and she refused to identify herself. After a short chase, Semmes ordered a shot from the *Alabama*'s 32-pounder fired across her bow as a warning, at which time one of his officers warned that there were women on her deck. Semmes ordered the Confederate flag raised. With the ships only six miles from neutral waters he feared he would have to stop her now. He ordered the shot fired but, in a concession to the presence of the women, he told Kell to make it a blank one.

The shot was fired but the fleeing ship gave no indication that the shot had even been heard. Women passengers or not, Semmes could not allow the vessel to reach neutral waters. "Send a solid shot through her rigging," he ordered. "Keep it high so there is no danger of hitting them."

This shot had its desired effect, and the ship turned into the wind and surrendered, identifying herself as the *Starlight*, another whaler.

Brought aboard the *Alabama*, the ship's captain, Samuel H. Doane, was furious. Semmes allowed Doane to vent his fury, then calmly told him that every whale killed put money in the Federal treasury and prolonged the war. Therefore, his ship would have to be burned.[9]

Armstrong served as prize master for the *Starlight*, accompanied by a well-armed boarding party. Before going to the *Starlight*, however, Armstrong was given explicit orders by Kell: nobody from the crew was to board the ship until Armstrong and the other officers went through her and either tossed all the liquor overboard or placed it in a safe place. Kell would have no looting, and there would be no liquor brought back on board the *Alabama*.

Despite these precautions, the *Alabama*'s cruise would be plagued by drunken crew members enjoying the liquor smuggled on board from captured prizes. Semmes and Kell would never be able to determine how they were accomplishing it.[10]

Next morning Fourth Lieutenant John Low and another boarding party went out to the *Starlight* and took the passengers ashore. Doane and his crew had already been placed in irons. Seven separate sails could be seen even as the passengers were being escorted to land.[11]

As soon as Low and the boarding party returned to the *Alabama*, one of the seven was singled out and chased. She proved to be the *Ocean Rover*, another whaler. With Armstrong still busy on the *Starlight*, Third Lieutenant Joseph Wilson took on the task of boarding the *Ocean Rover*. To Kell and Low fell the task of appraising her.

When confronted with the news that his ship would be burned, James M. Clark, captain of the *Ocean Rover,* asked Semmes if he and his crew could row themselves ashore in their own boats, despite being five miles from shore.

Semmes agreed to Clark's suggestion, and the captain and several of his men were allowed to return to the Ocean Rover to load the boats. When they returned for the rest of the crew, Semmes was amused to see that the boats contained more than simply supplies. The ship's cat and parrot were also on board. Before departing, Clark handed Semmes a fruitcake which he would no longer have a need for.[12]

As the Alabama lay to, taking on the supplies from the Starlight and the Ocean Rover, two more sails appeared. They belonged to the Alert and the E. R. Sawyer. Quickly, the Alabama's exhausted crew responded. Deciding to follow the Alert, their chase lasted for hours. The E. R. Sawyer, a schooner, disappeared as the Confederates focused their attention on the smaller bark.

Hoisting the British flag, the Alabama waited for a response from the Alert's captain, Charles Church. Getting none, Semmes ordered a blank shot fired. Still the little bark did not acknowledge the Alabama's presence. Semmes then ordered a shot to be fired just astern of the Alert, and this brought her around. The Alert proved to be one of the ships featured in the famous sea story Two Years before the Mast, which had been published some 16 years earlier. Despite her notoriety, Semmes ordered her to be burned with the Starlight and the Ocean Rover, their crews being allowed to go ashore. Among the items taken from the Alert were heavy winter underwear, something that would soon be needed by the men of the Alabama.[13]

On the morning of September 7, the firings began. The Starlight met her fate first, followed about two hours later by the Ocean Rover. Later in the afternoon, the Alert was torched. As the three ships burned, a fourth sail stumbled onto the scene. Realizing too late what was happening, she turned and ran, but after a short chase was captured and identified as the Weather Gauge, a whaler captained by a part owner of the vessel, Samuel C. Small. The Weather Gauge was assigned the same fate as the three ships already burning.

As Semmes checked Small's papers, another sail was reported, and again the Alabama gave chase as quickly as a boarding party could be placed on the *Weather Gauge*. In the gathering darkness, the small bark was soon overtaken. She identified herself as the Danish bark *Overman*. Not wishing to give away his position or identity to a neutral, Semmes ordered the American flag hoisted, identifying the *Alabama* as the United States Steamer *Iroquois*. The *Alabama* returned to the *Weather Gauge* and the three burning vessels, where the bone weary crew of the *Alabama* quickly fell asleep, exhausted by their busy day.[14]

Before turning in for the night, however, Kell watched the three burning prizes for some time. Years later he would recall the exhilaration he felt when watching a ship burn: "To watch the leaping flames on a burning ship gives an indescribable mental excitement that did not decrease with the frequency of the light, but it was always a relief to know the ships were tenantless as they disappeared in lonely grandeur, specks of vanishing light in the 'cradle of the deep'."[15]

Over the next three days, three more ships were chased and stopped. All proved to be neutral. The crew of the *Alabama* did not seem to mind, however. The excitement of the previous two days had at least partially satisfied their lust for some real action.

On September 13 two ships were spotted. The first one stopped was a Spanish bark. Undaunted, the *Alabama* turned and gave chase to the second. Their luck was better on this one, and when Semmes had the British flag shown, the other ship answered with the American flag and offered no resistance. She was the *Altamaha*, another whaling brig, under the command of Rufus Gray. She had been at sea nearly five months, and her voyage was now at an end.[16]

On the night of September 14, after Semmes had spent some private time at his shrine and then gone to bed, another potential prize was spotted. The two ships had passed one another, going in opposite directions. The *Alabama* turned and began pursuit. A quartermaster was dispatched to waken Semmes.

The chase lasted nearly two hours, by which time the *Alabama* had closed to within a mile. The ship failed to respond to a blank shot, but with a second shot the captain apparently realized his foe meant business. Captain William Childs ordered his ship, the *Benjamin Tucker*, stopped. This time, Fullam was in charge of the boarding party. As usual, the officers were put in irons, and the *Benjamin Tucker* was burned to the water line.[17]

It was two days before the *Alabama* stopped another ship. Early in the morning the *Courser*, a whaling schooner out of Provincetown, slipped out of the fog and into the view of the lookout on the *Alabama*. A two-hour chase ensued before her captain, Silas S. Young, saw the futility of trying to evade the faster Confederate. After examining the *Courser's* papers, Semmes gave Young the unhappy news that his ship would be burned. To the surprise and admiration of Semmes and his officers, Young did not protest, even though he was a part owner of the vessel. He snapped off a salute and an "Aye, aye, sir!" and left to inform his men.[18]

With the crews of the *Weather Gauge, Altamaha, Benjamin Tucker*, and *Courser* all on board as prisoners, the *Alabama* was quickly becoming overcrowded. Semmes feared that he would not be able to fight off a joint effort by the prisoners to overpower the men of the *Alabama*. Using whaleboats from the prizes, he had the prisoners sent ashore, breathing a sigh of relief when they had gone.

As the prisoners were loading into the whaleboats, Kell approached Semmes with one of them in tow. The young man had asked if he could join up with the *Alabama's* crew.

The surprised Semmes looked at the young man standing beside Kell. He was sturdy looking, and the crew of the *Alabama* was short-handed. Filling out the crew with prisoners was an option Semmes had not considered. The prisoner's name was Abram Norhoek, an able-bodied seaman. Semmes considered the situation. Finally, he agreed, and Abram Norhoek became the first of several prisoners to ship on with the *Alabama*.[19]

With the *Courser* sitting only a short distance away, and no longer burdened with his prisoners, Semmes decided that his gunners could use some target practice. He ordered the gun crews to their stations, and for the next several hours the guns of the *Alabama* fired at the *Courser*. Midshipman Edward Maffitt Anderson noted that the crew "made some very good shots considering it is the first time that we have tried our guns."[20] Satisfied that his gunners had improved their accuracy, and not wishing to waste any further ammunition, Semmes then ordered the *Courser* fired.

The next victim of the *Alabama* was seized early the following morning. Boarded by John Low, she was the *Virginia*, under the command of Shadrach R. Tilton. Despite her Southern name, she, too, was burned.

Less than a week earlier, Tilton had met with Captain David Gifford of the *Elisha Dunbar*, a whaling bark out of New Bedford, Massachusetts. The two ships had met in a squall, then passed some time together before departing on their separate ways. The two whaling captains were soon to meet again under more adverse conditions.

While the *Virginia* was still burning, the *Alabama*, flying British colors, encountered the *Elisha Dunbar*. Near dusk, and in rolling seas, Semmes feared Gifford may run under the cover of darkness. The Yankee ship was nearly twice the size of the *Alabama*, and for a short time, Semmes even considered not boarding her at all.

Rethinking his options, he finally dispatched two boats under the command of Lieutenant Joseph Wilson. With the *Elisha Dunbar* clearly an American vessel, Semmes chose to speed up the process by not checking her papers. Wilson left under orders to fire the ship before he returned. This is the only time Semmes is known to have fired a ship without first checking her documents.[21]

With the weather deteriorating rapidly, the sea got rougher. Semmes watched anxiously as his boarding crew struggled to get onto the *Elisha Dunbar*. Finally, all had boarded, and it wasn't long until the first flickers of flame could be seen. Wilson had carried out his orders well.

The burning of the *Elisha Dunbar* was one of the most spectacular blazes the *Alabama* had seen. With the skies darkening and the lightning flashing, the crew was almost hypnotized by the sight. At times, the sea was so turbulent that the men lost sight of their burning foe. Then, raised out of a trough, the flames became visible once more, only to disappear again when the next cycle of waves took over.

With the value of the *Elisha Dunbar* placed at $25,000 by Wilson, the *Alabama* reached her break-even point. Her 10 prizes totaled $232,000 in value, just exceeding the cost to build the *Alabama*. From this point on, every prize taken would be profit!

* * *

The sounds of raucous laughter emanated from the quarterdeck as George Whipple regaled the men of the *Kearsarge* with tales of his time aboard the *Sumter*. Whipple, along with several of his shipmates, had deserted the *Sumter* in March when the *Tuscarora* had trapped her. He had served on the *Tuscarora* for a short time, then shipped on with the *Kearsarge*.[22] He was an adept storyteller, and never lacked an audience on his new ship.

It was a Sunday, the day that the men had more leisure time. Earlier in the morning the decks had been scrubbed and holystoned while those in the engine room had polished the brass and cleaned the engines. After breakfast had come muster, with the officers lining up on the starboard side of the ship and the crew on the port side. Paymaster's Clerk Daniel Sargent had called roll and now, except for those who had duties, the rest of the day was free.

Knots of men dotted the deck, some playing checkers or chess, some reading. Here and there a crew member slept in the sun, but rarely on his back. The sleepers had all learned early in the cruise that sleeping on one's back led to sleeping with the mouth open. An open mouth became an invitation to the pranksters among the crew, who delighted in pouring water into the open cavity. The perpetrators then laughed uproariously as the choking crew member quickly jumped to his feet, coughing and sputtering. Once the rudely awakened sleeper had regained his breath and was able to talk, more often than not he cursed his tormentors and angrily chased them around the deck, to the amusement of those who had been watching the scene unfold. The officers usually were as amused as the crewmen and allowed the chase to go on, stepping in only when it was apparent that a fight was about to break out.

Now, above the sound of a nearby banjo, Whipple held court. The men around him hung on his every word as he told of his hatred for Raphael Semmes. Whipple resented the fact that Semmes never hesitated to put men in irons for the slightest offense. Many a man had spent the night hanging from the rigging for doing something wrong, although Whipple denied to his new crew mates that he had personal knowledge.

Now, his current captain was showing similar traits, and Whipple left his mates know he wasn't happy about it. Pickering had just issued an edict forbidding card playing, causing a great deal of consternation among the crew, including Whipple.

John Dempsey, captain of the afterguard, sympathized with Whipple. Dempsey was one of the many rowdies on board, and his incarceration record was becoming legendary among the crew. Most of Dempsey's problems began with liquor, which he somehow had become adept at smuggling on board. Once drunk, he seemed to have an obsession for fighting, a hobby that had kept him on Pickering's bad side for most of the cruise.

Dempsey also possessed a well-known opposition to giving freedom to slaves. As would be expected, the blacks on board didn't like Dempsey, and many of Dempsey's friends feared that it was only a matter of time until one of them attacked him when he didn't expect it. Sometimes even Dempsey himself wondered what he was doing on a Union ship, considering his proslavery beliefs.

* * *

It was now early July 1862, and the temperature hovered around the 100° mark. The *Kearsarge* was still guarding the *Sumter* at Gibraltar. Most of the officers had gone ashore at San Roque to watch the bullfights. Acting Master Eben Stoddard had been delegated by Pickering to serve as officer of the deck. Because of the heat, the crew had badgered Stoddard to allow them to go swimming, and Stoddard had finally relented.

Ordinary Seamen George Andrew and Edward Tibbetts, two of the better swimmers in the crew, had challenged one another to a race. Bets had been placed among those remaining on board, and crew members lined the rails to cheer for their favorite. The race had just started when one of the crew members shouted that he had seen a huge fish.

Others strained to see where the man was pointing when it appeared again. This time, several others also saw its shadow just below the surface, including Stoddard. He ordered a crew member to grab a harpoon and go after it, envisioning fresh fish for supper. Five crew members scrambled over the side into the dinghy and rowed toward the spot where the fish had last been seen. Another crew member with a better vantage point shouted that the fish was actually a shark!

The men in the water scurried to get up the side of the ship as the boat rowed toward the shark. The reflection off the water made it impossible for the men in the dinghy to see it, so they depended on those on deck for directions.

The rowers strained to bring the harpooner into range, their backs arched against the water's resistance. Andrew and Tibbetts, whose race had taken them further from the ship than the other swimmers, were now swimming back, probably unsure of the reason for the commotion on board. Perhaps they thought the shouting was for them as they raced for the finish. As they drew closer, they finally were able to distinguish the word "shark" as their friends screamed at them to get out of the water.

Now the dorsal fin of the shark was visible, and it was moving in the direction of the two racers. With the men on deck helpless to do any more than just shout and point, the dinghy rowers frantically made their way to Andrew and Tibbetts, hoping to bring them on board before the shark made an aggressive move.

As Andrew and Tibbetts, now nearly exhausted from their race, neared the *Kearsarge*, the shark turned and swam directly for Tibbetts. Shouts of encouragement, tinged with panic, came from on deck. Just as Tibbitts got to the ship, the shark lunged for him. Tibbetts instinctively punched the beast on the snout, hoping to fight it off. As he did, the dinghy was still several yards away.

Then Tibbetts screamed in pain as the shark struck his leg. As the men on board rushed to get a rope, the shark disappeared, then resurfaced, his dorsal fin making slow circles around his victim. The luckless Tibbetts, his leg broken and dangling helplessly, clawed frantically at the side of the *Kearsarge*, hoping to find a handhold which would allow him to pull himself out of the water. Desperate men leaned over the rail and reached for their friend, even though they knew there was no possible way they could extend down far enough to grab his hand.

The shark made one last pass, then turned and swiftly came at Tibbetts once more. The 19 year old barely had time to scream before he was pulled under the water. The crew drew deathly silent, every man straining to see any sign that Tibbetts had returned to the surface. The only sign of the struggle was the crimson color where Tibbetts had last been seen. After several minutes, Stoddard solemnly called off the search.[23]

Within a week those who were closest to Tibbetts gradually leaked the true story of their deceased friend. His name was not really Tibbetts, but was Edward Sampson. This neither surprised nor concerned the crew. It was not uncommon for a man to change his name if he was running from something, and many of them were.

As the story began to come out, the crew learned that Sampson, or Tibbetts as they still referred to him, had actually been a crew member on a merchant ship which had been captured by the *Sumter*. He, along with the other members of the vessel's crew, had been taken captive, then paroled on their promise to refrain from fighting against the Confederacy in any capacity until they were officially exchanged for prisoners held by the Union. Sampson, however, had not wanted to wait, and he had taken his new name so he could go to sea again. Hearing this, many crew members recalled how excited he had been when he had first spotted the *Sumter* at anchor. Now they knew why. They may have even pondered the irony of Sampson's death, coming as it did within sight of the ship that had captured him a year earlier.[24]

Scarcely more than a week after the shark attack, Dempsey found himself in trouble with Pickering once more. He and two companions had gone ashore. Returning drunk, Dempsey had been abusive and insubordinate to the officer of the deck. All three were put in irons, but Pickering had reached his limit with Dempsey, and on July 28 Lieutenant Thomas Harris, Acting Masters Stoddard, David Sumner, and James Wheeler, with Surgeon John Browne, gathered to conduct the first court-martial ever held on the *Kearsarge*. Huddled behind a hastily rigged sail for privacy, the five weighed the evidence, then stripped Dempsey of his rank, assigned him extra duty for a month, and ordered him to forfeit a month's pay. He was replaced as captain of the after guard by Francis Viannah.[25]

The court-martial did little to relieve the boredom that permeated the *Kearsarge*. It was apparent that the *Sumter* would not be sailing soon, if ever, yet the crew hoped against hope. If she set sail, they would have something to do.

Their opportunity finally came on August 6. However, it was not the *Sumter* that broke the boredom. Word had been received of a brig bound from Barcelona to the Confederacy, and the *Kearsarge* was ordered to search her out immediately. The *Kearsarge* set sail so suddenly that nearly a dozen men, in port on liberty, were left behind. Shorthanded, Pickering returned the next night to gather them back on board.

The brig was the *Mary Scaife*. The American consul in Gibraltar, Horatio Sprague, had relayed information to Pickering that she had left Barcelona carrying a load of miscellaneous articles. She was flying the British flag and was believed to be planning on running the blockade somewhere in the Carolinas. "If you find her, her captain will say she's bound for Cadiz," Sprague had told Pickering.

For a week the *Kearsarge* cruised a meandering route in the Strait of Gibraltar, not wishing to get too far from the *Sumter* in the unlikely event that she would attempt to leave port. Several vessels were stopped, but none proved to be the elusive *Mary Scaife,* and in mid-August, Pickering returned to port. While there, he opened his mail to read a letter from Sprague stating that the acting governor of Gibraltar, Sir Robert Walpole, had protested that the *Kearsarge* had no right to stop so many ships in the strait, no matter what the reason. He said it was a deliberate violation of British neutrality, and that if it didn't stop at once he would log a formal complaint.

Unimpressed by the threat, Pickering ordered his officers to prepare to sail again in the morning. No acting governor would force him to stop doing his duty! Before the *Kearsarge* could get under way, however, a messenger arrived bearing word from Sprague that the *Mary Scaife* had somehow been able to get past Pickering. A ship calling herself the *Good Luck* had arrived in Cadiz, a ship that had proven to be in actuality the *Mary Scaife*.[26]

The chase had provided a brief but welcome reprieve from the boredom of watching the *Sumter*, but the excitement was over, at least for now, and the men returned to their former routine of watching and waiting.

From the day the *Kearsarge* began her search for the *Mary Scaife* until August 19, fights broke out on a daily basis on the decks of the *Kearsarge*. Five men were placed in irons as a result. These five, Captain's Cook George "Ham Fat" Williams, Ordinary Seaman Thomas Buckley, Seamen Benedict Drury and Robert Motley, and First Class Fireman Henry Jamison, were in trouble almost as much as Dempsey, and would become accustomed to spending time in the brig before the cruise would end.[27]

With morale plummeting, Wardroom Steward Robert Scott, one of the 14 blacks on board, devised a plan to get off the ship. He decided to take some cash from the mess fund and tell everyone he was going ashore to get some sweets for the officers. But he did not plan on returning. He planned to go to the British governor and tell him that he was, in Scott's own words, a "runaway nigger." He would not only be off the ship, he would also have some money in his pocket. After much planning, Scott did just what he told friends he was going to do, and he was never seen again by the crew of the *Kearsarge*.[28]

Less than a week later the store ship *Release* arrived, bringing supplies and mail to the men of the *Kearsarge*. When the *Release*'s captain made known that he was bound for Boston, Surgeon Browne once again requested that three sick crew members be taken back to the United States. When the captain of the *Release* agreed, Seamen Edward Gilson and John Murphy, and Marine Private James Golden bade their friends a quick good-bye and were taken aboard the *Release* for the return voyage to America.[29]

With the three ill shipmates gone, and five others in irons, Pickering found his ship shorthanded once more. Duties had to be reassigned, and the extra duty each man received, combined with the boredom of watching the *Sumter*, led to a marked decrease in morale. Tempers were short, and it took very little to precipitate a fight. Nobody on the *Kearsarge*, including Pickering, even suspected that events in Washington were going to drive morale even lower, and in the not-so-distant future.

On September 14 the crew gathered for Sunday muster. Pickering took his position on the quarterdeck and informed his crew that on

September 1 the Congress of the United States had officially abolished the grog ration for ships at sea. Effective immediately, Pickering told them that there would be no more grog available for anything other than medicinal purposes. As would be expected, this order was not well received. Murmurs of discontent rippled through the crowd.

There was more, and Pickering spoke louder to make himself heard above the protests. When the clamor died down he continued with somewhat better news. Each man would be given an additional five cents daily in his pay to make up for the loss of his grog! It made little difference that Pickering had decided that medicinal purposes could conceivably cover a wide range of maladies, and thus had ordered that several barrels of medicine be kept on board."[30]

That night, their first with no grog as part of the evening's activities, saw the crew turn to their hammocks in a surly mood. Their demeanor did not improve when, after all had fallen asleep, they had been awakened by the long roll of the drum beating them to general quarters.

Each man raced for his battle station, not knowing what the emergency was. Confusion reigned as those who were in a position to have a view seaward strained to catch a glimpse of the unknown intruder they had been called upon to drive off. Gunners prepared their guns for loading and small arms were broken out. Fire hoses were strung along the deck. Officers kept a ready hand on the hilts of their swords on the chance that boarders would have to be repelled. After tensely waiting at their stations for more than an hour, the boatswain's whistle rang. The crew was being quieted down.

The men looked at each other quizzically until the realization hit them. It had been a drill! Recognizing this, and knowing that their sleep had been interrupted for no apparently good reason, the grumbling began anew. First the grog, now this. Few were in a good mood, especially when told by Pickering the reason for the drill: attacks can come in the middle of the night, and so can fires. The crew would have to be ready under all conditions. Cooler heads recognized that he was right, but only hours after taking away their grog, this was certainly not a good night for a drill.[31]

On September 28, 1862, while anchored in Algeciras, Pickering received a telegram from the United States minister at London. It told of a Confederate ship which had been terrorizing American merchant ships. The mysterious raider had already captured and burned 10 of them in the month of September alone.[32]

The *Kearsarge*'s coal bunkers were full. She had only to replenish her food supplies and she could be under way in search of this upstart. Pickering ordered his vessel headed for Gibraltar for the necessary supplies.

On September 29, an entourage from the nearby *Tuscarora* boarded the *Kearsarge*. The officers of the *Tuscarora*, led by their Captain T. Augustus Craven, had received a telegram similar to the one Pickering had received. Craven and Pickering had gathered their officers to discuss the strategy they would employ to hunt down the rebel raider. After a discussion of several hours, the *Tuscarora*'s officers returned to their ship, and it was not long before both American vessels were under way.

As the *Kearsarge* neared the open sea Pickering had the boatswain pipe the crew to the deck. After all had gathered, he told them where they would be going. It would not be blockade duty, but something even better; something which promised the action so many had sought when they signed on. Their new assignment would be to join the *Tuscarora* to hunt down and destroy a Confederate raider that has been burning their merchant ships. This raider called herself the *Alabama*, and her captain was a man named Raphael Semmes.

They would be going to the Azores in search of her, and Pickering ordered every crew member to pay attention while on deck. Any sails were to be reported. Pickering planned to stop every one of them until he found his foe. And when he did, he would sink her!

The *Kearsarge* and the *Tuscarora* would not be alone in their search. Secretary of the Navy Gideon Welles had dedicated a small armada to the task. In addition to the *Kearsarge* and the *Tuscarora*, Welles had also ordered the *Dacotah, Wachusett, St. Lawrence, St. Louis, Santiago de Cuba, Octorora, San Jacinto, Cimarron, Tioga, Sonoma,* and *Vanderbilt* into the effort. He had even sent the USS *Alabama*, an old ship-of-the-line, to join the search, perhaps hoping one *Alabama* would attract the other.[33]

Despite the concentrated effort, nobody even suspected just how long it would be until Semmes and the *Alabama* would be located.

CHAPTER SIX
OCTOBER 1862

Following the capture of the *Elisha Dunbar*, the *Alabama* found few ships for nearly two weeks. The whaling season had come to an end and so had the presence of the whalers. Where the *Alabama* previously had her choice of several sails to chase, now there were few sails to be seen. This did not bother Sailing Master Arthur Sinclair, Jr. Capturing 10 ships in slightly less than two weeks had been enough excitement for him. He wrote that invariably he would just fall asleep after a four-hour watch when one of the quartermasters would hold a lantern to his face to wake him and tell him that he was needed to board a prize.[1]

Jack spent much of his time fishing when Semmes wasn't finding new things for him to do. The men shuddered when they saw Kell approaching with a piece of paper in his hand. They knew he had been talking to Semmes and was now preparing to post the latest assignments on a nearby bulkhead.[2]

Semmes himself slept little, consumed most of the time with working over charts in his cabin. He also spent a great deal of time before his shrine. His crew made fun of this routine, joking about "keeping all them little saints and angels lit up all the time with them wax candles in the cabin."[3]

After several days of frustration, Semmes gathered his officers to tell them of a new tactic he had devised. The whalers were gone. There would be few ships in the area until the weather improved. The *Alabama* would turn toward Newfoundland, where she would cruise the main trade route between North America and Europe. Semmes had calculated that there would be an abundance of Union merchant ships hauling grain along that route, just ready to be boarded.

Second Lieutenant Richard Armstrong spoke up. While he agreed with his captain that there would be many Union merchant ships, Armstrong feared that also would mean there would be an abundance of Federal cruisers. After all, he reasoned, they certainly weren't going to let their merchant ships unprotected. Armstrong was a graduate of the United States Naval Academy in Annapolis and had served only a short time in the navy when war had broken out. With no hesitation he had resigned and gone home to Georgia to offer his services. He had served under Kell on the steamer *Savannah* and with Semmes on the *Sumter*, and he was not uncomfortable challenging Semmes when he thought he was right.

Semmes admitted that Armstrong was correct, but the *Alabama* would have to go where the ships are. If the Federal cruisers happened to be there, too, the *Alabama* would just have to be careful because Semmes had no intention of challenging them. That was not his mission. If they encountered merchant ships they would strike quickly and leave the area before word got back to Washington where they were. By that time, Semmes would be far away. What Armstrong did not know was that Semmes had already spotted a pattern: the Union ships were invariably heading to where he had already been seen, not to where he was going. The *Alabama* would capitalize on that throughout her entire cruise.[4]

Semmes put his plan into action, and the *Alabama* made her way toward Newfoundland. The prisoners from the *Virginia* and the *Elisha Dunbar* remained on board, under the watchful eye of Marine Lieutenant Beckett K. Howell, a brother of Mrs. Jefferson Davis. With their cruise concentrated in the Azores it had never been a problem to put prisoners ashore. Now, however, in the open sea, this was not possible.

Shadrach Tilton, captain of the *Virginia*, complained bitterly about his treatment. Kept in irons below deck, Tilton protested to Semmes that he and his crew spent much of their time soaked with incoming seawater. Semmes was unmoved, saying that the Union had once captured his purser and had his head shaved, and retaliation of some sort was in order.[5]

On September 29, the crew of the *Alabama* had their hopes momentarily elevated when a sail was sighted. When the ship was overtaken, however, they found her to be a French bark.

Then the *Alabama*'s luck changed, making Semmes look like a genius to his officers and men. They were, indeed, back among the Union shipping channels. The *Emily Farnum*, commanded by Captain N. P. Simes, had the misfortune of becoming the first prize captured by the *Alabama* in more than two weeks. She was captured while the *Alabama* was sailing under the British flag. Before she could be dealt with, however, a second sail appeared and was halted with a shot across her bow. The second unfortunate vessel was the *Brilliant*, under Captain George Hagar. The *Emily Farnum* and the *Brilliant* had been sailing together. Now, they sat together as prizes of the *Alabama*.

Lieutenant Armstrong boarded the *Emily Farnum*, while Master's Mate James Evans did the same on the *Brilliant*. Both captains were ordered to gather their papers and report to Semmes.

For the first time, Semmes was faced with a difficult decision concerning a prize. The papers on the *Emily Farnum* proved with no doubt that, while she was a Union ship, her cargo was neutral.[6] The fact that the *Alabama* was still carrying 68 prisoners may have made the decision a bit easier. Semmes ruled that the *Emily Farnum* would be spared, much to the consternation of the officers and crew of the *Alabama*. She would be used to take off the prisoners, with Captain Simes promising to take them to Liverpool.

The *Brilliant* was another matter, however. Captain Hagar explained to Semmes that his cargo of grain was British, but he had no papers to prove it. Semmes was unsympathetic, perhaps still chagrined that he had been forced to release the *Emily Farnum*. He ruled that the *Brilliant* would be fired.

For the next several hours usable items were transferred from the *Brilliant* to the *Alabama*. At dusk, the order was given and the fire was set. As she burned, three crewmen from the *Brilliant* plus another from the *Emily Farnum* decided to cast their lot with the *Alabama*. John Allen, William Clark, and David Thurston, all seamen, and Ordinary Seaman David Williams were now in the service of the Confederacy.

The burning of the *Brilliant* touched off a huge outcry back in the United States. Captain Hagar had proven to be both knowledgeable and articulate, and his eventual report from Liverpool triggered a special meeting of the Chamber of Commerce of the State of New York. In the official proceedings, the issue of British involvement was raised once more, the first time it had become an issue since the *290* had set sail. In part, the chamber stated that ". . . this act awaits the judgment of neutral nations, whose opinion thereon will doubtless be expressed in due time."

The proceedings also included a detailed description of the *Alabama*, with a request that it be publicized so that she would be easily recognized. The officers were also named.

The chamber adopted several strongly worded resolutions, one of which characterized the burning of the *Brilliant* as a crime against humanity. Although the chamber expressed a desire to maintain cordial relations with the people of Great Britain, it noted that vessels were being fitted out in Great Britain and manned by British sailors. The chamber also charged that England was permitting and encouraging acts of destruction against American shipping. The resolutions included a thinly veiled threat, warning the merchants of Great Britain that any repetition of such acts would produce ". . . the most wide-spread exasperation in this country." The resolution called for all who valued peace and good will to prevent any additional vessels from leaving the ports of England. Copies of the proceedings were sent to the Boards of Trade in London and Liverpool, and the American minister in London, Charles Francis Adams, was told to use his own judgment in presenting the protest to the British Foreign Office.[7]

During the period that the Chamber of Commerce of the State of New York was meeting and drafting its proceedings, the *Alabama* continued her work. Her first victim following the firing of the *Brilliant* was another ship out of New York, the *Wave Crest,* under the command of John E. Harmon. Before she was fired she was used as a target by the *Alabama*'s practicing gunners.

As the *Wave Crest* burned, another ship approached. Seeing the smoke, her suspicious captain, Samuel B. Johnson, chose to run. She was the brigantine *Dunkirk*, and the swifter *Alabama* quickly overhauled her. Fullam and Midshipman William Sinclair boarded Johnson's ship. As was the custom, Johnson was ordered to gather his papers and go with the *Alabama*'s officers to meet with Semmes.

When Semmes introduced himself, Johnson cursed his luck. He had heard of the *Alabama* but thought she was still in the Azores. Resigned to his fate, he returned to his ship one last time, where he informed his crew that they were now prisoners of the Confederacy.[8] The prisoners returned to the *Alabama* not knowing what would become of them. Those who had heard of Semmes feared the worst. After all, he was a pirate! They gathered in a poorly dressed line on the deck of their captor, where Semmes and his officers looked them over in the gathering dusk.

Semmes slowly walked the length of the line, examining each man and expressing quiet thanks that none of them was in his crew. Then he halted and returned to the man he had just passed. A closer examination of the man's face revealed an ex-crewman from the *Sumter*, Able-Bodied Seaman George Forrest.

Forrest realized that there was no escaping. He had indeed been on the *Sumter*, but had chosen to desert. While he had always hoped to see Semmes again, he had longed for different circumstances. After a brief conversation Semmes reminded Forrest of the punishment for desertion in wartime: the offender would be put to death.

Forrest was not certain how serious Semmes was about all this, and he wisely refrained from arguing. It may have saved his life. Semmes ordered him to be put in irons until a court-martial could be convened. Forrest may hang, but he'd be given a fair trial first.

Perhaps he feared similar treatment, or maybe he decided he really wanted to fight for the Confederacy. For whatever the reason, Seaman David Leggett chose to sign on with the *Alabama*.[9]

The *Dunkirk* proved to be an interesting capture from another perspective, as well. An examination of her papers suggested that she might have been involved in a smuggling operation. Smuggling was a common means of supplementing profits, and the boarding party gave it little thought. The product being smuggled, however, surprised even Semmes. Several copies of the New Testament, translated into Portuguese, along with religious tracts in the same language, were discovered. On one of the bundles the instruction was written to avoid taking them ashore, as it was against the law. Interestingly, however, someone had drawn a line through this admonition, adding a handwritten instruction to report anything of interest that may occur in the distribution of the testaments and tracts. It also suggested taking orders for additional Bibles and forwarding them to the New York Bible Society.[10]

On October 9, 1862, at 10:00 A.M., a court-martial was convened in the wardroom. An apprehensive George Forrest, still in irons, was led into the room. First Lieutenant John McKintosh Kell presided over the hearing. Others who sat on the court-martial board were Second Lieutenant Richard Armstrong, Master Arthur Sinclair, Surgeon Francis L. Galt, Lieutenant of Marines Beckett K. Howell, and Captain's Clerk William Breedlove Smith, who served as judge advocate.[11]

About three hours into the court-martial the lookout reported a large sail. The hearing promptly adjourned and the *Alabama* began her pursuit. No prize would be lost because of the indiscretions of a former crew member.

Late in the afternoon, the ship, the *Tonawanda*, was overtaken. The prize in hand, the court-martial was reconvened. Within 30 minutes a verdict was reached.

While Forrest may have been cursing his luck at having been captured, a more objective view would have told him that luck was actually riding on his shoulder. With most of the officers knowing him from the *Sumter*, even though he had deserted, mercy was shown. His sentence: to serve on the *Alabama* for the duration of her cruise with no pay, except that necessary for clothing and liberty money.[12] He may have thought it harsh, but it was better than hanging. Despite the mercy shown, Forrest vowed to get even with everyone involved in the court-martial. He would prove to be a troublemaker for the remainder of his time on the cruise.

Back on deck the crew was amazed at the size of the *Tonawanda*. Captained by Theodore Julius, she dwarfed the *Alabama*. She was carrying 75 passengers, 30 of them women and children, and their terror was apparent from the cries which carried across the hundred yards between the ships. Fourth Lieutenant John Low was the boarding officer.

Semmes and Low consulted when the fourth lieutenant returned to the *Alabama*. The presence of the women and children presented a dilemma. There was no way of disposing of them ashore, and the *Alabama* certainly couldn't accommodate them on board.

Semmes pondered his options, which were few. Finally, he reached a decision. Even though the *Tonawanda* wasn't neutral, he would release her on bond. But the *Alabama* was going to cruise in her wake, and if they found a prize of lesser value Semmes would transfer the passengers and crew to that one, then fire the *Tonawanda*.

Then Low made Semmes aware of one more thing he could not have anticipated. One crewman from the *Tonawanda* wanted to join the *Alabama*, which was not all that unusual, but there was also a slave from Delaware on board with his master. Low suggested that Semmes claim him as a prize of war.

A short while later, Ordinary Seaman William Halford stood before Semmes, prepared to sign the muster roll. Beside him stood a young slave, who was obviously terrified. He gave his name as David White. He thought he might be about 16 or 17 years old, but he was not sure.

Semmes decided he could use a mess steward, and Dr. Galt could always use another pair of hands. When presented with the options, White probably didn't see many choices, and he agreed to become a part of the crew, albeit with little enthusiasm.

During the remainder of the *Alabama*'s cruise, the young slave would go ashore many times with the wardroom steward to purchase supplies. Although he would be enticed by the American consul or his representatives to jump ship on many occasions, he never did, choosing to remain loyal to Semmes and the *Alabama*.

The next day, Captain Julius was brought on board from the *Tonawanda* as a hostage, an added precaution in the unlikely event that the boarding party would be overpowered and the *Tonawanda* taken back. The two ships cruised in tandem for two days, during which time an English brig and a Mecklenburg ship were stopped but allowed to proceed when their nationalities were established.

On October 11, the cry "Sail, ho!" came down from the lookout. Within two hours the speedy *Alabama* had overhauled her and identified her as the *Manchester,* commanded by John Landerskin. She was only two years old and was in excellent condition. Low was assigned to head the boarding party, and he valued the *Manchester* and her cargo of grain at $164,000. This would not be the ship of lesser value that Semmes had in mind when he talked of transferring passengers.

As the *Manchester* burned, Semmes read newspapers taken from the *Manchester* to learn how the war was going. It also provided him with much entertainment that he shared with his crew. Several editorials labeled the *Alabama* a pirate ship, and demanded that Semmes be hanged. More importantly, however, was the intelligence information he gathered. One of the newspapers was a *New York Herald* less than a week old. Incredibly, it listed the size and number of the Union gunboats! Kell looked over Semmes's shoulder as he perused the list of nearly two hundred gunboats, listed by name and type.[13]

Semmes took a pencil and crossed out the name of a sidewheeler, commenting to nobody in particular that the sidewheeler was too slow to ever be a problem to him. Kell pointed to another name on the list that he thought could be scratched off. Semmes agreed, and the two spent the next hour evaluating the ships on the list. When they were done, the original list had been pared down to only 13 ships that Semmes believed he had any need to worry about. The others could come around as they pleased. The *Alabama*, either faster or better equipped, would have no difficulty in fending them off or capturing them. Having to watch for only 13 ships as opposed to nearly two hundred was valuable information indeed, and it was all provided by the Northern press.

Back in Washington, Gideon Welles was seeing the same news, and it made him furious. His temper did not improve any when he received a suggestion from a shipowner that all future ships be convoyed because it was apparent that the navy was incapable of locating the *Alabama*. Many owners went so far as to forge counterfeit foreign registers,[14] and even Admiral David Porter complained that the navy always sailed to where Semmes had been, as if expecting him to wait.

On October 13, a large vessel was spotted approaching very rapidly. The conclusion on the *Alabama* was that she was either a whaler or a man-of-war. The rebel crew hoped almost unanimously that it was the former, not only because there would be no battle, but also because the oil-soaked whalers made the best fires.

Semmes ordered his gunners to cast loose the guns and get them loaded in the event that the stranger was less than friendly. Excitement mounted as the ship drew nearer, a long pendant now visible on her masthead. The prisoners were to be disappointed, however, as the approaching vessel turned out to be only a Spanish merchant ship, adorned with an ornament of a man-of-war. The crew of the *Alabama* looked at her with contempt, many grumbling that she appeared more interested in appearance than good maritime etiquette.[15]

Next day, the Danish ship *Judith* was chased and overtaken by two shots across the bow. A French schooner and an English ship were also hailed. The captain of the English ship, spying the St. George's Cross flying from the *Alabama*'s mast, saluted her, a greeting returned by Semmes. The *Alabama*'s practice of flying the flags of other nations was not at all uncommon, and had been done by ships of most countries for many years as a means of disguise. The practice would come to be condemned by the Northern press, however, as it became known that this deception was responsible for the demise of several Union vessels.

The weather was now becoming a concern to Semmes. The barometer was dropping and the wind was increasing. It wasn't long before the rain began to fall. Semmes was faced with the decision of what to do with the *Tonawanda* and her passengers. If the threatening gale materialized, he could lose the *Tonawanda* in the storm. Captain Julius agreed to sign a ransom bond in the amount of $80,000, binding the owners to pay that amount to the Confederate government, and the *Tonawanda* was released, leading to a joyous demonstration on the part of her passengers.

With the winds howling and the rain blowing at times horizontally, the *Alabama* pressed on. The sight of a sail was too much to resist, however, and the bark *Lamplighter* soon became the *Alabama*'s next victim. The seas were becoming rough, and Semmes and his officers agreed that the *Lamplighter* could probably have gotten away if she had tried. Her captain, O. V. Harding, appeared to be a skilled seaman, as was his crew. Harding chose to accept his fate, and the boarding party was sent over.

Their efforts were rewarded when they realized the *Lamplighter*'s cargo was tobacco, a luxury in short supply on the *Alabama*. The cargo was transferred and the prize set ablaze.

As the weather worsened, Semmes ordered that only essential sails be used, and that others be furled before it became too dangerous to send men aloft. Lifelines were strung and quarter boats swung in and secured.[16] By October 17 the *Alabama* found herself in the throes of a full-fledged hurricane. The weather bumkin, or boom, could not take the strain of the wind and the twisting of the sails, and it snapped with a loud crack. The main yard, now unsupported, lurched forward and also broke, ripping the topsail in the process. A giant wave carried the whaleboat away. With several of the yards and sails now gone, it was becoming difficult to keep the *Alabama*'s head into the wind. The pressure of the foretopmast staysail threatened to swamp the floundering vessel. Fortunately, Captain of the Foretop William Morgan saw what was happening. Climbing quickly to the staysail halyards he cut the sail away, relieving the pressure and averting what threatened to be a disaster.

Semmes would later estimate the diameter of the hurricane to be between one hundred sixty and two hundred miles. It appeared that the *Alabama* had sailed directly through it at its widest point. After several hours the winds died down, leading many on board to believe that the storm was over. However, Semmes knew that, rather than having passed through the hurricane, they merely were in the center of the vortex. Semmes ordered the hatches battened down and told the crew to prepare for heavy seas. Although he would not tell his men, he feared that the *Alabama* was doomed, knowing that few had ever sailed directly through a hurricane. For 45 minutes the *Alabama* received a respite, but then the winds picked up once more, this time from the opposite direction, as the ship passed out of the hurricane's eye and into the swirling winds again. If anything, the storm was worse on this side, and the barometer dropped to 28.64. Semmes reported that it rose and fell rapidly, never fluctuating above 29.70.

The crew cowered anywhere they could find shelter from the stinging spray of the sea. At times it was necessary to cover their faces just so they could breathe. Semmes ordered the wheel double manned, with both men lashed to it. Several times the *Alabama* actually lay over on her side, then righted herself. Sea foam sprayed in all directions, giving the appearance of a snow storm. Lightning struck the masts and passed into the water with a hissing sound. By evening the storm had passed, although the seas remained rough. There had been several minor injuries, but nothing serious, and nobody had been swept overboard.

It would not be until the next day that damage could be assessed.[17] The hurricane had taken its toll. The main yard had been lost along with its sail, and a cutter had been smashed. Rigging became a makeshift clothesline for the crew's saturated clothing. Semmes's collection of 17 United States flags, each representing a captured Union ship, had also been soaked. The quartermaster brought them topside to dry on the signal halyards. The display, while it must have been impressive, must also have appeared strange even to the experienced sailors on board.

There would be plenty of work for the boatswain, gunners, sailmaker, and carpenter over the next several weeks. As the crew worked to bring the *Alabama* back to trim, the lookouts maintained their vigils, spotting four ships over the next week. All were neutral. One, the English bark *Heron*, was chased with the British colors flying. When Semmes realized the *Heron* was neutral, he called off the chase. The captain of the *Heron*, eager to learn who had been pursuing him, asked for her name. Semmes replied that his ship was Her Majesty's Steamer *Racehorse*.[18]

On October 23, the *Alabama* chased another ship that proved to be an English brig. As the chase was ending, the lookout gave the familiar cry, "Sail ho!" The new vessel was a beauty, impressing even Semmes. After a short chase and a blank warning shot, the quarry halted, seemingly resigned to her fate. She was the *Lafayette*, out of New Haven and commanded by Alfred T. Small. The *Lafayette* had set sail just three days earlier and was bound for Belfast with a load of wheat and corn. Semmes convened his officers in what he was now calling the Confederate States Admiralty Court. Kell and Low were given the unofficial titles of associate justices. Reviewing the sworn affidavits with their consular seals, it was the court's duty to determine if the papers were genuine. The affidavits swore that the cargo was assigned to British concerns in Belfast, but Semmes's experience in admiralty law helped him recognize that the shippers were, in fact, an American branch of those companies. This meant, in effect, that the shippers were actually sending the cargo to themselves. International law stated that even a neutral merchant, if stationed in an enemy country, could be classified as an enemy merchant. Semmes knew this, and it did not take long for him to render his verdict. The ship would be burned. This action would give rise to British protests, claiming that Semmes and the *Alabama* had committed an act of piracy against a British-owned cargo. It was not the first time and would certainly not be the last time that Semmes would be accused of piracy.[19]

With the weather getting colder, Semmes ordered the prisoners to be housed in the forward fire room, rather than under a canopy on the main deck. In that location they were protected from the weather, but would have no view of the next day's chase, which proved to be an English brig.

On October 26 a Union schooner was observed. After a short chase, two shots were fired over her at a distance of about three miles. Her captain, William Nelson, saw the folly of trying to escape, and the *Crenshaw* became the Alabama's 19th prize. Armstrong commanded the boarding crew, and the *Crenshaw* soon lit the evening sky.

Newspapers captured from the *Crenshaw* carried an account by George Hagar, captain of the *Brilliant*, of how poorly he and his crew had been treated by the *Alabama*. If the crew of the *Crenshaw* had read those papers, it had little effect on them. Three ordinary seamen, James Clements, Walter Van Ness, and Martin Miditch, signed on with the *Alabama*. This brought the number of men who had signed with the *Alabama* from enemy crews to 11.

The next sail spied belonged to another American vessel, the *Lauretta*. Captained by Marshall M. Wells, she, as had the *Lafayette*, carried neutral papers. The first packet Semmes read carried a Portuguese seal, which he threw to the floor with a curse. The second packet, which happened to be Italian, received the same treatment. Semmes examined the third packet, which carried the British seal. In it was a bill of lading for pipe staves and nearly one thousand barrels of flour, all shipped by a British subject named H. J. Burden. Semmes was suspicious and he demanded that Wells tell him whether Burden was truly an Englishman. When Wells replied in the affirmative, Semmes let out another oath and indicated quite vocally that he did not believe Wells, and he immediately ruled that the ship and its cargo should be burned.[20]

As the *Lauretta* burned, the *Alabama* continued to augment her crew with enemy sailors. Ordinary Seaman Alfred Morris left his crewmates on the *Lauretta* and became the newest member of the raider's crew.

The next afternoon a sail was sighted off the starboard bow. She turned out to be a Dutch bark, but while the *Alabama* was evaluating her, five additional sails came into view. Selecting one of the ships, Semmes chased her down in the gathering darkness.

The ship was the *Baron de Castine*, a brig just 10 days out of Bangor, Maine. Her captain, John Saunders, made no claims of neutrality. With 44 prisoners on board, however, Semmes saw an opportunity. Saunders agreed to sign a ransom bond, and Semmes allowed him to sail away intact, carrying off the prisoners. It was, no doubt, a satisfactory agreement for both parties. Saunders carried a taunting message to the New York Chamber of Commerce from Semmes that stated, by the time they read the message, Semmes would be sitting in New York harbor.[21]

This was no idle boast. Semmes actually intended to sail within sight of New York City and burn a few vessels in full view of the city, striking quickly and sailing away just as fast. On October 30, Semmes gathered his officers in the wardroom and told them of his intentions. This was something the officers had wanted to do for some time, and they toasted the plan. Almost as quickly, however, someone pointed out that the *Alabama*'s coal supply would only last four days, and Semmes reluctantly had to call off the plan. Instead, the *Alabama* turned southward for a rendezvous with the *Agrippina*.

* * *

It took nearly a week for the *Tuscarora* and the *Kearsarge* to reach the Azores. Several ships had been stopped but none had been the *Alabama*. Unknown to Pickering and Craven, their quarry had captured two more American prizes since the search had begun.[22] On the evening of October 5 the *Tuscarora* and *Kearsarge* entered the harbor of Terceira in the Azores.

Inquiries revealed that the *Alabama* had not been seen, so the two left almost immediately for the island of Fayal. At the port of Horta, their luck improved, but just barely. Merchants boarded the *Kearsarge* to sell their wares, and Pickering immediately bombarded them with questions about the *Alabama*. Yes, they said, there had been a ship in Horta which called herself the *Alabama*, but she had departed nearly a month ago.[23] This would not be the last time the *Kearsarge* found herself several weeks behind the *Alabama*.

On October 8, the *Kearsarge* left Horta, hoping somehow that the *Alabama* had remained in the area. Pickering knew that the weather would soon turn foul, driving the American whaling ships from the vicinity as they followed the whales to warmer climates, but the whalers had not yet departed. Most likely, the *Alabama* would follow the same pattern.[24] Pickering had guessed correctly.

Only a few hours out of Horta a sail was spotted and the *Kearsarge* immediately gave chase. Pickering looked at his prey through his glass and was immediately disappointed. She was a sidewheeler. The *Alabama* had been reported to be much more sleek, and probably a lot faster than a sidewheeler. The chase was not called off, however. Any ship in this area could be Confederate. She didn't have to be the *Alabama* to be sent to the bottom.

As the chase continued, the officers speculated on the identity of their elusive target. Finally, they reached the consensus that she was probably the *Hero*, a known blockade runner. Sinking her would give the crew only slightly less satisfaction than sinking the *Alabama*. At this point, they just wanted to make contact with the enemy.[25]

The pursuit lasted several hours and some two hundred miles before Pickering gave up. It was apparent that they were no longer gaining on the strange sidewheeler, and Chief Engineer William Cushman was developing grave concerns for the condition of his engines. At Cushman's request, Pickering ordered the engines stopped and the sails set, while the exhausted engine room crew received a medicinal stimulant in the form of a special ration of grog.[26]

Ironically, they put in at Angra de Heroismo on the island of Terceira, unaware that the *Alabama* had taken on her guns and supplies there while she was still known as the *Enrica*. It was October 11, and at about the same time the *Kearsarge* was limping into the harbor, the *Alabama*'s boarding crew was clambering onto the *Manchester*.

The next morning the crippled *Kearsarge* left for Horta. There, Chief Engineer Cushman had the time to make a thorough inspection of his engines, after which he informed Pickering that he would need a minimum of five days to make the proper repairs.

While Cushman and his crew worked on the engines, supplies were brought aboard. With the supplies came water snakes, which crawled up the anchor chain and onto the ship. By now, crew members were becoming accustomed to watching for the snakes as they walked the decks.[27]

Meanwhile, back in Washington, Gideon Welles was having his fill of the *Alabama*. Almost daily, reports were pouring in that had the Confederate ship in several places at once, if the reports were to be believed. It seemed that every unidentified ship was thought to be the *Alabama*.

Finally, having reached his limit, Welles sent a dispatch to Acting Rear Admiral S. P. Lee, commander of the North Atlantic Blockading Squadron. The dispatch included photos of the *Alabama*. The *Emily Farnham* and the *Brilliant* had just been burned, and the *Brilliant*'s Captain Hagar had informed Welles that Semmes might be headed for Cape Breton to meet an English vessel. Hagar thought that the *Alabama* might be taking on additional rifled guns there. Welles ordered Lee to send the *San Jacinto* to look for the rebel ship.[28]

His engine repairs made, Pickering and the *Kearsarge* set sail on October 15. The next day she anchored at Sao Miguel, to allow Pickering to meet with the vice-consul there. While in port, apparently having had enough excitement for one cruise, Ordinary Seamen Daniel Lahie and Thomas Jones deserted.[29]

The next two days were uneventful, but on the third a sail was sighted. A brief chase ensued and ended when the *Kearsarge* fired a blank shot in the unidentified ship's direction. Pickering sent a boat to bring the captain back. When the captain arrived, he gazed up at the fluttering Stars and Stripes and hoped the flag was not a ruse. He climbed aboard, trepidation accompanying every step. When Pickering demanded the name of the ship the captain told him she was the *Eddystone*. The terrified man begged Pickering not to set fire to his ship.

A puzzled Pickering responded that the *Kearsarge* was not in the habit of firing vessels, to which the relieved captain responded that he had been sure the *Alabama* had captured him. As the *Eddystone* finally sailed away, the men of the *Kearsarge* laughed about the story the captain would someday tell his grandchildren.

Stopping at Madeira the next day, the *Kearsarge* took on additional supplies despite just having done so a few weeks earlier. Technically, a belligerent ship was not permitted to take on supplies in neutral ports more often than every three months, but the local officials were not sticklers for international protocol. Several bottles of wine found their way on board, despite Pickering's edict against it, and the effects of the secret supply would be seen at regular intervals over the next few months.[30]

On October 24 the *Kearsarge* made her way into the Straits of Gibraltar, passing the famous rock. Anchoring well after midnight, Pickering paid little heed to the silhouette of the *Sumter*, still anchored where he had last seen her several weeks earlier. For the next week the *Kearsarge* observed the *Sumter*, with the crew grumbling daily about the folly of watching a ship rust away when they could be chasing the *Alabama*. The surprised crew would soon learn that, not only was the *Kearsarge* to watch the *Sumter*, they were also going to have help. That assistance soon arrived in the form of the USS *Chippewa*.

At the Department of the Navy, anyone reading Gideon Welles's diary would have sensed the anger and frustration that was beginning to mount. "The ravages by the roving steamer *290*, alias *Alabama*, are enormous," he wrote. "England should be held accountable for these outrages. The vessel was built in England and has never been in the ports of any other nation. British authorities were warned of her true character repeatedly before she left."[31]

CHAPTER SEVEN

NOVEMBER–DECEMBER 1862

On November 1, 1862, while the *Alabama* was en route to a rendezvous with the *Agrippina*, the lookout reported seeing a sail. A chase ensued and a blank cartridge brought the quarry to a halt. The prize was the *Levi Starbuck*, a whaler. This was the first whaler sighted by the *Alabama* since the *Elisha Dunbar* had been burned in mid-September, nearly two months earlier. Under the command of Thomas Mellen, she had left New Bedford only a few days earlier, and her holds were stuffed with such delicacies as cabbage, turnips, and other antiscorbutics. The *Alabama*'s crew would find these a welcomed relief from the diet of salt pork, dried beef, and navy beans that they had been eating for more than two months. Following removal of the desired items, the *Levi Starbuck* was destined to burn, just as most of her predecessors.[1]

It was six days before another sail was sighted. Flying American colors, she showed no alarm when the *Alabama* did the same. When the Yankee vessel signaled a greeting and asked what the *Alabama*'s name was, Semmes signaled back, "The USS *Ticonderoga*."

There was no suspicion on the part of the Union ship, at least until the *Alabama* fired a blank and raised the Confederate ensign. The captured prize was the *Thomas B. Wales*, commanded by Edgar Lincoln, who so impressed Semmes with his excellent grammar and pronunciation that the latter commented on it to his officers.

The *Thomas B. Wales* carried valuable cargo, valuable in the sense that it would have contributed to the war effort if it had gotten through. She carried saltpeter, jute, and linseed oil. The saltpeter was a valuable ingredient in the production of gunpowder, and the jute was probably a replacement for cotton, which was becoming quite scarce in the North. Telling themselves that the jute could have been made into Union uniforms, the officers felt quite proud of having intercepted such an important cargo. That pride grew even stronger after Kell placed a value of $245,625 on the captured ship. This was significant because it meant that the *Alabama* had now passed the $1 million mark in the value of ships destroyed.

Perhaps of more importance, however, was the fact that the *Thomas B. Wales* carried the U.S. Consul at Mauritius, George H. Fairchild, and his family. Captain Lincoln's wife was also aboard. Semmes ordered his officers to vacate their quarters, allowing Mrs. Lincoln, Mr. and Mrs. Fairchild, and several children to be placed in the *Alabama*'s wardroom.[2]

The Fairchilds and Lincolns spent much of their time with Semmes, apparently showing no ill will to the Confederate captain. Their friendship would prove invaluable to Semmes after the war, when an official inquiry into the behavior toward prisoners on board the *Alabama* would find no evidence that any mistreatment had taken place.[3]

It was not only the Fairchilds and the Lincolns who were made to feel at home on the *Alabama*. Eleven crew members of the *Thomas B. Wales* chose to sign on. Samuel Brewer, William Burns, Louis Dupois, Henry Godson, Joseph Neal, Juan Ochoa, James Raleigh, Michael Shields, Charles Steeson, James Williams, and Joseph Martin all became members of the *Alabama*'s crew, bringing the complement to 26 officers and 110 men, only 10 short of a full crew. No other prize taken by the *Alabama* had more men sign on.[4]

Before the *Thomas B. Wales* was fired, her main yard was measured. It appeared to be similar in size to the hurricane-damaged main yard of the *Alabama*, and with little modification it would serve as a more than adequate replacement. Boatswain Benjamin McCaskey and

Carpenter William Robinson were given the task of supervising the changeover. Their craftsmanship had the *Alabama* back in full trim within a few days.[5]

On November 11, nearing the Tropic of Cancer, the *Alabama* stopped two English ships. The first of these, which was never mentioned by name by Semmes in any of his writings, was out of New York. She was boarded by Fullam, who was surprised to find no evidence that the ship was American. Semmes had little choice but to let her go free. The ship's captain mentioned before leaving that he was familiar with the *Alabama* and what she had done to several Union merchant ships.

The second vessel chose to run from the Confederates, and it took a shot through her rigging to bring her to a halt. A boarding crew was sent over, which returned much sooner than Semmes would have expected. They reported that the ship, the *Princess Royal*, was a floating deathtrap, with many of the crew infected with yellow fever.[6]

The tiny Caribbean island of Dominica was spotted on November 17. This, however, was not the destination that Semmes had in mind. Although low on coal, he ordered the *Alabama*'s propeller lowered as they cruised along the coast. This order tipped off the crew that they were about to enter a port somewhere, because Semmes would never waste coal if he didn't have a plan to replenish it.

Less than 24 hours after the first land was sighted, the *Alabama* anchored in the port of Fort-de-France, Martinique. There, they spied the *Agrippina*. The crew immediately realized then that Semmes had known all along that he would be meeting the tender, which was carrying mail and coal.

Once in port, Semmes went ashore to pay his respects to Governor Moussion de Conde, whom he had met while on the *Sumter*. Their previous meetings had been less than cordial and Semmes was not sure he would be welcomed. This time, however, Conde extended his hospitality. He told Semmes that he had been expecting the *Alabama*, which surprised the rebel captain. It didn't take long for the governor to reveal the source of his information. He stated that the *Agrippina* had been in port for more than a week, and that a drunken Captain Alexander McQueen had been bragging to all who would listen that the *Agrippina* was a tender for the *Alabama*, and that the rebel ship would be arriving soon. Conde suggested to Semmes that he bring the *Alabama* further into the harbor, where she would be better protected.

Once safely docked, badly needed provisions were hastily loaded on board and prisoners were placed ashore. The *Alabama* prepared to leave port, less than 24 hours after she arrived. While in port, however, the men had eaten well, as Wardroom Steward Richard Parkinson had been given a free reign to cook whatever he wanted. It had been a long time since the crew had seen anything more than dried beef, and it could be a while before they would see a good meal again. Of course, the men did not spend all their time eating, and a considerable amount of liquor found its way back to the ship. One of those who had been responsible for bringing the liquor on board was George Forrest. Although he had not been permitted ashore, he had slipped down a cable when the officers were busy elsewhere. Entering the water, he swam to a nearby bumboat, where he bought five gallons of rum. Back on board, he passed it around without drinking any himself.

As the crew made short work of the rum they got louder and more raucous, Forrest finally instigated them into rushing the main deck. As they did, Forrest shouted, "Mutiny! Mutiny! We're taking the ship!"

The officers rushed to the forecastle, a belaying pin narrowly missing Kell. The angered first lieutenant ordered the sober crew members to arrest those who were causing the trouble, but he was ignored. Knives appeared, but those who were wielding them were too drunk to exhibit any degree of accuracy.

Semmes had been in his cabin enjoying a cup of tea and some fruit that Bartelli, his steward, had brought him, when the commotion began. Hearing the ruckus, he now appeared on deck. Turning to Kell, he ordered him to have the drummer "Beat to quarters!"

The drum and fife immediately began the beat, and the crew rushed to their respective quarters. Conditioned to respond under any circumstances, they were now reacting on instinct. Those who were most drunk presented a comical sight as they struggled to get to their assigned posts. Had it not been for the seriousness of the situation, Semmes probably would have permitted himself at least a grin.

However, mutiny was serious business and had to be treated accordingly. Slowly, order was restored as each man made his way to his assigned location. Armed with no more than belaying pins and sheath knives, they knew they would no longer be a match for the armed officers.

Semmes and Kell slowly made their way through the assembled ranks three times, each time looking closely at each man to be sure they had not missed anyone. After the third pass, Semmes ordered the men taken to the gangway.

Turning to his quartermasters, Semmes ordered them to get their draw-buckets and fill them with water. Then, he told them to dump the water over the mutineers. They were to keep the water coming until told to stop, and Semmes insisted that none of them be missed with the dousing.

The mutineers laughed. This wouldn't be so bad. "Come on with your water," they mocked the quartermasters. "We're not afraid of it."

Semmes had used this form of punishment before, unknown to the drunken protesters, and had found it to be quite effective. Obliging those who called for more water, the quartermasters soon had a veritable bucket brigade in full swing, keeping the water steadily coming. The more vocal miscreants came under closer scrutiny by their captain, who had them doused one at a time so they could have their own personal dunking.

Semmes signaled for the quartermasters to move even faster, and now the water was a never-ending stream. As the water crashed down on each man, bucket after bucket, it became difficult for the mutineers to breathe. One by one, they began to choke and sputter, punctuated by curses directed at the quartermasters, then at Semmes. The more they cursed and sputtered, the faster the water continued.

The men began to fear that they would be drowned, and they begged for mercy. Semmes ignored them. When another implored the bucket brigade to stop, his answer was another bucket of water. Semmes knew that stopping too soon would defeat his plan. A few more buckets wouldn't hurt them, he decided.

Finally, Semmes gave the order to the quartermasters to stop their deluge. The gasping mutineers collapsed to the deck, now somewhat more sober than they had been when the shower had started. The amused crew watched as Semmes ordered each man's irons taken off. Their fetters removed, the humbled victims slowly filed off to their hammocks, trailing a small river of water behind. The entire episode had lasted more than two hours, and the crew had been grateful for the diversion. For sometime after, the sailors had a saying: "Old Beeswax is hell on watering a fellow's grog!" For his part in the mutiny, Forrest was ordered trussed up in the rigging, spread-eagled, for two hours on and two hours off, until further notice.[7]

As the *Alabama* prepared to leave port, Semmes's fears concerning McQueen's loose tongue were realized. Conde's warning of Union ships patrolling the area had been correct, as the heavily armed *San Jacinto* stood between the *Alabama* and the open sea.

William Ronckendorff, commander of the *San Jacinto,* was not known for backing down. After all, this was the ship that had instigated the famed Trent Affair in the early stages of the war. If she had not been afraid to take on the British diplomatic corps, there was little doubt that she would not be intimidated by the *Alabama*'s reputation.

Semmes's former nemesis, the governor of Martinique, came to the assistance of the *Alabama*. Conde issued notices forbidding anyone in the town to communicate with the *San Jacinto*, and no supplies could be sent out to her. He also sent a message to Ronckendorff that he would have to either anchor or move outside the three-mile limit. Ronckendorff knew that if he anchored, he would be bound by the 24-hour rule, requiring him to wait a full day after the *Alabama* had departed before he could give chase. He chose to move further out to sea, but still close enough that he could watch the harbor exits.

The French gunboat *Fata* anchored near the *Alabama* as a thinly disguised signal to Ronckendorff that he could do nothing to the rebel steamer while she was in port. The *Fata*'s captain also showed Semmes the best escape routes out of the harbor.[8]

While the crew of the *Alabama* did not fear the *San Jacinto*, they also did not look forward to a direct confrontation with the more heavily armed vessel. Semmes sent the ship's gold ashore for safekeeping. He did not want it falling into Ronckendorff's hands. His plans were dashed, however, when the local bankers wanted to keep five percent for their trouble. "I'll let the *San Jacinto* have it first," Semmes fumed, and ordered the gold returned to the ship.[9]

Meanwhile, Ronckendorff asked a nearby American brig, the *Hampden*, to go in the harbor and watch the *Alabama*. The captain of the *Hampden* was to send up a rocket in the general direction of the *Alabama*'s flight. That night, with a light rain falling and clouds obscuring the moon, the *Alabama* silently slid out of the harbor. Each man strained to hear or see any evidence that they had been observed by anyone. The gunners stood tensely at their stations, prepared to return fire if the *San Jacinto* attacked. At 8:10 P.M., the signal was given indicating the *Alabama*'s exit from the harbor, but by then she had safely made her escape.[10] All Ronckendorff would get for his efforts was a severe reprimand from Welles for allowing the *Alabama* to get away.[11]

On November 21, nearing Blanquilla, Semmes spotted the *Agrippina*. Signaling McQueen to follow, the *Alabama* made her way toward the harbor. There a schooner lay at anchor. As the *Alabama* approached, the schooner hoisted the American flag. The *Alabama* did the same in answer. While the crew appeared fascinated by flamingos parading on the beach, Semmes and Kell focused their attention on a different activity.

The crew of the schooner had pitched a large tent on the beach, under which boilers were rendering blubber from a whale that lay alongside the ship. Shortly, the schooner's master approached in a small boat and requested permission to board the *Alabama*, commenting that it was good to see a ship from back home. Ignoring the comment, Semmes inquired as to the quality of the anchorage, whereupon the Yankee assured Semmes that he'd have no problems, and that he'd even be willing to pilot him in if he wished. The appreciative Semmes took him up on his offer. Spying the *Alabama*'s deck guns, the captain let out a low whistle, then remarked that his host would be able to give "that pirate Semmes" fits if they would meet. He also expressed his hope that somehow that might happen.

Then as the man watched, Semmes gave the quartermaster the signal to pull down the Stars and Stripes and run up the Confederate ensign. As the dumfounded man looked on, his mind struggled to grasp what he was seeing. Semmes said, "I am the pirate Semmes, and you are on the decks of the CSS *Alabama!*"

The captain realized there was no turning back. He could not deny what he had said. Looking panic-stricken, he waited for the announcement that his ship was to be burned, as he had heard so many times from others who had met such a fate.

However, this was to be his lucky day, and Semmes knew it as well. The schooner was in Venezuelan waters. While Semmes would like nothing better than to burn the ship, he realized he could not do it legally. Of course, he could capture it and release it later, but that would serve no purpose. As a result, the whaler would be set free.

When the relieved captain thanked Semmes, Semmes waved his hand and told him not to be too thankful yet. Semmes could not afford to take the chance that the ship would run under cover of darkness and report the *Alabama's* presence. To prevent that, Semmes ordered the captain and his mate to come aboard the *Alabama* every evening while the ship was in the harbor. They were allowed to return to their own ship each morning, but it was understood that they would come back to the *Alabama* each night. If they didn't, Semmes promised the captain that he would find a way to get the whaler out beyond the limit, at which time he would burn her to the water-line.

The captain reluctantly agreed. He did not relish the thought of spending every night with the piratical crew, and he knew his mate would feel no differently, but it was better than his only other choice. And thus it was that the *Clara L. Sparks* became one of the few Union ships to encounter the *Alabama* and suffer no ill effects.[12]

On November 25 another schooner, this one showing British colors, was sighted at anchor. Semmes sent a boarding party, which reported back that the captain of the British ship had told them that he had just left Barbados four days earlier, and that the *San Jacinto* had left the same port a day before that. He did not know where she was headed.

That same day, three new hands transferred from the *Agrippina* to the *Alabama*. George Yeoman, Martin Molk, and William Robinson all became ordinary seamen on the rebel ship.[13] The crew size actually decreased, however, as Edward Fitzsimmons, Michael Kinshlea, Thomas Walsh, and William Price were discharged as invalids.

The evening of the 26th, all hands were called to muster. The purpose was to read the sentence of the general court-martial of George Forrest, who had been found guilty of insubordination and inciting a mutiny. As the crew looked on, Forrest was ordered to forfeit all pay and prize money, return all clothing except for that which he owned when he had been captured, and that he be dismissed from both the ship and the Confederate navy. The master-at-arms was directed to take him ashore. As he left the ship, the unrepentant Forrest defiantly shook his fist in the general direction of Semmes and shouted that he'd get even some day.[14]

The coaling completed, the *Alabama* prepared to leave Blanquilla. Before leaving, Semmes told the captain of the *Clara L. Sparks* that he should not let the *Alabama* catch him again. "If I do," said Semmes, "it will not go as well for you the second time." The *Clara L. Sparks* quickly departed, taking with her the disgraced George Forrest, now a crew member.

Semmes now set his sights on one of the California mail-steamers, believed to be carrying a million dollar gold shipment. Newspapers from captured prizes showed the shipping routes and schedules, so he determined that it would not be all that difficult to intercept one of the steamers. In his exhilaration, he told the officers and crew of his intentions. The crew adopted his excitement, and each man spent every free moment at the rail, scanning the horizon for any sign of the treasure, as well as the several Union warships that were pursuing the *Alabama*.

On November 30, a sail was reported. In midafternoon the ship was captured and boarded. However, the *Parker Cook*, commanded by Thomas M. Fulton, carried no gold. Well into the night the crew of the *Alabama* relieved the *Parker Cook* of all her provisions until, at 9:00 P.M., she was set afire.

Over the next five days, nine ships were hailed. All were foreign, much to the disappointment of the crew. On December 5, while cruising between Cuba and St. Domingo, a schooner showing Yankee colors was spotted. The *Union*, under the command of Joseph H. Young, offered no resistance and was quickly boarded. The reason for the *Union*'s lack of resistance was quickly learned, as Semmes's admiralty court determined that the cargo was English. The decision was made to release her on a ransom bond of only $1,500, the amount reflecting the lack of value of her cargo.[15]

Before releasing the *Union,* the prisoners of the *Parker Cook* were transferred over to her. If Semmes had to release her because of a neutral cargo, she would at least serve a purpose of carrying off the prisoners that now clogged the decks of the *Alabama.*

Two days later, on December 7, 1862, with the crew mustered in clean uniforms for Sunday services, the cry "Sail ho!" came down from the lookout. The ship was a large steamer brig similar to the description of the gold ship! Semmes lifted his telescope to get a better look. She appeared to have no guns. There was no indication that she was a warship. Semmes continued to evaluate his prey while Kell ordered, "All hands work the ship!"

Boilers were fired and the propeller lowered. Each man scampered to his assigned post. Adrenaline flowed, as every crew member contemplated the fact that they could all be rich men within the hour.

Semmes had the United States flag run up, hoping the steamer would respond. There was no answer, however, and Semmes had the *Alabama* move across her path. The steamer was faster than Semmes had anticipated, and she passed before the *Alabama* could get into position. As she passed, Semmes noticed that the decks were full of passengers, many of them women. Several could be seen peering back through opera glasses.

At 2:45 in the afternoon Semmes had the gunners fire a blank cartridge as the quartermaster hoisted the Confederate flag. Several women on board the steamer screamed as they saw the six broadside guns trained on them. Passengers scurried to get below decks, replaced by marines at the rail.

As the steamer tried to escape, Semmes ordered the pivot guns fired. A second order was quickly given to fire at her smokestack. Both guns fired nearly simultaneously, one of which struck the foremast about 10 feet above the deck. Most of the mast was carried away, splinters raining down onto the marines below. The steamer's captain realized that he was no match for his adversary, and he ordered the ship to surrender. The marines, drawn up in fighting formation, reluctantly lay down their arms to avoid placing the passengers in danger after given the order by USMC Captain David Cohen.

Semmes sent a boarding party over, which reported his miscalculation. She was not carrying gold. The ship was the *Ariel,* a mail packet carrying 500 passengers, 140 marines, and a crew of 60. Captain Albert J. Jones, master of the *Ariel,* had no idea who his captor was. The *Alabama* had the ability to lower her smokestack, and Semmes had ordered this done. Thus, Jones saw no evidence at that point that he had been captured by a steamer. Only when Semmes ordered the smokestack raised did Jones begin to suspect that he had run afoul of the infamous Raphael Semmes.

Lieutenant Richard Armstrong, Coxswain George Freemantle, and a well-armed boarding party of about 20 men under the command of Fourth Lieutenant John Low held the *Ariel* while Jones and his papers were taken aboard the *Alabama.* While Jones was on the *Alabama,* his first officer, R. C. Thomas, wrote an account of the capture that would appear in *Frank Leslie's Illustrated Newspaper* a month later. The headline would read: "The Capture of the California Steamer *Ariel* by the Rebel Pirate Ship *Alabama*".[16] A similar article, no more complimentary, would also appear in *Harper's Weekly.*[17]

Armstrong did not just happen to be on board the *Ariel.* When the original boarding party reported the panic among the women, Semmes had summoned Armstrong. The handsome 19 year old was ordered to don his best uniform and get the best sword he could find. Semmes ordered Bartelli to get Semmes's best sword knot for Armstrong to wear. In a matter of minutes Armstrong looked resplendent.

Looking him over with approval, Semmes ordered him to go and use his charm to calm the ladies. He was also to do what he could to convince them that the men of the *Alabama* were not pirates, but Southern gentlemen who would protect them. Midshipman William Sinclair, who himself was young and attractive to the fair sex, would go along to assist.

Once on board, Armstrong and Sinclair began to work their way through the crowd, charming all the women but reserving special attention for the prettiest. Shyly, one young lady touched Armstrong's hand and asked if she could have one of his buttons as a remembrance of her encounter with the *Alabama*. Armstrong agreed and cut a button from his coat. Others, seeing the young lady's success, made similar requests and Armstrong and Sinclair were kept busy removing their brass buttons. Distracted, they did not see the men who were hiding their money and watches.[18]

The *Ariel* had been carrying $10,000 in its safe, which Semmes took. Passengers' personal items were left untouched. The question of what to do with nearly seven hundred prisoners now confronted Semmes. They would not all fit on the *Alabama*, he knew, so burning the *Ariel* was out of the question, at least for now.

Temporarily letting the boarding party in charge, Semmes and the *Alabama* gave chase to another vessel that proved to be neutral. As he returned to the *Ariel*, Semmes gave great thought to the dilemma. The problem was made more complicated by the fact that Commander Lewis C. Sartori of the United States Navy was one of the passengers. He could hold Sartori as a prisoner of war and release the others, or he could release everyone. He decided against keeping the marines on board the *Alabama* because of the uncertainty of being able to control them.

Semmes finally decided to parole Sartori while keeping all the passengers and disarmed marines on board the *Ariel*. The two ships would move together under sail for the next several days. To prevent the *Ariel* from escaping under steam in the event the *Alabama* should spot and chase another sail, Semmes had several of the prize's valves removed so that steam could not be generated.[19]

With his prize in tow, Semmes had his helmsman turn for Kingston, Jamaica, hoping to put his seven hundred prisoners ashore if the governor there would permit it. He could then burn the *Ariel*. Semmes knew that getting permission to land the prisoners could be difficult, however. International law prevented passengers from prizes from being taken into neutral ports, although Semmes suspected that Jamaica's governor would not be particularly stringent about this.

Early that morning the *Alabama* briefly detained an English schooner, then resumed her journey. Some 12 hours later, a brig was sighted in the darkness. The chase began, and Semmes ordered a shot fired at her. Just as the shot was fired and a boat lowered, word came from the engine room that the *Alabama*'s engine had failed when a valve casting had given way. The *Alabama* now had no steam power, and thus was unable to continue the chase. Firing another shot risked hitting the boat that was now under way to meet the stranger.

Fortunately, the winds died down and the small boat was able to overtake the brig. Reporting back, the crew stated the quarry was German. More importantly, however, they also reported that she had just left Kingston, where yellow fever was rampant. Obviously, the passengers could not be placed ashore where they would likely fall victim to the epidemic. Faced with this problem, and recognizing that his ship had no usable engine, Semmes made the decision to release the *Ariel* under ransom bond, payable by the ship's owner, Cornelius Vanderbilt, to the Confederate government within 30 days of the end of the war.[20]

No longer encumbered by their prize, the *Alabama* sailed around the northern side of Jamaica as Chief Engineer Miles Freeman, First Assistant Engineer William Brooks, Second Assistant Engineer Matthew O'Brien, and Third Assistant Engineer William Robertson labored to get the engine repaired. It would take them two more days. As the repairs continued, Semmes had the crew practice firing, boarding, and repelling enemy boarders.

On December 23, with the thoughts of the crew turning toward the Christmas holiday, the *Alabama* met up with the *Agrippina*. The two anchored in crystal clear water and the transfer of coal began almost immediately. As the *Alabama* took on the fuel, several of the crew were assigned the task of scraping the barnacles from the copper bottom. Others caulked openings in the deck, while the gunners fired the guns several times to test the powder. The tests were successful.[21]

Christmas provided the crew with a day off work and an extra ration of grog, but little else to mark the holiday. For Semmes and those who had served with him on the *Sumter*, it marked their second Christmas away from home. The crew amused themselves by fishing, swimming, and robbing sea gull nests of eggs. Some of the crew found some nets in an old fishing hut on shore, which they set in hopes of catching some turtles, but the eggs were the closest they would get to a Christmas treat.

Semmes noted in his journal that many of the crew apparently thought they were joining a privateer when they had signed on, hoping to have what Semmes described as a "jolly good time and plenty of license." He went on to write that he had finally worked them into a well-disciplined group. He closed his journal on December 29 with the observation that "it has taken me three or four months to accomplish this, but when it is considered that my little kingdom consisted of 110 of the most reckless sailors from the groggeries and brothels of Liverpool, that is not much."[22]

* * *

On the first day of November, Pickering received a telegram from Gideon Welles ordering him to continue to watch the *Sumter*, but to also visit the Azores and Madeira as often as he could. Pickering, reluctant to test his engine screw without extensive repairs, ignored the order and made for Cadiz instead, planning to perform the necessary maintenance. The *Chippewa* remained behind to watch the *Sumter*.

On November 4 the lookout reported a sail. Probably realizing that Welles would not be happy with his decision to go to Cadiz rather than searching in the Azores for the *Alabama*, Pickering gave the order for the crew to prepare to attack. If this ship happened to be the *Alabama*, he could meet the demands of Welles while still getting to a dry dock in Cadiz.

The unsuspecting ship came closer as the tension mounted. Finally, Pickering had her hailed. To the disappointment of every man on board, she proved to be a British mail packet. It was well after midnight, and there would be no *Alabama* tonight.[23]

By morning, the *Kearsarge* reached Cadiz, where she was forced to wait nearly a month before a dry dock would become available. As they waited, the crew amused themselves as best they could, bartering on a daily basis with the occupants of the bumboats which constantly hovered around the ship.

On November 7, Pickering was surprised to see the *Chippewa* entering the harbor. Her captain had come to Cadiz to inform Pickering that he had received word that the *Alabama* was on her way back to the Azores. Actually, the rebel steamer was near Bermuda. Once again, the mystique surrounding the *Alabama* had her in several places at once.

For the next four weeks, as the *Kearsarge* patiently waited to be accommodated in dry dock, the crew grew more restless. Several were punished over the next few weeks for various offenses ranging from drunkenness to insolence. Officers were not exempt, and some of them were on the receiving end of Pickering's discipline as well.[24] Finally, on November 29, word was received that a dry dock berth had become available. A local pilot was engaged to guide the *Kearsarge* upriver, running her aground in the process.

As the *Kearsarge* was sitting in dry dock, the political scene was humming. The United States consul at Glasgow reported that Glasgow was a hotbed for the building and outfitting of Confederate warships, specifically mentioning the *Alabama* and the *Oreto*. His counterpart in Liverpool said essentially the same thing, reporting that Confederate sympathizers were making formidable preparations for further operations at sea. His report also noted that the names of existing ships were being changed to make it more difficult to trace them.[25]

At that same time, C. H. Marshall, chairman of the New York Chamber of Commerce, was asking the exasperated Welles just what measures were being taken to capture the *Alabama*. Welles had to be less than happy to hear the chamber's suggestion that the government grant commissions to private vessels which would be fitted out for that purpose.[26] The obvious inference was that private shippers had lost confidence in the navy and were ready and willing to take matters into their own hands.

Nor was the Northern press doing anything to improve the secretary of the navy's mood. On the one hand they printed detailed routes and schedules of the very ships that were hunting the *Alabama*, articles which helped Semmes immeasurably to avoid detection. On the other they complained that not enough was being done.

The *New York Times* editorialized that " . . . the success of the *Alabama* will probably lead to the fitting out of a dozen such steamers, and as only the fleetest will be used, even when found it will not be easy to overtake them. A stern chase with a steamer is a long one, and escape is almost a certainty."[27] The editor was careful to avoid any mention of the fact that one of his paper's regular columns, titled *Marine Intelligence*, provided detailed descriptions of the various ships, their dates of departure, their destinations, and other information that Semmes found most valuable.

The newspapers also spared no space in verbally attacking the British. In one editorial the *Times* stated, "If the present outrages go on, England may depend upon it that the day of reckoning will come." The same editorial complained, "There is substantially no difference between allowing a ship of war like the *Alabama*—built, owned, manned by Englishmen—to sail from an English port, under an English flag, to burn American ships, than to allow an English man-of-war itself to do it."[28]

With pressure being applied by the Northern press, insurance companies, private shippers, the chamber of commerce, and politicians, it is little wonder that Welles was reaching the end of his patience. Until the *Alabama* could be captured or sunk, and the pirate Semmes held accountable, he would have no peace.

The message from Pickering, stating that the *Kearsarge* would have to go into dry dock rather than pursue the *Alabama*, was the final straw. Welles believed that the *Kearsarge* was already spending too much time in port, and now she would be going into dry dock for who knew how long? Furious after reading the message, he ordered the USS *Vanderbilt* to leave as soon as possible with a replacement for Pickering.[29]

The unsuspecting Pickering, still unaware that his days as captain of the *Kearsarge* were numbered, continued his daily activities. Even as his replacement was steaming across the Atlantic, the propeller and shaft were removed and the *Kearsarge* was floated out of dry dock until the repaired parts were ready to be reinstalled.

The removal of the propeller had taken a week. It had been another week before the shaft had been taken out. The conditions of both made it apparent that the *Kearsarge* would be out of commission for an extended period of time. With little to do to pass the time, the crew members did what they did best when on liberty, and it was a rare day that did not see several of the men either arrested by local authorities or punished by Pickering. On December 23, crewman Robert Motley turned his back on the *Kearsarge* and deserted, never looking back.

The beleaguered Welles closed out his diary for the year with a passage which left no doubt that his frustration was mounting: "We had yesterday a telegram that the British pirate craft *Alabama* captured the *Ariel* . . . We shall, however, have a day of reckoning with Great Britain for these wrongs, and I sometimes think I care not how soon nor in what manner that reckoning comes."[30]

CHAPTER EIGHT

JANUARY–FEBRUARY 1863

The crew of the *Alabama* ushered in the new year, 1863, by caulking and painting. The latest storm had revealed new openings through which the blowing water had found its way, soaking those unfortunate enough to be in the wrong place. Tar was smeared on lavishly, probably more by those who had been forced to wear wet clothing until the sun returned.

Semmes became philosophical and wrote in his journal, "The first day of the new year; what will it bring forth? The Almighty, for a wise purpose, hides future events from the eyes of mortals, and all we can do is to perform well our parts and trust the rest to His guidance. Success, as a general rule, attends him who is vigilant and active, and who is careful to obey all the laws of nature. It is useful to look back on this first day of the new year and see how we have spent the past; what errors we have committed and of what faults we have been guilty, that we may avoid the one and reform the other."[1]

The new year also heralded President Lincoln's Emancipation Proclamation, declaring all slaves held in states currently waging war against the Union free. Lincoln had issued his preliminary proclamation in September, but it did not become effective until January 1.[2] On that date, the steerage officers found their own way to offer commentary on Lincoln's edict. Using an old plank two feet wide by four feet long, they wrote a mock epitaph, placing the "tombstone" ashore where anyone passing would see it. "In memory of Abraham Lincoln," it said, "President of the late United States, who died of Nigger on the brain. 1st January, 1863." They signed it simply, "*290.*"

Then, on a piece of paper, they added a note in Spanish and placed it so that it would be protected from the elements. "Will the finder kindly favor me by forwarding this tablet to the U.S. Consul at the first port he touches at." Semmes, who was the only *Alabama* officer fluent in Spanish, probably had a hand in writing the note. There is no record of the tombstone ever reaching any consulate.[3]

That same day the *Alabama* put to sea once more, heading northward toward the coast of Texas. This route was not randomly chosen. From newspapers taken from prizes, Semmes had learned of an expedition of thirty thousand troops, to be led by General Nathaniel P. Banks, to capture the city of Galveston. Some one hundred ships were to land the men. Semmes planned to mount a bold surprise night attack on the fleet, sinking as many as he could and slipping away in the confusion.

However, unknown to Semmes, the Confederacy had already retaken Galveston. Under Major Leon Smith, they had surprised Union troops in Galveston on January 1, and the city was again in Southern hands. Instead of a fleet of troop transports, the Union now had only six heavily armed ships sitting offshore performing blockade duty.

Shortly after 3:00 in the afternoon of January 11, the lookout reported five vessels, two of which appeared to be steamers. The vessels were the Union blockaders, and they spotted the *Alabama* at about the same time. Believing that another blockade runner was about to try to reach Galveston, Commodore H. H. Bell of the USS *Brooklyn* signaled Lieutenant Commander Homer C. Blake on the USS *Hatteras* to give chase.

Spying the *Hatteras* leaving the fleet, Semmes decided to draw her still further from the protection of the other ships. He knew darkness would not be long in coming, and he planned to use it to his advantage. The *Hatteras* was a converted river excursion boat, a sidewheeler with her engines dangerously exposed. Not built for speed, the slower *Hatteras* could not keep up with the *Alabama,* and Semmes had his ship slowed several times to allow the *Hatteras* to close the distance. Knowing his sidewheeler should not be able to gain on the sleek-appearing stranger unless the other vessel allowed it, the suspicious Blake correctly began to think that he may be on the trail of the notorious *Alabama*. Carrying two short 32-pounders, one 30-pounder rifled Parrott gun, and one 20-pounder rifled gun on the side toward the *Alabama*, Blake planned to get into close range where his guns would be most effective if he needed to use them.

Just after dusk, at about 6:20 P.M., the *Alabama's* crew was beat to quarters. The tension mounted as those on the starboard battery loaded their guns with five-second shells. As the shadows of night enveloped the two ships, the *Hatteras* drew closer until only one hundred yards separated the two. There was no moon, and each appeared only as a silhouette to the other. Both ships idled their engines, creating an eerie silence broken only by the sound of the waves striking the sides of the vessels. Many on the *Alabama* were no doubt reminding themselves that they had been referred to as a bunch of pirates by much of the Northern press, and as the scum of England by others. It was now time to show the North what they really were. Kell reported to Semmes that all were ready for action.[4]

The ships were now close enough that voices could be heard coming from the *Hatteras*. Then, someone from the *Hatteras* shouted, "What ship is that?"

Kell raised his trumpet and answered, "This is Her Britannic Majesty's steamer *Petrel!*"*

After a short delay Blake shouted, "If you please, I'm sending a boat on board of you!"

Kell answered, "Certainly. We'll be pleased to receive your boat."[5]

The sound of a cutter being dropped into the water could be heard by those on the *Alabama*, and as the little cutter moved slowly through the darkness, Kell shouted, "What ship are you?"

Blake answered, "This is the United States Steamer ——."

---

* Acting Master S. H. Partridge of the *Hatteras* would later report that he heard the name *Spitfire* given, rather than *Petrel*.[6] Captain Blake's report indicated that he had heard the name *Vixen*.[7] Semmes's memoirs[8] and the log of the *Alabama*[9] both say that the name *Petrel* was given, and it is this name that most historians agree on.

The officers on board the *Alabama* looked at one another and asked, "What did he say?" None had heard the name.

The question was asked again, and still the men on the *Alabama* could not make out the name. It did not matter. The words "United States Steamer" had come through quite clearly. Semmes turned to Kell and said, "We must not strike them as British. Tell them who we are and order a broadside at the name."[10]

Kell nodded and raised his trumpet once more. "This is the Confederate States Steamer *Alabama!*" He then gave the signal to fire, and immediately the guns of the *Alabama* came to life. Quickly, the guns of the *Hatteras* returned the fire. Their first volley sailed harmlessly over the masts of the *Alabama*.

The *Alabama*'s first barrage found its mark, and already two of the *Hatteras*'s guns were out of service. Then, a huge hole appeared at the *Hatteras*'s water line and a fire broke out in her sick bay. The battle was quickly becoming one-sided. A blast struck the engine room, sending scalding steam in all directions and forcing the engineers of the *Hatteras* to leave the area as fast as they could run. Another fire erupted in the hold.

On the *Alabama*, Semmes ordered his crew to aim low. With each volley the crew members bellowed, "This is from the scum of England!" or "Here's one from the wharf rats of Liverpool!" The Northern press had obviously struck a nerve with their derogatory comments about the *Alabama*'s crew.

Blake, realizing that his ship was about to sink, ordered all his armament on the port side thrown overboard. He might lose his ship but he refused to let his guns fall into enemy hands. That done, he ordered the magazines flooded, to reduce the chance of explosion. As the sea rushed into the magazine, he ordered a lee gun fired as a sign of surrender. The battle had lasted less than 15 minutes.

Hearing the lee gun fire, Kell shouted, "Have you struck?"

"Aye, we have," came the answer. Immediately a cheer arose from the throats of the Confederate crew. Kell ordered a cease fire.

"We're sinking fast," Blake shouted. "Can you help us?"

Boats were launched from the *Alabama* and the 17 officers and 101 men of the *Hatteras* were quickly rescued. Coming on board, Blake offered his sword to Semmes, saying, "I do this with deep regret."

Semmes accepted the sword, bowed, and said, "I'm glad you are safely on the *Alabama*. We will try to make you as comfortable as possible."[11]

Blake requested a quick account of his crew, determining that Firemen John C. Cleary and William Healy, both Irishmen, had been killed. Five more were wounded: Fireman Edward McGowan had suffered a severe wound of the thigh; First Cabin Boy John White had received a slight wound of the leg; Captain's Mate Edward Mattock had been slightly wounded in the hand; Seaman Christopher Steptewick had taken a slight wound in his back; and Landsman Patrick Kane had a minor wound of his leg.[12] Acting Master S. H. Partridge and five others who had been on the small boarding craft were missing, and Blake incorrectly presumed they had been caught in the crossfire and were lost. Actually, they had rowed furiously when the first volley was fired and had been able to avoid detection. They would eventually get back to the fleet, where they would give an eyewitness account of the sinking.[13]

Only Carpenter's Mate William Rinton had been slightly wounded on the Confederate ship, having been struck on the cheek by a shell fragment.[14]

The officers and crews of both ships quietly watched the *Hatteras* slowly sink bow first. She went down so quickly that Semmes did not have time to send a boarding crew to bring back the customary chronograph and flag.

As all observed the final struggle of the *Hatteras*, lights were reported in the distance. Semmes looked back in the direction of Galveston, but with more than one hundred prisoners on board, decided against any further encounters for this evening. He ordered all lights turned off, and the *Alabama* vanished into the night.[15]

At daylight, the *Alabama*'s damage was assessed. It turned out to be minimal. She had been struck 13 times, with the most potentially damaging hit coming from a shell which had narrowly missed the middle starboard gun crew. Another shell had passed through the funnel, while a third remained lodged in her timbers under the main chain. The other 10 hits had done minimal damage.[16] Back at the site of the fight, only the tops of the *Hatteras*'s masts were visible to the USS *Brooklyn*, USS *Sciota*, and USS *Cayuga*, who had come in search of their sister ship.

Giddy with the success of their first fight, the crew and officers of the *Alabama* set out for Jamaica, where Semmes planned to get rid of his prisoners as quickly as he could. These men were fighters, and their numbers approximated those of the crew of the *Alabama*. Semmes warned his officers to watch for any signs of trouble and take action immediately, fearing a possible takeover of his own ship if Blake and his crew got the opportunity. His fears were unfounded, however, and the crews appeared to take a liking to one another over the 10 days it took to reach Jamaica. Blake and Kell, it turned out, had known one another in the old navy, and they renewed their acquaintance.[17]

En route a ship was sighted and Semmes ordered a chase. The ship turned out to be the *Agrippina*, and after a short reunion the two parted ways. Semmes did not wish to give his prisoners any indication of the relationship between the *Alabama* and the *Agrippina*, and thus did not spend much time with her. He would never see his tender again.

For nearly a week the *Alabama* labored toward Jamaica, following in the path of a string of squalls and gales. Excepting an English brig hailed on January 17, no other ships were sighted. The prisoners mingled with the crew of the *Alabama*, and Blake was given a berth in Semmes's cabin. The *Alabama*'s surgeons assisted those of the *Hatteras* in tending to the wounded, even supplying medicine to replace that of the *Hatteras*, which had gone down with the ship.

On January 20 the lookout reported land just ahead, the western tip of Jamaica. It had been nine days since the battle. Hoisting French colors, a pilot was brought on board and the *Alabama* was soon anchored in Port Royal harbor, Kingston.

There, the *Alabama* enjoyed a hero's welcome. As Semmes awaited permission from the governor to land the prisoners, boats of every size and shape made their way from shore, their occupants all eager to see the famous pirate ship. Invitations were extended to all on board to visit the natives in their homes. Officers from three British ships, the *Reindeer*, the *Jason*, and the *Greyhound*, which were also anchored in the harbor, came on board, each anxious to hear the story of the battle.[18]

Local police escorted many of the *Alabama*'s men back from liberty. Several had to be placed in irons for their actions, either in town or on board ship. Kell would later write, "Carried away with victory, many got gloriously drunk, and gave me a good deal of trouble to get them back and properly sobered."[19]

The crew of the *Alabama* fraternized with the crew of the *Hatteras*, their former prisoners. They got drunk with them, fought with them, and were arrested with them. Some of those who were brought back to the ship managed to slip away and go back into town, where they were arrested again.[20]

Over the next few days Ordinary Seamen William Halford, Joseph Neal, Thomas Walsh, Gustave Schwalbe, John McAlee, and Valentine Mesner, along with Firemen John Latham, Thomas Potter, and David Roach would desert. These men were all trained mariners and took badly needed skills away with them. Potter would return four days later, however, and remained with the *Alabama* for the duration of her cruise.[21]

The biggest loss was not a crew member, but an officer. Paymaster Clarence Yonge took some gold from the *Alabama*'s sea chest and went ashore, where he openly consorted with personnel from the *Hatteras*. Worse, he began a dialogue with the United States consul, arranging to defect to the Union. When he heard of this, Kell sent an armed party ashore to arrest the errant officer.

Semmes immediately ordered a court-martial which found Yonge guilty, whereupon he was stripped of his sword and dismissed.[22] Semmes was so embittered toward Yonge that he would never utter his name again, nor would he include him by name in any of his writings, saying that to do so would honor him.

Surgeon Francis Galt was appointed to serve as paymaster with Yonge's departure, and Assistant Surgeon David Llewellyn took over Galt's duties. The loss of the deserters was eased a bit with the signing on of James Adams, Albert Gilman, William Jones, and James Maguire. Gilman apparently did not find the *Alabama* to his liking, though, and he himself became a deserter some six months later.

While the *Alabama* was in port, the United States demanded once more that the British seize her. Their grievances were ignored. Seeing little hope that any action would be taken against the Confederate ship by local authorities, the *San Jacinto* and *Iroquois* were ordered to cruise the area and watch for the *Alabama* when she left port. However, on the night of January 25, the *Alabama* quietly slipped out of Kingston unobserved by either of the Federal ships.

At noon the next day a sail was sighted. A short chase ensued, and was brought to an end by the firing of a blank cartridge. The *Golden Rule*, a Union merchant ship out of New York commanded by Captain Peter H. Whiteberry, was condemned to be burned.[23] The fire was visible from the shores of Jamaica.

Part of the *Golden Rule*'s cargo included rigging, masts, and spars that were being transported to the United States brig *Bainbridge*, which had suffered extensive damage in a storm. The *Alabama* took some of the rigging for her own use and burned the rest with the *Golden Rule*, keeping the *Bainbridge* in port for several more months.

Less than 24 hours later, a schooner was boarded which proved to be Spanish. Eight hours after that, however, another sail proved more fruitful. She was the *Chastelaine*, out of Boston and commanded by James Warren. The *Chastelaine*, too, fell victim to the torch.

On January 28, Semmes entered port in the old city of Santo Domingo in the Dominican Republic, where he put the prisoners from the *Golden Rule* and *Chastelaine* ashore. A Yankee brigantine sat anchored tantalizingly nearby, untouchable in a neutral port. After receiving fresh provisions, the *Alabama* put to sea once more, where several crew members were court-martialed for various offenses.

On February 2 a brigantine was stopped and boarded, with the *Alabama* again passing herself off as the USS *Iroquois*. The brig proved to be the *Ida Abbott,* a neutral. Later in the day a second neutral vessel was hailed, a Hamburg bark.

That afternoon a potentially disastrous occurrence took place. The relative calm on deck was disturbed by Paymaster Steward Frederick Johns, who rushed from the hold shouting that there was a fire in the spirit room! Any fire on board ship is dangerous, but this was especially so because of its location. Situated immediately adjacent to the magazine, the fire would ignite the powder if it spread that far. Semmes, from his position on the quarterdeck, ordered all hands to quarters.

In the spirit room, Captain of the Hold James Higgs beat at the flames with a blanket. Others rushed to help, knowing the consequences if the fire should spread. On deck, crew members scurried to carry a hose to the site of the fire. Before they could accomplish this, however, Higgs and his companions had extinguished the fire.

Semmes, hearing that the danger had passed, rushed to the spirit room as quickly as he could, hoping to assess the damage and determine what had happened. Higgs immediately took responsibility, explaining that he had come in to draw off some liquor, and when he did, the candle apparently ignited the fumes. At the mention of a candle Semmes bristled. One standing order of the ship was that nobody ever took candles into the spirit room. Higgs knew he had been wrong in breaking the rule, but he explained that he had been unable to see, and that he had taken pains to avoid getting it too close to anything. Having sent 23 ships to their watery graves by burning them, Semmes recognized the irony of almost having suffered the same fate himself. He ordered Higgs placed in irons for his poor judgment.[24]

At 2:30 the next afternoon the lookout reported an approaching vessel. The United States flag was hoisted, a gesture which was answered with the same flag from the approaching schooner. Semmes quickly hove her to. Under the command of Oren H. Leland, she was the *Palmetto*, a three-year-old craft that had left New York only 10 days earlier.

Leland insisted that he did not know who owned the cargo, although he could provide no proof that his ship was neutral. The *Palmetto* was loaded with provisions that the *Alabama* could use, and the boarding crew removed crackers, cheese, and other foodstuffs before she was fired.

For the next 18 days only a Spanish brig and two English schooners were sighted. On February 21 the *Alabama* sailed into the midst of several vessels. A chase was begun as two of the vessels were observed signaling to one another and then parting company. Going after the ship showing American colors, Semmes ordered a blank cartridge fired to stop her. The shot was ignored. Steam was brought up and the propeller lowered, and the rifled gun crew was called to their station. They fired a shot over the rigging of the stranger, which was also ignored. Angered by the insolence of the Yankee, Semmes ordered a third shot fired, which the gunners were about to do when the ship's captain finally decided that further resistance was futile.

Kell dispatched a boat to the prize, the *Golden Eagle*. The boarding officer, George Fullam, ordered the *Golden Eagle*'s captain, Edward A. Swift, to follow the *Alabama*, which had already started after the second vessel, the *Olive Jane*.

The *Olive Jane* was quickly overtaken and stopped with a blank cartridge. Her captain, Robert Kallock, was summoned to Semmes's Admiralty Court, where his ship was condemned. His papers indicated that he was carrying, among other delicacies, a large supply of brandies and French wines. Fearing what would happen if any of the liquor found its way onto the *Alabama*, Semmes sent Arthur Sinclair on board the *Olive Jane* with strict orders to make sure that not one drop of the liquor was brought back.

Sinclair, unsure of how successful he would be at stopping the smuggling of at least a small amount of the liquor, suggested that an orderly dinner on the *Olive Jane* for the boarders might be the best means of prevention. Using the canned meats, cheeses, and olives from the *Olive Jane*'s stores, along with a limited amount of the brandy and wine, the feast was spread, and the boarding crew arrived back on the *Alabama* only mildly tipsy.[25] Hearing what had transpired, Semmes merely smiled and said he felt bad that Bartelli and the wardroom stewards had not gone along.[26]

After torching the *Olive Jane*, the *Alabama* returned to deal with the *Golden Eagle*. Finding her to also be carrying American cargo, Semmes ordered her to the same fate as the *Olive Jane*. As the *Alabama* sailed away, her officers and crew could look to either side and see the results of their work, flames lighting the night sky. Before they departed, though, two new crew members, Ordinary Seamen Jean Veal and Jacob Verbot, were mustered in from the prizes.

Over the next few days it was apparent that the *Alabama* had sailed into an area of high maritime activity. Three neutral ships were hailed on February 22, four more on February 24, two on February 25, and six on February 26.[27] On these occasions Semmes alternately used the aliases USS *Iroquois* and USS *Dacotah*.

On February 24 two crew members were honorably discharged, their enlistments having expired. Boatswain's Mate George Horwood and Fireman James McFadden, both original members of the crew, became the only *Alabama* crewmen to be sent home when their enlistments expired at sea.[28]

On February 27, while hailing the English ship *Henry*, a second ship was sighted. After a short chase, she stopped abruptly when a shot struck just five feet from her bow. The ship was the guano-laden *Washington*, out of New York. Her captain, Joseph G. White, was brought before the Admiralty Court in Semmes's cabin.

When handed the bills of lading, Semmes frowned. They indicated that the guano was owned by the Peruvian government and was consigned to an agent in Antwerp. By all appearances the cargo was neutral. White confirmed as much. That neutrality was enough to save the ship. White was asked if he was willing to sign a ransom bond, and if he would take the *Alabama*'s prisoners off the ship. If he agreed to those terms, Semmes would allow him to go. White quickly agreed to the bond of $50,000, transferred the prisoners, and was on his way before Semmes could change his mind.

One more English ship was stopped that day, and two more the next, closing out one of the busiest months in the entire cruise of the Confederate raider.

* * *

While the *Alabama* was enjoying one of her busiest months ever, the *Kearsarge* was languishing in La Carraca at the mercy of the Spanish repairmen. Even the bars and brothels ashore were no match for the boredom experienced by the men of the American ship. Surprisingly, only three men deserted in the first two months of 1863: Daniel Clarke, James Mellus, and Christian Smith. Mellus had been one of the original crew members.

The Northern press, however, had taken no such hiatus. On the first day of the new year the *New York Times* reprinted an article from the *London Globe* that had said that the United States had only to furnish prima facie evidence that the construction of the *Alabama* had violated the Foreign Enlistment Act, but had failed to do so. Had they done it, according to the *Globe*, the English would have taken immediate action.[29] This contention did little to improve the mood in the offices of the Navy Department.

Evenings saw the men assembled on the forward deck, where they passed the time singing and dancing. Plays were improvised, most of them not very good, but they occupied the time. A glee club was formed, and the singers and audience alike looked forward to the concerts, even though the group only knew a few songs. Those who had no talent for singing or acting found their idle time spent spinning yarns. Each evening a crowd would gather, pipes and cigars sending a cloud of smoke into the rigging. The officers sat on stools while the crew lounged on the topgallant forecastle.

Occasionally, Pickering allowed a few men to take liberty. Their behavior, however, usually meant an end to the free time in town for several days. Pickering would mellow after a week or so and allow another group to go ashore, most often with the same results.

In mid-January word got back to Welles's office in Washington that the *Alabama* had sunk the *Hatteras*. Welles immediately demanded to know what Admiral Charles Wilkes had been doing when the *Alabama* attacked. Welles bellowed that despite the fact that Wilkes had seven ships at his disposal looking for the *Alabama*, Semmes had been able to slip in and sink one of the navy's own! It was bad enough that the *Alabama* was burning the merchant fleet, but Welles believed that a naval vessel should have been able to fend her off.

At about the same time, the British were responding to the complaint that they were furnishing munitions to the Confederacy and allowing British subjects to be recruited for service on the *Alabama*. The Union bought more munitions from England than the South did, they said, in an inadvertent admission that they had violated the law by dealing with either party. Accusations were also hurled that the Union had attempted to recruit the crew of a captured blockade runner off the coast of Charleston in a violation every bit as blatant as the signing of British subjects onto the *Alabama*.[30]

On February 7 a message arrived in Welles's office that the *Sumter* had taken advantage of the *Kearsarge*'s absence and escaped. Although the *Chippewa* had been watching her, the *Sumter* had eluded the Union ship, which possibly had become complacent in the daily routine of watching the Confederate ship sitting in port. The *Sumter* was now owned by a British concern and had been renamed the *Gibraltar*. On February 10 a report from Captain B. F. Sands of the USS *Dacotah* pointed out a weakness in the Union blockade which could easily be exploited by the *Alabama*. The *Dacotah* was part of the blockade along the Cape Fear River in North Carolina. Sands noted that the blockade in that area was sparse, and if he were to send a vessel to chase a blockade runner it would leave a gap through which the *Alabama*, or any other ship so inclined, could slip and wreak havoc. In addition to the vulnerable gap, he bemoaned the fact that much valuable coal is wasted in a chase. He concluded his report by saying that the Confederates, if they were to learn of this weakness, could use a small boat to lure his boats out where they could be attacked by a waiting *Alabama*. Amazingly, Sands's report met with little concern in Washington.

On February 15, Lieutenant Commander Thomas Harris left the decks of the *Kearsarge* for the final time, having been ordered to return to the United States to take command of the USS *Chippewa*. Happy not only to be taking command of his own vessel, Harris was also ecstatic over no longer having to share the boredom of life in dry dock.

Meanwhile, the battle of words continued with regard to the construction of ships by the British. Quoting a letter from an anonymous source to Lord Palmerston that had originally been printed in the *London News*, the *New York Times* wrote, "Does anybody outside of a lunatic asylum believe that the emperor of China is in immediate want of a fleet of war steamers?" The letter told of a covered shed at the Lairds' shipyard where two warships were being built for the emperor of China under the supervision of one James Bulloch. The article charged that several other British shipbuilders were also doing similar work for the same customer.[31]

Despite these charges and countercharges, nothing changed. Ship construction continued in England, the *Alabama* continued her mission on the high seas, and the *Kearsarge* repined in a Spanish dry dock.

CHAPTER NINE

MARCH–APRIL 1863

On March 1 the *Bethiah Thayer*, her commanding officer Thomas Mitchell Cartney, was boarded by a party from the *Alabama*. Although she was out of Rockland, Maine, her cargo of guano was neutral. Semmes had no choice but to allow Cartney to sign a ransom note and go on his way.

Two other ships, both neutral, were boarded that same day: the English bark *William Edward* and the Maltese bark *Nile*. In hailing the *William Edward*, Kell used the alias *USS Ticonderoga*, perhaps as a way to taunt the Federals.

When Fullam boarded the *Nile* he was informed that a United States ship of war was in the area. Telling Semmes of this news when he reported back to the *Alabama*, the officers of the *Alabama* concluded that the vessel was most likely the USS *Ino*, a clipper that had already seen some measure of success against the *Sumter*.*

Twenty-seven ships had been stopped since the last ships, the *Golden Eagle* and the *Olive Jane*, had been burned. That dry spell was about to end. On March 2, 1863, the *Alabama* took possession of the

---

* While the *Ino* was, indeed, searching for the *Alabama,* she was not in the South Atlantic. She was further north, closer to New York.

John A. Parks, commanded by Captain John S. Cooper and hauling a cargo of lumber. Holding the customary Admiralty Court session, Semmes was faced with a difficult decision. Cooper appeared to have an authentic certificate of neutrality, but Semmes was suspicious. Searching through the mailbag from the *John A. Parks*, Semmes found a letter that indicated that the cargo was actually American. Armed with this information, Semmes condemned the *John A. Parks* to a fiery end. Before the blaze was started, Carpenter William Robinson sorted through the lumber in the hold of the *John A. Parks* and picked out the best pieces for use on the *Alabama*.[1]

Around dusk that same day another vessel was spotted and brought to a halt. She was the *Miss Nightingale*, an English bark. Semmes asked the captain to take the prisoners off the *Alabama*, but he refused. Finally he relented to take Captain Cooper of the *John A. Parks*, his wife, and his two nephews. He could not be convinced to take the crewmen, however.

On March 15 the familiar cry came down from the lookout, "Sail, ho!" The sail belonged to the *Punjaub*, an American ship which stopped after a blank cartridge was placed near her bow. Her captain, Lewis F. Miller, was brought aboard the *Alabama* for the customary hearing. Carrying an English cargo, she was ransomed after agreeing to take the prisoners from the *John A. Parks*. Semmes was amused to note that the ship's papers showed the owners of the *Punjaub* to be Thomas B. Wales and his son, Thomas B. Wales, Jr.[2] It had only been four months since the *Alabama* had burned a ship of the same name and owned by the same owners.

Eight days later the *Morning Star*, stopped in a driving rainstorm, was also rewarded with a ransom release. Carrying a neutral cargo, she was ransomed despite her Boston origin.

Later in the day the frustration was relieved with the capture of the *Kingfisher*. A small whaling schooner, her owners had the good fortune to have had the *Kingfisher*'s cargo of whale oil transferred to a neutral vessel just a short time earlier, and her only cargo was a meager 20 barrels of oil. Her captain, Thomas F. Lambert, was chagrined to learn that his ship was to be burned.

Kell ordered the boarding party to take any supplies that the *Alabama* could use, in addition to the customary chronometer and flag. That accomplished, the fire was set. The heavy rain caused the fire to burn sporadically, blazing when the fire reached some oil-soaked portion of the ship, then ebbing as the rain drenched the flames.

Two days after the firing of the *Kingfisher*, the crew of the *Alabama* got the opportunity to set another fire. Master's Mate James Evans, stationed at his lookout post, called down that sails were approaching. Evans had the uncanny ability to differentiate between Union and foreign vessels, and many were the times that Semmes did not bother chasing a sail simply because Evans believed it was a neutral. He was rarely wrong.[3]

When asked if the approaching ship was Yankee, Evans replied in the affirmative, but there were two ships, not one. And, he shouted, they were both Yankee. As usual, he was correct. The ships were the *Nora*, commanded by Charles E. Adams, and the *Charles Hill*, commanded by Franklin Percival. Both were carrying salt. Adams produced papers declaring the cargo to be the property of W. N. deMattos of London, making the shipment neutral. There was no consulate's signature, however, and Semmes decided that the certificate was invalid. This decision was supported when papers found on the *Charles Hill* included a letter from Percival to the owners of the vessels, telling them to declare their cargo as British and get the certificate signed by the British consul.[4] Semmes condemned both ships, transferring 35 tons of coal from the *Charles Hill* to the hold of the *Alabama* before setting the blaze. Two more chronographs now graced the growing collection in Semmes's cabin.

The *Alabama*'s crew talked to the crews of the *Nora* and *Charles Hill*, trying to coax them into joining the *Alabama*. They spoke of double the pay, good food, plenty of tobacco, the possibility of prize money, and plenty of grog.[5] The efforts paid off, and 10 badly needed crew members were recruited: John Hughes, Albert Hyer, Peter Jackson, William McClellan, Joseph Minor, Frederick Myers, William Nordstrom, Charles Olson, John Benson, and Charles Coles. Of these, Hughes, Hyer, Jackson, Nordstrom, and Coles would all desert within the year.[6]

On March 28 the English bark *Chili* was boarded. Seeing that the cargo was neutral, Fullam, in charge of the boarding party, allowed the bark to go on her way without revealing that the *Alabama* was not really the Union vessel she had purported to be. Before Fullam and his crew left the *Chili*, the *Chili's* officers had extended a warning that the *Alabama* was believed to be in the area and that she had whipped a vessel twice her size. The officers strongly recommended that Fullam's ship not try to fight her if they should meet. Fullam thanked the officers and returned to the *Alabama*, presumably keeping a straight face until he was out of sight of the *Chili*.[7]

On March 29 the *Alabama* crossed the equator for the first time. Sinclair enjoyed the spectacle of the midshipmen trying to determine the latitude with their sextants, not knowing that they were directly over the equator.

Needing more coal, Semmes planned to meet the *Agrippina*, not knowing that McQueen had sold the coal and kept the money. Upon learning of this at a later date, Semmes and Sinclair accused him of selling the coal to Federal ships, although this could never be substantiated.[8]

As was often the case with Semmes, luck seemed to follow him. On April 4 the *Louisa Hatch*, out of Rockland, Maine, was stopped and boarded. Her cargo: coal from Cardiff! Her captain, William Grant, told Semmes that he had departed Cardiff about a month earlier and was bound for Point de Galle. Not only had Semmes obtained the coal he needed, it was high-quality Welsh coal, smokeless and difficult to detect on the open ocean.

The *Louisa Hatch* was condemned, but she was not burned immediately. It would take time to transfer the coal. Fullam replaced Evans on board the *Louisa Hatch*, and he followed the *Alabama* as Semmes made for the island of Fernando de Noronha, off the coast of Brazil. The island included a penal colony, housing some of Brazil's most infamous criminals. Because there was no way off the island, the criminals roamed freely, living in their own huts.

On April 7 the weather took a turn for the worse, the rain coming down so hard that it was difficult for the two ships to keep one another in sight. Fullam wrote in his journal, "Whole sheets of water pouring down, in fact the heaviest rain ever seen by any on board."[9]

Early the next day Semmes hooked a towline to the *Louisa Hatch* and attempted to transfer coal by shuttling boats between the two. When this did not work, the *Alabama* towed the prize into the harbor of the island, using the captain of the *Kingfisher*, Thomas Lambert, as his pilot. Lambert's expertise proved invaluable in the tricky currents and tides of the area. At 2:45 in the afternoon of April 10, the two ships anchored in 78 feet of water and began the coaling process, with the two lashed together by spars extended between them.

By 7:30 the next morning, however, the heavy swells had caused the two ships to slam together too many times, despite the spars, and they separated. The shuttle boats resumed the coaling.

Semmes and Galt, the newly appointed paymaster, went ashore to inquire about provisions while the coaling process continued. The island was so far out of the way that the island's governor, Sebastiao Jose Basilo Pyrrho, was excited to have visitors. Semmes, knowing he had violated international law by bringing the *Louisa Hatch* into the neutral port, tried to explain to the governor that the law wasn't so strict that the *Louisa Hatch* couldn't be kept there for a few days. Fortunately for Semmes, the governor was not concerned with international law, and he believed that the *Alabama* was within her rights to claim the *Louisa Hatch* as a prize of war.[10]

Later in the day, the governor made an effort to establish diplomatic relations between his island and the *Alabama*. The overture was made in a letter carried by two emissaries. Semmes received them with great fanfare, asking his steward, Bartelli, to break out the ship's best champagne. The meeting was quite cordial, with much laughter and many champagne toasts. Cigars were lit, and one of the emissaries let it be known that he was actually not a government official at all. Rather, he was one of the convicts, a fact that disturbed Bartelli so much that he made his exit as soon as the opportunity allowed.[11]

The *Louisa Hatch* carried more than one thousand tons of coal. The *Alabama* could only hold three hundred tons, however. Regrettably, Semmes was forced to burn more than eight hundred tons of valuable coal because he had no room to carry it.[12]

The coaling was not completed until April 15. The work had scarcely been completed when two whalers, obviously American, came into view. Anchoring some five miles offshore, the two captains came ashore in boats. Pulling alongside the *Louisa Hatch*, they spied Fullam, who welcomed them aboard. The two captains declined but asked if they could trade some whale oil for some provisions, identifying their ships as the *Lafayette* and the *Kate Cory*.

Then, Stephen Flanders, captain of the *Kate Cory*, asked Fullam if he had seen the *Alabama*. Fullam lied, telling Flanders that the *Alabama* had last been reported in Jamaica. Pointing toward the *Alabama*, the captain of the *Lafayette,* William Lewis, then asked Fullam if he knew her name. Again Fullam had to lie, saying the ship was a Brazilian mail packet that had brought in a load of convicts a day earlier.

After some more small talk, Fullam asked what had brought the two ships into the harbor, with the answer being that they had sprung a bad leak during the last gale and they had been forced in for repairs. As the gale was discussed, one of the men happened to spy a small Confederate ensign on board the *Alabama* that had been hung out to dry.

"Give way, men!" he shouted to his crew in the small boat. "Give way for your lives!"

The men in the small whaleboats strained as they pulled on their oars, desperately trying to reach their ships. The amused Fullam watched briefly, then signaled the *Alabama*. The raider ignored the two small boats and went directly to the *Lafayette* and *Kate Cory*, capturing both.

The first mate of the *Lafayette* hurriedly threw the ship's papers over the side as the *Alabama* approached. In so doing he destroyed any chance the *Lafayette* had of being spared, and the Admiralty Court determined both ships should be burned, even though both had been taken inside the marine limits.

The *Lafayette* was the second ship of that name captured by the *Alabama*. The first had been captured the previous October. In addition to sharing a name, the two *Lafayettes* also shared the same fiery fate. From shore, the governor and several convicts enjoyed the spectacle.[13]

In addition to two more chronometers and United States flags, four men from the two ships decided to join the crew of the *Alabama*: George Getsinger, Robert Owens, James Wallace, and Maurice Bright.[14]

While still in Fernando de Noronha, a shipboard fight developed between two powder monkeys, Robert Egan and Thomas Parker. Egan in particular had been a problem for Semmes almost from the day he stepped on board, and he had been the instigator on this occasion. For his effort, Semmes had him spread-eagled in the mizzen rigging, although he could have been forgiven if he had decided to send Egan ashore to stay in the penal colony. Egan would eventually desert the *Alabama*, and Semmes would make no effort to find him.[15]

On April 22 the *Alabama* prepared to get under way once more. Before she left, Governor Pyrrho came aboard bearing a turkey, roses, and tropical fruits as going-away gifts. The gifts could have been easily interpreted as bribes, particularly when the governor asked Semmes if he would write an official affidavit testifying that the *Lafayette* and *Kate Cory* had been captured outside the marine limits. Both Semmes and Pyrrho knew that had not been the case, but the governor, having either a fit of conscience or fear of punishment, thought it might prevent his being accused of ignoring the neutrality laws. The amused Semmes, perhaps wishing to show his appreciation for the island's hospitality, did as he was asked.[16]

Two days later the *Alabama* chased and boarded the *Nye*, a whaler carrying five hundred barrels of oil. Her captain, Joseph B. Baker, said they had been at sea for nearly 11 months, and therefore had only a scant notion that the *Alabama* even existed. He made no effort to hide the fact that the *Nye* was American. In a matter of hours his ship had been burned.

Within 48 hours another Yankee ship, the *Dorcas Prince*, was boarded. A blank cartridge fired near her bow brought her to a halt, and the boarding party removed provisions from her before she was fired. Her captain, Frank B. Melcher, and his wife were placed in the wardroom of the *Alabama*. Had they been housed in the captain's cabin they would have been able to admire the new home of the chronometer from the *Dorcas Prince*, which had been placed alongside those of 34 others.

* * *

It was now early March and still the *Kearsarge* sat idle. Pickering, tiring of the delays and frustrated in his attempts to maintain some semblance of discipline among his crew, confronted the Spanish dock superintendents. Threatening to take the propeller and its shaft back on board, finished or not, Pickering told the superintendents that he was going to set sail soon, with or without their help. Miraculously, the shaft was completed within hours, and on March 3 the workers began wrestling it into position. A week later the *Kearsarge* left dock for a test run, returning for only a few minor repairs.

On Sunday, March 15, the *London Times* issued the latest in a continuing series of denials of England's responsibility for the actions of the *Alabama*. Admitting that the *Alabama* had been built in Liverpool, the *Times* rationalized that " . . . It is the use that has been made of the *Alabama*, not her origin, that has rendered her dangerous, and for this we are not in any way accountable."[17] Despite the denial of responsibility, Welles must have felt some degree of vindication, as this first tacit admission of the *Alabama*'s construction site was published.

Finally, on March 17, the *Kearsarge* set sail, albeit without two of her crew members, Ordinary Seamen Frank Wilson and William Spencer, who had deserted. Landsman William Clark would join them on the roles of those leaving the *Kearsarge*, deserting as soon as the ship landed in Cadiz the next day. While in Cadiz the men were denied liberty, Pickering hoping to retain as many as possible for the new captain. For the next two days powder and shell were brought back on board, having been removed when the *Kearsarge* had gone into dry dock. A storm came up on March 24, the day that Pickering had planned to set sail, delaying departure until March 26.[18]

On March 28 a strange set of sails was spotted. Commander Craven of the *Tuscarora* had told Pickering that there would be no Confederate ships of war in the area because of the difficulty in obtaining coal in this region of the world. This strange ship, obviously not running under steam, appeared to be conserving fuel. Although he recalled Craven's report, Pickering decided that the ship could be an enemy cruiser.

The crews were immediately beat to quarters, and guns were made ready. The United States flag was run up, an action which was answered by the stranger's flag, an unusual pattern never seen by any of the officers before. Pickering asked Acting Master James R. Wheeler, who stood beside his captain at the rail, if he recognized the flag. Wheeler was baffled, having never seen that particular flag design before. The flag was green with a white cross, and it contained what appeared to be a depiction of a plant of some sort in the center of the cross. The two studied the flag as the ship drew closer, then passed. She was certainly not Confederate, they agreed. Pickering felt uneasy at having allowed the stranger to pass without challenging her. Finally, his concern got the better of him and he ordered the *Kearsarge* turned around. He wanted to confront this stranger and see just where she had originated.

With crew members certain that they would never be able to catch the stranger, the *Kearsarge* put her new propeller to the test. Within a few hours they caught up with the ship with the strange flag, and Wheeler shouted to the ship, asking her name.

The answer was muffled, and some thought she had identified herself as the *Sea King*, while others insisted that she was the *Peking*. It really didn't matter; the flag was that of the China Tea Company, rather than some unknown country, and the *Kearsarge* returned to her original course.[19]

As Pickering was putting his men through their paces one last time, Welles was resisting the efforts of President Lincoln and Secretary of State William Seward, who were trying to convince him to use privateers to catch the *Alabama*. Welles refused to consider it, still believing his navy could do the job.

The beleaguered Welles feared that the war would last a long time, no matter who chased the *Alabama*. "I close my book and this month of March," he wrote in his diary, "with sad and painful forebodings. The conduct and attitude of Great Britain, if persisted in, foreshadow years of desolation, of dissolution, of suffering and blood."[20]

Back on board the *Kearsarge*, Pickering set his sights on the Azores, where he had been ordered to report. Sailing through rough seas, seasickness once again hit the crew and officers. Finally, on April 1, land was sighted through the falling rain. It was the tiny island of Santa Maria in the Azores. Pickering's command was drawing down to the last few hours.

The *Kearsarge* put in to get away from the storm, extending Pickering's command somewhat. On April 4, the storm was over and the *Kearsarge* resumed her journey, anchoring off Horta on April 5. That afternoon the American consul escorted the new commander and first lieutenant aboard.

The captain was 52-year-old John A. Winslow, ironically a Southerner, having been born in North Carolina. He called Massachusetts home, however, and had married his first cousin, Catherine Amelia Winslow, who was a native of Boston. Now sporting a graying beard, he had obtained a commission at the age of 16, being appointed a midshipman through the influence of Daniel Webster. A lighthouse inspector when the war broke out, he had offered his services to the Union. Commodore Matthew C. Perry himself had praised him for his gallantry in the attack on Tobasco during the war with Mexico, and his reputation was such that his offer was readily accepted.[21]

Winslow had been assigned to the Mississippi River, where he had supervised the construction of gunboats. Later, assigned to command the *Benton*, he had been badly injured when his ship ran aground. In the process of getting her afloat, an iron hawser had come apart and struck him in his left arm, severing tendons and tearing muscles completely into the bone.[22]

It was not his arm that bothered him this day, however, as he met Pickering for the first time. He had been fighting inflamed lungs for several weeks, and while waiting to take over command of the *Kearsarge* Winslow had developed an infection in his left eye. It still had not healed, and he would eventually lose the sight in that eye.[23] Like Semmes, he was a religious man, although he did not build a shrine in his cabin as had the captain of the *Alabama*.

Winslow's arrival on board the *Kearsarge* was hardly looked on as a promotion by Welles, who had meted out the assignment. Sending officers to chase enemy raiders provided Welles with the perfect opportunity to eliminate officers who had offended him, which Winslow had done. His first offense had been the voicing of his displeasure at David Porter's promotion to acting rear admiral. Welles had been willing to overlook that indiscretion until Winslow had foolishly offered a negative assessment of the Confederate victory at Second Bull Run. After the Union defeat, a frustrated Winslow had been quoted as saying that he wished the Confederates would "bag old Abe."[24]

Winslow had admitted that he had indeed said that, but in a different context. He explained that his actual words had been that he " . . . wished the rebels had bagged old Abe, for until something is done to arouse the government we shall have no fixed policy."[25]

Welles had not been appeased by Winslow's explanation, and sending Winslow to replace Pickering had been his way of showing it. Winslow, nursing a lung condition to accompany an infected eye, found himself on the deck of his new ship, determined to show Welles that he was the right man for the job. He may be indiscreet, but he had never been a coward, and he planned to show his mettle if the occasion arose. He especially wanted to encounter the *Alabama*.

Winslow's first lieutenant was to be the replacement for the departed T. C. Harris. James S. Thornton, 36 years old, was not thrilled to be on the *Kearsarge*. He had wanted to remain on blockade duty, an assignment he enjoyed and which he thought would be more exciting than his new duties.

A 22-year navy veteran, Thornton was accompanied by a good reputation. At the battle of New Orleans he had taken command of the *Hartford* when her captain had been killed. Admiral David Farragut had praised his actions, saying that Thornton had saved the ship and the victory. At Mobile, Semmes's home city, Thornton had commanded the gunboat *Winona*, chasing down and destroying a rebel steamer while under fire from nearby Fort Morgan.

By mutual agreement, it was decided that the formal change of command would take place on April 8. This made Pickering nervous because it gave the crew time to take on more liquor and create problems. To keep the crew's minds and hands occupied, Pickering had them load more coal and clean the ship until it fairly glistened. While this went on, the ever-present bumboats swarmed about the *Kearsarge*, their occupants selling and bartering their wares to those on board.

The morning of April 8 saw Pickering, Winslow, and Thornton inspecting the crew. Then, the inspection completed, the sad goodbyes commenced. In spite of all his discipline, the men had grown to like Pickering, and many thought he had been treated unfairly. They had never gone into port unnecessarily, they said, and it hadn't been

Pickering's fault that the propeller had failed. The name of Gideon Welles was cursed by more than one sailor as Pickering gave his men one final salute, climbed into the captain's gig, and made for shore amid a chorus of cheers from his former crew. The scene was repeated to a lesser degree a scant 24 hours later when Captain's Clerk Charles Muzzey left the *Kearsarge* to return to the United States.

The crew had their first real introduction to their new captain the next morning when Winslow appeared on deck to watch the *Kearsarge* make for the open sea. Captains normally didn't leave their cabins with any great regularity, and the men were surprised to see Winslow out and about.

Winslow had the *Kearsarge* stop at Angra do Heroismo so he could see where the *Alabama* had taken on her equipment after sailing from Liverpool. Then, four days after taking command, he did something that the men had not seen before on the decks of the *Kearsarge*: he preached the Sunday sermon.

Back in the United States it appeared that all the protests concerning British comportment may have finally had a positive effect. The *New York Times* reported that the British House of Commons had recently debated the problem of having built the *Alabama*, and what might happen if they continued to turn a deaf ear to the protests.

The question was also raised as to why the *Alabama* had not been detained in Port Royal after her battle with the *Hatteras*. Of course, the *Times* sarcastically noted, the question was not raised until after the rebel raider had long departed.[26]

The ship had scarcely anchored in Angra when a steamer was sighted, raising Winslow's suspicions that a blockade runner was planning to enter port to take on coal. The *Kearsarge* set out to challenge the steamer but could not gain on her because of overheated bearings. Raising Portuguese colors, the *Kearsarge* fired a shot that was ignored by the fleeing vessel. Over the next several hours, two more shots had the same effect. The chase was finally called off and the *Kearsarge* returned to Angra where it was learned that they had been chasing a British mail steamer.[27]

As the *Kearsarge* lay at anchor in Horta, Thornton's mind drifted back one year to his time on the *Hartford*. That ship had stored her spare anchor chains by draping them over the sides. This not only freed up space in the hold, it also protected the boilers from any shells that an enemy may fire at the sides. He wondered why the same had not been done on the *Kearsarge*.

After he proposed his idea, it was only a few days until the crew of the *Kearsarge* had followed through. There was enough chain on board to allow about 49 feet along the length of the ship, on both sides, to be covered. From the main deck to the waterline, chains were fastened with large bolts, effectively turning the *Kearsarge* into an ironclad.[28] This would give rise to great controversy when the *Kearsarge* eventually met the *Alabama* some 14 months later.

Fearing that the rough surface created by the chains would induce too much drag, Carpenter's Mate Mark Ham was directed to encase the chains with boards. Once completed and painted to match the rest of the ship, it took a keen eye to notice the slight bulge created by the armor.

While those back in the United States may have been impressed if they had seen the *Kearsarge*'s new profile, the stinging criticism of the navy's failure to stop the *Alabama* continued. Near the end of April the *New York Times* quoted several letters which had been printed in the Liverpool *Mercury*. These letters said that private sources, apparently having lost all confidence in Welles and his department, were raising funds that would be sufficient to purchase the necessary vessels to put an end to "that pirate."[29]

The Combatants

**Raphael Semmes,
commander of the *Alabama***

Courtesy of William Stanley Hoole Special
Collections Library, University of Alabama

**John Winslow,
commander of the *Kearsarge***

Courtesy of National Archives and Records
Administration, NARA #111-B-3680

**Confederate
Secretary of the Navy,
Stephen Mallory**

Courtesy of Library of Congress,
Prints and Photographs Division,
LOC #LC-B812-1743

**United States
Secretary of the Navy,
Gideon Welles**

Courtesy of National Archives
and Records Administration,
NARA #111-B-1189

The *Alabama*

Courtesy of National Archives and Records Administration, NARA #19-N-13042

The *Kearsarge*

CSS *Alabama* sinking the USS *Hatteras*, January 11, 1863

Courtesy of U.S. Navy Photographic Center

**The capture of the mail steamer *Ariel* by the
Alabama as it appeared in *Frank Leslie's
Illustrated Newspaper*, January 10, 1863**

Courtesy of William Stanley Hoole Special Collections Library, University of Alabama

A typical inspection on the *Kearsarge*

Courtesy of Library of Congress Prints and Photographs Division,
Detroit Publishing Co. Photograph Collection, #LC-D4-20473

Sunday morning services on the *Kearsarge*

Courtesy of Library of Congress Prints and Photographs Division,
Detroit Publishing Co. Photograph Collection, #LC-D4-20474

CHAPTER TEN

MAY–JUNE 1863

On May 2, 1863, Semmes waxed nostalgic. It was his wedding anniversary, the third consecutive one he had spent away from his wife and family. At times he thought this inconvenience may be what inspired him to exact such revenge on the Union merchant fleet.[1]

The last four ships that had been boarded, the *Lafayette, Kate Cory, Nye*, and *Dorcas Prince*, had all been burned. The pendulum now swung the other way for the Confederates, as the next five ships stopped were neutral. On May 3, luck reversed itself once more. Two vessels were spied at about the same time. Shortly after noon the first was hailed and boarded by a crew commanded by Evans. She was the *Union Jack*, commanded by Charles P. Weaver. With Evans serving as prize master on the *Union Jack*, the *Alabama* gave chase to the second ship, bringing her around some two hours later.

The second ship, the *Sea Lark*, would prove to be the most valuable ship destroyed by the *Alabama*, valued at $550,000 by Kell.[2] Her captain, W. F. Peck, could do no more than watch helplessly as his ship was plundered by the men of the *Alabama*. Working from a list prepared by Dr. Francis Galt, the new paymaster, they grabbed soap, candles, clothing, and other items while ignoring more valuable cargo that was

133

not needed on the *Alabama*. Of course, the chronometer was removed and taken aboard the Confederate raider.

With the prisoners from the *Sea Lark* and the *Union Jack* added to those from the *Nye* and the *Dorcas Prince*, the *Alabama* was now laden with more than one hundred prisoners. This not only taxed the ability of the ship to handle so many additional people, it also posed a potential problem with respect to maintaining control of the ship. The prisoners nearly outnumbered the *Alabama*'s crew, and Semmes constantly feared an uprising.

Faced with that possibility, Semmes directed the helmsman to aim for Bahia. In spite of his overloaded craft, Semmes still hailed and boarded seven ships, all neutral, before reaching his destination on May 12. He had scarcely arrived when visiting health officials informed Semmes that there were at least three Union ships of war immediately off the coast.

While port officials reluctantly allowed Semmes to land his prisoners, the president of the Department of Bahia delivered a proclamation to him. The proclamation denounced Semmes and the *Alabama* for violating the neutrality laws in the captures of the *Lafayette* and *Kate Cory*. Further, it demanded an apology.

Having read the proclamation, Semmes calmly asked Bartelli to fetch him a pen and some paper, whereupon he dashed off a reply. Pulling no punches, Semmes wrote that the proclamation was a complete lie. "I can be a trifle careless in my choice of words," he said to Bartelli with a devious grin. "We have the heaviest guns in the harbor."

He also noted that the Confederacy could retaliate against Brazil after the war, a possibility that the president had not considered before. Deciding that an apology was not really in order, he backed down and directed local officials to extend all freedoms of the port to the *Alabama*.[3]

Not to be outdone, the United States consul officially demanded that the *Alabama* be detained and offered up to the United States government, which planned to hold her responsible for what were described as the ravages committed on their commerce. The Brazilian government wanted no part of it, however, and the demand was ignored.

Semmes, knowing that an English mail boat was anchored in the harbor, also wrote another letter to O. S. Glisson, commander of the USS *Mohican*. The *Mohican* was searching for any Confederate raider, but wanted the *Alabama* in particular. Semmes believed the *Mohican* to be one of the ships he had been warned about by the health officials.

"If the *Mohican* will come to where I can conveniently meet her," Semmes taunted, "I would have great pleasure in paying some attention. Circumstances do not permit me to go out of my course to meet anything."[4] This last statement referred to Semmes's mission, which was to seek out enemy merchant ships rather than warships. He then had the letter taken to the British mail packet for delivery.

At dawn on May 13, the officers of the *Alabama* became concerned about a steamer that had anchored some two miles from the *Alabama* during the night. The first light revealed that she was a brig-rigged screw steamer, apparently a ship of war. The officers gathered along the rail and watched anxiously as the light improved. At about 8:00 A.M. someone noticed the ensign flying from her mast. Remarkably, it was a Confederate flag!

Semmes was summoned. Rushing to the main deck he ordered a signal given to the ship. The signal was answered, and the newcomer got up steam and moved closer to the *Alabama*. She was the CSS *Georgia*, commanded by William Lewis Maury, and a reunion of sorts was effected, with many of the officers of the two ships having served together on the *Sumter*.[5] The *Georgia* would be the only Confederate ship the *Alabama* would ever encounter on her voyage.

While both Confederate warships were in port, Semmes received an edict that he had 24 hours to depart. Semmes informed the messenger that he would be willing to comply with the order only if he could get 30 tons of coal on board. Without the coal, however, Semmes planned to stay.

When the official asked where he planned to obtain that coal, Semmes was ready with an answer. The *Castor* was already in port to provide coal for the *Georgia* and she was carrying enough to also supply the *Alabama*. However, his plan was summarily dismissed. Port officials feared that the *Castor* may be carrying more than coal. They believed that she also brought with her a quantity of arms from Liverpool which were to be transferred to the *Alabama*. If the British wished to violate the international laws by sending the *Castor* to outfit Semmes, that was their business, but the Brazilians would not allow the sanctity of their neutrality to be breached.

Semmes rejoined that he had no choice then but to remain in port. At that, the official suggested that he get his coal from shore. He could allow that, but he could not allow the *Alabama* to take on arms from the *Castor* or anyone else. He noted that the Brazilians were already receiving protests from the United States concerning a train excursion and gala held in honor of the Confederates.* Under no circumstances would Semmes be allowed to stay any longer than necessary.

Semmes could see that there was little to be gained by arguing, and it really didn't matter to him where the coal came from as long as he got it, so the bunkers were filled with coal from shore. Semmes got the coal he wanted and the officials happily believed they could now tell the United States that no preference was given, and that, in fact, the *Alabama* had not been permitted to take on coal from a British vessel.

With coal being loaded, it was apparent to the crew that their time in Bahia was limited. Seeing their chance, two deserted. One of these, Ordinary Seaman Peter Henney, deserted on May 17. The other was Master-at-Arms James W. S. King, who departed May 20. Both were among the original members of the crew. The day after King deserted, the *Alabama* put to sea, hailing three neutral vessels in the first four days at sea. Then, on May 25 a large ship was sighted. Running the Stars and Stripes up the mast, the *Alabama* signaled "I want to talk to you."

The ship, also showing American colors and unaware of the trap that was about to be sprung, turned towards the *Alabama*. The unsuspecting merchant ship was the *S. Gildersleeve*, commanded by John McCallum. Semmes and his Admiralty Court quickly condemned her, and the *S. Gildersleeve* was burned.

Later that day another ship, the *Justina,* was chased and boarded. Since she was not carrying any cargo, Semmes could not justify burning her. *Justina*'s acting master, Charles Miller, signed a $7,000 ransom bond. The *Justina* was then used to transport the prisoners from the *S. Gildersleeve.*

---

* United States Minister J. W. Webb and the United States Consul at Bahia, Thomas Wilson, both filed protests over the perceived royal treatment given the men of the *Alabama* and the *Georgia*. As usual, the protests fell on deaf ears.[6]

One more ship, a Dutch bark, was stopped that day, and over the next three days three more neutrals were hailed. One of them, the English ship *Lady Octavia*, carried American newspapers that were only a few weeks old and provided valuable information.

On May 29, a sail was sighted off the starboard bow and another chase ensued. It took two blank cartridges to bring her around. Fullam headed the boarding party, which learned that the latest victim was the *Jabez Snow* out of Buckport, Maine. Her captain, George W. Guin, could do little more than protest as the boarding party took what provisions they could carry. It took little time at all for the Admiralty Court to condemn the *Jabez Snow* and her cargo of English coal, since Guin could produce no evidence that the cargo was neutral.

Three days later a sail was spied at 3:20 A.M. followed by an eight-hour chase that ended with three shots. She was the *Amazonian*, a bark carrying a general cargo. Fullam headed the boarding party and brought the captain of the *Amazonian*, Winslow Loveland, back to the *Alabama* for the customary legal proceedings. For whatever reason, Loveland failed to bring his papers with him when he boarded the *Alabama*. With no papers to back his claims of neutrality, the Admiralty Court had hardly convened when the verdict was reached to burn the *Amazonian*.[7]

On June 3, a neutral ship, the *Widna*, was stopped. Semmes asked her captain to take all the prisoners from the *Alabama*, but the man was reluctant. "I don't want to offend Lord Russell," he argued. Semmes then offered the captain one of the chronometers from his growing collection to sweeten the deal. With the chronometer considered the ultimate trophy during the 1860s, the captain was quickly swayed and the passengers were transferred, along with a week's worth of provisions. Sinclair, who was responsible for the task of keeping the chronometers running, silently said a prayer of thanks. That would be one less he would have to wind.[8]

Forty-eight hours after leaving the *Widna*, another ship laden with coal was stopped. Again, a blank cartridge was required to bring the *Talisman* to a halt. She was bound for Shanghai from New York, and her captain was D. H. Howard. The *Talisman* carried five passengers in addition to her cargo. One of those was a photographer named Lorenzo F.

Fisler. Fisler had signed a contract with a firm in Shanghai to do photographic work. In return, Fisler was to be paid his expenses plus a fee which could be paid in one of two ways. He had his choice of receiving $100 in Mexican money each month or one fourth of the business's profits. Fisler had opted for the latter.

When the *Talisman* burned, Fisler's equipment burned as well. After the war Fisler filed a successful claim for his equipment and clothing. Because he could not work without his equipment, he also felt justified in claiming a reimbursement for business delays caused by the loss. This portion of his claim proved to be unsuccessful.*

The next three vessels that were stopped proved to be neutral. On June 16, a bark was stopped whose papers proved to be very interesting to Semmes. She was identified in the papers as the *G. Azzopadi,* and her captain, Frederick Thorndyke, carried papers saying she was British, but he himself was an American and his ship had the characteristic look of a Yankee. Semmes was suspicious and informed Thorndyke that, if his suspicions proved valid, his ship would be burned.

Thorndyke insisted that his papers were not falsified. Finally, he blurted out that the reason his ship looked like a Yankee was because it once was. A surprised Semmes asked for an explanation, which Thorndyke was more than willing to offer. He explained that the ship had been built in Portland, Maine, and was christened the *Joseph Hale.* The previous October she had endured considerable damage in a storm, so Thorndyke had put in at Port Louis, Mauritius. With no money to make the necessary repairs, she was sold to an Englishman, upon which the registry was transferred and the ship took on the name *G. Azzopadi.* Everything was done properly and legally, according to Thorndyke.

Semmes studied Thorndyke closely as he spoke. He appeared to be sincere. His papers all seemed to support his story, and they certainly had the look of authenticity. Finally, Semmes was convinced. The papers showed the transfer to be bona fide. Semmes decided to allow Thorndyke to proceed on his journey, warning him that, if it was learned later that he had lied, the *Alabama* would find his ship and no mercy would be shown. As the *G. Azzopadi* sailed away, Semmes still had

---

* Fisler's claim was filed as part of the Alabama Claims, Case 404, Lorenzo Fisler vs. United States.[9]

some lingering doubts, but it would turn out that Thorndyke had been truthful.[10]

As unusual as the story of the *G. Azzopadi* was, it would be repeated within 24 hours. A ship carrying three hundred passengers was stopped, requiring two blank cartridges and a shot. She was the *Queen of Beauty* out of London. The ship had previously carried the name *Challenger* and had been American.

On June 20 a ship with a very Yankee look was spotted. She was boarded at dusk. She was a 20-year old American bark carrying Argentinean wool. Fullam led the boarding party onto the Union ship's deck, where he learned he had just boarded the *Conrad*. Fullam quickly escorted her captain, William H. Salsbury, back to the *Alabama* for the customary adjudication.

It appeared at first that the cargo was neutral, despite the fact that the ship was American. Finally, Semmes decided that the cargo was Union, and he condemned the *Conrad*. Salsbury and his crew were removed to the *Alabama*. The *Conrad* was a sleek-looking bark out of Philadelphia. Handsome in appearance, Semmes felt it a shame to destroy her. He struck upon the idea of seizing her and outfitting her as a Confederate ship of war. When he broached his idea to his officers they immediately concurred.

If the *Conrad* were to become a Confederate raider, however, she would need a crew. Semmes felt confident enough in the potential for success that he placed 14 of his own men on board. John Low, the 26-year-old fourth lieutenant of the *Alabama*, was placed in command. Midshipman William Sinclair, a relative of Arthur Sinclair, was assigned to assist Low, as were Quartermaster Adolphus Marmelstein and Seaman Joseph Minor. The crew was completed with the transfers of Ordinary Seamen Martin Molk and Robert Owens, and Seamen Edwin Jones, Henry Legris, Samuel Brewer, William Rinton, John Duggan, Robert P. Williams, Sam Brown, and Thomas Williams. Ordinary Seaman Thomas Allman of the *Conrad* elected to remain with his old ship when she became the property of the Confederacy and, after mustering in, brought the total to 15 officers and crew.[11]

Immediately, arms and provisions were transferred to the new raider. Two of the guns transferred, both 12-pound brass guns, had been taken from the *Talisman*. It would seem that Semmes may have had something in mind when he took the guns, because he had no need for them on the *Alabama*.[12] Twenty rifles and six revolvers were taken from the *Alabama*'s hold, having been placed there when taken from the *Ariel*.

Saying it was appropriate to name a child of the *Alabama* after one of the state's towns, Semmes declared the new Confederate ship the *Tuscaloosa*.[13] The fledgling crew of the *Tuscaloosa* ran the Confederate flag up the mast and a gun was fired as the *Alabama*'s crew cheered in unison. Semmes then wrote out orders to Low, explicitly ordering him to sink, burn, and destroy.[14] With the departure of the *Tuscaloosa*, the crew of the *Alabama* recognized almost immediately that they were now shorthanded, and that those left behind would have to add to their work load. By placing 14 of his men on the *Tuscaloosa*, plus Allman, who had chosen to stay with his ship, Semmes actually hurt himself in two ways. A crew of 15 was not large enough to be very effective, and he was now badly shorthanded on his own ship. Worse, morale began to sink when it was learned that the men on the *Tuscaloosa* were ineligible to share in the *Alabama*'s prize money. Although that meant more for each man who remained on the *Alabama*, friendships had become more important than a few dollars, and the unfairness was a topic of conversation for some time to come. With the departure of Low, Arthur Sinclair was promoted to fourth lieutenant in his place. Midshipman Irvine Bulloch, builder James Bulloch's half brother, became the new master.

It was not long before the *Alabama*'s watch spotted a suspicious sail. Immediately Semmes had the men brought to their quarters. A short chase brought the vessel to a halt, only to show Semmes that the *Mary Kendall*, out of England, was neutral. Her captain immediately asked if the *Alabama* had a surgeon aboard, explaining in urgent tones that one of his crew members had fallen from aloft and was in pretty bad shape and the English ship had nobody to treat him. Kell quickly summoned Dr. David Llewellyn, the *Alabama*'s assistant surgeon. Llewellyn immediately took a boat to the *Mary Kendall* and performed the necessary treatment. When Llewellyn returned to the *Alabama*, he reported that the *Mary Kendall* was leaking badly and that several of her crew members were refusing to work on her any longer.

Semmes was tempted to take the disgruntled Englishmen aboard but feared eventual retribution for violation of the Foreign Enlistment Act. Instead, he asked the captain of the *Mary Kendall* to take his prisoners. The captain agreed and Semmes gave him a chronometer as a token of appreciation. Six of the prisoners, however, decided to remain with Semmes. William Wilson, George Percy, George Thomas, John Williams, John Miller, and James Wilson all became members of the *Alabama*'s crew.

On June 27 Semmes ordered a revision to the *Alabama*'s course. She had been steering for the Cape of Good Hope when weevils were discovered in the bread supply. With the need to replenish the contaminated bread, Rio de Janeiro became the destination.

Her route altered, the *Alabama* encountered and boarded an English ship, the *Vernon*. The *Alabama* used the alias USS *Dacotah* once again to gain the English vessel's confidence. Upon boarding, Fullam requested the ship's papers but the captain refused. By law, a belligerent could capture any neutral vessel that refused to identify herself. Fullam, unsure of what to do next, insisted on seeing the papers. The captain still refused. Semmes had given his boarding officers full authority to make any necessary decisions when on board another ship, and Fullam exercised that option. Nothing gave him reason to suspect that the ship was American, so he decided to allow the ship to continue on her way. When he returned to the *Alabama* he immediately explained to Semmes what he had done, and fortunately for Fullam, Semmes supported his decision.[15]

The month of June was closed out with the boarding of two more neutrals: the *Asshur* and the *Medora*, both English barks. Semmes was disappointed to see that the newspapers on the *Medora* were too old to provide any value as an intelligence source.

* * *

On May 8, 1863, the *Kearsarge* left Horta, arriving at Angra the next day in a downpour. Upon arrival, Winslow learned that two blockade runners had been there a short time before, coaling and leaving as soon as they were finished. Perhaps remembering that remaining in port had been Pickering's undoing, Winslow put to sea that same evening.

For several days the *Kearsarge* cruised the Azores, until at long last Winslow decided that there were no rebel prizes in the area. On May 18 a suspicious-looking steamer was chased for nearly seven hours. Again, it was a British mail steamer, this time the *Tasmania*. During the chase the troublesome bearings began to overheat once more, and the engine room crew spent much of their time pouring water over them to prevent them from burning up.[16] Disconnecting his propeller to reduce wear on the bearings, Winslow ordered the helmsman to make for Portugal.

On May 26 another ship was chased, this time proving to be a French transport. Now near Gibraltar, Winslow made the decision to put into port. Entering the harbor, the *Kearsarge* nearly collided with another vessel. The helmsman averted a collision but struck two other ships before veering into an anchored brig, causing severe damage to all three vessels in addition to crushing her own dinghy. The rails and smokestack also were damaged, and it took nearly an hour of maneuvering to get the luckless *Kearsarge* and the brig untangled.[17]

While in port, repairs were made, and Francis M. Trude, who had been with the *Kearsarge* since her maiden voyage, chose to desert. Not wishing to waste time looking for him, Winslow ordered the *Kearsarge* to sea after two days, entering Cadiz just two days later. Unlike Pickering, Winslow allowed several of the crew to go ashore. He quickly learned why Pickering had been so stingy with liberty. Several of those who went ashore, including some of the officers, failed to make it back to the ship when liberty was officially over. Some of those who were late had good reason to miss the boat back to the ship; they were sleeping off their revelry in the local jail.

It soon became time for the *Kearsarge* to depart, and the ship moved to the coal yard to begin taking on more coal, a two-day process. Two days after having filled her bunkers, the crew was jolted awake by the crash of a runaway barge striking against the hull. This time the damage was slight, and the *Kearsarge* moved to dry dock, where the job of removing algae and seaweed from the bottom of the ship began. New bearings were installed and two ill crewmen, James Carroll and Charles

Tirnan, were sent home, both judged to be too sick to be of any help on board.

After all repairs had been made, the *Kearsarge* set sail, making a brief stop in Gibraltar for supplies. On June 19, Winslow set out for the open sea, looking for the *Lord Clyde*, a new ship which was a known blockade runner. Before finding the *Lord Clyde* he encountered another suspicious steamer at the port of Funchal. She was the British steamer *Smoker* and she rode much lower in the water than Winslow thought she should. Her captain let slip that she was about to set sail on a route known to be a favorite of blockade runners trying to reach the Texas ports. Shortly after she left port, so did the *Kearsarge*.

Overhauling the *Smoker* within a short time, Winslow ordered a boarding party. This alone was enough to get the crew's adrenaline flowing. The *Kearsarge* had never sent out a boarding party before. The boarding party dug through the *Smoker's* coal bunkers for hours, not knowing what they were looking for but hoping to find something. Finally, they gave up, having uncovered nothing. Reluctantly Winslow allowed her to proceed.[18]

Unconvinced that the *Smoker* had not somehow been able to hide contraband, Winslow believed that Madeira was providing coal to blockade runners. Anchoring nearby, he waited, hoping to encounter one of the offending ships.

As he waited, he did not allow his crew to sit idle. Gun drills were conducted, and even those crew members who had never fired a weapon were included. First the big guns were fired, then small arms. During the afternoon of June 29 several marines and gunners placed a howitzer into a boat and took it ashore, where they simulated an attack. There was no time for shirking. This new captain knew what he wanted, and what he wanted most was for his crew to be well prepared.[19]

CHAPTER ELEVEN

JULY–AUGUST 1863

The *Alabama* opened the month of July 1863 with two chases. Nine other sails were sighted but were not chased because the Confederate raider was already involved in pursuit. The first chase involved a neutral English bark, but the second proved more fruitful. When this second vessel was boarded, the party learned she was the *Anna F. Schmidt*, out of Boston. The *Anna F. Schmidt* had given the *Alabama* an extensive chase. Her captain, Henry B. Twombly, had ignored the blank cartridge the *Alabama* had fired, and it had taken a live round from the 100-pounder Blakely to convince Twombly that his pursuer was serious.

Before Fullam and his boarding party had gone to the prize, several of the crew members had given the boarders instructions to look for specific personal items. The ship's rule was that nobody was to take anything from a prize for personal use. This rule, however, was ignored with nearly every prize. Depending on the cargo, the men sometimes got their order filled, sometimes not.[1]

On this day the boarders had to break open cases to determine what was available. Food, clothing, medicine, bread, boots, shoes, and other items were checked. The bread could be used to replace that which weevils had infested. Other items were compared to the official list of items needed on board the *Alabama*. The boots and shoes were badly needed and were taken to the raider, along with a few other items. Few personal items were found to match the requests, however.[2]

The *Anna F. Schmidt* was valued at $350,000 by Kell, making it the second most valuable prize ever taken by the *Alabama*, exceeded only by the *Sea Lark*.[3] Despite her value, the *Anna F. Schmidt* was not spared from the torch.

Later in the day, the English ship *Thorndeer* was boarded. Although the *Thorndeer* had been built in the United States, her registry was British and she had a Scottish captain. Her cargo of Welsh coal was also neutral, and she was allowed to proceed.

That evening another ship, a sleek frigate with the appearance of an American clipper ship, was encountered. At the peak of the chase the *Alabama* fired a blank cartridge. To the dismay of Semmes and his officers, the frigate fired a return shot of her own. All hands were immediately called to their quarters, and the propeller was lowered in preparation for battle. The gunners loaded the port battery with five second shell. Everything pointed to a probable encounter with this impudent stranger.

With a full head of steam, the *Alabama* soon overtook the frigate. "What ship is that?" shouted Kell.

"This is Her Britannic Majesty's ship *Diomede*," came the answer.

Another British ship! Shaking his head at the announcement, Kell ordered the crew piped down.

Then, from the *Diomede* came, "Who are you?"

As the crew left their stations, Kell answered, "We are the Confederate States Steamer *Alabama*!"

The disembodied voice from the *Diomede* then shouted, "We thought as much when we saw you by the light of the burning ship. Is that your work?"

Kell proudly replied in the affirmative, and after a short silence signaled the *Diomede* to go on her way, pleased that the men of the *Diomede* had recognized the name of the *Alabama,* as well as her work.[4]

It was four days before the next ship was boarded and added to the list of prizes taken by the *Alabama*. The *Express*, carrying a load of guano, was neutral according to her captain, William S. Frost. Frost, whose wife was also aboard, admitted that the ship itself was American but he was adamant that his cargo was owned by Belgians. Semmes ruled that Frost's claim was fraudulent and he condemned the *Express* to burn. Prisoners were taken aboard, along with bread and other provisions before the *Express* was set afire.

Frost and his wife were accommodated in the *Alabama*'s wardroom, and five new crew members were shipped from the *Express* and the *Anna F. Schmidt*. Fred Columbia, William Bradford, Henry Saunders, James Broderick, and John Williams all signed on, bringing the complement to 23 officers and 120 men. Williams was the second of that name to join, but he would end any confusion just two months later when he and Saunders would desert. On July 22 Semmes transferred Captain Frost and his wife, as well as Captain Twombly of the *Anna F. Schmidt*, to the *Star of Erin*, out of Belfast.[5]

For four days no sails were sighted. Then within 24 hours, an unnamed Dutch ship and three English vessels, the *Lillian, Havelock*, and *Rover* were boarded. All passed on their way after the customary exchange of pleasantries.

July 28 found the *Alabama* nearing a well-known navigational feature on Dassen Island, known as the Lion's Rump. Semmes was reluctant to approach the island which was infamous for its dangerous reefs. Then, encountering an English bark the next day, he learned that her master was familiar with the local waters. Bringing him on board, the *Alabama* then sailed into Saldanha Bay for some badly needed maintenance. Within three days Albert Gilman, William Nordstrom, and James Wallace had all deserted. Tragically, the crew was about to be reduced by yet another.

Even without going ashore it was apparent to the crew and officers that there was an abundance of game in the Saldanha Bay area. Ducks, geese, and other birds flew over the ship, and the ever present natives in bumboats spoke of antelopes, pheasants, wild boar, and other game. With a lull in the prize-burning activities, many planned to go hunting at the first opportunity.

Three of those were Master Irvine Bulloch, Fourth Lieutenant Arthur Sinclair, and Third Assistant Engineer Simeon W. Cummings. Since

August 3 was a day of liberty, they decided to spend the day duck hunting. They rowed to the head of the bay, and by afternoon they had taken
a fair share of ducks. For some inexplicable reason, Cummings grabbed
the muzzle of his gun, which had been resting on the seat of the boat,
and pulled it toward him. As the horrified Sinclair and Bulloch looked on,
the hammer of Cummings's gun caught on something and the weapon
went off with a roar, only a few inches from Cummings's chest. Cummings
did not utter a word, but a surprised and shocked expression came over
his countenance as he slowly slumped to the bottom of the boat.

Knowing that Cummings had been badly hurt, Sinclair and Bulloch
began rowing as quickly as they could back to the *Alabama* while screaming for help. A crew member rushed to get Assistant Surgeon David
Llewellyn, who was at the victim's side even as he was passed over the
rail. Taking Cummings below, Llewellyn worked feverishly, but to no avail.
The third assistant engineer died shortly after being brought on board.[6]

A native of Connecticut, Cummings had moved to New Orleans
when he was 14 years old. Despite his Yankee origin, he had chosen to
fight for the Confederacy. His action had estranged him from his family
and, sadly, he had never reconciled with them.[7]

At midafternoon the next day all hands were piped on deck for the
funeral service. The body was gently placed in a boat. The Confederate
flag on the *Alabama* flew at half-mast, the only time in her cruise it would
do so. Five small boats, carrying as many officers and crew as could be
spared from duty, lined up behind the boat that carried Cummings. Each
craft also had a Confederate flag at half-mast. Slowly, the sad procession rowed the short distance to shore where a wagon was waiting. The
body was moved onto the wagon and the pallbearers climbed aboard.
Because Cummings had served in the Engineering Department, three
of his pallbearers came from that group. Third Assistant Engineers Matthew O'Brien and John Pundt joined Chief Engineer Miles Freeman. The
fourth pallbearer was George Townley Fullam, the master's mate. An
honor guard followed in a second wagon, followed by the ship's officers
on horseback. Those crew members who had gone ashore walked at
the end of the procession.

The cortege slowly filed to the family cemetery of a Dutch farmer
who had graciously offered a small plot when he had heard of the

tragedy. Kell led a brief service, after which three volleys were fired and a temporary headstone was placed on the grave. After each man filed past the grave to pay his respects, the saddened group made its way back to the *Alabama.**

Semmes had not had a good week. In addition to the death of Cummings, his men had outdone themselves while on liberty. One had even drawn a gun on an officer. Because of this incident Semmes halted any further liberty, noting in his journal that "I have a precious set of rascals on board—faithless in the matter of abiding by their contracts, liars, thieves, and drunkards."[8]

On August 5 the *Alabama* set sail for Cape Town, following the coast. The crew was amazed to see the *Tuscaloosa* approaching. Unknown to them, when the two ships had departed nearly seven weeks earlier, Semmes had instructed Low to meet him near Cape Town to give him a report on the *Tuscaloosa's* activities.

Fullam was dispatched in a boat to bring Low on board, where he greeted his old friends before retiring to Semmes's cabin to give his report. Although the *Tuscaloosa* had sighted an average of more than one ship per day, nearly all had been neutral. Only one Union ship, the *Santee*, had been captured, and she had been released on bond. At the conclusion of the meeting, Low returned to his ship and the *Alabama* resumed her journey to Cape Town. Semmes wrote a letter to Governor P. E. Wodehouse in Cape Town, requesting permission to land his prisoners, take on supplies, and make more repairs.

This letter resulted in a great deal of excitement in the city of Cape Town. The *Alabama*'s reputation was well known, and the citizens of that city buzzed over the possibility of seeing the famed raider. When observers alerted the city that not only was the *Alabama* nearing the port, but an American bark was also approaching from the opposite direction, the excitement built into near frenzy proportions. To see the *Alabama* was exciting enough, but it now appeared that they would also get to see

---

* Sometime later, officers of the Royal Navy who were based in Cape Town replaced the temporary headstone with a permanent marker. This is believed to be the only monument to a Confederate in South Africa.[9] In 1994 Cummings's body was reinterred in Columbia, Tennessee, with full military honors.

her do what she had become famous for: capturing and burning a Union merchant ship.

Shortly after noon on August 5, a chase began which was to plunge the *Alabama* into even deeper controversy. The wind was light, which proved to be in the *Alabama's* favor. Had there been a strong wind, the American ship could have easily made it inside the three-mile limit. With British colors hoisted, the *Alabama's* engineers fired up her boilers as the propeller was lowered. The chase was a short one, a blank shot and a muzzle round convincing the American skipper that it was futile to continue to run. Fullam calculated that the ships were about five miles from shore.[10]

Master's Mate James Evans initially boarded the prize, the *Sea Bride*. He brought the captain, Charles F. White, back to the *Alabama* for the customary maritime trial. White was a part-owner of the *Sea Bride* and had a great deal to lose if she was burned.

Sending Fullam to replace Evans, Semmes instructed the master's mate to cruise back and forth as long as the weather permitted, but to refrain from entering the bay. Semmes knew that bringing a prize into a neutral port would be a clear violation of international law. However, Semmes also instructed Fullam and his boarding party to meet him in Saldanha Bay by August 15 if a storm should brew. Such a storm did come up and howled for two days. The *Alabama*, anchored in Table Bay, maintained her position throughout the gale.

Meanwhile, Semmes dispatched Lieutenant Joseph D. Wilson to go ashore and meet with the governor. The purpose of the visit was to confirm that Governor Wodehouse had received the letter Semmes had sent him, and to reiterate the request that the prisoners be put ashore.

Visitors quickly mobbed the *Alabama*, eager to see the vessel that had become so famous in such a short time. Local newspaper accounts noted that large crowds flocked " . . . to see the *Alabama*, her captain, and her officers."[11] A long line of visitors wanted to meet with Semmes, and Bartelli stood at his door to screen those who wished an audience.[12] Late in the afternoon the English mail steamer *Lady Jocelyn* arrived, adding to the festive air by giving the crew of the *Alabama* a cheer as she passed.

On August 7 United States Consul Walter Graham filed a protest, saying that the capture of the *Sea Bride* had been made in territorial waters. Captain White supported Graham's claim. The charges would be weakened by a report to Governor Wodehouse from Captain Charles G. Forsyth of the nearby neutral ship *Valorous*, who said that he thought the capture had been at least six miles off shore. Captain H. Wilson, Table Bay's port captain, agreed with Forsyth. Rear Admiral Baldwin W. Walker of the Royal Navy at Simon's Bay relied heavily on the reports of Forsyth and Wilson in his examination of the circumstances, as well as Fullam's readings.

With the Cape Town area decidedly pro-Confederate, Graham's official protest had little chance. In fact, even as Admiral Walker was conducting his investigation, British officials who showed no concern for any appearance of non-neutrality were entertaining Semmes and his officers. After all, the ship had been built in England and her crew was predominantly English. It was no surprise to Graham when his protest was not acted upon.

On August 9, the *Alabama* steamed out of port, bound for the British naval station at Simon's Bay, where the *Tuscaloosa* would be waiting. Less than three hours into the voyage a sail was sighted, and the *Martha Wenzell*, an American bark, was quickly overhauled. The customary check of the ships' locations, however, revealed that the *Martha Wenzell* had been captured inside the three-mile limit. Overjoyed when told his ship would be released, the captain thanked Semmes profusely. The *Martha Wenzell* would be the only ship that Semmes ever officially admitted had been captured illegally. [13]

Her prize released, the *Alabama* continued on to Simon's Bay, where once again she received a warm greeting. The next morning Semmes proceeded to the home of Rear Admiral Walker, where he immediately apologized and explained that his capture of the *Martha Wenzell* inside territorial waters had been unintentional. Walker believed Semmes and so reported to the secretary of the British Admiralty. Perhaps of greater importance, Walker also warned Semmes that the Union's *Vanderbilt* was in the area. "Her captain says he does not intend to fire on you if he finds you," Walker said ominously, "but he will run you down and sink you."

This was not an idle threat. The *Vanderbilt* was much larger than the *Alabama* and nearly as fast. Semmes was familiar with this vessel, but unintimidated. The *Vanderbilt* was a converted passenger ship, a large paddle wheeler. If the two should meet, Semmes had already decided, the *Alabama* would place a shot into her wheel and disable her.

That evening, Semmes enjoyed dinner on the *Kwantung*, a Chinese gunboat anchored nearby. Joining Semmes were the commanders of the *Kwantung* and the HMS *Narcissus*. Semmes and the *Kwantung*'s commander must have had much to talk about, as their ships had a great deal in common. Similar to the *Alabama*, the *Kwantung* had been built in Liverpool by none other than the Laird brothers.

While in port, the crew caulked and painted, as they did at every opportunity. On shore, Consul Walter Graham worked hard to convince any *Alabama* man on liberty that he should remain on liberty. Graham would do his job well. Beginning with Thomas James, Alfred Morris, and Thomas Weir at the end of July, and continuing through the end of September, 21 men of the *Alabama* would desert, many convinced to do so by the consul.[14]

On August 14, only one day before Semmes planned to put to sea, 20 men were still absent from the *Alabama*. Many of them were reported to be hiding at Black Sophie's bordello in Cape Town.[15] Semmes offered rewards for their immediate apprehension, and several suddenly appeared in the hands of the police, who tried to claim the reward. Some of those who returned smuggled liquor onto the ship, contributing to a considerable number of continuing problems.

On August 15, with the *Alabama* ready to sail, Semmes was still missing 14 of his crew, and was forced to take on nine new recruits. These men were James Welsh, Philip Wharton, Frank Mahany, Richard Ray, Nicholas Maling, John Russell, John Adams, Samuel Valens, and Russell Hobbs. Semmes was obviously not impressed with his new recruits, and he noted that it would take weeks to make sailors out of them, as well as to work the grog out of the rest of the crew before they settled down into "good habits and cheerfulness."[16] To get around the law against recruiting in a neutral port, the nine men were considered stowaways.

They were hidden deep in the bowels of the ship and would not be sworn in until the vessel was safely beyond the three-mile limit.

Semmes also recruited two others, both of whom had been ship-wrecked near Table Bay. Baron Maximilian von Meulnier and Julius Schroeder had been serving in the Prussian navy when their ship had foundered, and they had eagerly rushed to the *Alabama* when they learned she was in port. Recognizing their experience, Semmes was willing to ignore the Foreign Enlistment Act, as so many others on both sides did throughout the war, and he signed them on. Both men would prove to be valuable assets to the *Alabama*.

With his crew as complete as possible for the time being, Semmes ordered the *Alabama* to cast off at 11:00 A.M. in a light rain. By 2:30 the first sail was sighted, and soon the *Saxon*, an English bark was boarded. Satisfied of her neutrality, the *Alabama* allowed her to proceed, then signed on the nine "stowaways." Semmes could not have known at that time that the *Alabama* was entering one of her leanest periods in her entire cruise, and would not burn another American prize for three months.[17]

The first ship stopped after the *Saxon,* the *Broughton Hall,* proved to be another English vessel. One of those summoned to board her was Dr. Llewellyn, who was asked to tend to the captain's ailing wife. With Surgeon Francis Galt's time being increasingly occupied by his duties as acting paymaster, the *Alabama* was fortunate to have Llewellyn on board to take over the medical duties.

On August 23 Semmes called a court-martial for Chief Boatswain's Mate Brent Johnson. Johnson had pulled a knife on a superior officer but offered the defense that he had been drunk and should not be held accountable. He was nevertheless found guilty. Johnson was sentenced to be disrated to seaman, placed in solitary confinement for three months, and then discharged in disgrace, forfeiting all pay and prize money.[*]

On August 28 the *Alabama* anchored in 15 fathoms at Luderitz Bay in present-day Namibia. The *Tuscaloosa* and *Sea Bride* were already

---

[*] Semmes would reduce the sentence one month later, dropping the remainder of the solitary confine-ment and returning Johnson to duty as a seaman. Johnson quickly worked his way back through the ranks, becoming quartermaster on Christmas Eve, 1863.[18]

there. The officers assumed the *Sea Bride* would be burned after the prisoners were put ashore, but Semmes had another idea. When Semmes had captained the *Sumter* he often took his prizes into Cuba, where he would sell them. When he later learned that the government had returned the prizes to their original owners, he began the practice of burning them instead. Now, Semmes was in a port which was not under any foreign power. Luderitz Bay was ruled by the Hottentots, who neither were aware of international laws nor cared of their existence. He planned to sell the *Sea Bride* to any South African parties who may be willing to make such a purchase.

The initial contacts had been made in Cape Town, where Captain Thomas Elmstone, who represented a group of English speculators, had shown interest in purchasing the *Sea Bride*. Elmstone and Captain Loete met with Semmes and Galt in Semmes's cabin, shortly after the *Alabama*'s arrival in Luderitz Bay. Elmstone explained to Semmes that he had brought Loete along to command the *Sea Bride* if an agreement could be reached.

The likelihood of an agreement being reached was excellent. Semmes was prepared to sell the *Sea Bride* at a bargain price. He told Elmstone that he had not found one prize on the journey from Cape Town to Luderitz Bay, and he'd like to have something to show for his journey. Semmes hoped to sell the *Sea Bride* and her cargo, as well as the cargo that still remained on the *Tuscaloosa*.

Naturally, Elmstone was interested in learning what the cargoes contained, and Semmes obligingly told him that there were cloth and notions on the *Sea Bride* and wool on the *Tuscaloosa*. He estimated that the *Sea Bride* and her cargo were worth about $75,000. Elmstone balked at the mention of $75,000, explaining that his clients were not willing to spend that much, particularly with the risk of possible confiscation involved.

Elmstone and Semmes bargained for several hours until a final price was negotiated. The agreement: Semmes would sell the *Sea Bride* and her cargo, as well as the wool from the *Tuscaloosa*, which had never been removed when she had been converted from the *Conrad*, for the equivalent sum of $16,940.[19] As part of the agreement, the wool would be resold in London and the Confederacy credited with two-thirds of the proceeds. Elmstone also agreed to purchase any future prizes Semmes brought in.[20]

Elmstone's clients, Robert Granger and Company, painted the *Sea Bride* and renamed her the *Helen*. Registered in Hamburg, she would sail between Madagascar and Mauritius, eventually sinking off the coast of Madagascar.

Semmes, meanwhile, had second thoughts after the sale. "Our mission is to destroy enemy commerce," he said. "It is not to sell ships." He would not sell another prize for the remainder of the cruise.

* * *

On July 3, as the battle in Gettysburg was winding down, the *Kearsarge* turned for the Azores. There was no celebration on July 4, but two days later the *Kearsarge* put in at Madeira. There, Lieutenant Commander James Thornton bought enough chicken and ale for every man to eat and drink his fill.

Winslow proved to be a no-nonsense sort who took his duties seriously. Several times over the next few days he ordered steam so he could chase some ship that was possibly the *Alabama*. With a great deal of physical labor involved in firing the boilers, the men grumbled with each chase, particularly those involving ships that didn't even resemble the *Alabama*. The complaints grew louder each time they chased yet another ship that turned out to be neutral.

On July 17 a sidewheeler anchored in Horta, not far from the *Kearsarge*. She appeared to be British, but Winslow was suspicious. For one thing, the stranger's captain got into an argument with the port officers, refusing to show his papers. The officials retaliated by placing the ship under quarantine, meaning nobody could come ashore. Seeing this unfold, Winslow suspected that the ship would soon depart. He ordered the *Kearsarge* turned around and all men to their quarters. The crew was instructed to be ready to follow if the sidewheeler made a run.

Early in the afternoon, just as Winslow had thought she would, the stranger quickly made for the open sea. Already idling under steam, the *Kearsarge* was ready. Before the anchor could be brought up, however, the engineers thought they heard the order to engage the propeller. The

Kearsarge suddenly lurched forward with her anchor still embedded in the mud.

In the engine room the crew labored to get the ship moving, not knowing that the anchor was still doing what it was designed to do. They only knew the ship was not moving as fast as it should, so more steam was ordered. The anchor broke loose and soon the *Kearsarge* was churning after the suspicious sidewheeler, albeit at a much reduced speed, dragging the anchor behind.

With no such encumbrance, the stranger easily pulled away. Thornton ordered his gunners to fire a shell, but the distance between the two was already too great and the shell fell considerably short. The officers implored Winslow to let them cut the chain but he refused. The chase continued until after dark, even though the stranger had long since disappeared. Approaching Terceira in the darkness, Winslow ordered all lights doused. Slowly the *Kearsarge* eased her way into the roadstead near Angra, where the crew was surprised to see the silhouette of their quarry outlined in the moonlight. Winslow immediately ordered the fires banked and the *Kearsarge* prepared to spend the night.

The presence of the *Kearsarge* did not go unnoticed, and in the morning the stranger's captain, John Taylor, angrily approached the Union ship and asked to come aboard. Confronting Winslow, Taylor demanded to know why the *Kearsarge* had fired on him the previous day. Winslow, refusing to be intimidated, told Taylor that he had intended to bring him around. Winslow then demanded the name of the ship.

"We're the *Juno*," said Taylor, "and we are not carrying anything that you would be interested in. You may come and inspect us if you wish."

Winslow thought the captain of the *Juno* was too cooperative and deduced that Taylor had probably already put his contraband ashore, planning to take it back on board after Winslow made his inspection. The Yankee captain politely declined, telling Taylor that the *Kearsarge* would simply wait until the *Juno* put to sea again. Then he'd find out for himself. Taylor, not realizing that the *Kearsarge* had been dragging her anchor, told Winslow that he had run from him once and would do it again.[21]

The two vessels stayed at anchor for two days while the *Juno* took on coal. Winslow kept a man poised with an ax, ready to drop the anchor at a moment's notice. A marker buoy had already been attached so it could be located later. Observing this, Taylor tried to fool the *Kearsarge* into dropping anchor, feigning a departure by lunging his ship forward, then cutting his engines. Winslow, however, would have none of it. On July 22, after several bluffs, the *Juno* finally made her move. Winslow responded and the *Kearsarge* steamed away quickly.

The sidewheeler took a route that followed the coast, passing through a route that was too narrow for the *Kearsarge*. Winslow took a wider swing, giving the *Juno* a lead of more than a mile. With no anchor to hold her back this time, the *Kearsarge* overtook the *Juno* after a very short chase. A surprised Taylor offered to let Winslow come aboard and make his inspection, but Winslow refused, noting that the two were still in Portuguese waters. Winslow preferred to wait until his foe was past the three-mile limit.

Taylor, chagrined that Winslow had realized his attempted ruse, waited for a while but then struck for open waters once more. The American ship again overtook her quarry. Taylor, seeing that boarding was inevitable, tried unsuccessfully to destroy his papers. The heavily armed boarding crew had orders to thoroughly search the ship until her contraband was discovered. The American flag was run up the *Juno*'s mast to signify her capture, and the two ships made for Horta. There, Winslow ordered the *Juno* to remain outside the three-mile limit, under command of the boarding party. Nobody was going to accuse him of bringing a prize of war into a neutral port. The *Kearsarge* anchored inside the bay.

Captain Taylor sent word to the British consul on Fayal that he had been captured illegally, and the consul demanded that Winslow set the *Juno* free. Winslow had no intention of giving up his prize and stalled as long as he could while his men dug through the coal bunkers in search of anything which may have been hidden there. Nothing had been found by late afternoon and the consul was becoming more demanding. Winslow had little choice but to allow Taylor to return to his ship and depart. Before leaving, the defiant Taylor made a show of taking down the American flag and running up his own British ensign.*

---

* Seven months later a member of the *Juno*'s crew would admit that seven tons of powder had been concealed in the bottom of her hold, and that Winslow would have almost certainly found it if he had been allowed more time to search.[22]

A frustrated Winslow ordered the *Kearsarge* to return to the island of Terceira, where more gunnery practice was ordered. At the end of July, Winslow returned to Angra to retrieve the *Kearsarge*'s anchor. Even that did not go well, despite the foresight of marking the spot with a buoy. As the anchor was raised, the rope snapped and the anchor and its chain dropped to the bottom of the bay. It would not be retrieved until the next day.

At the same time, progress was noted in the effort to hold England accountable for the damages caused by the *Alabama* and her sister ships. The *New York Times* reported that the House of Commons had held an animated debate about two ironclads preparing to leave Liverpool for Confederate service. The delegates discussed the fact that they had been built in England for a belligerent, and they feared that their departure may lead the United States to declare war against England. For the first time, England showed signs of concern, and it was reported that the American minister had made a " . . . formal claim upon England to indemnify American shipowners for their losses."[23]

As the debate raged on, the men of the *Kearsarge* went ashore in groups of 40, many returning late, many returning with injuries, and many not returning at all. Some of those who had been injured in bar fights suffered such serious wounds that Surgeon John M. Browne implored Winslow to stop all liberty until further notice. Bar fight injuries would prove to be the least of Browne's concerns, however. In mid-August Landsman Mark Emery fell seriously ill and did not respond to Browne's best efforts at treatment. The popular 22 year old was a rarity among the crew as he had never been punished by either Pickering or Winslow for any infraction.

Emery's condition deteriorated to the point of hallucination. His fever rose so high that he no longer recognized old friends. Browne applied all his medical knowledge, but to no avail. On August 19, Emery died.

All hands were piped to the quarterdeck that afternoon for the funeral. Emery had been placed inside his hammock and covered with the flag he had served so well. As Winslow conducted the burial service, several crew members hoisted the young man from Maine onto a plank placed on the gangway. At the appointed moment the head of the plank was raised and the body slid off and disappeared silently into the sea.[24]

Emery was not the only man on board who became ill. Over the next several days, 15 more men were afflicted with the mysterious illness. While some of those exhibited only mild symptoms, others were far more serious. Despite these illnesses, the *Kearsarge* hosted a party at Horta. As the festivities continued into the night, Coal Heaver Clement Boener's condition worsened. By the time the music had stopped for the night, the German teenager had slipped into unconsciousness. Just before dawn, Boener became the second member of the crew to die within a week.

With the *Kearsarge* so close to shore, Boener's body was prepared for a land burial. A crude coffin was constructed and, in a scene eerily similar to the burial of the *Alabama*'s Cummings just three weeks earlier, the body was transported ashore.

Flags on the *Kearsarge* and the launch were at half-mast as the burial party accompanied their ship mate to his final resting place. Once on shore, the crew members took turns carrying the coffin to a church that sat more than a mile inland. Behind the church, in a small cemetery, Boener was placed in a newly dug grave. His shipmates placed a simple marker at the head of the grave, paid their last respects, and sadly retraced their steps back to the boat that would return them to the *Kearsarge*.[25]

CHAPTER TWELVE

SEPTEMBER–OCTOBER 1863

September 1863 began strangely for the men of the *Alabama*. On September 2 a large sail was spotted just as dawn was breaking. The vessel appeared to be American, and she was signaled to stop. The ship, the *Punjaub,* did so with no resistance. Her captain, Lewis F. Miller, was taken to Semmes, who thought he recognized Miller. As Semmes perused Miller's papers he soon realized why his adversary looked so familiar. The *Alabama* had captured the *Punjaub* once before! Semmes was now in a dilemma. He had never allowed a ship to go free twice. Semmes shuffled through his packet of ransom bonds until he found the bond for the *Punjaub*'s first capture. "March 15, 1863," he read. "The *Punjaub*. Released on $50,000 bond. Signed by a Captain Miller." When asked, Miller confirmed that he was the signer of the first bond.

Miller had put up the ship and all his tackle as security for the ransom bond the first time his ship had been captured by the *Alabama*. It would do no good to offer it as security a second time. And the *Punjaub*'s cargo of cotton and saltpeter appeared to be owned by a British firm, making it neutral. There appeared little that Semmes could do. He perused the papers, looking for any indication that Miller was not telling the truth about the neutrality of his cargo, but found nothing.

Finally the frustrated Semmes realized that his options were limited. Against his judgment it appeared that he recommended to the makeshift court that the *Punjaub* be released. The "judges" nodded their agreement, much to Miller's relief.

Semmes then reminded Miller that his was the first ship he had ever released twice. He also added that he wouldn't even consider releasing him a third time. Miller, not wishing to give Semmes time to change his mind, beat a hasty retreat from the cabin. Even Bartelli had to struggle not to laugh when Miller left. He had enjoyed the exchange thoroughly. He almost hoped they would see the *Punjaub* a third time, just to see what Old Beeswax would do.[1]

On September 3 another ship was boarded after being halted by a blank cartridge. No Union vessel had been halted for nearly three weeks, and the *Alabama*'s luck did not change with the boarding of this ship. She was the *Isle O'May*, a coffee-laden English bark. Although the week was destined to be a busy one with eight more vessels challenged, all of them proved to be English, and the crew's frustration mounted.

On September 11 the English bark *Flora* was stopped. Her captain was in a foul mood and had ignored the *Alabama*'s three signals and blank cartridge before finally realizing the futility of running. The *Alabama* was flying the Stars and Stripes when Fullam boarded the *Flora*, and he identified his ship as the USS *Ticonderoga*. The *Flora*'s captain met Fullam at the rail and demanded to know why he had been stopped. Before Fullam could say a word, the captain launched into a tirade. Apparently several Union boarding crews had already stopped him several times on his voyage. Believing the *Alabama* was another Union vessel, he turned his ire toward Fullam.

Fullam listened attentively as the British captain vented his frustrations about the many delays he had encountered since leaving Manila. First he had been confronted with high winds and heavy seas. Then, he had been repeatedly stopped by Union ships, all of which had found his ship to be neutral. Now he was being boarded again. When the Englishman finally stopped to catch his breath, Fullam asked him if he knew who had boarded him earlier. The frustrated captain did not, but he remembered the last ship was a "big two masted warship with long funnels," remarkably like Fullam's, he added. It also flew the United States flag.

The English captain continued to rail against Yankees in general as Fullam and the boarding crew examined the ship's papers and cargo. Finding everything in order, Fullam ordered the boarding party back to the *Alabama*, apologizing to the captain of the *Flora* for the inconvenience. With the anti-Yankee harangue still emanating from the *Flora* as the small boat worked its way back to the *Alabama*, the crew broke into laughter. One of the crewmen suggested facetiously that maybe they should burn the ship just to give him more reason to hate Yankees!

Back on board the *Alabama*, Fullam related the encounter to an amused Semmes, after which the officers concluded that the CSS *Georgia* must have been the offending "Yankee" who had stopped the *Flora* two days earlier.[2]

Five days after boarding the *Flora,* the *Alabama* made her way into Simon's Bay, South Africa, anchoring late in the afternoon. In Simonstown, Semmes learned that the *Georgia* had been there a short time earlier, lending support to the supposition that it had been the *Georgia* which had delayed the *Flora* two days prior to the *Alabama*'s boarding.

Semmes intended to replenish his ship's coal supply in Simonstown, but when he attempted to make the arrangements he learned that there was none to be had. The reason for the shortage of coal? The USS *Vanderbilt*, under the command of Charles H. Baldwin, had taken it all just a few days earlier!

Although the lack of coal concerned Semmes, he was bothered more by the fact that the *Vanderbilt* was in close proximity. Newspapers taken from prizes indicated that Baldwin's primary mission was to intercept the *Alabama* and sink her. This itself did not strike any fear in Semmes, but he preferred not to encounter a Union warship if he didn't have to.

One of those interested in the *Alabama*'s presence in Simonstown was American consul Walter Graham, the same consul who had been frustrated with the *Alabama* following her controversial capture of the *Martha Wenzell*. Exacting a measure of revenge, Graham was able to convince 16 members of the crew to desert during the *Alabama*'s short stay in Simon's Bay. Three of the 16, Nicholas Maling, Richard Ray, and Samuel Valens, had only been on the *Alabama* about a month. Semmes appealed to the local authorities, asking that the United States be forced to return the men, but to no avail. Although the local officials sympathized with Semmes, neutrality forbade their interference.

While he had no desire to violate the Queen's neutrality, he argued that no man should be forced to do what he doesn't wish to. If Simonstown soil was sacred and could not be violated, then it must work the other way, too. A war ship is part of a country's territory, Semmes argued, and if some of the Queen's subjects came aboard and decided to stay, he should not be required to try to force them off.[3]

The thinly veiled threat was not lost on the officials, but they feared retribution from the United States if they took action. Their refusal to interfere enabled Semmes to enlist the services of a local crimp, a man who could obtain sailors for a price. The typical crimp employed methods that were not always within the bounds of legality, but Semmes had little choice. Within a few days of his request, the crimp arrived at the *Alabama* to tell Semmes he had found 13 "volunteers" who had been boarding with him.

Semmes asked the crimp if he was aware that the *Alabama* could not ship seamen in a neutral port, to which the crimp replied that he did know that. However, he suggested that Semmes was permitted to take passengers to sea if they wished to go. Semmes immediately realized what the crimp was saying; and passengers could be asked to work as crew members to pay for their passage. Semmes fixed a steely glare on the crimp. He didn't like this man, and he didn't enjoy dealing with him, but he could not sail without replacements for those who had deserted. Semmes then inquired if the crimp expected a fee for bringing the 13 men aboard.

The crimp took on a hurt expression, as if Semmes had figured his motives incorrectly. He insisted that he only asked a token payment, merely what the men already owed him for lodging and drinks. Semmes did not respond as the crimp fished in his pockets, pulling out a scrap of paper. Referring to it, the man began to read aloud each man's debts. Semmes, uninterested in the crimp's litany, quickly stopped him and instructed Kell to take the man to the paymaster for payment. Meanwhile, Dr. Llewellyn gave each a cursory physical examination, pronounced them fit enough to serve despite their varying degrees of drunkenness, and sent them off to clean up.[4]

All of the new hands were ordinary seamen, and Semmes described them as "vagabonds, hungry and nearly shirtless." The 13 new crew members were Thomas White, John Wilson, John Mehan, Andrew Pfeiffer, John Smith, John Welham, Henry Angel, Thomas Brandon, George Conroy, Richard Evans, Richard Hambly, James Hart, and Thomas Kehoe.[5]

On September 24, with what would prove to be an erroneous warning ringing in his ears that the *Vanderbilt* was nearing Simon's Bay, Semmes put to sea. Within 24 hours six vessels were sighted, any one of which he feared could be the *Vanderbilt*. One of the sails was chased but proved to be neutral. That same day, unknown yet to Kell, his daughter died in Georgia, a victim of diphtheria.[6]

Semmes stayed out of the usual shipping lanes, taking a route that would help him avoid the *Vanderbilt*. As a result, few ships were spotted. The men passed their leisure time fishing for dolphins, although many fished only for the sport, since they feared possible poisoning if they should eat the meat.

A common fear of mariners was that a dolphin, or any other fish for that matter, which had eaten barnacles from the bottom of coppered ships, would give a man a fatal fever if eaten. To determine if the catch had eaten such barnacles, a silver coin was placed in the frying pan with the fish. If the coin turned black the meal was tossed overboard. Some of the more cautious crew members wouldn't eat the meal no matter what the crude test showed.[7]

Dolphins were not the only quarry for which the men fished. Cape pigeons and albatross flew around the ship, waiting for garbage to be tossed over from the galley. The birds seemed to sense when the stewards were about to get rid of the refuse, appearing almost on cue. When the garbage was dumped, the pigeons swooped down and feasted on the floating debris. As they did, the crew members tried to catch them on open hooks. The "fishing" was halted any time an albatross approached, as the men watched in awe as the graceful birds glided almost effort-lessly into the meal. Jack was no different than any other seaman of the time, fearing bad luck if an albatross were harmed.[8]

Now in the Indian Ocean, storms arose quickly and with little warn-ing. One gale after another buffeted the craft, although they did provide favorable winds that had the *Alabama* racing across the sea. On Sep-tember 27 Semmes celebrated his birthday. Now 54 years old, it was just one more day away from home and his family.

On October 3 only the second sail in nearly a month was sighted. Steam was raised and the chase began. The boredom of the past sev-eral weeks was quickly forgotten and the crew prepared for what they hoped would be an encounter with the enemy. Late in the morning, using the alias USS *Dacotah*, they stopped their quarry. The crew and officers were soon disappointed to learn that the ship they had been chasing was the *Mona*, an English steamer. The disappointment would have been even greater had they known it would be more than three weeks before they would see another ship.[9]

On October 12 the lookout spotted land. Consulting his charts, Semmes determined that the island was St. Paul. Although he planned to spend some time on the island, the never ending gales blew him off course and he sailed past the island rather than try to fight the winds. Four days later another squall ripped into the *Alabama*, filling the gig. The storm was so fierce that it was impossible to save the gig, and it became necessary to cut it loose.[10] Had Semmes chosen to read back through his journal he would have noted that it was one year to the day since the horrendous cyclone which had almost sunk the raider ship.

It was nearly a week before the weather finally improved, prompting Fullam to record the presence of a brilliant rainbow.[11] Three days later the Tropic of Capricorn was crossed, and what remained of the foul weather abated almost immediately. The men of the *Alabama* could not relax however, despite the weather's improvement. The USS *Wyoming* was in the area, and she was known to be looking for the *Alabama*. The *Wyoming*, although carrying less armament and not nearly as fast as the *Alabama*, still presented a threat that could not be ignored. Her com-mander, David McDougal, had zeroed in on the *Alabama*'s whereabouts, and he had notified Welles when Semmes had left South Africa. McDougal's crew, no doubt, was also in a foul mood and probably would not have run from a fight with the Confederates. Only three months earlier, the *Wyoming* had fought a battle with a Japanese ship in which four of her crew had been killed and seven others wounded. The battle, in the Straits of Shimonoseki, had been prompted by an earlier Japanese attack on the USS *Pembroke*.[12]

McDougal had also notified Welles that many American vessels were changing their flags because they were experiencing difficulty in obtaining cargoes. McDougal said he knew of three that were currently sailing under Portuguese colors, and he had only seen three others since leaving Macao. The captain of one of those had told him that he was also going to change his colors when he arrived in Bangkok. The *Alabama* and her sister ships were accomplishing their objective!

Anticipating a possible encounter with the *Wyoming*, Fullam and William Breedlove Smith, the captain's clerk, suggested that a seventh gun be added to the broadside pivot port by moving one of the 32-pounders from the aft. Permission was granted and the move was arranged. In addition to Smith and Fullam, Lieutenant of Marines Beckett K. Howell, Boatswain Benjamin McCaskey, and Master's Mates Maximilian von Meulnier, James Evans, and Julius Schroeder volunteered to help with the move.

On October 29 a Dutch ship, the *Anna, was stopped*. Fullam took von Meulnier with him when he boarded, figuring the German would be a useful interpreter. Fullam was shaken to learn from the *Anna*'s captain that the Dutch vessel had been boarded six days earlier by the USS *Wyoming*. Reporting this information to Semmes on his arrival back on board the raider, the officers and crew surmised that it was only a matter of time until they encountered the American ship.

With the weather calmer, although brutally hot, Semmes resumed gun drills, hoping to train his Cape Town recruits while, at the same time, refreshing the alcohol-soaked minds of those who had sampled the fruit of the vine while in that port city. Fresh paint was applied which quickly dried under the tropical sun. Semmes was becoming more concerned about the condition of the copper bottom of his ship, however. Several seams had come loose and the copper was beginning to curl up in rolls. Until he could reach dry dock, nothing could be done to correct this problem, and his speed was being compromised. Knowing this, Semmes probably harbored mixed feelings about the advisability of encountering the *Wyoming* at this time.

The month of October ended with the boarding of several neutral ships. In each instance the *Alabama* passed as the USS *Mohican*, telling the neutrals that they were there to relieve the *Wyoming*.

* * *

In early September 1863, Winslow received word of the arrival of the CSS *Florida* in Ireland. Commanded by John Maffitt, the *Florida* had dropped off an officer who was charged with traveling to Paris to seek permission for the Confederate ship to put into a French dock for repairs. Maffitt had then taken his ship to Brest. Winslow immediately put to sea in search of the *Florida*. Fighting heavy seas, the *Kearsarge* used more coal than normal. Her bunkers getting perilously low, Winslow headed for El Ferrol on the coast of Spain.[13]

Upon reaching El Ferrol, Winslow learned that the *Florida* had put in at Brest. Hastily loading his coal, he prepared to head for the French city when he realized that the Spanish officials had blocked off the harbor exit by placing a boom across the narrow opening. Eventually a harbor tug would open the harbor long enough for the *Kearsarge* to make her exit.[14]

On September 17 the *Kearsarge* arrived at Brest, only to learn that the *Florida* had already entered dry dock. Winslow looked at that with mixed emotions. Certainly the *Florida* would not be going to sea anytime soon, and that was a good omen for American merchant vessels. However, Winslow had harbored hopes of an encounter with the rebels, ending with his foe on the bottom of the sea.

The *Florida* had been granted the rights of a belligerent, which meant that she could make repairs but was not permitted to take on armament or any munitions. On the other hand, Winslow was told by port officials that he must abide by those same rules, and could not leave port for 24 hours after the *Florida* put to sea. Faced with this stipulation, Winslow decided to wait outside the port where he would not be obligated to abide by the 24-hour rule. The entrance to the port was lined on either side by reefs that extended some 15 miles seaward on the south end, and even further on the north. The harbor was such that there were three active entrances, or exits in this case, which would have to be watched. Undaunted, Winslow and his men began their wait.[15]

The wait was not long. On September 22 the *Florida* slipped out of dry dock, anchoring near the entrance to the harbor. This activity prompted Winslow to assume that the *Florida* may be ready to sail, and he refused all requests for liberty. He could not afford to be caught with crew members away from the ship if the *Florida* got under way. With no opportunity for liberty, the bumboats became even more important to the crew, and the bartering continued in earnest throughout the day. Among the more popular items was a local beer, which predictably was to cause more problems aboard ship.

On September 25, with the *Florida* still where she had anchored and showing no signs of preparing to flee, Winslow cautiously allowed a small contingent to go ashore. There, they encountered crew members from the *Florida*, and a fight broke out between the members of the rival crews.

One enterprising crew member from the *Florida* hitched a ride in a bumboat that was going out to the *Kearsarge*. Arriving at the Union ship, he offered his services as a crew member. After passing an examination by Surgeon John Browne, he was given an advance pay of $8. This proved to be a mistake, as the young man disappeared and was never seen again. He was on the *Kearsarge* such a short time that his name was not even recorded in the muster roll.[16]

As the *Kearsarge* waited, Winslow ordered the bilge cleaned, the engines painted, and new sails to be taken on. Installing the sails, Ordinary Seaman Zaran Phillips lost his grip on the slimy rigging and fell to the quarterdeck. Miraculously, he survived with nothing more than a broken collarbone and a few bruises and contusions.[17]

Winslow conferred with the port authorities on a daily basis and soon concluded that the *Florida*, although out of dry dock, would not be fit for sea duty for some time. In the midst of all the work being done on the *Florida*, Captain Maffitt, in poor health, had requested to be relieved. Winslow knew that a new captain would be unlikely to take his new ship to sea without first becoming familiar with both the vessel and the crew.

With the *Florida* out of service, most of her crew spent their idle time on shore waiting for *Kearsarge* crew members to arrive, whereupon another fight would inevitably break out. Winslow sent letters of complaint to both the admiral of the port and the new captain of the *Florida*, indicating that he planned to arm his men when they went ashore and that they would have permission to use their weapons if assaulted by the crew of the *Florida*. The letter, although not accepted by the captain of the *Florida*, would prove to have done its job and there were few fights between the crews for the remainder of the time the *Kearsarge* was in port.[18]

Winslow learned that the *Florida* needed a number of engine parts which would not be available for some time, possibly another two months.[19] Armed with this piece of intelligence, he loosened his liberty policy, allowing the men to go ashore in groups of 20. He felt certain that the word had gotten to the crew of the *Florida* that the *Kearsarge*'s men could be armed, and he no longer feared that his men would be set upon as soon as they reached shore. For their part, the men of the *Kearsarge* never seemed to mind the confrontations as much as did their captain.

As the men enjoyed their liberties in the bars and brothels of Brest, the debate raged on in England concerning the advisability of continuing to build ships for the Confederacy. In a letter to the *London News*, respected Oxford College professor Goldwin Smith wrote: "The Americans have already, it is true, one war on their hands; but, as experience shows, it is a mistake to think that they will not, if provoked, go into another." Professor Smith predicted that "If a war with America comes, it will bring devastation and misery to both sides." His letter concluded with the warning that " . . . these people are a nation with our blood in their veins; and no nation with blood like ours in their veins ever bore, even in extremity, such outrages as these."[20] Presumably, a letter from a person of Smith's stature gave rise to much consideration in the halls of Parliament.

Unknown to Winslow, the *Georgia* had passed nearby as the *Kearsarge* continued to observe the *Florida*. Winslow would only learn of the Confederate steamer's presence through a conversation with a British ship captain who told him that the *Georgia* had boarded him just a short time before. Realizing that the *Florida* was not about to leave port, Winslow ordered all hands back on board and set out to find the *Georgia*. On October 31, with a gale blowing, the *Kearsarge* put to sea in search of a Confederate vessel to sink.

CHAPTER THIRTEEN

NOVEMBER–DECEMBER 1863

Early in November 1863, Captain David McDougal of the USS *Wyoming* boarded the British steamer *Mona*, in the Sunda Strait. The *Mona's* captain mentioned to McDougal that the USS *Dacotah* had also boarded him on October 3. McDougal knew the *Dacotah* had not been in the area and deduced that the ship had, in fact, been the CSS *Alabama*. He was closing in on his quarry.

Knowing of stockpiles of coal on Christmas Island, he suspected that it was only a matter of time before the *Alabama* or some other Confederate ship of war put into that port to restock. He turned his ship in that direction, planning to intercept his elusive foe when she came in for coal.[1]

While McDougal prepared to spring his trap, the *Alabama* chased down one neutral ship after another in the Java Sea, boarding the English ship *Janet Mitchell*, the French ship *Jules Cezard*, the Dutch bark *Frans & Elise*, and the English ship *Burmah* in rapid succession.[2] Then on November 6, the long string of neutrals was broken as the bark *Amanda* was stopped with two blank cartridges.

Fullam and Evans boarded the *Amanda* as a team. Isaiah Larrabee, the captain of the *Amanda*, immediately protested and pleaded that his cargo was neutral. Fullam and Evans were noncommittal, taking Larrabee to the *Alabama* for adjudication. There, in the dim light of Semmes's cabin, he presented his case. Pointing to his documents, Larrabee emphasized that he was carrying sugar and hemp that was owned by Ker and Company of Manila, British subjects. He continued his argument as he pointed to another paper that revealed that the cargo was consigned to Halliday, Fox and Company that was headquartered in London.

Semmes read the documents carefully in an effort to determine their legitimacy. Finally he glanced up at Larrabee and asked to see his affidavit. If the cargo was truly owned by British subjects, as Larrabee claimed, they should have attested to that fact under oath and provided Larrabee with the evidence. For all Semmes knew, with no affidavit of proof, Larrabee could have filled the papers out himself, and he told Larrabee as much. Larrabee protested, saying Semmes could not condemn a ship on such a technicality. His plea fell on deaf ears, however, and Semmes ruled that, even if it was a technicality, he had no choice but to destroy both the ship and its cargo.[3]

Semmes allowed Larrabee and his crew to gather any personal belongings they wished to keep. Larrabee fixed a look of contempt on Semmes as he was led from the cabin. Semmes warned him that, if stopped again, the result would be the same unless he carried proof that was attested to under oath.

Larrabee was taken back to the *Amanda* where he and his crew salvaged what little they could carry. As they did so, the crew of the *Alabama* swarmed over the *Amanda*, taking what could be of use on their own ship. Shortly after midnight, the *Amanda* became the first prize burned by the *Alabama* since July 6, when the *Express* had met the torch.[4] As the *Amanda* burned, the lights of several vessels, approaching the flames for a closer look, were seen from the decks of the *Alabama*. None appeared to be worth chasing.

On November 8, looking for a place to anchor within sight of Sumatra, Semmes was surprised to learn that the ocean floor could not be reached, despite casting out the line to a depth of 75 fathoms. The rebel raider continued under sail for another 12 hours before sandy bottom was discovered at about 16 fathoms. The anchor was dropped but retrieved about four hours later when a bark, the *Java Whistle* of the Netherlands, approached. From her captain Semmes learned that the *Wyoming* had been spotted in Batavia.

Two days later, under both sail and steam, the *Alabama* moved through the Strait of Sunda, hoping to avoid an encounter with the *Wyoming*. On the chance that the *Wyoming* might appear, the quarter boats were swung inward and the battery prepared. Gun crews stood at the ready. Nobody doubted that they could defeat the *Wyoming*, but all wondered at what cost.

The crew grew tense with each sail that was sighted, only to relax again when the vessels were reported to be neutral. During the midafternoon, the lookout spotted what appeared to be an American clipper ship approaching through a heavy squall. The officer of the deck sounded the alarm and the nervous crew manned their stations in anticipation of a fight. After 20 minutes the clipper hove to, and Fullam and the boarding crew cautiously rowed to their quarry, unsure of what to expect. On board the *Alabama*, all eyes watched intently.

Then came the signal that the clipper was not the *Wyoming* after all, but was the *Winged Racer*, captained by George Cumming. Cumming was taken to the *Alabama*, where he freely admitted that his ship was American. Denial would not have done any good, as he surely must have known. His registry was American and he had been flying the Stars and Stripes when boarded.

Semmes was pleased to notice that the *Winged Racer*'s manifest listed many items that could be used on the *Alabama*. The *Alabama*'s supplies of sugar, coffee, and tobacco were nearly depleted, and he reasoned that the *Winged Racer* would no longer have any need for them. For nearly 12 hours the supplies were shuttled from the *Winged Racer* to the hold of the *Alabama*. As the *Alabama*'s crew ferried back and forth from one ship to the other, so did the ever present bumboats. Native merchants swarmed around the two ships, selling fruits, vegetables, chickens, and pigs to anyone who was interested. Only when the flames arose from the *Winged Racer* did they cut their lines and hurriedly make their exits.[5]

As the Yankee clipper burned, Cumming approached Semmes with a request. Since the sea was fairly calm and they weren't far from land, he asked if Semmes would permit Cumming and his crew to go ashore in their boats. Semmes looked at the burning ship, then at Cumming, and asked if he would be willing to take the crew of the *Amanda* with him. Cumming agreed, and Semmes told him to ask Larrabee if he was agreeable to such an arrangement. Within minutes Larrabee had agreed, and the prisoners were soon on their way to shore.[6] Once there, Cumming and Larrabee sought out the American consul and Captain David McDougal, of the USS *Wyoming*.

By the time McDougal heard the story, however, the *Alabama* was well under way. When he arrived on the *Wyoming*, all that was there to remind him of the *Alabama* were the burned-out wrecks of the *Amanda* and *Winged Racer*, the *Alabama*'s disappearance just one more stinging insult from his adversary Semmes.

As McDougal searched for the *Alabama*, the rebel ship was miles away, where her lookout spotted a clipper ship that was almost certainly American. When the *Alabama* drew close enough, the American flag was run up. The clipper answered with the same flag but when the *Alabama* hoisted the Confederate flag, the American made her sails and began to run. A chase was not what Semmes wanted at this time. His ship was deteriorating and his speed was compromised. The copper bottom was curling up in rolls, and the boilers were badly corroded.[7] There was little choice, however, as the stranger showed no inclination to stop.

Semmes ordered the steam brought up, and he vowed to continue the chase as long as his boilers held out. His foe was sleek looking, and her impressive appearance was exceeded only by her speed. Semmes and Kell agreed that she was one of the prettiest ships either had ever seen. As they watched, the clipper unfurled even more canvas. The *Alabama* struggled to keep up, even though all sails were filled and the boilers were operating at full capacity.

Semmes shouted for more steam. Third Engineer Matthew O'Brien told him the boilers were working for all they were worth. He feared that pushing any harder would possibly cause the boilers to explode. Semmes shook his head and reluctantly told O'Brien to just do the best he could."[8]

Forty-five minutes into the chase Armstrong fired a shot from the rifled gun. It fell short, spraying water over the clipper's quarter deck. The crew was called to move some of the forward guns aft, hoping that the weight in the rear may help lift the bow enough to gain some desperately needed speed. The chase continued unabated until the wind began to diminish. The *Alabama* slowly gained some of the distance back as the clipper desperately worked her sails. A shot from the *Alabama*'s bow gun sailed through the American's rigging. With the wind now reduced to little more than a breeze, the clipper had no choice but to surrender and wait meekly for the boarding party.

The clipper was the famous *Contest*, one of the most beautiful ships on the sea. Her captain, Frederick George Lucas, was brought aboard for the customary hearing. As he boarded he was greeted by Semmes who, with an outstretched hand, commented admiringly that Lucas had made a beautiful run. For a while Semmes had actually thought the *Contest* was going to outrun him. When he mentioned that to Lucas, the captain of the *Contest* replied that he would have if the wind hadn't turned against him. Semmes only nodded, knowing full well that Lucas was right in his assessment of the relative speeds of the two vessels.[9]

As the *Alabama*'s crew plundered the *Contest*, the officers paid her the ultimate compliment, going aboard just to look her over.[10] Semmes even considered for a time whether to convert her to Confederate use, as he had done with the *Conrad*. He finally concluded that he didn't have enough guns to spare, and reluctantly ordered the sleek clipper ship fired.[11] Two boatloads of men were sent to the *Contest* to do the firing. The first flame leaped skyward at 9:00 P.M., with Lucas watching silently at the *Alabama*'s rail. Before long the ship had burned nearly to the water line, and she slowly sank into the sea.

The officers of the *Contest* stayed on the *Alabama* for more than a week. They did not waste their time, quietly observing the conduct of the *Alabama*'s crew, their skills, and the general conditions on board. Sometime later one of the officers would testify: "Crew much dissatisfied, no prize money, no liberty and see no prospect of getting any. Discipline very slack, steamer dirty, rigging slovenly . . . crew do things for which they would be shot on board American man-of-war; for instance, saw one of crew strike a master's mate . . . was told by at least two-thirds of them that (they) will desert on first opportunity." Commenting on the gun drills, the same officer went on: "Have given up on small arm drill, afraid to trust crew with arms. While on board saw drill only once, and that at pivot guns, very badly done; men ill disposed and were forced to do it; lots of cursing."[12]

On November 13 Semmes called for the cigars which had been taken from the *Winged Racer* to be brought out and distributed among the officers and crew. As the crew smoked, some of the older crew members vented their dissatisfaction that the cigars were the first time they had seen anything resembling a reward for their efforts. Having been promised gold, they were not to be satisfied with tobacco. Seaman Frank Townshend became particularly incensed, and convinced those around him to throw the cigars overboard as a protest. Townshend was thrown in irons for his efforts. Seamen Albert Hyer and John Riley were also arrested. A court-martial was held the following day and the three were reduced to ordinary seamen, forfeited three months' pay, and placed in solitary confinement on bread and water for 30 days.[13]

On November 19, the *Alabama* passed herself off as a Dutch surveying vessel, and an English ship, the *Avalanche,* was boarded. The ruse was discovered only when Fullam and von Meulnier went aboard to make arrangements for the prisoners to be transferred. After some discussion the captain of the *Avalanche* not only agreed to transport the prisoners, he also furnished recent newspapers which told of the decline of American maritime commerce which, by now, had nearly vanished.[14]

The next day, November 20, saw two more neutrals boarded: the Siamese bark *Amy Douglas* and the French bark *Aloinir.* Four more were boarded over the next three days as the *Alabama* crossed the equator.[15] Almost immediately the winds became calm and the *Alabama*, low on coal, was forced to resort to kedging to maintain any movement at all in the tranquil waters.*

---

* Kedging consisted of taking a small anchor out in a boat and placing it ahead of the ship. The ship was then pulled up to the anchor, at which time the process was repeated. This process was extremely slow, and many crewmen wondered if the energy expended was worth the relatively short distances moved.[16]

For the next three days the winds remained calm, picking up momentarily as if to tease, then dropping back to a barely discernible breeze. The tropical rains came, drenching the men as they struggled to keep the ship moving. Semmes, fearing the arrival of the *Wyoming* at any time, resisted the thought of sitting becalmed until the winds returned. On November 30 the wind finally picked up and brought with it heavy squalls. The sails were set in a driving rain. Despite the rain, the crew welcomed the opportunity to cease kedging.

December 2 saw the *Alabama* anchored in 18 fathoms near the island of Pulo Condore. Semmes harbored thoughts of claiming the island as Confederate territory, planning to use it as a naval base. Unknown to Semmes, it had been ceded to France some two years earlier and was governed by a French ensign, Monsieur Bizot. When the need for repairs was presented to Bizot he quickly agreed to allow the *Alabama* to remain in the bay. Unsure of the *Wyoming*'s whereabouts, Semmes ordered the ship to anchor with her broadside turned to the harbor entrance while Bizot, in a gesture of friendship, came aboard and met with Semmes in the captain's cabin.[17]

Meanwhile, the ship's sailmakers, gunners, boatswain, and carpenters were kept busy making repairs, and the decks were soon littered with tools and spare parts. Lieutenant Kell and Carpenter William Robinson rigged up a hydraulic caisson that allowed crew members to work underwater, and badly needed repairs began on the copper and timbers of the hull without the need for a dry dock.[18]

A mail packet arrived on December 10, much to Semmes's chagrin. He knew that the packet would probably relay word of the *Alabama*'s whereabouts at her next stop, making it dangerous for the *Alabama* to remain in port. The *Wyoming*, or any other Union ship in the area, would most likely steam for Pulo Condore as soon as they heard the legendary raider was there for repairs. Reluctantly, because repairs had not been completed, Semmes decided to put to sea.

On December 15 the *Alabama* was once more under way, en route to Singapore, and reached the island on December 21. Upon entering the harbor, the crew observed more than 20 American ships, partially dismantled and showing no signs that they would be leaving port soon.

The scenario was readily apparent. The American ships, hearing that the *Alabama* was in the area, had hurriedly put into the nearest port. This explained why the rebels had encountered no Union ships for the past six weeks. As the officers contemplated the scene before them, they realized that they had, in effect, stopped American commerce in the China Sea.[19]

In Singapore, Semmes was surprised to learn that he had been following the *Wyoming* all over the South China Sea, and had entered ports just days apart.

The next morning, Semmes had his ship move to the wharf to take on coal, a process that took 12 hours. As the bunkers were filled, nine of the crew deserted. Richard Hambly, Frank Mahany, John Allen, James Williams, Henry Cosgrove, John Doyle, Albert Hyer, James Smith, and John Grady all jumped ship. Four new crew members signed on: Robert Devine, Thomas Watson, James King (the second crew member with this name), and Henry Higgins joined the *Alabama* for the remainder of her cruise.[20]

On Christmas Eve, at 10:00 A.M., the *Alabama* weighed anchor, taking five fewer crew members with her. The four new crewmen got their first taste of life on the *Alabama* five hours later, when a large bark showing British colors was encountered. Fullam led the boarding party. Once on board, Fullam examined the ship's papers and found them to be irregular. Fullam requested that the captain accompany him to the *Alabama*, but the captain refused to go. Indignantly, he told Fullam that he was a British subject and his vessel was a British ship. As such, he believed he was not compelled to accompany Fullam anywhere.

When informed of this, Semmes angrily went to board the stranger himself, the only time in the cruise of the *Alabama* he would do so. The captain of the bark, Samuel B. Pike, showed papers indicating his ship was the *Martaban*. Semmes immediately began to interrogate Pike, asking him why his British flag was so new that it still had the fold lines. Before Pike could answer, Semmes pointed out the decidedly American lines of the *Martaban* and asked why Pike's galley was preparing potatoes and codfish for the evening meal, a meal that no Englishman would order. Pike was also asked to explain why his paint was so fresh, including the name on the side of his ship, why every signature on Pike's crew roster was made out in the same handwriting, and why most of the crew spoke with New England accents.

Pike had not expected such an onslaught. Unprepared, he tried to formulate some kind of answer which Semmes might accept. He began to explain that the *Martaban* had been the American ship *Texan Star* until 10 days ago, when it had been sold to a British firm. That explained the fresh paint.

Because Pike carried no bill of sale among his papers to prove his contentions, Semmes decided to burn the ship. Pike was incensed, insisting that Semmes could not burn a ship under a British flag. Semmes was not moved. Further, because the cargo was being carried under false colors, it too would meet the torch. Semmes gave Pike and his crew 30 minutes to gather anything they wished to take with them, except for their flag and chronometer. Those now belonged to the *Alabama*.[21]

True to his word, within 30 minutes the first flames flickered on the *Martaban* as Pike and his crew, now prisoners of war, watched from the *Alabama*. With a sigh of resignation, Pike explained that a month earlier he had received a message from the owners of the ship, Samuel Stevens and Company out of Boston. The message warned Pike that the *Alabama* was in the same waters that he was in, and that he should execute a sham sale, transferring the *Texan Star* to a British company and changing her name.

Pike decided to change the registry before he sailed, and made out a transfer of the title to a company named M. R. Currie and Company. The temporary transfer was balanced by a mortgage of 80,000 rupees, and Currie and Company would get one percent as a commission for allowing Pike to use their name.[22]

The next morning the prisoners were put ashore. It was Christmas day, and Semmes used the special occasion to allow the men to splice the main brace. The entire crew drank a toast to their wives and sweethearts. That evening, in a steady rain, two neutral vessels were boarded. They were the *Gallant Neill*, an English bark, and the *Puget*, of Marseilles.

On December 26 a steamer and six other vessels were observed at 6:10 A.M. One of them, the American clipper ship *Sonora*, was becalmed, her crew scrubbing her decks. As the *Alabama* bore down on her with a blue British ensign flying in the breeze, the *Sonora*'s captain, Lawrence W. Brown, peered through his glasses in an effort to identify the approaching stranger. The men stopped scrubbing and watched intently, and one of them recognized a boat that he thought had been taken from the *Contest*, his former ship. That boat had been taken by the *Alabama*. Unfortunately for Brown and the *Sonora*, the crew member was correct, and Semmes added the *Sonora*'s chronometer and flag to his growing collection.[23]

Before the *Sonora* could be burned, however, another clipper appeared. Quickly chased down, she was the *Highlander*, commanded by Jabez H. Snow. Snow's namesake had been captured and burned by the *Alabama* on May 29, 1863, and he was quite familiar with the *Alabama*. After some conversation, Semmes agreed that Snow and Brown could keep their boats to try to reach Singapore, some four hundred miles away. As the two crews rowed off, singing a sea chanty, the *Highlander* and the *Sonora* were put to the torch.[24]

On December 27 a letter was sent from Major General J. Bankhead Magruder to Semmes, suggesting that the *Alabama* proceed to the Gulf of Mexico. There, Magruder believed that Union transports were plentiful and there was great opportunity to inflict serious injury and profit from prize taking.[25]

Without the benefit of having received the letter, Semmes opted to head for Brazil, then for Barbados where he would take on coal. By now, his boilers were in such a condition that he ordered his engineers to keep the fires lit, not wishing to stress them further by cooling them down and reheating them. The ship's seams were opening up, and the copper bottom was peeling off. The *Alabama* was feeling the effect of a cruise which was now well into its second year.

* * *

Anxious to track down the *Georgia*, the *Kearsarge* had put to sea in the midst of a driving storm. Had Winslow known that the gale was not about to blow itself out, he might have waited in port. As it was, the ship bobbed like a cork on the rolling sea, out of control at times. For two days the storm had its way with the *Kearsarge,* when the lookout finally spotted a distant lighthouse shining through the late afternoon darkness. Other lighthouses appeared as the *Kearsarge* worked her way along the Irish coast. On November 3, Winslow and his ship anchored in the harbor at Queenstown. It wasn't long before the vessel was crowded with visitors who were anxious to view this sleek-looking American.

Winslow had a two-fold purpose in docking at Queenstown. He needed coal and recruits. Coal would be easy to find, but recruiting in a British port was against the Foreign Enlistment Act. Both sides, however, had learned quickly that there were ways around the Act.

As with the *Alabama*, the *Kearsarge*'s crew seemed to shrink with every port visited, as men found liberty more to their liking than duty on board. Queenstown was no exception, and within 24 hours, John Thompson and John Kelly left the ship with no intentions of returning.

With Winslow in Cork on an official visit, a port official arrived at the *Kearsarge* to order the ship out of port within 24 hours, to comply with British laws regarding belligerents. James Thornton, lieutenant commander of the *Kearsarge*, received the official. He promptly told the man that he would not take the ship out until his captain told him to, and that Winslow was not on board.

Thornton's response quickly reached the ears of the local news media, which promptly urged local officials to use the Queenstown fleet to force the *Kearsarge* to leave. The media, however, apparently had failed to remember that the Queenstown fleet consisted of two old British frigates, a few small boats, and a training ship. Local officials had no intention of using them against a ship of war, and the idea quickly died.

By the time Winslow returned, his crew had mysteriously grown by 16 members. The truth surrounding their arrival on board may never be known. Thornton later swore that they had come to the *Kearsarge* to enlist in her service, at which time Thornton told them that if they were physically qualified they might remain on board until Winslow arrived. Winslow, on his return, had told him not to enlist the 16 and they were ordered to leave. Winslow offered information that supported Thornton's story.[26] Others would say that the applicants had been welcomed aboard and hidden in the hold by several petty officers.

However it happened, the *Kearsarge* put to sea once more, still in search of the *Georgia*, on November 5. Before weighing anchor, all visitors were ordered off the ship. Officers said they combed the ship and found a number of stowaways, with all removed and sent ashore.

On November 6 the 16 men were discovered secreted on board, possibly assisted by some of the crew.[27] These men all hoped to sign on with the Union ship, in much the same manner as Semmes had gained his new recruits at Simonstown several weeks earlier.

Winslow wanted to get his ship back to Brest in order to observe the *Florida*, and so could not immediately return the stowaways to Queenstown. Instead, he took them to Brest, where he ordered them held so they could not sign on with the *Florida*, intending to take them back to Cork when the *Kearsarge* made her return.[28]

However, they all pleaded destitution and asked to be permitted to remain on board. Some have speculated that this was all according to Winslow's plan to avoid the Foreign Enlistment Act. Whether by design or by chance, Winslow allowed that he could not force the men to leave in such a penniless state, and thus permitted them to stay on the *Kearsarge*.

Throughout the month of November the *Kearsarge* stood off the coast, watching the three possible exits the *Florida* may use if she decided to leave port. It was cold and rainy, and the mood of the crew was as bad as the weather. The stowaways blended into the crew, standing watch and performing their duties alongside the rest of the men.

On November 19 William Dayton, the United States minister to France, told Winslow to return the new crew members if they weren't needed for the operation of the ship. Dayton feared the French may correctly view the additions as justification to allow the *Florida* to also add to her crew. He believed the *Florida* probably had already done this and he planned to protest to the French as soon as the rebels left port. If the *Kearsarge* had already done the same he correctly feared his argument would be considerably weakened.[29]

On Thanksgiving the cooks did their best to relieve the boredom by cooking up a meal of roast goose and mincemeat pie. The following day an impromptu race between the captain's gig and one of the cutters further helped to brighten the mood, and Winslow apparently looked the other way when the crew began to play cards, violating the ship's rule against such diversion.

Winslow and several of his officers stood at the rail watching in the general direction of the *Florida*. The captain commented to nobody in particular that he hoped the *Florida* didn't surrender because he really would like to destroy her. One of his officers chuckled and said that he seemed to recall that when Horatio Lord Nelson was losing a battle his admiral sent up a signal for him to surrender. Nelson had put his glass up to his blind eye and said he didn't see any signal, so he stayed to fight, and eventually he won the battle. Perhaps Winslow could do the same. Winslow, whose infected eye had now deteriorated to the point where it was effectively blind, laughed along with his officers, and agreed that he could repeat Nelson's tactic and go on to sink the *Florida*.[30]

On December 5, convinced that the *Florida* was still unable to go to sea, Winslow and the *Kearsarge* left Brest, still carrying the Irishmen who had boarded in Queenstown. Two days later the Queenstown harbor was sighted, and the *Kearsarge*'s officers signaled for a pilot. The pilot boat *Petrel* soon arrived, whereupon Winslow ordered the stowaways onto the little boat. The *Petrel*'s captain was instructed to take the men ashore, accompanied by a letter from Winslow to Rear Admiral Sir Lewis T. Jones, commander of the British naval forces in Ireland. The letter certified Winslow's testimony as to how the men happened to be on board the *Kearsarge*.[31]

The controversy would not end with the landing of the stowaways, however. Jones would initially report that only 15 men returned from the Kearsarge, then change his mind later and state that, indeed, all 16 had come back on the *Petrel*. One of the stowaways, however, reported that Michael Ahern had stayed on board the *Kearsarge*, and that Ahern had actually signed on with the *Kearsarge*'s crew. How he happened to be on the *Kearsarge* to sign on remains open to conjecture.

The stowaways, resplendent in their Union uniforms, became local heroes, telling their stories to all who would listen, most often in the pubs of Queenstown, where tongues were loosened by the seemingly endless draughts of ale bought for them by admirers.

The *Kearsarge* departed Queenstown without ever entering the harbor. The stowaway incident had left Winslow in a foul mood, and he hoped to take it out on any Confederate raider he found. On December 9 he passed the breakwater at Cherbourg where the *Georgia* sat anchored. It would be several more days before Winslow received word from Edouard Liais, the American consular agent, that the *Georgia* was taking on coal and water and appeared nearly ready to depart.[32]

On December 11, vilified in the Irish press, Winslow penned a letter to Charles Francis Adams, United States envoy in London. In it he explained the stowaway incident and charged that the Irish newspapers were not printing the facts. Winslow further charged that Confederate agents were capitalizing on the affair and feeding the news media with their own version of the incident.[33]

The *Kearsarge* continued on to Portsmouth, England, where Winslow hoped to trap the *Agrippina* as she waited with supplies for the *Florida, Georgia*, and *Alabama*. But she had already sailed, and the frustrated Winslow ordered the *Kearsarge* back to Brest to determine the status of the *Florida* and to recoal. Taking on coal was a dirty job at best, and the mood of the coal heavers did not improve when the captain of the coal brig seemed determined to account for every shovelful, and it took nearly three days to accomplish the job of filling the *Kearsarge*'s bunkers.

Winslow recognized the low morale that existed among his crew, and he permitted them to go ashore on liberty while in Brest. He did so, knowing full well that some may desert. Once ashore, the men were reluctant to return, and most overstayed their curfews by several days. One, Zaran Phillips, who had not yet completely healed from his earlier fall from the rigging, returned with a new gash on his forehead that he seemed unable to explain.

Fights with the crew of the *Florida* were not unusual in the bars and bordellos of Brest, and more than one crew member returned to the ship much the worse for wear. The police of Brest were kept busy, with crew members of both ships spending a fair share of time in the local jails. Those who remained on board had their share of problems, as well, as the records showed drunkenness, fights, insubordination, and the inevitable desertions.[34]

The winter weather was unforgiving, and a cold rain was a constant companion. The crew seemed to be wet all the time, and Surgeon John Browne found himself treating a variety of illnesses that could be attributed to the conditions.

Christmas Day 1863 saw the crew treated to another sumptuous feast of roast goose, but it did little to relieve the morale problem. That was soon to change. On December 26 a tug was observed moving the *Florida*. Word quickly spread throughout the *Kearsarge*. Anxious for any relief for the boredom that permeated the crew, the men lined the rail to see what the *Florida* was doing.

For two days there was little or no activity on the *Florida* which gave any hint of her intentions, although there was little doubt in anyone's mind that she was about to leave port. On December 28 those suspicions were confirmed when provisions and ammunition were loaded.

Aware of the *Kearsarge*'s presence and intent, the port admiral sent a line-of-battle ship to anchor between the adversaries. There would be no breaking of international law if the port admiral had any say. However, Winslow had no plan to attack the *Florida* in French waters. Still sensitive to the criticism he had received from all quarters after the stowaway incident, he planned to avoid at all costs any suggestion that he had violated any laws. He ordered the *Kearsarge* to the open sea where he could operate with impunity.

On December 29 Gideon Welles, having discussed the stowaway incident with Charles Adams, sent a letter to Winslow directing that the *Kearsarge* captain file a full report on the matter. Adams had forwarded Welles a complaint from the British government, and Welles needed an explanation.[35]

Winslow closed out the year by cruising back and forth in international waters, waiting for the *Florida* to exit her haven. Unfortunately, it was impossible to view all three exits from this far out, and Winslow worried that the *Florida* would also be watching him, waiting for her opportunity to use the one exit that he could not see.

CHAPTER FOURTEEN

JANUARY–FEBRUARY 1864

January 1, 1864, greeted the men of the *Alabama* with a slight south-westerly breeze, a breeze which increased as the day progressed. At 7:30 that evening a heavy squall struck. Semmes allowed the men to splice the main brace to ward off any chill caused by the storm.

Two days later, January 3, Semmes ordered the Articles of War read. It was the first Sunday of the month and he probably felt the need in light of the desertions in Singapore. He was not sure if it would have the desired effect, but it made him feel as if he was doing something.

The next day the English bark *Glennalice* was hailed but not boarded. A French ship was chased later in the day. The *Lady Harriet*, another English bark, broke the monotony on January 8, but there was little to see except a few whales for the next several days. On January 11 Semmes reminded the crew that it had been exactly one year since the *Alabama* had sunk the *Hatteras*. A celebration was in order, and the main brace was spliced once more. Because it was a special occasion, the officers allowed the men to double up on their drinks.

On January 14 the first American ship of the new year was sighted. She was the *Emma Jane*, under the command of Francis C. Jordan. Jordan had his wife on board. The *Emma Jane* was registered as a

United States vessel, and because she was in ballast there was no cargo to evaluate. Semmes was pleased to note that the reason the *Emma Jane* was in ballast was because the *Alabama* was known to be in the area. Jordan and his wife were accommodated in the *Alabama*'s ward room and the crew placed in the hold. The *Emma Jane* was then burned.[1]

By now Semmes was beginning to show the strain of his cruise. Tugging on his mustache, he paced in his cabin, coming out less frequently than before. Although he was worried about the *Alabama*'s condition, he was also more than a little homesick. He missed his family and became more despondent each time he thought of them.[2]

The scarcity of Union merchant vessels, while fulfilling the mission of the *Alabama*, did nothing to improve Semmes's spirits, nor that of his men. More out of boredom than necessity, duties became repetitious. Gun crews were trained almost daily, Boatswain Benjamin McCaskey spent a great deal of time inspecting his tackles, Gunner Thomas Cuddy supervised the polishing of the guns until they glistened, and Sailmaker Henry Allcot checked his sails over and over. The boredom was becoming palpable.

McCaskey also devised a makeshift bath house that provided safety from sharks. He took a large square sail and placed it just below the surface of the water. He then placed a solid shot in the center and triced up the edges, forming a large bag. Crew members then took their baths inside this enclosure, safe from even the most aggressive sharks.[3]

Arthur Sinclair welcomed the quiet time, unlike most of the others. Studious, he would take a book aloft, straddle the topsail yard and settle his back against the mast. There he would read for hours unless he had duties to perform. Occasionally he looked up from his reading to scan the horizon for sails, hoping to see one before the lookout called it out. There were few sails to be seen, however.

Down on deck the crew members regularly checked the prize book to see how much money had accrued. The men became accomplished mathematicians as they calculated their share of the prize money. Tiring of this, some sought out William Breedlove Smith, the captain's clerk, who served as unofficial librarian of the ship. Those who could read borrowed books from Smith to wile away their off-duty hours.

Back in the Confederacy, all men between the ages of 18 and 45 were being conscripted. Even if the crew of the *Alabama* knew of this, it probably would have meant little. Most of them had never been in the Southern states in their life, nor would they ever.

While the *Alabama* was welcomed in many ports, and even treated as well as any royalty ever was, not everyone looked forward to the rebel's arrival. The *Times of India*, a newspaper in Bombay, told its readers that the *Alabama* was "not unlikely" to land in Bombay. The newspaper urged the citizens to "show no favor to the pirates."[4]

On January 29 a curious phenomenon was observed, one that proved unnerving to many of the superstitious crew members. With no land in sight, the lookout screamed that the *Alabama* was about to run aground. Kell, knowing that no shoals or reefs appeared on charts of the area, raced to the rail and peered over the side. As far as he could see the water appeared to be milky white, with a brilliant phosphorescence. It looked as if the ship was almost touching the sandy bottom. "All hands reef the topsails," he shouted. He had to get the ship stopped before the ocean's bottom tore out the *Alabama*'s fragile copper hull.

Semmes was summoned as the raider slowed, each man bracing for the expected grinding against the rocks. Semmes ordered soundings taken around the perimeter of the ship, but bottom was never reached. Puzzled, the soundings were repeated with the same result. Wordlessly, officers and crew alike focused their gazes on the white surface of the water. Someone threw a bucket overboard, hauling it up for a closer inspection. The water in the bucket appeared normal. Still, the milky appearance of the ocean extended as far as anyone could see.

The unnatural condition of the water was becoming alarming to the crew. As the *Alabama* inched her way through, the crew drew anxious. For several hours the *Alabama* slowly, almost imperceptibly, glided through the strange appearing water until it finally disappeared behind the ship. Few words had been spoken, and the only sounds had been the slapping of the waves against the hull and the creaking of the masts as they swayed in the light breeze. The superstitious crew was neither satisfied nor relieved at having passed through the crisis. The never before seen phenomenon was a bad omen, they thought. The most common theory was that the *Alabama*, now doomed by bad luck, would soon sink. They were more accurate than they realized.[5]

On January 30 the *Alabama* recrossed the equator. There had not been a repeat of the phosphorescence that had been experienced a few days earlier, but still the crew was edgy. No good would come of something like that, they reasoned. It was a topic of conversation at every opportunity, discussed even more than the oppressive heat that bore down on them.

On February 9 the heat had become nearly unbearable, and the breezes stopped completely. It became necessary to fire up the boilers, using valuable coal, and lower the propeller. The engine room became nearly uninhabitable from the temperature, and the engineers spent as little time as possible at their stations. At 1:35 P.M. the *Alabama* anchored off the coast of Johanna Island, a dependency of Madagascar. Fresh provisions were brought aboard, and many of the men went for a swim in an effort to cool off.

For all intents the *Alabama* was becalmed and would have to remain at Johanna until the breezes resumed. With no liquor on the island, Semmes feared little that he would lose any of his men. Most stayed on board and ate the tropical fruits that were so plentiful.

Finally, on February 15 the breezes became stronger. Coming lightly from the north, they provided some relief from the heat, and more importantly, they were strong enough to propel the ship. At noon, the *Alabama* weighed anchor and put to sea under steam. Once away from land, the propeller was lifted and the ship was under full sail. Despite the heat, business on board had to continue, and on February a court-martial was held for John Adams, Thomas Brandon, Henry Higgins, and Thomas White. All were reduced to the grade of landsman, forfeited a month's pay, and were blacklisted for two weeks. All four had been charged with desertion.

As had been the case for several weeks, not another sail was sighted by the lookouts. Day after day the rebel ship cruised, alone on the sea. Not until February 25 was another sail sighted. Hoisting the French flag and calling herself *L'Invincible*, the *Alabama* hailed her. She was the English ship *Caspatrick*. It mattered not to the crew and officers of the

Alabama that she was neutral. They had finally spotted a ship after 39 days. Next day the ship was rocked with a tropical storm, accompanied by incessant lightning and heavy thunder. Most of the men stood on the deck and allowed the rain to drench them, cooling them off in the process.

On February 27 a heavy sea provided evidence of the previous day's storm. Ordinary Seaman Henry Godson, who had been sick for some time, was carried up on deck for some fresh air. He was placed on the topgallant forecastle to enjoy the tropical sunshine in hopes that it might prove beneficial to his health. The pitching and rolling sea, however, soon tossed him overboard. He struggled to stay afloat, no mean feat for even a healthy man under the heavy waves. Lieutenant Joseph Wilson, serving as officer of the deck, shouted to bring the ship to a standstill. "Hard down your helm!" he shouted. Then, "Brace aback! Lower the lee lifeboat!"

A lifeboat was quickly put over the side to make an attempt to rescue the struggling Godson. The *Alabama* shuddered to a halt as Godson fought to stay afloat. Michael Mars grabbed two gratings and threw them over the side, just as Kell made an appearance. Kell tried to dissuade Mars from entering the water, preferring to let the boat make the rescue. Ignoring Kell, Mars jumped over the rail and swam to Godson's side, pulling him onto one of the gratings. Mars then swam back to the ship, pulling the grating which held the nearly drowned Godson. Cheers greeted him as he neared the stern, where both were picked up by the lifeboat.[6]

* * *

The *Kearsarge* continued her to and fro traverse, watching for the moment when the *Florida* would make her run. After several days, however, it appeared that nothing was going to happen anytime soon, and Winslow ordered the *Kearsarge* to the island of Ushant. The harbor there offered a good view of the entrance to Brest harbor, and a reward was offered to the first man to spot the *Florida* leaving the harbor.

The sea grew heavy on New Year's Day, tossing the *Kearsarge* about and causing Winslow to direct a second anchor to be dropped. The help given by the second anchor was only marginal, and Winslow decided that the harbor was becoming too dangerous. If the *Florida* should pick that time to leave, the *Kearsarge* would have considerable difficulty leaving the rocky harbor, he reasoned.

Although it was dark and he did not have a pilot to guide him out of the harbor, Winslow chose to leave as soon as he could. The men were called out of their hammocks to raise the anchors, a task that took more than an hour. The anchors aboard, the *Kearsarge* got under way, Winslow on the forecastle, carefully slipping through the rocky waters. Somehow the ship made it through with no damage, much to the dismay of the crew.

Once in open water, the sea smoothed enough for Winslow to feel more comfortable about his ability to chase the *Florida*. Less than 24 hours after slipping out of the harbor at Ushant, two steamers were seen. James Wheeler called for Winslow and ordered the *Kearsarge* to give chase. When Winslow arrived on deck his pulse quickened. Believing that one ship had to be the *Florida* and the other a French escort, he had the crew beat to general quarters.

The chase continued for nearly two hours. Then, through his telescope, Winslow saw that both ships were flying the French flag. Neither ship was the *Florida*. The chase was called off and Winslow directed the helmsman to turn the ship back from where they had come.[7]

Returning to Brest, Winslow could see the *Florida* where she had been when he had last seen her. Had they known of the *Kearsarge*'s wild goose chase, the officers of the *Florida* would have enjoyed themselves immensely.

Reaching Ushant the *Kearsarge* anchored where the lookout could watch the harbor at Brest. She would remain there for nearly two weeks, during which time the crew practiced their duties in the event of a battle. While there, the United States consul at Havre, France, James O. Putnam, sent an urgent-sounding letter to Winslow. In it he noted that information had been received that the *Florida* was waiting for the *Georgia* and *Rappahannock* to join her in Brest, where the three Confederate ships planned to join forces and attack the *Kearsarge*.[8]

Unaware of the threat, natives of Ushant came to the ship to sell their wares, and the crew supplemented their bland diet with many island delicacies. Provisions were becoming scarce, and the additional food was welcomed. However, by mid-January Winslow had little choice but to sail to Cadiz for supplies. Water was particularly needed because the condenser had failed once more.

Armed with the information that the *Florida* was still experiencing engine problems, Winslow decided that it was safe to leave, and on January 17 the *Kearsarge* bade farewell to Ushant.[9] Three days after the *Kearsarge*'s departure, William L. Dayton sent Winslow a letter reinforcing the one sent earlier by Putnam. In it, Dayton reported that the captain of the *Florida* had been quoted in the newspapers that he planned to fight the *Kearsarge* early in February. Although Dayton had earlier ordered Winslow to take his Irish stowaways back to Queenstown, he now gave Winslow permission to do whatever he had to do to enlist the men he may need.[10]

With the *Kearsarge* already shorthanded, another crew member would be lost when John Netto, a landsman, deserted. To add to the problem, many of the crew were approaching the end of their enlistments. Winslow exercised his authority as captain, refusing the men's request to go home. The enlistments were extended through the end of the cruise, the news tempered by an increase in their pays of 25 percent.[11]

On January 23 the *Kearsarge* reached Cadiz, having followed the Portuguese coastline as much as possible to conserve coal. Almost immediately the engineers set to repairing the boilers, while others began the task of shoveling coal from the coal barge into the *Kearsarge*'s bunkers. The condensers were soon repaired and supplies were replenished.

At Cadiz several unscrupulous merchants tried to eliminate old merchandise by sending it to the *Kearsarge*, but the vigilant assistant paymaster Joseph A. Smith would have none of that. When he discovered insects in the flour and beans, as well as moldy sugar and meat, he immediately rejected it. The crew took care of returning it to the merchants by tossing it overboard into the harbor, where the owners could come and get it if they so chose. None did.

Winslow met with the American consul to ask about recruiting new crewmen, and seven new recruits signed on almost immediately. Meanwhile, Freeman H. Morse, U.S. consul in London, provided additional information to Putnam that rebel ships were being outfitted for a coming battle with the *Kearsarge*. He said that the *Florida* alone had taken on two steel Blakely rifled cannon to go along with the 80-pounder Whitworths she already had. Without offering proof, he said an English yacht had transported them. He also charged that about 150 additional men had been sent from England to supplement the *Florida's* crew, bolstered by offers of bounties and half the value of the prize if the *Kearsarge* could be sunk. Morse's message also suggested that the *Alabama, Rappahannock*, and *Georgia* would probably join the *Florida*, with the action against the *Kearsarge* to take place early in February. Morse then offered the idea to replenish the *Kearsarge's* crew with Americans recruited from the Liverpool area, which would not violate the Foreign Enlistment Act.[12]

On January 26 William Dayton sent a message to Winslow alluding to a possible confrontation with the rebel ships. In a thinly veiled reference to the Queenstown stowaways, he told Winslow in a postscript, "If you need men, let nothing which has occurred heretofore prevent your shipping them."[13] Although Winslow had not yet received Dayton's message, he had anticipated it and had already begun to recruit. William Alsdorf, William Bell, Thomas Blake, Charles Blees, Jonathan Brier, Jean Briset, William Brown, Joshua Collins, James McBeth, Charles Mattison, and John Pope became new members of the crew over the next few days. Although many of them would eventually desert, those who stayed on proved to be capable seamen.

On February 4, Winslow penned two messages in reference to the rumored battle. Enclosing copies of the letters from Dayton and Morse, he sent a short note to Gideon Welles in which he requested permission to borrow two guns from the *St. Louis* if the two should meet. His second letter was to Morse, in which he stated that he had not received any challenge from the *Florida*, contrary to published newspaper accounts. He also noted that "printed bombast" served no purpose when the *Florida* already had every opportunity to engage the *Kearsarge*. Then, he ominously noted that, if indeed the *Florida's* armament and crew had been increased, it would not be prudent to allow her to join the *Georgia*, implying that he would do whatever was necessary to prevent it.[14] Welles endorsed Winslow's words, stating that "To accept or send a challenge would be to recognize the pirates on terms of equality, elevating them and degrading our own."[15]

Armed with Welles's endorsement as well as Dayton's permission to add to his forces as he felt the need, Winslow sent James Wheeler ashore to find willing crew members. Wheeler did his job well, signing on Thomas Alloway, William Barnes, Timothy Canty, George English, Vanburn Francois, Jose Iguacio, Alexander Joseph, Peter Ludy, Heinrich Meinsen, Antonio Rousserz, John Shields, and Phillip Weeks. These men, added to the 12 men who had signed over the previous two weeks, brought 24 badly needed crewmen aboard. Although new men were being added, old ones were also leaving. Master's Mate William Yeaton was put ashore on February 12 due to an illness that would keep him off the *Kearsarge* for six months.

On February 13 Winslow had the *Kearsarge* leave Cadiz, hoping to return to Brest to continue his watchful vigil. Just two nights before, taking advantage of a heavy fog, the *Florida* had slipped out of port. Arriving in Brest, Winslow was chagrined to find his foe nowhere in sight.

There was little to do but notify Washington that the *Florida* had escaped, although it did indicate that the *Florida* never really intended to fight the *Kearsarge*. On board the *Kearsarge* there was more than the usual grumbling. It now appeared that the past several weeks had been wasted, and that the hoped for confrontation with the *Florida* would not be.

"If the U.S. Minister had just sent us supplies when the captain asked for them, we wouldn't have had to go to Cadiz for provisions," was the familiar refrain.[16] The 24-hour law also came in for its share of condemnation, the crew reasoning that they should have been allowed to go into the harbor and attack the *Florida* rather than cruising back and forth outside, trying to watch three exits.[17]

It wasn't long before Winslow learned that the *Georgia* had also departed from Cherbourg. There would be no rebel ships trapped in port this time. Had he known, however, he could have taken consolation in the fact that the *Georgia* did not leave on her own. Pressure applied by the United States had caused the French to rethink their policy of leniency. The marine minister had, in turn, applied pressure to the *Georgia*, letting her captain know in no uncertain terms that the rebel cruiser was no longer welcome.[18] At long last, the complaints of the United States were being heard by foreign governments.

With the French policy tightened, there were also consequences for the *Kearsarge*. On February 19 Winslow was approached by a French official who told him that he also would have to leave port within 24 hours, unless he was taking on provisions or making emergency repairs. Choosing to do neither, the *Kearsarge* weighed anchor and departed from Brest, bound for Cherbourg, arriving at the small port city two days later, on a cold, blustery morning. Almost immediately a steamer was spied, and Winslow ordered a chase. The effort went for naught, however, with the ship proving to be a French ironclad, and Winslow returned to Cherbourg.

A breakwater, providing two entrances to the port, protected the Cherbourg harbor. Winslow chose to stay outside the breakwater where he could monitor the ships going in and out without having to follow the 24-hour rule. As the *Kearsarge* watched, a ship started to leave the harbor but, spying the *Kearsarge*, quickly turned and returned to port. Suspicious, Winslow sent a boat to find out what the ship was trying to hide. If he was lucky, she may even prove to be one of the Confederate raiders he had been hoping to encounter.

Luck was not with him, as the ship turned out to be a Union merchant ship which was just as suspicious of the *Kearsarge*. Fearing the strange vessel hovering just outside the breakwater may be the *Alabama*, the captain had decided to remain in port rather than risk being captured.

With no signs of any Confederate activity in the area, the *Kearsarge* set off for England where they could take on coal with only minimal violation of the international laws.[19] The winter weather remained foul, and the *Kearsarge* struggled the entire trip, sighting the famed cliffs of Dover on February 25. There, dozens of other vessels were already taking refuge.

Having already taken on coal within the past three months, Winslow requested that a coal brig sail out to meet the *Kearsarge*, where the coal could be transferred outside the territorial waters. While he waited, the customary crowd of visitors came to visit the ship, including a man who claimed he had served on the *Florida*. He offered to use his contacts to locate the raider, and promised to deliver her up to the *Kearsarge* if

Winslow was interested. Ever suspicious, Winslow figured the man for a spy whose real mission was to divert the *Kearsarge*'s attention from the *Rappahannock,* which lay at anchor at nearby Calais. Winslow chose to ignore the offer.

Late in February the coal brig arrived, meeting the *Kearsarge* off the coast of Boulogne. The brig brought more than coal, as it had stocked up on a supply of rum before sailing. The entrepreneurs on board the brig quickly sold their liquid cargo to willing hands on board the *Kearsarge.* Now fortified against the ravages of the weather, the crew began the job of transferring the coal to the bunkers of the *Kearsarge.* More than one crew member paused during the process to duck into the hold and rinse the coal dust from his throat with the contents of his newly purchased bottle. The usual drunken fights broke out before the bunkers had been half filled, and several crewmen were placed in irons by the furious Winslow, who still did not know how the liquor had come aboard, since he had permitted none of the crew to go ashore.

CHAPTER FIFTEEN
MARCH–APRIL 1864

March 1864 began the same way that February had ended for the *Alabama*: heavy seas, only light winds, and not a sail in sight. By the third day, however, the breezes had turned into winds, and by evening a gale came in from the northwest. All sails were taken in and the *Alabama* hove to, hoping to ride out the storm. The storm moderated somewhat the next day, and by March 5 the weather had become mild once more, although the sea was still heavy.

On Sunday, March 6, the Articles of War were read, as was the custom on the first Sunday of the month, after which Semmes read a General Order in which he praised Michael Mars for his gallant conduct in jumping overboard to save Henry Godson. Mars was embarrassed and hoped that this would be the last public recognition of his act.

On March 7, for only the second time since January 17, a sail was sighted, but she was an English ship.[1] The next day three more were seen, although they were too far in the distance to justify chasing. Activity increased on March 9, when eight sails were sighted. Two were halted. One was a French ship whose name was not recorded, the other the Dutch bark *Van der Palau*.

Two days later the *Alabama* passed the Cape of Good Hope, with favorable winds. At 3:00 P.M. a sail was made on the starboard beam, and the English flag was run up the mast. The ship answered with the Dutch flag. The *Alabama* was once again back in the shipping lanes, and by evening she was within 20 miles of the Cape lighthouse.

An English mail steamer was spied the next day, but nothing that looked like an American. On March 13, passing herself off as the USS *Dacotah* once again, a large ship was hailed and hove to. Perhaps simply because no ship had been boarded for several weeks, Semmes ordered Fullam to head a boarding party. When the party arrived on board they learned that they had stopped the *Scottish Chief*, a British ship. The identity verified, some time was spent on pleasantries, after which the *Alabama* resumed her cruising.

By midafternoon another sail was sighted and a chase was initiated. In less than three hours the vessel was stopped. Once again using the alias *Dacotah*, the crew was disappointed to learn that their quarry was the *Orion*, out of Hamburg. It had now been two full months since the last Union vessel, the *Emma Jane*, had been burned.[2]

The next day a large double topsail yard ship was sighted and chased, but the speed of the *Alabama* had been reduced drastically by the deterioration of her hull, and the ship eluded Semmes and his men. After five hours the chase was called off, to the disappointment of everyone on board.

No sails were observed over the next three days, but March 17 proved to be a special day. With so many Irishmen on board, it was impossible for St. Patrick's Day to pass without some sort of celebration. Semmes did not require much convincing to allow the crew to splice the main brace in honor of the Emerald Isle's patron saint.[3]

The next day, with many of the crew nursing St. Patrick's Day headaches, the *Alabama* gave chase to a bark which showed Spanish colors. When boarded by Fullam and his party, her captain identified her as the *Manila*. Later in the day another chase was initiated, this time in a heavy fog. Within a few hours the quarry had eluded the *Alabama* in the mist, and the chase was called off. A squall had blown in, accompanied by flashes of lightning and claps of thunder, and the crew did not protest when the chase ended. They could now go below deck and get out of the storm.

On March 20, with more favorable weather, three sails were sighted and intercepted. Two were English and one Dutch.[4] One of the English ships, the *Sardinia*, had run and it took a blank cartridge to bring her to. The other two had offered no resistance, and the day ended uneventfully with the rebel raider sitting just off the coast of Cape Town.

Under cover of the French flag, the *Alabama* entered port. With yet another gale brewing, two anchors were dropped. Once in Cape Town, Semmes learned that the *Tuscaloosa* had been seized by the British as an uncondemned prize which had been taken into neutral waters illegally. The British purportedly planned to return the ship to her Philadelphia owners.[5]

Semmes spent the next two days preparing a legal brief, to be presented to Governor Wodehouse in Cape Town. Semmes argued that Wodehouse himself had once ruled that a nation could not legally inquire into another country's warship's history. The sympathetic Wodehouse agreed with Semmes, but took no immediate action. Meanwhile, unknown to either, the British government ruled that the seizure of the *Tuscaloosa* was, in itself, an illegal act, and had ordered the ship turned over to Semmes. That word would not be received until after the *Alabama* sailed from Cape Town, and the *Tuscaloosa* was destined to sit out the remainder of the war in Simon's Bay.[6]

While Semmes argued for the *Tuscaloosa*'s release, he must have done it with mixed emotions. Manning and outfitting the *Tuscaloosa* had been a mistake when viewed against her lack of success, and if he won her release he may have had to augment her crew with some of his own before sending her back out to sea. The *Tuscaloosa* had already deprived him of the services of several good crewmen and officers, and to give up additional men would have compounded his error. The news was not all bad, however. The *Tuscaloosa*'s wool had been sold, as had the *Sea Bride*, and the proceeds were waiting for Semmes when he arrived.[7]

While Semmes and his officers were cordially received in Cape Town, such was no longer the case throughout the rest of the British Empire. Support for the Confederacy was eroding as the United States government continued to apply pressure to England. Charles Adams, United States minister to Great Britain, had demanded that Parliament authorize payment of damages for the American ships destroyed by vessels built in England.[8] It was believed that his arguments were no longer falling on deaf ears.

The *Alabama* remained in Cape Town until March 25, Good Friday, during which time her decks buzzed with activity. Boat after boat arrived alongside carrying visitors wishing to view the famous raider. Although they were disruptive, Semmes and his men received them all, perhaps recognizing that the Confederacy needed to keep any friends they still had.

As the *Alabama* weighed anchor, a Union merchant ship steamed into port, probably unaware that the Confederates were also there. Had the *Alabama* put to sea just a few hours sooner, the Union ship would have become a prize. As it was, however, once in port she would not venture out again until the *Alabama* was well out to sea, and Semmes didn't even consider waiting for her. Fullam wrote that the lost opportunity was "the unkindest cut of all."[9]

Before leaving, four new hands were brought on board. Since they were not sworn in until the ship had passed beyond the territorial limits, technically Semmes had not violated any international rules. This ploy kept both the Union and the Confederacy within the letter of the law on more than one occasion. Once at sea, Nicholas Adams, John Buckley, Fred Lennon, and Henry McCoy officially became the latest members of the *Alabama*'s crew. Somehow Semmes avoided losing any crew members to desertion this time, so the four men represented a net gain in strength.

With her bow pointed in the general direction of England, the *Alabama* creaked and groaned her way through the waves. By now her bottom was covered with barnacles and had curled up at the seams, her boilers were corroded badly from the effects of the sea water, and even her beams had started to split. The effects of nearly two years at sea were becoming more apparent with each passing day, and it took every effort of the crew to keep her moving.

Semmes and his men approached the island of St. Helena on April 7. This tiny island, famed as Napoleon's place of exile, was only a speck in the ocean, more than seven hundred miles from land. The *Alabama* remained in this area for several days, hoping to catch some Union merchant unaware. Like an injured animal, Semmes now preferred to lie in wait for his prey rather than chase it down. He knew he would likely come up short on any chase, considering the condition of his ship.

It had been a long cruise. The ship was falling apart, the men were ready to go home, and Semmes himself felt that it was time to return to Mobile and his family. With such little activity in the shipping lanes he spent most of his time in his cabin, writing letters to his wife and catching up on his reading.

Not until April 17, with the helmsman heading toward Brazil, did the *Alabama* come across any ships, neutral or American. On that day two were stopped. After a short chase the Italian bark *Carlo* was stopped, believing the USS *Dacotah* had pursued her. Later in the day the *Formose*, a French ship, hove to, again believing that the ship which had signaled her was the *Dacotah*. Officers on both ships provided new information to Semmes regarding the lack of activity in the shipping lanes. The *Carlo* said that less than a half dozen American ships were in port at Buenos Aires when she had departed that city just a few days earlier. The captain of the *Formose*, who had recently been in the Chincha Islands, reported seeing not one American there.

It was now apparent that American ships were no longer a force on the world's oceans. Owners were selling their vessels off to foreign interests, or at the very least, holding them at anchor until it was once again safe to resume shipping. In some respects the *Alabama* was now the victim of her own successes, but it also pointed out that her mission had been accomplished. The next day saw the *Alabama* stopping the Hamburg bark *Alster*, which was hauling a cargo of palm oil to Falmouth. Her captain had seen no Americans, either.

Late in the morning of April 22 a sail was sighted. A square-rigger, she looked to be an American. Semmes ordered the helmsman to give chase, and for the next several hours the *Alabama* labored to gain on the stranger. By nightfall the *Alabama* seemed to be close enough to overtake her, but Semmes chose to wait until the next morning when it would be easier to see and safer to board.

In the dim light of dawn on April 23 Semmes ordered the Stars and Stripes run up. A blank round was fired and the ship, which had answered the Stars and Stripes with an identical banner, came around. She was the *Rockingham*, under the command of Captain Edward A. Gerrish, who was accompanied by his wife and child.

Gerrish produced papers which showed that his cargo of guano was neutral. However, with the *Rockingham* being the first American ship stopped by the *Alabama* in nearly three months, the Admiralty Court was not about to let her slip away. The papers were unsworn, which was good enough for Semmes. The *Rockingham* was quickly condemned, and Gerrish and his family were transferred aboard the *Alabama* along with his crew.

Once the boarding party had brought back those provisions needed on board the *Alabama*, Fullam and his boarding party prepared to go back on board the *Rockingham* and set their fires. But Semmes had another idea. The sea was smooth and the weather favorable. He asked Kell if he thought the men would benefit from some target practice. Kell recognized that he had not been asked a question. Rather, he had been given an order in the form of a question, to which he quickly responded. The crew was beat to general quarters, and the target practice began.

Each gun fired two shots and two shells at a range of about five hundred yards. Although Fullam noted that the firing was excellent, some problems quickly became apparent. Some of the shells had not exploded, while others exploded with a muffled sound, rather than the characteristic sharp report. Semmes expressed concern about his fuses and ordered the remaining fuses and caps examined. Those that didn't look right were tossed overboard. Nothing was done with the powder.[10]

The gunnery practice completed, the *Rockingham* was set ablaze. With the guano-laden ship still burning behind her, the *Alabama* resumed her journey. Later in the day the *Robert McKensie*, a ship out of Liverpool, was boarded, and three more English vessels were boarded over the next few days: the *Kent*, the *Bertha Martha*, and the *La Flor del Plata*.

On April 27 the Confederate cruiser encountered the last prize she would ever take. Near the equator the *Alabama* hailed the clipper ship *Tycoon* which was carrying a valuable general cargo to California for the gold mining industry. Commanded by Edward Ayres, she also carried some passengers. Ayres made no claims of neutrality, and his ship and cargo were quickly condemned. As the crew and passengers were moved onto the *Alabama*, the boarding party took supplies from the *Tycoon* for use on the Confederate raider. Shortly after midnight on April 28 the crew of the *Alabama* burned their last ship.

Robert Longshaw, first mate on the *Rockingham*, and Edward Burrell, a crewman on the *Tycoon*, signed on with the *Alabama*, the last two who would do so.[11] The officers of the *Alabama* noted a marked change in attitude among the crew now, the high hopes of two years earlier having been displaced by uncertainty and a feeling of pending disaster.[12]

* * *

Winslow and the *Kearsarge* remained off the coast of Boulogne for a few days after coaling. While anchored, a suspicious officer noted that several of the passing fishing boats came much closer to the ship than he thought was necessary. Watching them pass, he decided they may be Confederate sympathizers bent on forcing their way onto the *Kearsarge*. He discussed it with other officers and several pistols were loaded and kept handy. The engineers rigged up a hose to one of the boilers, planning to spray scalding water onto any unauthorized boarders. No such attempt was ever made, however, and the precautions were found to be unnecessary.

On March 2, still fearing a possible attack on the *Kearsarge* by a force of Confederate ships, Gideon Welles sent a message to Winslow. Saying he did not believe an attack was probable, he was still relying on the *Kearsarge* to defend herself if one came. He repeated his contention that to acknowledge any challenge would be to recognize the enemy, raising them but lowering the Union.[13]

Before the message was received, however, the *Kearsarge* departed Boulogne and headed for Calais, hoping to catch the *Rappahannock* still in port. In need of repairs, the Confederate would be easily blockaded, but Winslow and his men arrived after dark. Unable to determine if the *Rappahannock* was still there, and not permitted to enter port at night, Winslow decided to continue sailing.

Setting his sights on England, Winslow dropped two officers off at the tiny port of Deal, giving them instructions to go on ahead. Their mission was to obtain permission from the British to bring the *Kearsarge* into a government dry dock in London.

Unwilling to leave the area without determining the whereabouts of the *Rappahannock*, Winslow took one last cruise past Calais, where he finally confirmed the rebel ship's presence. Hoping to have better luck against the *Rappahannock* than he had against the *Florida*, Winslow ordered a full-scale drill. Held after all had turned in for the night, the sleepy crew did their best to work through it.

With the 24-hour rule being strictly enforced by the French, Winslow was reluctant to enter the port. Instead, he hired a local tugboat named the *Annette,* on which he posted Wheeler with instructions to signal the *Kearsarge* if the *Rappahannock* made a move out of the port.

Satisfied now that the *Rappahannock* would not slip out of Calais the way the *Florida* had done at Brest, Winslow moved his ship to Dover. Against his judgment, Winslow allowed a few men to go ashore each day. Many failed to report back when they were due, which was not unusual. Facing punishment when they finally did return, many extended their unauthorized leaves even longer, and Thomas Burns, deciding that he liked being ashore better than he liked life aboard the *Kearsarge*, never did return.[14]

On March 27 the *Kearsarge* headed back for one last check of the *Rappahannock* before leaving for London. There Winslow learned that the rebel faced impoundment by the French government. Even if the impoundment threat was not carried out, Winslow knew that the diplomatic wrangling which would inevitably accompany the threat would last for some time. He saw little need to remain on watch but still kept Wheeler at his post on the *Annette.*

Needing a dry dock, the *Kearsarge* departed for London. Within hours the *Kearsarge* received another lesson on the fickle nature of the winter weather in the English Channel. Hit with another bad storm, the foretopmast snapped off and crashed to the deck, creating a maze of rigging, shattered mast, and sail. The crew spent the major portion of the storm on the deck, cutting away the debris.[15]

On March 30 the *Kearsarge* and her crew reached the mouth of the Thames River. By midafternoon they had sailed upriver to Woolwich, where they took their powder off for storage in a shore magazine. By morning, all the powder had been removed and the *Kearsarge* made her way to the Victoria docks in London.

Perhaps he had hoped that the British had forgotten the Queenstown stowaway incident. If he did, Winslow underestimated the determination of the British government to make both sides more accountable to the Foreign Enlistment Act. With Michael Ahern still aboard from the original group of stowaways, the British had their evidence sailing up the Thames to meet them.

Several of the stowaways had provided affidavits that Ahern had not returned from the *Kearsarge* with them. Armed with this information, officials ordered that Ahern be arrested if he stepped ashore, but that no effort should be made to go aboard to get him. Presumably, he remained on board, because there is no record that he was arrested while the *Kearsarge* was in London.

Once in dry dock the crew and officers of the *Kearsarge* received good news. The bottom of the ship was not in bad condition, as they had feared. With only minor bottom repairs needed, and with the boilers restored to safe operating conditions, Winslow hoped to turn his attention to more extensive repairs. However, the British would not allow it. Saying that the *Kearsarge* had arrived before permission had been granted, Winslow was ordered to leave port, and on April 6 the *Kearsarge* left the dry dock, leaving behind Ordinary Seaman Martin Roach, who had deserted.

Sailing downriver, the *Kearsarge* once again stopped at Woolwich, this time to reload their powder. That task complete, Winslow sailed for Dover where he was thwarted once again by the British government. Charging that the *Kearsarge* was beginning to use Dover as a base, national officials strongly suggested that Winslow find a different port from which to operate.

No longer permitted to stay in Dover, Winslow sailed across the channel for France with the little tug *Annette* trailing behind. The *Annette* was towing a coal barge loaded with Welsh coal for the *Kearsarge*. Anchoring near Boulogne once more, the task of transferring coal began.

Again, liquor found its way from the barge to the *Kearsarge* as enterprising colliers supplemented their income with the proceeds from sales to the Union ship's crew.

Mindful of the potential for an enemy attack, Winslow refused to allow the men to have idle time on their hands while in Boulogne. Gunnery practice kept the men too busy to think about anything else, and Winslow reminded them that they still were not sure if the ship would be attacked by a flotilla of rebel cruisers. The prospect of having to fight off several enemy ships at one time seemed incentive enough for the crew to take the practice seriously.

While gunnery practice was in progress, Ordinary Seamen John McCarthy and George Baker, with an unnamed companion, overstayed their liberty in Boulogne. Twenty-four hours later the *Kearsarge* left port. A vigilant lookout spotted the three rowing desperately in the *Kearsarge*'s wake in an attempt to get back aboard before the ship went under steam. The officer of the deck ordered the ship halted long enough to allow the three to catch up, putting them in irons as they climbed over the rail. The three were court-martialed and reduced to landsmen for their effort.[16]

With all on board, the *Kearsarge* steamed for Belgium, where friendlier waters awaited. The Belgians had not yet issued any prohibitions against Union ships coming into their ports, and Winslow hoped to take advantage of that. Signaling for a pilot to come aboard to guide him through the narrow inlet at Ostend, he hoped to make the repairs that had been denied him in London.

The pilot immediately directed the engine room to give him eight knots, a speed which the crew thought to be foolhardy at best, given the restrictive space through which the ship had to maneuver. Against their judgment the engineers did as directed, and within minutes the *Kearsarge* paid the price, becoming entangled with a small fishing sloop.

The undaunted pilot backed the *Kearsarge* out of the ensnarement and asked for eight knots once again. This time the Federal ship struck a small footbridge, tearing out a large portion and running aground in the process, damaging the head gear. To complicate matters, the tide was going out and the stern of the ship dropped lower than the bow, which was now firmly planted in the mud. With the deck at an odd angle, it was apparent that nothing would be accomplished until the tide came back in.

The crew was directed to move as much weight from the bow as they could, and the day was spent in shifting spare chains, provisions, and even an anchor to lighten the load. With the incoming tide Winslow hoped to float the *Kearsarge* free and continue on into the port, where the repairs that he had planned would now, most likely, be even more extensive.

With the engines straining in reverse and every available hand manning the capstan, the *Kearsarge* groaned and creaked but failed to move. The crew was ordered to the stern, in hopes that their combined weight might lift the bow high enough for the ship to be backed out, but still the rocks refused to give up their prize. Finally, well after dark and several hours after running aground, the *Kearsarge* worked herself free. The pilot, however, had had enough. He refused to try a third time, and Winslow saw no need to talk him out of his decision. A second pilot was brought aboard, and it was nearly midnight before the battered vessel finally made it into port.[17]

At daylight an inspection was made. Although the copper bottom had been torn, there appeared to be no structural damage. More importantly, the ship was still watertight. Winslow directed that the originally planned maintenance be carried out, after which he left for Brussels with Surgeon John Browne and Paymaster Joseph Smith. In his absence the ship was cleaned and painted, working around the customary visitors. Ashore, those on liberty conducted themselves in the usual manner, with at least one escorted back to the ship by the local constable.[18]

On April 22 Winslow received word in Brussels that the *Rappahannock* was preparing to leave port. Provisions were being taken on and all crew members had been recalled, the agent's message said. Winslow immediately sent a telegram to Thornton to prepare to sail while he, Browne, and Smith returned. Thornton did as directed, taking the ship out some three miles from her berth so that no time would be lost when Winslow and the others arrived. For their part, the crew was not unhappy to leave. Recalling the ill-fated attempts to enter the port, several of them vowed never to return.[19]

With Winslow's return the next morning, last-minute preparations were made and the *Kearsarge* got under way by afternoon. The engineers gave her a full head of steam and the Union vessel raced for Calais, hoping to intercept the raider before she left. Winslow need not have hurried, as it turned out, because his information had been false. Arriving in Calais, he was frustrated to see the *Rappahannock* sitting just as she had several weeks earlier. Winslow concluded that the agent who had sent the message had felt guilty at having no information, and so had simply sent a message.

Winslow's agreement with the tender *Annette* had run out by now, and he saw little need to renew it. The tug had shipped some mail and provided some coal, but beyond that had done little. After considering the situation, Winslow decided to recall Wheeler and allow the *Annette* to go on her way.

The *Kearsarge* sat watchfully for three days before Winslow decided that there was no need for such vigilance. He decided to return to Dover, hoping that he could take on some additional recruits. His effort to add to his crew was unsuccessful, but the trip to Dover was not wasted. There, Winslow picked up newspapers which outlined the whereabouts of the *Alabama*, the *Georgia*, the *Florida*, and the *Rappahannock*, the four ships which ostensibly had planned to attack him. He had known where the *Rappahannock* was, but now he knew what the others were doing, as well.

The *Florida* was reported in Havana, and although this was not accurate, Winslow reasoned that she would not be a problem for him. That left only the *Georgia* and the *Alabama*. Of those two, only the *Alabama* caught his attention, as the news reports said she was heading for the English Channel. With luck, Winslow hoped to run across her.

CHAPTER SIXTEEN

MAY 1–JUNE 18, 1864

PREPARATION FOR BATTLE

At 3:15 P.M. on May 2, 1864, the *Alabama* crossed the equator for the fourth and final time. Knowing they were on the final leg of the cruise, the crew became more spirited. They were going home.

The *Alabama*, slowed by the curling copper on her bottom and the presence of barnacles and seaweed, lost even more speed as the winds died down. For several days Fullam made no entries in his journal except for references to the wind.[1]

Nearly becalmed, Semmes wished to use the time constructively. Shells were brought onto the gun deck and gunnery practice commenced. As with the shots and shells fired at the *Rockingham*, many of these failed to explode.

Even after the winds picked up there was little chance for success now for Semmes and his partially crippled ship. Throughout the entire month of May the *Alabama* stopped only a dozen ships, and all of those were neutral.[2] Not an American vessel was seen, and if one had been spied, the *Alabama* was in no condition to give chase. Her decks were leaking, her bilges filling with water, her boilers barely able to make steam. Repairs, major repairs, were needed. Even neutral vessels were ignoring the rebel ship, sailing past as if she didn't exist. The once proud scourge of the seas had been reduced to a caricature of a ship of war.

Late in May strong gales buffeted the ship, opening up still more leaks. The crew could do little more than hunker down and take all that came their way. They were losing what little fight they had left. On June 4 a brig was signaled, and Fullam boarded her to check her papers. Again, the ship was neutral. She was the *Julie Caroline*, and once more Fullam didn't bother to tell the captain the true identity of the ship which had stopped him. He used the pseudonym HMS *Scourge*.

Over the next several days more neutrals were boarded. Although the boardings gained nothing, Semmes was able to obtain current newspapers. From each, the news was nearly the same. The Confederacy was strangling. The cause appeared to have been lost. The news left the officers saddened, but the crew, few of whom had any particular allegiance to the Confederacy in the first place, took the news in stride. They were more interested in the fact that they were to get several months' leave as soon as the *Alabama* put into port. With so many repairs needed, their services would not be required for some time.

On June 9 the *Alabama* boarded her last ships. The first was the Genoese barkentine *Raffaeline*, the second was a Dutch bark whose name was not recorded. Over the entire cruise, Fullam noted that 447 ships were "seen, spoken, and boarded" by the *Alabama*.[3] The records are sketchy in support of this number, but more than 300 can be verified.[*]

That same day Semmes ordered the crew to rig up some spare yards, most of which had been taken from prizes. These were fashioned onto the mizzen. New topsail and mainsail yards were pieced together and added. The purpose of all this was to disguise the *Alabama* to look like a full-rigged ship rather than the bark she was known to be. If Semmes could no longer chase the enemy, perhaps he could fool him and bring him close enough for capture.

On June 10 Semmes, now suffering from a cold and fever, took on a pilot to bring the *Alabama* into the English Channel. It was well after dark and Semmes made the decision to wait until morning light before entering port. He retired to his cabin and, as was his custom, knelt

---

[*] Refer to Appendix A for a listing of these ships.

before his altar before going to bed.[4] Tomorrow, the *Alabama* would enter the port of Cherbourg, where finally the necessary repairs could be made.

On June 11 the pilot guided the *Alabama* into Cherbourg harbor, still carrying 37 prisoners from the *Rockingham* and *Tycoon*. Semmes immediately put on his full dress uniform and went ashore to meet with Port Admiral Augustin Dupouy. There, he asked Dupouy for permission to land his prisoners and put into dry dock for badly needed repairs. Dropping off the prisoners would present no problem, he was told, but allowing a belligerent warship to dock in a neutral port was a touchy matter. Dupouy decided that he could not make the ruling, saying it would be up to Emperor Napoleon III, and he was vacationing in Biarritz. Dupouy said the emperor was not expected back in Paris for another week.[5]

Unlike many port cities in Europe, Cherbourg had no commercial docks. Instead, the French navy owned the docks, as the government had built a naval base there in 1858. Perhaps Semmes selected Cherbourg over the commercial docks at other nearby harbors because he knew the emperor had always appeared to be pro-Confederate. If that were the case, Semmes most likely believed that he would have fewer legal questions concerning the Foreign Enlistment Act if he docked in France, rather than England.

For whatever reason, Semmes felt comfortable docking in Cherbourg, and he planned to give his crew at least a two-month leave. However, until he was sure he would be able to stay, he would have to keep the crew under his command. Finally, after much discussion, Dupouy agreed to relax the rules and allow the *Alabama* to remain in port until the emperor made a decision.

Still, Semmes was reluctant to release his men. He knew most of them would probably never report back, but that in itself was of little concern to him. Their desertion simply meant the prize money would be divided among fewer crew members, and most of the crew had done little to distinguish themselves lately anyway. However, rumor had it that the *Kearsarge* may be coming to Cherbourg, and if that rumor was true, Semmes would need every hand, especially if it was ruled that he had to leave port. Knowing the *Alabama* could not hope to outrun an enemy ship in her current condition, he ordered additional gunnery practice.

He also notified Confederate Commissioner John Slidell and Flag Officer Samuel Barron, the ranking Confederate naval officer, of his arrival in Cherbourg. His note to Barron began with a description of the repairs that the *Alabama* would need, and proceeded to say that he intended to give his crew and officers an extended shore leave. Then, putting into words what he had been thinking for a long time, he closed his note to Barron with a cryptic statement. "As for myself," he wrote, "my health has suffered so much from a constant and harassing service of three years, almost continuously at sea, that I shall have to ask for relief."[6]

Meanwhile, the *Alabama*'s arrival had not gone unnoticed by American Vice Consul Edouard Liais, and while Semmes notified his superiors, Llais did likewise. In Paris, American Minister William Dayton immediately initiated diplomatic action upon hearing from Llais. He demanded that the French invoke the 24-hour rule and either force the *Alabama* to leave within a day or block her in so she couldn't leave at any time in the near future.

On June 14 Semmes wrote once more to Barron. In his note he stated that the French had been courteous but they had been incorrect when they had charged that Confederate cruisers were showing too much partiality to French docks, using them instead of those in England. As evidence, Semmes pointed out that he frequented English ports quite often, and that Cherbourg had been the first French port where he had asked for permission to make repairs. He also felt compelled to point out that it was a uniform practice of all nations, in war or during peaceful times, to allow the use of their public docks when private ones were unavailable.[7]

* * *

On May 4, 1864, the *Kearsarge* set sail for Holland. Repairs could be made there without the political ramifications found in France or England. Twenty-four hours later the crew was removing her powder at Westerschelde in preparation for entering Flushing.

On May 6 a Dutch pilot came aboard to escort the *Kearsarge* into port. Unbelievably, the pilot ran the *Kearsarge* aground, striking a pier in the process. For the next several hours the crew labored to free the hapless ship, and it was late in the afternoon when she finally slid loose and made it into dry dock.[8]

Once in dry dock the damages to the *Kearsarge* were assessed and found to be relatively minor despite the beating she had taken over the past few weeks, mostly at the hands of the pilots. More than 50 sheets of copper had been ripped from the hull, but once again the hull itself had escaped damage. Dutch craftsmen could easily make the repairs in a few days. The engine repairs which Winslow had wanted to have done in London would have to wait once more.

With the crew's presence not needed, most of the men took liberty. For the next few days there were more visitors on board than there were crew. Winslow had gone to Belgium and most of the officers had taken off for some much-needed relaxation. With nobody in charge, the crew ran wild and few of them bothered to return to the ship at night.

When Winslow returned on May 10 he found few of his crew present. Unknown to the captain, several languished in the local jail. Winslow only learned of their whereabouts when he asked police to try to locate his men. The police gladly returned the crewmen when they found them in the bars and brothels, and Winslow had them thrown in irons to prevent them from going ashore again. Finally, the bulk of the crew was once more on board.

On May 12 the *Kearsarge* was seaworthy once again, and she slipped out of dry dock at high tide and under a full moon, bound for Calais. After cruising in the familiar waters around Calais for a few days, Winslow ordered the ship to Dover to pick up mail, after which the ship returned once more to keep an eye on the *Rappahannock*.

Nine days later Winslow's authority was again tested when David Sumner, the normally soft-spoken acting master, refused to perform a task that Winslow had ordered. Sumner's refusal probably surprised Winslow, but the captain could not afford to play favorites, and he reported Sumner to the Navy Department. For the next week, as Sumner sat out his punishment in his stateroom, the *Kearsarge* continued to watch the *Rappahannock*. Reports stated that the rebel's departure was imminent, and Winslow was determined to see that there was no repeat of the *Florida*'s escape.

On May 23 the *Rappahannock* ran the Confederate flag up her mast, a move that was answered by the crew of the *Kearsarge*, who not only ran up the Stars and Stripes but also the British flag in honor of the queen's birthday.

Three days later, however, Winslow received the surprising news that the *Rappahannock*, rather than leaving port, was removing the coal from her bunkers. The news gave Winslow the opportunity he needed to make the repairs to his engines. He immediately gave the word to his officers and crew to prepare to return to Flushing. Within hours he was under way, and the *Kearsarge* arrived in Flushing on the last day of May.

A week later to the day, with the crew relaxing on the forecastle, a messenger arrived with a telegram for the captain. Winslow was summoned and quickly arrived on deck. Taking the telegram, his good eye scanned it briefly. Turning to the officer of the deck he ordered the gun fired, signaling those on liberty that they must return to the ship. Before the puzzled officer could put the order into effect, Winslow was calling for Cushman to build up his steam.

The *Kearsarge* soon was steaming upriver, bound for the open sea and some as yet unknown destination. A Dutch band serenaded the ship as it passed upriver.[9] The crew, having become quite fond of the bars and brothels of Flushing, would require a good explanation for the rapid departure.

Once at sea the men were called to muster. With the crew drawn deathly silent, Winslow told them that he had received a telegram from the United States minister in Paris, William Dayton, in which Dayton reported that the *Alabama* had arrived in Cherbourg. The *Kearsarge* was under orders to go there and wait for her. Winslow did not elaborate, nor did he have to. Boatswain James Walton piped the men down, at which time bedlam erupted. If there was anything better than liberty in Flushing it was a possible confrontation with the *Alabama*.

Three cheers were given for the *Kearsarge*, then three more for Winslow. A simple message had raised spirits on the *Kearsarge* like nothing had ever done before. Sinking the *Alabama* would more than make up for all the earlier frustrations. Certainly the *Florida* had slipped away, and the *Sumter* had somehow given them the slip. Even the

Georgia had evaded them, also leaving from Cherbourg. And the *Rappahannock*, well, who knew if they would ever see her on the open sea? But this was the *Alabama*. The name was magical. Defeating her would be more than the equal of losing the other four.

By morning the *Kearsarge* was in Dover, where mail was picked up and new sails taken on. From Dover, Winslow sent a message to the *St. Louis*, asking her captain, George Preble, to come to Cherbourg from Gibraltar "with all possible haste"[10] and assist in watching the harbor entrance. It had taken two years for any Union ship to catch up with the *Alabama* and Winslow wanted to leave nothing to chance.

That evening the *Kearsarge* left Dover for Cherbourg. By late the next morning the breakwater which protected the Cherbourg harbor was in sight. Officers and crew alike lined the rail, all straining for a glimpse of the legendary rebel. Finally she came into view. It had taken two years, but there she was. She couldn't run any longer. Not wishing to be caught up in the 24-hour rule, Winslow ordered the *Kearsarge* to come to rest outside the breakwater. He was a patient man; he could wait for the *Alabama* to come to him.

* * *

From the deck of the *Alabama*, Semmes and his men watched the sleek black Union ship of war on the other side of the breakwater. Figures could be seen along her rail, and Semmes knew one of them had to be his old shipmate, John Winslow.

Still fighting the cold and fever which had dogged him for the past several weeks, Semmes was growing concerned. What if the ruling from the French government did not go in his favor? He knew he would not be able to outrun the *Kearsarge* if he did not get the repairs he needed, but if he could not remain in Cherbourg he may have to do just that. Or, he could stand and fight. Semmes believed his chances were better doing the latter.

Semmes went below to his cabin, and then asked Bartelli to find Kell. In the solitude of his quarters and in front of his shrine, he considered his request to Barron that he be relieved of his duties. His thoughts were interrupted by the arrival of Kell. Semmes motioned Kell to a seat, then told him the reason for having called him in: he wished to discuss the advisability of fighting the *Kearsarge*. Kell's eyebrows lifted but he said nothing. His captain would let him know when it was time for him to speak.

Semmes laid out his position, recognizing that the arrival of the *Alabama* at Cherbourg had been telegraphed to all parts of Europe. Within a few days Yankee cruisers would effectually blockade Cherbourg. It was still uncertain whether or not he would be permitted to repair the *Alabama* in Cherbourg, and in the meantime, the delay would not be to the *Alabama*'s advantage. Semmes told Kell he thought they may be able to whip the *Kearsarge*, the two vessels being made of wood and carrying about the same number of men and guns. Besides, even though he had been ordered to avoid entanglements with the enemy's cruisers, he said he was tired of running from what he referred to as "that flaunting rag." Kell knew without asking that Semmes referred to the American flag.[11]

Kell, on the other hand, was not so sure they should fight the *Kearsarge*, and he candidly said as much. He knew that the powder had gone foul. Every third shot at the *Rockingham* had failed to explode.

Semmes countered that one lucky shot could do the trick, with two of the *Alabama*'s guns capable of sinking any wooden ship afloat. Kell quickly pointed out that the *Kearsarge* had the same capability. Carrying two 11-inch pivots, she was a man-of-war, built to fight. The *Alabama* once could match her speed, but not now.

Semmes admitted as much, but he continued to insist that he could win a fair fight. At the worst, he believed they had an even chance. He saw nothing rash in offering battle to Winslow. The ships were well matched and the *Alabama* carried one gun more than the *Kearsarge*, although the latter threw a slightly heavier broadside. He had considered everything.

As they talked he finalized his decision. He intended to fight. He ordered Kell to notify the men to clear the ship for action. As Kell carried out the order, Semmes prepared to make a formal request for coal and to notify the port admiral that he hoped to complete all the arrangements by Saturday night, or sooner if possible.[12]

After Kell departed, Semmes wrote another note to Flag Officer Barron, informing him of the plan. Semmes then ordered coal, knowing he would need all the steam he could muster if he was to engage the *Kearsarge*. A puzzled Admiral Dupouy wondered if that meant that Semmes no longer wished to make repairs, as he could only do one or the other. Before Semmes could make his final decision, however, it was made for him.

The Minister of the Marine and the Colonies in Paris sent a message to Dupouy with the answer that Semmes had feared. Reasoning that the *Alabama* had not been forced into Cherbourg by an accident, and that she could just as easily have gone to Spain, Portugal, Holland, or any other country, the French government ruled that the *Alabama* would have to go to a commercial dock to make her repairs, that the principles of neutrality did not permit France to allow a belligerent to rebuild itself or to augment her crew.

The message also directed Dupouy to tell Semmes that any prisoner placed ashore would be considered free as soon as he touched French soil, and that none would be delivered up to the *Kearsarge*, as Winslow had requested.[13] This last information gave Semmes some minor semblance of victory, coming in response to a letter of protest he had penned to the French when he had heard of Winslow's request.

After reading the message that had sealed his fate, Semmes retired to his cabin. He then wrote a note asking the Confederate agent in Cherbourg to pass a message along to Winslow by way of the American consul. That message became the basis of the challenge that Semmes issued to Winslow. "Sir," he wrote, "I hear that you were informed by the U.S. consul that the *Kearsarge* was to come to this port solely for the prisoners landed by me, and that he was to depart in 24 hours. I desire to say to the U.S. consul that my intention is to fight the *Kearsarge* as soon as I can make the necessary arrangements. I hope these will not detain me more than until tomorrow evening, or after the morrow morning at the furthest. I beg she will not depart before I am ready to go out. I have the honor to be, very respectfully, your obedient servant, R. Semmes, Captain."[14]

* * *

Winslow received the news that Semmes wanted to fight, and he anxiously considered the possibility. This is what he had been dispatched to do, and finally the time was at hand. He may not be allowed to pick up the *Alabama*'s prisoners, but he could make prisoners of Semmes and his entire crew, and given the chance he fully intended to do it!

Winslow had not yet responded to Semmes's challenge, perhaps recalling the message he had received from Welles when there was a possibility that the *Kearsarge* was to be the victim of an attack by several rebel cruisers. It is also possible that Winslow felt no need to respond, that the fight was going to take place with or without an answer.

He ordered all hands piped to the deck. When all had assembled he held up the message from Semmes so each man could see it. Reading it to the crew, Winslow finished by saying that he did not know when the *Alabama* planned to come out, but that all hands should be ready to fight at any time. His remarks were greeted with a rousing chorus of cheers.

The plan laid out, Winslow ordered all hands to prepare the ship for battle, and all were dismissed to carry out his orders. Loose items that would not be needed in a fight were stowed and the gun crews went through their routines. There would be no time to think about what to do next, once a battle started. Surgeon Browne asked that a place be prepared where he could treat the wounded, hoping that such action would not be necessary.

* * *

In preparation for the battle Semmes sent four and one-half sacks of gold sovereigns ashore, along with the paymaster's last payroll and a sealed package of the ransom bonds from the prizes he had released. These were deposited with the Confederate agent in Cherbourg, Mr. Ad. Bonfils.[15] The chronometers from his burned prizes were sent ashore on the English yacht *Hornet*. The *Hornet*'s commander, Captain Hewitt, took the chronometers to Liverpool where they would eventually be sold.[16]

After considerable delay Semmes received permission to take on coal, and on June 15 the process began. While the coal was being transferred, the crew cleaned guns, arranged powder, shot, and shell where it could be quickly retrieved, and sharpened pikes and cutlasses in the event that they would either board the *Kearsarge* or be called upon to repel boarders themselves. This was all done as visitors thronged the decks, making the work all the more difficult. For his part, Bartelli brought out the ship's glasses, polishing them for what he was sure would be a victory celebration after the *Kearsarge* was sunk.[17]

As the news spread that the *Alabama* intended to fight the *Kearsarge*, Confederate officers across Europe made plans to rush to Cherbourg to offer their services. Among them were William Sinclair, the handsome midshipman Semmes had used to calm the ladies on the *Ariel* when that ship was captured. Sinclair had been one of those who had transferred to the *Tuscaloosa* and he was eager to rejoin his friends on the *Alabama*, especially if it meant a good battle. He was accompanied by his father, Captain George Sinclair, who also planned to fight.[18]

In nearly every instance, however, French authorities refused to allow these officers to board the *Alabama*. Two exceptions were Maximilian von Meulnier and Julius Schroeder, the Prussian master's mates who had shipped onto the *Alabama* at Cape Town the previous September. They had already started home on leave when they got word of the pending battle, and because they were officially still part of the crew, French officials allowed them to board.[19]

Schroeder and von Meulnier, if they had chosen to do so, could have climbed up with the lookout and seen their foe cruising slowly back and forth beyond the breakwater. Within 72 hours they would get a much closer look.

* * *

Captain Evan P. Jones maneuvered his yacht past the *Alabama*, gazing admiringly at her as he passed. Smaller, he was able to get closer to shore, where he anchored. His yacht, the *Deerhound*, of the Royal Yacht Squadron, had arrived in Cherbourg to pick up the yacht's owner, John Lancaster, and his family. The Lancasters had been vacationing and were to arrive in Cherbourg by train on June 18.

It would be another day before the Lancasters arrived, so Jones and several of his officers took a boat back out to the *Alabama*, hoping to go aboard and get a closer look at the famous cruiser. Pulling alongside, however, he was turned back with the explanation that too much remained to be done for the *Alabama* to entertain any more visitors. Disappointed, Jones returned to the *Deerhound*.[20] He had hoped for a better reception, since the *Deerhound* and the *Alabama* had both been built by the Lairds.

* * *

On the morning of June 18, William Dayton, Jr., the son of the U.S. minister in Paris, took a boat out to the *Kearsarge*. The younger Dayton had been issued a pass by Admiral Dupouy only after promising to report back to Dupouy in person after his visit to the American vessel, as proof that he had not signed on to fight. Carrying a dispatch from his father, Dayton immediately sought out Captain Winslow upon boarding. He handed Winslow the message from his father.

The elder Dayton had quickly written the note after conferring with French officials. Dayton had originally met with them to protest the *Alabama*'s presence and to demand that no accommodations be given to the rebel. The French had already decided not to, but they voiced concerns that the *Kearsarge* would initiate the battle as soon as the *Alabama* crossed the three-mile limit. The three-mile limit had been imposed years earlier when weapons had limited range, but both ships carried guns which were capable of hitting targets more than that distance away. French officials feared that shells could land on French soil unless the battle took place further off shore.

Dayton had pointed out that the three-mile limit was internationally recognized, but after some discussion he had agreed that to move further out would pose no risk to the *Kearsarge*. It was this advice that he had written in his note to Winslow. He suggested that Winslow take the battle out some six or seven miles, but only if it did not hurt the *Kearsarge*'s chances for victory. Dayton also warned Winslow not to sacrifice any advantage.[21] It was a warning that Winslow did not need.

After Dayton left the ship, Winslow called his officers together to discuss the coming battle and the strategy they would follow. At the meeting's conclusion, Winslow and his officers agreed " . . . not to surrender, but to fight until the last and, if need be, to go down with colors flying."[22]

* * *

George Sinclair, William Sinclair's father, boarded the *Alabama* as a visitor. A recognized ordnance expert, he hoped to share his expertise with Semmes. It had not been an easy task to gain permission from French officials to come aboard, and he suspected that they were watching him quite closely to make sure that he didn't become part of the crew. Sinclair and Semmes spent several hours in Semmes's cabin discussing various scenarios and possible battle situations. Sinclair offered advice on whether to use shot or shell under the various conditions.[23]

Following the meeting with Sinclair, Semmes called his crew together. After warning them that they must return to the ship with clear heads, he gave them liberty. The men left the ship, passing through cheering throngs of onlookers who had lined the docks to get a glimpse of the men of the *Alabama*. Once ashore, the men were treated as heroes, with local citizens all lining up for the honor of buying them drinks. The crew seemed bent on making the most of what could be their last liberty, and twenty-year-old Third Lieutenant Joseph Wilson observed that they were "fattening up for the slaughter."[24]

That evening Semmes called his officers to his cabin, where he saluted each one individually. The atmosphere was tense, and a deathly silence permeated the cabin. Finally, Semmes spoke.

"Gentlemen," he said, "tomorrow we fight the *Kearsarge*. Only the good God knows what the outcome will be. Thus far, He has shielded us. I believe He still watches over us. I have taken this responsibility alone. It was the only way out with honor. If I have done wrong, if I fail, the fault will be mine. The *Alabama*'s record speaks for itself. You can be proud of it. It is my intention, with God's help, and yours, to sink or capture the *Kearsarge*."[25]

Murmurs of agreement rose from the officers. Each pledged to do his part. Semmes then continued, telling them he would be sending the ship's treasure chest ashore. He suggested they all place their valuables in it. Solemnly, he added that those who owned property may wish to make out their last will and testament. Joseph Wilson spoke up, saying that all he owned was a guitar, and it wouldn't fit in the chest. He asked to keep it to bolster his spirits, a request that Semmes granted.[26]

Kell reported to Semmes that he had thoroughly inspected the entire ship. She was ready for a fight, he pronounced. After a brief discussion of strategy, Semmes dismissed the gathering. He still had something he felt compelled to do, and he could not do it until everybody had departed.

Now alone, he left the ship and went ashore. There, he found a small Catholic church. Entering, he paused a few moments to allow his eyes to grow accustomed to the dim light. Then, he walked down the small aisle to a pew near the front, where he spent the next hour in prayer.

Returning to his beloved ship at 10:00 P.M. he found most of the crew already there, with the rest not far behind. For the first time in the two-year cruise of the *Alabama*, there had been a liberty with no drunken brawls, no fighting, and nobody arrested. Each man had done as his captain had requested and returned to the ship with a clear head. All knew the importance of tomorrow.

* * *

John Lancaster, his wife, their four children, and a niece had boarded the *Deerhound* on June 18 as planned. They had enjoyed their vacation on the continent and were now ready to return to England. They had heard of the coming battle and were caught up in the excitement.

Knowing their yacht had come from the same shipyard as the *Alabama*, they naturally felt a kinship with Semmes and his crew. Discussions centered around the battle, the *Alabama*, and what the family should do in the morning, which would be a Sunday. Lancaster and his wife strongly suggested that the family attend church, despite the seeming importance of the battle. The three boys of the family, however, disagreed. They could attend church anytime, they argued. They wanted to see the battle.

The debate continued for several minutes until Lancaster said he would put it to a vote. When he asked who would like to go to services, Lancaster, his wife, and their niece raised their hands. The next question was, who wanted to go out to see the battle? The three boys vigorously raised and waved their hands, perhaps hoping their enthusiasm would sway the vote.

The vote was a tie: three votes for attending services and three for going out with the ships and watching the fight. But one hand had not gone up for either. Catherine, the Lancasters' nine-year-old daughter, had not voted. Catherine knew what she wanted to do, but she feared offending her parents. Finally she timidly noted that she'd like to watch the battle.

Her brothers shrieked with joy. Catherine had broken the tie, and she had done it in their favor. The brothers each gave her a hug as their parents watched in amusement.

Stifling a smile, Lancaster said that the majority had spoken. They would forego attending church in favor of going out to see the fight.

The family retired that evening with visions of the next day's battle passing through their minds. Young Catherine Lancaster slept soundly, unaware that her vote had placed her family in a position to play a major role in the coming battle.

CHAPTER SEVENTEEN

THE BATTLE

Sunday, June 19, 1864, dawned brightly. Except for a slight haze, it promised to be a perfect day. An azure blue sky greeted the crews of both ships as they gathered on their respective decks. A gentle westerly breeze pushed up small whitecaps on the water, whitecaps which were too small to present any concern to a sailing vessel. On any ordinary day this would be viewed by mariners as the ideal day to be a sailor. But today was no ordinary day, not for the crews of the *Alabama* and the *Kearsarge*, at least. Today they would meet in battle. Today they would become a part of history. Today, some of their crew members would leave this earthly life for a better place, one where the seas were always calm and the winds forever favorable.

On board the *Alabama*, the crew members took their customary locations for the morning mess, eating quietly and nervously. The men were attired in fresh uniforms, except for the gun crews, many of whom had already stripped to the waist in anticipation of the heat on the gun deck. Few words were exchanged as each man retreated into the recesses of his mind. Thoughts of home, of the coming battle, of what might be the outcome occupied the thoughts of every member of the crew, from the highest officers to the lowliest powder monkeys. Many were too nervous to eat, yet they forced themselves. A prolonged battle would afford them little opportunity for another meal.

As the men of the *Alabama* ate in silence, a small boat approached, from which a smartly dressed French naval officer signaled that he wished to come aboard. Once on deck, he was greeted by Kell. Semmes had not yet come up from his cabin.

His demeanor stern, he saluted Kell, who returned the gesture. The French officer then proceeded to inform Kell that the ironclad frigate *La Couronne* had been assigned to accompany the *Alabama* to the marine league where she would anchor. Her instructions were to take whatever measures were necessary to ensure that French waters were not violated during the fight.

Kell was uncharacteristically subdued, and he barely replied. The French officer ignored Kell's terseness. This was, after all, a man who was going into battle. He could not be expected to be engaged in small talk. The officer wished Kell and his crew good luck, saying that the people of France were praying for the safety of the *Alabama*.

Kell voiced his appreciation as the French officer saluted once more. Kell returned the salute, and the officer turned sharply and strode for the rail. As he disappeared over the side, the crew members returned to their breakfast, seemingly unconcerned by what the *La Couronne* might do if the *Alabama* should happen to carry the fight back into French waters. Their battle would not be with the French frigate; it would be with the *Kearsarge*. They did not intend to run for the French coast, nor would they allow the *Kearsarge* to do it.

On shore, the crowds were already assembling, as if for a picnic. Blankets were spread and picnic baskets opened as the spectators enjoyed a breakfast in the French countryside. Occasionally, someone could be seen pointing to the *Alabama*, but for the most part it could have been any Sunday morning crowd enjoying a day along the coast. The air was festive, and the throng grew rapidly as the morning trains arrived from Paris. The hotels and rooming houses had been filled for days, and many had been forced to sleep in barns or in the open, under the summer skies. Faces peered from windows, and the crew of the *Alabama* could see spectators sitting on rooftops or climbing trees to gain a better vantage point.[1]

Suddenly, Semmes appeared on deck, resplendent in a crisp, new gray uniform. Gold epaulettes adorned his shoulders, and the sun glistened on three rows of gleaming brass buttons. His mustache had been perfectly waxed by Bartelli, coming to two symmetrical points. As he walked, his sword swung jauntily at his side. He saluted the deck officer, who returned the salutation.

Placing his hands on his hips and looking up at the nearly cloudless sky, he said to Arthur Sinclair, without looking at him, "If the bright and beautiful day is shining for our benefit, we should be happy at the omen." Turning his gaze on Sinclair, he continued, "Mr. Sinclair, how do you think it will turn out today?"

Sinclair had not expected this particular question, and searched for an answer. He answered, slightly flustered, "I cannot answer the question, sir. But I can assure you the crew will do their full duty and follow you to the death!"

Semmes paused, then nodded almost imperceptibly. "Yes," he said softly, "I know they will."[2]

With breakfast ended, the men made last-minute preparations. Gear was stowed, boilers were fired, and each man went to his battle station. Decks were sanded to provide better traction, and tubs of water were placed at strategic locations in the event they would be needed to fight fires. Assignments were reviewed, and every man vowed to do his part to bring glory to their ship.

At 9:45 in the morning, the *Alabama* weighed anchor and steamed for the harbor's western entrance, her Confederate flag waving proudly. Spying the ship's movement, the crowd lining the shore cheered loudly, the men waving their hats as a gesture of bon voyage. Fathers hoisted small children to their shoulders so they could see over the heads of those in front. Miniature flags were waved. There was no doubting which ship the crowd favored.

The *La Couronne* followed in the wake of the Confederate warship, while the crew of the French line-of-battle ship *Napoleon* gave three resounding cheers as the *Alabama* passed. The *Napoleon*'s band struck up a French rendition of "Dixie." Three small pilot boats followed the *La Couronne*, carrying French harbor officials and naval officers who hoped to use their ranks to gain a better vantage point. As the *Alabama* churned to the harbor entrance, one of Cherbourg's churches offered a mass for the safety of Semmes and his crew.[3]

Almost unnoticed was a small yacht, bearing the English ensign and the pennant of the Royal Yacht Squadron, which fell into the rear of the procession. John Lancaster and his family were on the verge of becoming a part of history.

* * *

At the harbor entrance the *Kearsarge* cruised slowly and methodically from one end to the other. Although Winslow planned to conduct the fight some six or seven miles off the coast, he had no intentions of allowing the *Alabama* any extra space through which to escape, nor did he wish to provide any opportunity for a surprise attack by his Confederate counterpart.

The crew of the *Kearsarge* had prepared for the fight by dressing in their blue mustering clothes. They had holystoned the deck until it glistened in the morning sun, and they now prepared for Sunday morning services. As the bell tolled to signal the crew to service, Winslow stood before the assemblage as was his custom on every Sunday morning. He had just opened his Bible and was preparing to read the scripture when the cry came down from the lookout: "The *Alabama*'s coming out!"

As the drummer beat the crew to quarters, the men scurried in all directions, each to his assigned station. Acting Master's Mate Ezra Bartlett was one of the first to his station. In charge of the shell supply, he had ordered grape and canister stored on deck in the event that close quarter fighting became necessary. He would not have the battle lost for his inefficiency.[4] It was now 10:20 A.M. Gunners cast loose their guns and prepared for the first volley. The battle was about to begin!

On shore the crowd gaped incredulously as the *Kearsarge* veered from her back-and-forth course and headed for the open sea. Several guffawed and shouted that the Yankee ship was running away already! But the *Kearsarge* was doing no such thing. Winslow's plan was to conduct the fight in open waters, keeping his promise to French officials that it would take place at least seven miles off shore. He hoped that this would also make it more difficult for the *Alabama* to reach territorial waters if Semmes chose to make a run.

As the *Kearsarge* steamed away from the coast, Winslow was sure that his crew was ready, but perhaps no more ready than those who had been excused for illness or injury. To a man, they left their sick beds and stood at their quarters. They would fight that day as well as their illnesses and injuries allowed.[5]

The two ships were evenly matched in fire power. The *Kearsarge* carried into the fray four 32-pounders in her broadside, two 11-inch Dahlgrens pivoted on the deck, one 28-pounder rifled gun pivoted on the top-gallant forecastle, and a 12-pounder howitzer. For her part, the *Alabama* countered with six 32-pounder guns in her broadside, one 8-inch smoothbore of 112 cwt, and one 7-inch 100-pounder rifled gun (Blakely pattern) on pivots. It was this last weapon that dictated Semmes's battle strategy more than any other.[6] Although Winslow's two 11-inch Dahlgrens gave the *Kearsarge* a close-range advantage, Semmes knew that he could inflict a great deal of damage with his Blakely long before the *Kearsarge* could get close enough to hurt him, and he intended to use that to his advantage.[7] For his part, however, Winslow intended to run the *Alabama* down if he could, or if that could not be achieved, " . . . to close in with her."[8]

With the coal taken on in Cherbourg, the *Alabama* now rode lower in the water. Semmes hoped this would make him a smaller target, although in fact, it actually created additional drag and resulted in a reduction in speed and maneuverability. This was in addition to the drag already created by the copper bottom which, in its deteriorated condition, had curled up in rolls at the bends. To compound Semmes's problems even further, the *Alabama*'s boilers had become so corroded by salt deposits that only a moderate head of steam could be attained.[9]

As the *Alabama* steamed out to meet her foe, a 32-pounder was shifted to the fighting side to give additional fire power. This created a starboard list of nearly two feet, further compromising the *Alabama*'s speed and maneuverability.[10]

At the three-mile limit the *La Couronne* stopped and anchored. The *Deerhound* and the pilot boats halted nearby, leaving the *Alabama* to continue on alone.

Semmes took a position on the horseblock abreast the mizzenmast, from where he would direct the battle. As the *La Couronne* and the smaller boats dropped back, Semmes ordered the boatswain to pipe all men aft. When all had assembled he looked across the faces gathered before him and calmly addressed them.

"Officers and Seamen of the *Alabama!*" he began. "You have, at length, another opportunity of meeting the enemy—the first that has been presented to you since you sank the *Hatteras*! In the meantime, you have been all over the world, and it is not too much to say, that you have destroyed, and driven for protection under neutral flags, one half of the enemy's commerce, which, at the beginning of the war, covered every sea. This is an achievement of which you may well be proud; and a grateful country will not be unmindful of it. The name of your ship has become a household word wherever civilization extends. Shall that name be tarnished by defeat? The thing is impossible!"

Shouts of "Never! Never!" rose from the crew.

Semmes paused and peered at the upturned faces of the men gathered in front of him. He continued, "Remember that you are in the English Channel, the theater of so much of the naval glory of our race, and that the eyes of all Europe are at this moment, upon you. The flag that floats over you is that of a young Republic, who bids defiance to her enemies, whenever, and wherever found. Show the world that you know how to uphold it! Go to your quarters!"[11] Enthusiastically, the crew members raced to their stations. Once there, Kell instructed his gunners to lie down on the deck and rest.[12]

At about 11:00 A.M.,* about 45 minutes after the *Alabama* passed through the breakwater, the ships were approximately seven miles northeast of Cherbourg. Suddenly and without warning, the *Kearsarge* turned and headed directly for the *Alabama*, apparently attempting to make good on Winslow's plan to ram her. Failing that, Winslow's backup plan was to pass on her stern and rake her.

At 1,200 yards Semmes coolly checked his watch and turned to Kell. "Are you ready, Mr. Kell?"

"Aye, aye, sir," Kell responded. "Ready and willing!"

Semmes then ordered, "Then, you may open fire at once!"[13]

---

* Time estimates vary from 10:57 to 11:10, depending on the account.

Kell gave the signal to Armstrong, in charge of the 100-pounder Blakely, who in turn gave the signal to the big gun's crew to open fire. With a roar the Blakely came to life. Seeing the puff of smoke belch from her muzzle, the crowd on shore let out a cheer. The action had finally begun.

As the crew watched, they saw their opening shot fall short, sending a spray of seawater high into the air. Wilson then gave the signal for his 32-pounders to join in, and a deafening starboard volley resulted, shaking the entire ship with its violent recoil. The shots were all high, passing over the forecastle and under the foreyard, causing only minimal damage to the *Kearsarge's* rigging.

The *Alabama*'s gun crews frantically cleaned and sponged the barrels of their guns, quickly reloading and preparing to fire again. When ready, once more the signal was given and the 32-pounders responded with another deafening blast. The gun deck was now awash with smoke and the pungent smell of sulfur. The results were similar to the earlier volley. Still the *Kearsarge* had not responded.

Finally, at 900 yards, the order was given that the *Kearsarge's* crew had been waiting for: "All the divisions! Aim low for the waterline. Fire!" The 11-inch guns, now within their effective range, fired with a tongue of flame leaping from each muzzle. Their deadly missiles fell short, however, much as had the first volleys from the *Alabama*. On the Confederate ship, a cheer rang out.

The marines in charge of the 28-pounder rifled gun on the *Kearsarge's* topgallant forecastle fired next, and their aim was true. Their shell struck the *Alabama* near her port bow, striking a slide rack and sending out a shower of wood and splinters. An *Alabama* crewman screamed in pain as his leg was ripped open, but he was more fortunate than his gun mate, who fell dead, believed to have been struck by one of the *Alabama*'s own shot. The marines' first shot had also inflicted the first casualties of the battle. There would be more to come on both sides.

As the ships approached one another, each worked her starboard batteries. Another fierce volley from the *Kearsarge* caught the *Alabama* fully broadside. Winslow directed his helmsman to cross the *Alabama*'s stern. "Prepare for raking fire!" came the order to the gunners.

However, Semmes was no novice, and he quickly figured what Winslow had in mind. "Swing to port!" he screamed to the helmsman. "They're going to try to rake us!"

The *Kearsarge* responded to the *Alabama*'s move, but it was too late to carry out the deadly battle plan. The *Alabama* had successfully neutralized the *Kearsarge*'s attack, forcing the two vessels into a circular orbit around one another, their starboard sides facing. Before the battle would be over, the ships would have circled one another seven times as the current swept them westward, each circular path narrowing the distance between the two.

The barrage continued, enveloping the two adversaries in a cloud of smoke. Circling, they quickly came out of the dense atmosphere, only to enter another cloud with the next volley. On board the *Alabama*, Kell seemed to be everywhere, shouting out directions, providing encouragement, and checking with the engine room.[14]

Meanwhile, on board the *Kearsarge*, Thornton passed from gun to gun. He encouraged his gunners to make every shot count, reasoning that every shot that hit was better than 50 wasted.[15]

Both ships now lay down a continuous fire. The *Kearsarge*'s rigging was cut in several places, sending yardarms askew and threatening to drop them to the deck. One 32-pound shell fired from the *Alabama* fell short but skipped off the water and lodged under the forward 11-inch pivot gun without exploding. Another, a shell from the 100-pounder Blakely, passed directly through the *Kearsarge*'s smokestack, exploding as it exited but causing no injuries.[16] The chief engineer would later report that the shell ripped a three-foot diameter hole in the smoke pipe and carried away three chain guys. He also said the top of the engine room hatch was cut completely through and across, but no other damage was noted.[17]

The *Alabama* was now firing two shots for every one from the *Kearsarge*, but it appeared that the gunners on the *Kearsarge* were aiming better. An 11-inch shell burst through the *Alabama*'s gun port, immediately wiping out half of the gun's crew " . . . like a sponge from a blackboard," as Kell would later remember.[18] Body parts and gore spattered the remaining crew members, the shock of which rendered Third Lieutenant Joseph Wilson unable to continue with his command. Michael Mars looked at Kell and signaled for permission to clear the butchery

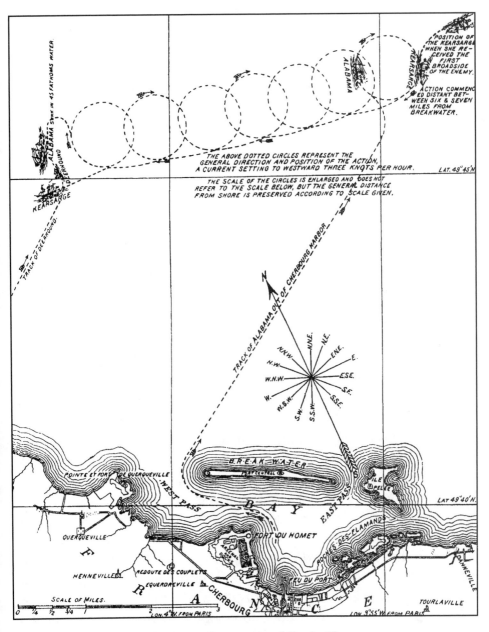

**Contemporary map of the battle
showing ship positions and movements**

Reprinted from *Official Records of the Union and Confederate Navies in the War of the Rebellion*,
Series I, Volume 3, with permission of the Department of the Navy, Naval Historical Center.

from the deck. Understanding Mars's signal, Kell nodded his assent, whereupon Mars grabbed a shovel and deftly scooped up the carnage, tossing it over the side and quickly, but calmly, resanding the deck.[19] The dazed Wilson, unable to grasp what he had just seen, was replaced by Midshipman E. Maffitt Anderson on Kell's order. Eight men from another gun crew quickly rushed in to take the places of their unfortunate shipmates.

Another shell killed one man and wounded a second. The *Kearsarge*'s fire was devastating. The *Alabama*'s decks were littered with wreckage and wounded men, her smokestack nearly full of holes. The spanker gaff, which carried the *Alabama*'s colors, was torn away, bringing the colors to the deck. Another flag was quickly hoisted at the head of the mizzenmast, even before the cheers of the Federal gunners had died down.

At about the same instant, the *Kearsarge* took a direct hit on her hull. Believing they had just destroyed the *Kearsarge*'s engine room, the gun crew on the *Alabama* gave a loud cheer, followed by curses and groans as they realized that the damage was minimal. Semmes, also watching in disbelief, shouted to Kell, "Mr. Kell, our shells strike the enemy's side, doing little or no damage, and fall into the water. Try solid shot."[20]

Kell complied, and shot and shell were then alternated as the *Alabama* tried desperately to find a lethal combination. One shell crashed through the *Kearsarge*'s hull below the main chains, wounding three men. One of those who was badly wounded was Ordinary Seaman William Gowin. Unable to walk, he dragged himself to the forward hatch, refusing all efforts to help and shouting to those who offered to come to his assistance that they should stay with their guns. His face contorted in agony as he struggled to get to safety. Despite the bones protruding through his trouser leg, he did just that.[21] Casting sidelong glances at the crawling Gowin as they continued to work their guns, the crew gained inspiration from the courage he was showing. Reaching the surgeon, he gasped, "I can fight no more, so I come to you. But it is all right; I am satisfied, for we are whipping the *Alabama*. I will willingly lose my leg or my life if it is necessary." On the gun deck, a cheer arose with every telling shot into the *Alabama*. With each cheer, Gowin feebly raised his arm and did his best to join in. His friends had no way of knowing that he would succumb to the effects of his wounds just nine days later, becoming the only fatality on the *Kearsarge* in her fight against the *Alabama*.[22]

The same shot also badly wounded Quarter Gunner John Dempsey. The surgeon's report would later indicate that the Irishman had suffered a compound comminuted fracture of the right arm and, although he would eventually lose the limb as a result, he continued to fight as best he could with his remaining good arm, his injured arm dangling helplessly by his side. Ordinary Seaman James McBeth also fought valiantly despite being badly wounded with a compound fracture of his own, just below the knee.[23]

Shortly after the shot which badly wounded Gowin, Dempsey, and McBeth, a shot from the Blakely severed the chains and imbedded itself in the side of the *Kearsarge*. This was quickly followed by another shell which passed through the roof of the engine house, narrowly missing the engineer.[24]

Fifteen minutes into the battle, Armstrong's Blakely lodged a 100-pound shell in the *Kearsarge*'s sternpost, near the rudder. The entire ship shuddered at the impact. Semmes watched through his telescope, waiting for the explosion which would rip out the stern of his opponent, but the explosion never came.[25] Another Blakely shell did explode on the *Kearsarge*'s quarterdeck, near the aft 11-inch Dahlgren, and two more shots passed through gun ports. However, they inflicted no discernible harm. Still another 32-pounder made a direct hit near the forward 11-inch gun, but just as with the shell which had lodged in the *Kearsarge*'s sternpost, that one also failed to explode.[26] Despite the occasional successes, for the most part the *Alabama*'s gunners were firing wildly, and their shots were causing little damage.

It was also apparent to observers that the *Alabama*'s powder had deteriorated. Back on the pilot boats, a French officer nudged the man next to him and pointed. "The powder smoke from the *Kearsarge* is white," he observed, "but the *Alabama*'s is dark." His companion nodded assent, both recognizing the telltale appearance of a poorer grade of powder. On the *Deerhound*, a similar observation was made.[27]

Small fires broke out on the *Kearsarge* but were quickly doused. The rifled gun on the forecastle of the *Kearsarge* fired faster than any of the others, but about 30 minutes into the battle a potentially disastrous situation developed. One of its shells stuck about halfway home and could not be rammed in any further. If fired, the gun would probably burst, but somehow the crew managed to free the jammed shell and the gun continued to operate.[28]

On the *Alabama*, several of the guns had slowed their firing. In the excitement of the battle, with adrenalin pumping through every man at full capacity, some of the gunners had fired their guns before the ramrods were removed. Now the gunners waited helplessly until new ones could be brought from the hold.[29]

On deck, Semmes had been struck in the hand by a shell fragment. He called to one of his nearby quartermasters, who quickly bound the wound and fashioned a makeshift sling for his captain.[30]

As the ships had continued to circle one another, they had closed to within 500 yards, well within the range of the *Kearsarge*'s 11-inch Dahlgren. Deadly accurate now, their eyes burning and the smoke making it all but impossible to breathe, the Federal gunners somehow found the will to step up their pace. The roar of the guns was deafening and the crews all gasped for their next breath, yet Thornton would later report that they acted almost as if they were on an exercise.[31]

Sensing victory, Winslow continued shouting his orders. "Eleven-inchers fire at her waterline. You 32-pounders, sweep her decks." The gunners responded as directed.

The *Alabama* was now suffering badly from the effects of the fight. Her fires were going out, her ensign had been shot away, and major rudder and propeller damage were making it difficult to control her direction. Now, the unthinkable was happening. As Semmes watched helplessly, he could see seawater splashing over the gunwales. He hoped to get yardarm to yardarm, where his men could swarm over the *Kearsarge* and fight hand to hand. But even as he prepared for his next move, it was apparent that his plan would not be possible to carry out.

His only opportunity now appeared to be to run for the three-mile limit. The *Kearsarge* would surely not dare to fire on him in French waters. On the seventh circle around the *Kearsarge* Semmes, wincing in pain from his wound, summoned Kell. "Mr. Kell," he shouted, "as soon as our head points to the French coast, shift your guns to port and make all sail for the coast."

Kell nodded his understanding. At the appropriate time, he yelled to John Roberts to loose the jib. Roberts hastened to carry out his orders. Returning to his station he was struck by a shell. Screaming in agony, he died even as he stumbled toward his gun.

Miles Freeman ran to Semmes, shouting that he could no longer work his engines. The fires were flooding out. Hearing this, Kell raced to the hatch and shouted down to the engine crew to give more steam. Matthew O'Brien heard the demand and responded, "Aye, sir. We'll give her the steam. We'll blow her up before we let the Yankees have her!"[32]

As the *Alabama* sluggishly plodded in the general direction of the coast, Winslow quickly moved to cut her off. Despite the *Kearsarge*'s own damage to her sternpost, she was able to get between the Confederate vessel and the coast.

Seeing his retreat cut off, Semmes ordered his first lieutenant to go below and see how long the ship could stay afloat. Kell ran below, encountering Surgeon David Llewellyn working frantically over a badly wounded man. Before Kell could speak, a shell from the *Kearsarge*'s 11-inch Dahlgren blasted through, carrying with it the operating table and the hapless crew member lying on it, leaving only the dazed Llewellyn. Kell and the surgeon gaped incredulously at the damage, then at each other, before Kell raced back up to the deck to report that they would be able to stay afloat for perhaps another 10 minutes.

Semmes looked at the tattered flag he had served so well. He knew what had to be done, but he could not bring himself to give the order. Finally, he said, barely loud enough to rise above the battle noise, "Then, sir, cease firing, shorten the sail, and haul down the colors. It will never do in this nineteenth century for us to go down and our decks covered with our gallant wounded."[33]

Kell passed the order and a quartermaster reached for the halyard. He just as quickly pulled back when several men shouted that they would never surrender. One of them drew his cutlass, threatening to kill the first man who dared try to bring down the colors. Kell pulled his pistol and shouted that it must be done. Realizing that Kell was right, two crew members reluctantly reached for the halyard.

As the colors came down, several more shots emanated from the *Kearsarge*. As the men turned in the direction of their foe and cursed, Kell shouted at them, "Don't flinch, men. Stand to your quarters!"

Turning to Captain's Coxswain George Freemantle, he sadly ordered that a white flag be flown from the stern. Two crew members grabbed what little remained of the white Confederate ensign and held it at the stern of the ship. A leeward shot was fired as a sign of surrender. An answering boom thundered from the *Kearsarge* in acknowledgment. It had only been about an hour since the opening volley had been fired.

On the deck of the *Kearsarge*, Winslow gave the order to cease fire. As the Federal gunners milled about their guns congratulating one another, two more shots rang out from the deck of the *Alabama* as two rebel gunners, either not hearing the surrender order or choosing to ignore it, fired at their conqueror.

"Give it to them again, boys!" Winslow screamed. "They're playing us a trick!"[34]

Immediately the gunners fired a broadside, inflicting still further damage on the crippled Confederate vessel, as the rebels frantically waved the surrender flag from the stern. By now the *Alabama*'s bow was slowly rising, making it difficult to stand upright on the deck without grasping some solid object. An eerie silence now descended over both ships. Semmes, in a dejected voice, ordered Kell to dispatch an officer to the *Kearsarge* and ask that they send boats to save the wounded. The *Alabama*'s boats had been disabled.

Kell immediately ordered a dinghy, which somehow had escaped the bombardment with only minor damage, to the *Kearsarge* to ask for help. Fullam jumped into the boat as several seamen grabbed the oars. As the boat wended its way through the *Alabama*'s flotsam toward the now silent Union warship, several crew members from the *Alabama* jumped overboard as the water splashed over her stern.

Reaching the *Kearsarge*, Fullam observed that she was in a perfect position to rake the *Alabama* if the battle resumed. From the deck above, Winslow watched as Fullam dropped his sword overboard in a ceremonial sign of surrender. Winslow was still wary, recalling the stories he had heard about the manner in which the *Alabama* had lured the *Hatteras* to her doom.

Fullam was assisted on board by two Federal crew members, where-upon he immediately told Winslow that the *Alabama* had surrendered and was now sinking. He asked that the *Kearsarge* send boats to assist the rebel ship's wounded.

Winslow only had two boats that were in any condition to be used, but he willingly agreed to send them. He gave the order to launch the boats on their mission of mercy, as Fullam looked up and down the deck.

"Where are your dead and wounded, sir?" he queried.

Winslow followed Fullam's gaze. "We've only had three men wounded," he replied, "and they are below."

"Three wounded?" Fullam exclaimed in amazement. "My God, it's a slaughterhouse over there!"[35]

The shaken Fullam then asked permission to return to his ship so that he might assist with rescue efforts. Winslow agreed.

Making his way back to the foundering ship which just an hour be-fore had been the pride of the Confederate navy, Fullam heard her shud-der and creak. As he watched helplessly, the *Alabama*'s main mast snapped, and her stern began to slowly settle under the waves.

CHAPTER EIGHTEEN

THE RESCUE

Aboard the *Alabama* the situation was becoming grim. Fullam had not yet returned from the *Kearsarge* and no rescue boats appeared. His crew quickly surrounded Semmes as the *Alabama* shuddered and listed once more. It was apparent that it would be only a matter of time before Semmes would have to give the order to abandon ship. It was an order he dreaded giving, and so he refrained from giving it as long as he could.

Michael Mars asked desperately if there was anything he could do. Remembering his diary and papers, Semmes asked him to go to the captain's cabin and fetch the ship's papers and Semmes's journal. He must save them, if nothing else.

Mars turned and sprinted for the cabin without another word. Meeting Bartelli along the way, the two of them waded through waist deep water to get to the captain's cabin. Bartelli knew where the papers were kept, and in only a few minutes the papers were on their way back up to the quarterdeck, where Mars handed them to Semmes.

Taking the two packages of papers, Semmes examined them briefly, then handed one of the packages back to Mars, the other to Captain's Coxswain George Freemantle. Mars loyally assured Semmes that he would protect the papers with his life. Semmes mumbled his thanks, now having a difficult time talking in the face of the imminent demise of the ship he had come to love.

Spying Bartelli, Semmes asked his servant if he had been injured. Bartelli assured him that he was fine, but the captain's cabin had been destroyed. Even his painting of the *Alabama* was gone. Semmes could only nod, placing his hand on Bartelli's shoulder.

By now the water on the deck was ankle deep. Semmes whispered something in Kell's ear, whereupon Kell nodded and gave the order all had dreaded: "All hands overboard! Save yourselves! Grab an oar or a spar or a grate to hang on to."

The men scrambled for the rail. Already, several were in the water. Before more could join them, Kell boomed out in an afterthought, "And stay out of the vortex!" to warn all to get away from the ship so the suction created when she went under would not pull anyone with her.

Two crew members helped Semmes take off his boots and coat. Semmes unbuckled his sword and looked at it with affection. No Yankee hands had ever held it, nor would they. Holding it high above his head, he tossed it into the churning waters. Gideon Welles would later complain that the sword belonged to the United States government and Semmes had no right to throw it away.[1]

Kell stood beside Semmes, who was wearing a life preserver. The two looked at one another, then entered the water together. The water was extremely cold for mid-summer, and it seemed alive as men frantically swam all around them in an effort to get away from the ship before she went down.

Looking back toward the *Alabama* Semmes observed Bartelli and David White, the young slave boy who had shipped on from the *Tonawanda*, both standing at the rail and looking apprehensively over the side. Unknown to Semmes, neither knew how to swim.

Rescue boats were now in the water, and the men of the *Alabama* desperately tried to stay afloat long enough for the boats to reach them. While Semmes watched, the *Alabama*'s bow rose high into the air, wreckage sliding down the deck and off the stern. Then, her funnel fell away, followed by the snapping of a mast, sending out a crack as loud as any rifle shot. Finally, less than 90 minutes after the first volley had been fired, the mighty *Alabama* slipped beneath the waves. With her went

Bartelli, White, and several others who had been unable or unwilling to get off in time.

Moments after the ship disappeared, Kell shouted to the survivors to stay as close together as possible. He knew the men would be weakening in the icy water. Even as he spoke, a body drifted by, still clinging to a makeshift raft of shell boxes. It was Assistant Surgeon David Llewellyn.

Looking back to where the *Alabama* had been just moments before, Kell recalled sadly that, except for a grand total of 22 hours, he had spent the entire two years of the cruise on her decks.[2]

Semmes looked around at his men, now struggling to stay afloat. Michael Mars, true to his word, was taking care of the captain's diary as best he could. Swimming with one hand, the other was extended high over his head, still grasping the journal.[3]

Young Eugene Maffitt, a nonswimmer himself, tried to convince the rapidly tiring Kell to take his life preserver. Kell, knowing that to do so was to condemn the midshipman to a certain death, refused. Despite Kell's refusal, Maffitt tried to push it toward the lieutenant, who pushed it back and insisted that Maffitt keep it.[4]

As he fought to keep his head above water, Kell could not help but think of the *Hatteras* and how every man had been saved. Now, he angrily thought that he was going to die because the *Kearsarge* was making no effort to rescue the men of the *Alabama*. He was wrong, however. Unknown to Kell, only two boats from the *Kearsarge* were usable, the others having been damaged in the battle. Those two boats were in the water now, rowing toward the flailing men of the *Alabama*.

The *Deerhound*, which had slowly worked her way out to get a better view of the battle, was now within hailing distance of the *Kearsarge*. Pointing toward the crew of the *Alabama*, Winslow shouted, "For God's sake, do what you can to save them!"[5] The *Deerhound* turned and steamed to assist, reaching the first man within minutes. The *Deerhound's* crew lowered boats into the water and began picking up survivors.

In one of the rescue boats the *Deerhound's* chief steward, William Roberts, shouted that he had spotted Semmes. Semmes, who was about to go under, shouted back that he feared he would not be able to keep up any longer. A crew member grabbed Semmes's outstretched hand and dragged him aboard. Semmes, every ounce of energy expended, lay on the bottom of the boat and begged his rescuers not to put him on board the *Kearsarge*. He pleaded with them to take him to the yacht. Someone quickly covered Semmes with a sail to hide him from unfriendly eyes, as others pulled Kell over the side.[6]

As the rescue effort progressed, French pilot boats arrived to assist. No other vessels were close enough to be of any help. One of the first to be rescued by a pilot boat was the *Alabama*'s second lieutenant, Richard Armstrong. Armstrong would report that one of the *Kearsarge*'s boats had ignored him and left him to drown, choosing instead to focus the search for a particular person, probably Semmes.[7] In quick succession William Brooks, Henry Allcott, Charles Godwin, James Welsh, George Egerton, Thomas Murphy, William Robinson, Maurice Bright, and Michael Mars were pulled into the pilot boat.

Although Arthur Sinclair would claim that the *Kearsarge* had failed to help, Mars later refuted Sinclair's statement, saying he had been quickly rescued by the *Kearsarge*'s cutter, but had jumped overboard when he had the chance, swimming to the French pilot boat before the Federals could react.[8] He still retained Semmes's papers.

Those rescued by the boats from the *Kearsarge* were returned to the Union ship. Winslow, who had chosen not to wear a good uniform during the fight, stood at the rail to greet them. As the weary survivors struggled aboard, one of them spotted Winslow and asked if he was the steward of the ship. Winslow answered politely that he was actually the captain. Instantly the rescued crewman apologized, stammering that he had meant no disrespect, and that he had only wanted to ask for some whiskey because he was feeling faint from spending so much time in the cold water. Winslow immediately directed one of the boys to fetch some whiskey. He then turned back to the exhausted man from the *Alabama* and said, "My man, I am sorry for you." Pointing to the United States flag that fluttered above, he continued, "That is the flag you should have fought under."[9]

Watching from a perch high on the topgallant forecastle was George Whipple, holding a Sharps rifle. He peered intently as each man climbed over the rail. He was looking for one man in particular, checking his rifle to make sure it was loaded. As he did so he was hailed from below.

Whipple did not answer, perhaps recalling the time Semmes had ordered him strung from the rigging by his thumbs when the two had been on the *Sumter*. Semmes would never come aboard this ship alive, Whipple thought, and if he didn't appear today, there would be another time.[10]

As he waited for Semmes, Whipple was shocked to see a familiar figure brought aboard. It was Carpenter William Robinson, two brawny crewmen handing his body up. Whipple and Robinson had been friends on the *Sumter*, and the usually gruff Whipple found himself brought to tears as his old friend was placed gently on the deck. Surgeon Browne examined the body carefully, and finding no bullet wounds pronounced him a drowning victim.[11]

Third Lieutenant Joseph Wilson spied Lieutenant Commander James Thornton of the *Kearsarge*. Wilson offered his sword to Thornton in a conciliatory gesture. Just as quickly, Thornton refused to accept it, saying, "I always appreciate a gentleman, no matter what circumstances we meet under."[12]

Some of the rescued crewmen apprehensively looked up to the main yardarm as they came aboard. They later informed their captors that Semmes had told them they would be hanged as pirates if taken captive. They were greatly relieved to hear that they were to be treated as prisoners of war.[13]

Back on the *Deerhound* an exhausted Semmes was taken to the yacht's cabin, bleeding badly. Hot coffee and rum were passed out to him and his men. In due course Kell came to check on his captain. Kell asked, in a concerned tone, whether he had been injured. An affirmative answer came in a voice so weak that Kell hardly recognized it.

John Lancaster sidled up to Semmes and told him that every man had been picked up. He asked Semmes where he would like to be taken. Semmes looked at his benefactor and said, "I am now under English colors and the sooner you put me, with my officers and men, on English soil the better!"[14]

Lancaster nodded and gave the order to Evan Jones. Within minutes the *Deerhound* gradually edged leeward, still giving the appearance that she was seeking survivors. Slowly she made her way outside the search area, then fired her boilers and made for the English coast.

On the *Kearsarge* a disbelieving Winslow watched as the *Deerhound* moved off toward the horizon. Several officers pointed and shouted that the *Deerhound* was running. The crew of the 32-pounder aimed at the *Deerhound*, waiting for the order to fire. That word never came. Winslow still believed that the yacht would either bring the prisoners to him or surrender them when they got ashore. This time the venerable captain had guessed wrong, however, and he would not see the *Deerhound* or her prisoners again.

As the *Deerhound* disappeared into the distance, Winslow turned his attention to the shivering survivors. Speaking to his crew, he said, "We have won the battle without loss of life, and God must have been on our side. The *Alabama*'s men have been in the water and you are requested to give them some of your clothing. Report any expense to me. These men have surrendered and I want you to use them as brother shipmates. Your dinner will soon be served to you. Share it with them!"[15]

Winslow then went to his cabin, leaving his frustrated officers and crew to grumble about how they could have also sunk the *Deerhound* had they just been given the word. Their moods were slightly assuaged when the grog tub appeared, and with the splicing of the main brace they turned their conversation to the excitement of the battle.

By 3:00 P.M. the *Kearsarge* was back in Cherbourg, arriving to a huge crowd.[16] After anchoring near the French frigate *Napoleon*, Winslow sent Second Assistant Engineer William Badlam ashore to gain permission to allow the wounded to be landed. Badlam was met by the younger William Dayton, and the two sought out Admiral Augustin Dupouy.

Dupouy said that he would allow the injured to come ashore, but the moment they touched French soil they would no longer be considered prisoners by the French government. Badlam and Dayton said they would have to discuss the terms with Captain Winslow, and they returned to the ship. There, Winslow agreed to Dupouy's terms, and the wounded from both ships were soon on their way to the Marine Hospital. As the wounded were escorted ashore, Winslow turned his attention to filing his initial report, which would go to Gideon Welles.[17]

When his report was finished, Winslow had to decide what to do with the uninjured prisoners, and he sent a telegram to the elder Dayton in Paris, asking for guidance. Dayton wired back that he should retain all the prisoners until the *St. Louis* arrived, at which time they could be conveyed to the United States. This was not what Winslow wanted to hear. His ship was too crowded with so many extra men, and he preferred to release them. After considerable thought, he decided he would do just that. All prisoners except the four officers were released. Those officers, Third Lieutenant Joseph Wilson, Acting Chief Engineer Miles Freeman, Third Assistant Engineer John Pundt, and Boatswain Benjamin McCaskey, were permitted to go ashore with the understanding that they would return when Winslow wanted them.

Welles did not take the news of the prisoners' release well. Winslow quickly sent him a list of reasons why it had not been practical to retain the prisoners. Winslow stated that the berth deck was of insufficient size even when it held only the men of the *Kearsarge*, and was even more crowded now that it was covered with the bedding of the wounded. He said the quarterdeck was also crowded, and that the spar deck was filled with prisoners who required guarding. Guards could not be spared, he said, because other Confederate ships were believed to be in the area and he needed all hands to return the ship to a state of readiness. He also noted that not only were his rigging and hull damaged in the battle, but also that the shot which had lodged in his sternpost had raised the transom frame and bound the rudder so badly that it took four men at the helm to steer the ship.[18]

Whether Winslow's arguments changed Welles's mind or whether it was because Welles eventually realized that Winslow had just removed the navy's biggest nemesis, the incident was soon forgotten. Besides, there would be other, far greater, controversies on which to focus.

With the *Kearsarge* safely anchored and her gangplank down, the inevitable swarm of visitors arrived. Each wanted to discuss the battle, with most stating they knew all along that the *Kearsarge* was the better ship. Many of those saying this, however, had lost money betting on the *Alabama*.[19]

Among the visitors were the officers and crew of the *Rockingham*, who were pleased that the *Kearsarge* had avenged their capture. These men also told the officers of the *Kearsarge* that the *Deerhound* had, in fact, been a tender for the *Alabama*. They said they were positive that the yacht had brought experienced English gunners with her who had volunteered to serve on the *Alabama*. They even went so far as to identify the ship they had served on previously, the HMS *Excellent*.[20]

The officers of the *Kearsarge* listened courteously, then discounted the stories after the men of the *Rockingham* had departed. Once given liberty, however, they heard similar stories from other sources, sources they considered more reliable than the crew of the *Rockingham*. Having heard it from several sources, they chose to believe that the *Deerhound* was indeed a tender to the *Alabama,* rather than the innocent family yacht it was purported to be. How else could anyone explain why she had run after picking up the survivors? Winslow got the confirmation he needed several days after the battle, when, in his words, the prisoners verified that boats had shuttled back and forth between the *Alabama* and the *Deerhound* the night before the battle. The prisoners also stated that the next morning the *Alabama*'s crew noticed a number of strangers who had been made captains of the guns.[21]

For three days the *Kearsarge* remained in Cherbourg, patching her battle scars using her own crew. Except for one patch on the smokestack, which was made by a local boilermaker, the *Kearsarge*'s carpenters carried out all the needed repairs.[22]

Meanwhile, the *Deerhound* steamed for Southampton, where the men of the *Alabama* were treated as heroes. Semmes and Kell were given rooms in Robert Kelway's hotel, Kelway proudly informing them that the last guest in their room had been a prince.[23] Kelway also told them that he would accept no payment.

The crewmen, meanwhile, were treated with only slightly less reverence. The wounded were gently carried to the Sailors' Home for treatment, while local families took in many of the uninjured. Those who stayed in hotels and boardinghouses found that they were not expected to pay for their rooms.

Two great ships, two gallant crews, and two dogged commanders intent on seeing to it that only one would survive: the ingredients for a classic battle which would be talked about as long as ships go to sea. The *Alabama* was no more; the *Kearsarge* would sail again. Both, however, would be remembered not just for what took place on a day in June 1864 but for two distinctive and memorable cruises that would be held up as the standards for years to come.

The officers of the *Kearsarge*

Courtesy of Library of Congress Prints and Photographs Division,
Detroit Publishing Co. Photograph Collection, #LC-D4-20471

Plate rescued from wreck of *Kearsarge,* engraved with date of battle

Courtesy of Preble Museum, United States Naval Academy

**Captioned "The U.S. Ship of War 'Kearsarge' 7 Guns
Sinking the Pirate 'Alabama' 8 Guns"**

Courtesy of William Stanley Hoole Special Collections Library, University of Alabama

**Lithograph of the battle by A. Hoen & Co., Baltimore,
Allen C. Redwood, Publisher**

Courtesy of William Stanley Hoole Special Collections Library, University of Alabama

Confederate naval buttons worn by Raphael Semmes

Courtesy of Preble Museum, United States Naval Academy

A piece of an oar from an *Alabama* lifeboat

Courtesy of Preble Museum, United States Naval Academy

**The English yacht *Deerhound*, rescuer of many
Alabama crew members, including Semmes**

Courtesy of William Stanley Hoole Special Collections Library, University of Alabama

**The burning of the *Brilliant*, with the *Alabama* in foreground. The
caption on this print reads: "The pirate 'Alabama', alias '290', certified
to be correct by Captain Hagar of the 'Brilliant'." This appeared in
Harpers Weekly, November 1, 1862.**

Courtesy of William Stanley Hoole Special Collections Library, University of Alabama

Semmes with his officers from the *Sumter*, many of
whom also served under him on the *Alabama*.
Semmes is seated in the center of the first row.

Courtesy of Naval History Division, Office of Chief of Naval Operations

Winslow and his officers following the battle with
the *Alabama*. Winslow is third from the left.

Courtesy of National Archives and Records Administration

Engine room gong from the *Kearsarge*

Courtesy of Preble Museum, United States Naval Academy

Engine register from the *Kearsarge*

Courtesy of Preble Museum, United States Naval Academy

Captioned "The gun that sank the *Alabama*"

Courtesy of Library of Congress Prints and Photographs Division,
Detroit Publishing Co. Photograph Collection, #LC-D4-20470

Kearsarge ship's company

Courtesy of Library of Congress Prints and Photographs Division,
Detroit Publishing Co. Photograph Collection, #LC-D4-20472

Unexploded shell in sternpost of the
***Kearsarge*, behind a model of the ship**

Courtesy of Massachusetts Commandery Military Order of the Loyal Legion
and the US Army Military History Institute

EPILOGUE

The battle was over. The *Alabama* lay in 45 fathoms of water, a part of history, while the newspapers of the world picked at the carcass. "The Pirate Sunk off Cherbourg by the *Kearsarge*" trumpeted the *New York Times*. The accompanying article disputed all claims that the *Alabama* had voluntarily gone out to fight the *Kearsarge*, offering instead that Semmes had been ordered out of Cherbourg by the French minister prefect. Ignoring Semmes's true mission, the *Times* chortled that the *Alabama* had been sunk on her very first encounter with a naval vessel in battle, discounting the *Hatteras*, which the *Times* said had been lured into range by "falsehood."[1]

In another early account of the battle, the *London Star*, obviously now courting the favor of the United States, editorialized as follows: "The *Alabama* has at last met her well deserved fate. Her career of lawless destruction has ended in a short fight and an utter wreck. She has gone down under the guns of the first war-ship she has ventured to encounter. After preying for nearly two years upon unarmed merchantmen, and having performed nothing more worthy of her boasted prowess than the destruction of a gunboat lured by the display of false colors within range of her fire, she has fought her first and last battle."[2]

When the editors of the *New York Times* tired of flogging the *Alabama*, they turned their attention to England, focusing on the role of the *Deerhound* in the rescue of the rebel cruiser's crew. " . . . one thing which our naval officers will certainly not forget," they wrote, "is never again to trust the honor of a British sailor, present as a spectator. Some of that class might and probably would be honorable men, but the safest way will be never to trust them. Captain Winslow, when he found the *Deerhound* making off with his prisoners, ought to have ordered her back by a shot across her bows, and if that had not proved effectual he should have given her another amidships."[3]

A month after the battle, the *Manchester* (England) *Examiner* called for a reconciliation of sorts, saying, "Thus ends the career of one of the most notorious ships of modern times. Costly as has been her career to Federal commerce, she has been hardly less costly to this country. She has sown a legacy of distrust and of future apprehension on both sides of the Atlantic, and happy will it be both for England and America if with her, beneath the waters of the Channel, may be buried the memory of her career and of the mischief she has done."[4]

Despite the appearance of such joy on the part of the media, the *Alabama* had done her job. Semmes had fulfilled his mission. It would be decades before Union shipping recovered from the reign of terror inflicted by the *Alabama*. While the media chose to ignore that, there was no denying that the world's oceans had become safer with the demise of the rebel cruiser. Seven months after the battle, Jefferson Davis would say in a letter to Samuel J. Person, "The *Alabama* and the *Florida* alone sufficed to destroy or drive from the ocean three-fourths of the merchant marine of the enemy engaged in foreign commerce . . ."[5]

The *Kearsarge*, whose guns had never been tried under battle conditions, had carried 18 officers and 145 crew members into the battle and had suffered only three wounded. Quartergunner John Dempsey soon lost his arm from his wound, and James McBeth would forever walk with a limp because of his leg wound.

William Gowin, the ordinary seaman who had been such an inspiration to his mates when he refused all help after being badly wounded, did not fare as well. For nine days he suffered, showing enough spirit that those around him believed that his recovery was of no question. The bleeding took its toll, however, coupled with his debilitation from previous bouts with malaria. Then, phlebitis delivered the knockout blow. Resigned to his fate, Gowin told his friends that he was willing to die and that he would die happy, knowing his ship had won a glorious victory. On June 27, 1864, Gowin died, the only fatality incurred by the *Kearsarge*. He was buried in Cherbourg, and his shipmates raised enough money to place a monument on his grave. Not long after, Americans living in Paris contributed donations to erect a similar monument to Gowin in his Michigan hometown.[6]

That the men of both vessels fought bravely there is no doubt. As in all battles, however, some stood above all others. Seventeen men of the *Kearsarge* were awarded the Medal of Honor for their actions on June 19, 1864. Among them was Joachim Pease, one of the first black men to receive the honor. Others were Michael Ahern (the Queenstown "stowaway"), John Bickford, William Bond, James Haley, Mark Ham, George Harrison, John Hayes, James H. Lee, Charles Moore, Thomas Perry, William Poole, Charles Read, George Read, James Saunders, William Smith, and Robert Strahan.

The magnitude of the *Kearsarge*'s victory was summed up in a simple note sent to Winslow's wife by Admiral David Farragut, who told her, "I would rather have fought that fight with the *Alabama* than all I have done in the war."[7]

It is uncertain how many men the *Alabama* carried into the fray, if Winslow's contention that British sailors bolstered her ranks is to be believed. Assuming none did, the muster roles indicate that she had 25 officers and a crew of 120, slightly fewer than that of the *Kearsarge*. Fullam's statement to Winslow that the decks of the *Alabama* were a slaughterhouse was not an exaggeration. Nine of her crew were killed or mortally wounded: James Mair, Peter Duncan, George Appleby, John Roberts, Karl Pajorva, James King II, Charles Olson, Christian Pust, and James Hart. Another 20 were wounded, and 19 others either drowned or were declared missing. Among the missing was the captured slave boy, David White. Semmes's faithful servant Bartelli was confirmed drowned.

Of those who survived, 64 were believed rescued and taken captive by the *Kearsarge*. Winslow's report to Gideon Welles noted that he took on 70 survivors, including six officers, but that number is not supported by the records, nor can the number of those he claimed were rescued by pilot boats.[8] Forty were rescued by the *Deerhound* and another 12 by the pilot boats, although Winslow thought the latter rescued nine. True to their word, Mars and Freemantle saved Semmes's papers and eventually returned them to their captain.

Acting Master David Sumner, whom Winslow had found it necessary to place in confinement for refusal to carry out an order while the *Kearsarge* was watching the *Rappahannock*, volunteered his services when it was apparent that the battle was imminent. Winslow accepted his offer and Sumner performed so well that Winslow sent off a special report to Welles recommending that any action that the department had begun against Sumner be annulled.[9]

While *Kearsarge* Surgeon John Browne was in the process of amputating John Dempsey's mangled arm after the battle, Acting Paymaster and Surgeon Francis Galt from the *Alabama* introduced himself to Browne and offered to assist. Browne, seeing that Galt was injured himself, as well as suffering from exposure and fatigue, instead suggested Galt go to Browne's room and rest. Galt went to Browne's room, but instead of resting, he attended to the injured.[10]

On July 7 Gideon Welles, only one day after sending a congratulatory memo to Winslow, sent another to the *Kearsarge*'s captain. This one, however, was less cordial, asking for a more detailed report and reminding Winslow that no muster roll for the *Kearsarge* had ever been forwarded to the department, either by Winslow or by his predecessor, Charles Pickering.[11] Those messages were followed by others on July 8 and July 12 in which Welles rebuked Winslow for paroling his prisoners.[12]

Of the four officers held on the *Kearsarge*, Joseph Wilson was exchanged late in 1864, while John Pundt, Miles Freeman, and Benjamin McCaskey were held as prisoners of war at Fort Warren in Boston Harbor for the remainder of the war.

The crew of the *Alabama* had been well drilled, but because there was no way to replenish ammunition, they had not fired live ammunition except for two occasions. The first was in the sinking of the *Hatteras*, the second near the end of the cruise when live rounds were fired at the *Rockingham*. While this saved ammunition, it no doubt contributed to the *Alabama*'s defeat, as the gun crews showed a marked ineptitude at judging distances in their fight with the *Kearsarge*. During the battle the *Alabama* fired an estimated 370 shot and shell, with only 12 hulling the *Kearsarge*. Official damage reports stated that only 28 shot and shell struck the Yankee ship, with most hitting spars and rigging. In contrast, the *Kearsarge* fired only 173 shot and shell but made a higher percentage count.[13]

Arthur Sinclair would later write that he believed the *Alabama* would have had an even fuller history had Semmes not chosen to fight the *Kearsarge*.[14] This assumption is unlikely, however. The *Kearsarge* had the *Alabama* cornered, with the *St. Louis* and the *Ticonderoga* en route to assist. No doubt other Union ships would have steamed for Cherbourg as well, leaving Semmes little choice but to fight when the odds were the best they were going to get. The longer Semmes had waited the lower his chances would have been for success.

The *Tuscaloosa* was returned to her original owners at the close of the war. The *Sumter* was sold, and she eventually sank in the North Sea. Ironically, the *Alabama,* although having served the Confederacy far beyond expectations, never entered a Confederate port.

Although the *Alabama*'s officers estimated the value of the ships burned or ransomed at more than $5 million, the only prize money ever divided was from the proceeds of the sales of the captured chronometers.

The *Kearsarge* remained in Cherbourg for two weeks following the battle. During that time a commission of French officials swarmed over the ship, with the permission of the United States government. They took measurements and made drawings, actions that were protested by the *New York Times*. The *Times* went on to predict " . . . this combat, like that between the Monitor and Merrimac [*sic*], is going to create in Europe a second revolution in naval warfare."[15]

On July 5 the *Kearsarge* departed for Dover where she remained for another two weeks. In mid-July Winslow and his crew made one last trip to Cherbourg to pick up their wounded comrades. Returning to Dover, the *Kearsarge* received orders to proceed to the coast of Brazil to try to do to the *Florida* what had been done to the *Alabama*. Before the *Kearsarge* could locate the *Florida*, however, the USS *Wachusett* rammed the rebel cruiser and captured her. Winslow took on 17 prisoners from the *Florida*, promising to return them to the United States as prisoners of war.

Saying that they would all be home in time to vote for President Lincoln, Winslow had his helmsman turn the *Kearsarge* for home. With the *Alabama*'s shell still lodged in her sternpost, the *Kearsarge* steamed into Boston Harbor shortly after midnight on November 8, 1864. She had been at sea 34 months.

The city of Boston welcomed the *Kearsarge* and her crew with open arms, honoring them with a parade and a reception at Fanueil Hall. As a show of thanks, the *Kearsarge* put on an exhibition for six weeks for the benefit of the Sailors' Fair.[16]

After the war the *Kearsarge* served in the North Atlantic, hosting a reunion of the crew on the 29th anniversary of the battle, June 19, 1893. On January 27, 1894, she was sent to Nicaragua to protect Americans who were believed to be in danger because of trouble between Nicaragua and Honduras. Just a week later, on February 2, 1894, the *Kearsarge* slammed into the Roncador reef. Within minutes she was on her side. Her masts were cut away and her guns thrown overboard in an effort to right her. Although unsuccessful, the effort did provide time for the crew to safely abandon the ship.

Congress eventually appropriated $45,000 to raise the *Kearsarge,* and the Boston Towing Company went to the wreck site to fulfill the contract. By the time they arrived, however, the proud old *Kearsarge* had been looted and burned.[17]

Winslow became an overnight hero in the United States. He was appointed to the rank of commodore, retroactive to the date of the battle. Welles, however, still seething over the parole of Winslow's prisoners, held up the promotion until the weight of public opinion forced him to give in.

Another well-known figure, General William Tecumseh Sherman, chose to focus his criticism of Winslow on his lack of action against the *Deerhound*. In a letter to Major General H. W. Halleck, he said, "I have just received Secretary Stanton's dispatch, and do not understand how Semmes and crew were allowed to leave the sinking *Alabama* in an English yacht."[18]

Winslow rode out the criticism, however, and took over the command of the Gulf Squadron in 1866. Three years later he became commander of the Portsmouth Navy Yard, birthplace of the *Kearsarge*. By July of 1870 he had risen to the rank of rear admiral and was commander of the Pacific fleet. Within two years his health failed and he died in Boston on September 29, 1873. He was buried in Forest Hill Cemetery, his grave marked by a boulder from Mt. Kearsarge, New Hampshire.

James Thornton, who had so coolly moved from gun to gun during the battle exhorting his gun crews to stay calm and aim low, was recommended to the Senate of the United States for advancement "ten numbers in his grade."[19] After leaving the *Kearsarge* he became commander of the USS *Iosco*, and then executive officer at the Portsmouth Navy Yard. That was followed by a stint as commander of the *Monongahela*. In early 1874, during a severe storm, he was badly injured in a fall in his stateroom. The injuries would ultimately prove fatal, and he died on May 14, 1874. His remains were removed to Merrimack, New Hampshire, for burial.

Charles Pickering, the *Kearsarge*'s first commander and the man who had christened the ship at the Portsmouth Navy Yard, would enjoy none of the *Kearsarge*'s fame. He spoke little of his time on the ship and was virtually ignored by newspapers on both sides of the ocean in the years following the battle. He died in 1888 of kidney disease.

When Semmes appeared to have recovered from his ordeal, Confederate officials offered him a new ship. He refused. French newspapers persisted in keeping the story alive however, speculating that the ship would be built in France. Newspapers in the United States responded by saying they welcomed the spectacle of Winslow and his crew testing themselves against a French vessel, especially if Semmes commanded.[20]

Still revered by many in Europe, a group of British naval officers presented Semmes with a new sword to replace the one he had thrown into the sea. The inscription read: "Presented to Captain Raphael Semmes, C.S.N., by officers of the Royal Navy and other friends in England, as a testimonial of their admiration of the gallantry with which he maintained the *Alabama* in the engagement off Cherbourg, with a chain-plated ship of superior power, armament and crew, June 19th, 1864."[21]

Semmes toured Europe for several months, departing for Cuba in October 1864. From Cuba he sailed to Louisiana, and from there he returned to his family in Mobile. The *New York Times*, however, was not content to ignore him even though he was out of the limelight. Referring to his resignation from the United States Navy, the *Times* called him a traitor for violating " . . . not only his military oath, and his oath as a citizen of the United States, but also his oath of allegiance to his own state."[22]

After only a few months in Mobile he accepted an appointment as a rear admiral in the Provisional Navy as a reward for his "gallant and meritorious conduct in command of the steam sloop *Alabama*,"[23] and he was placed in command of the James River Squadron, relieving Flag Officer John K. Mitchell.[24] In Greensboro, North Carolina, in May 1865 when the Confederates surrendered to Joseph Johnston, Semmes signed a parole and returned to Mobile to open a law practice.

Still regarded as a pirate by many in the North, he was arrested on December 15, 1865, and taken to the Marine Barracks in Washington.[25] There he was charged with escaping after giving his "moral parole," taking prizes in neutral waters, being cruel to prisoners, burning Northern merchant ships, and raising foreign flags to deceive Northern vessels. Semmes wrote from his cell to President Andrew Johnson, claiming immunity under the military convention in Greensboro. Then, still unsure whether he would be hanged, an unexpected ally testified in his behalf. Former consul George H. Fairchild, whom Semmes had captured on the *Thomas B. Wales* in November 1862, came forward and said that Semmes had treated him, his wife, and their children with the utmost courtesy, and deserved mercy in return.[26]

The new secretary of the navy, John A. Bolles, after reviewing the evidence and possibly swayed to some extent by Fairchild's testimony, decided to drop the charges. Semmes was released in April 1866, whereupon he returned to Mobile and resumed his law practice. Two years later he was finally paroled as part of President Johnson's general amnesty.

On August 30, 1877, Raphael Semmes died at the age of 68, still a hero to the people he had served so well. In 1900 the citizens of Mobile erected a monument in his honor at the corner of Government and Royal Streets.

John McIntosh Kell made his way to Halifax on an English steamer, with plans to return to the Confederacy. Union spies, however, were not to be denied, and his every move was watched. On July 26, 1864, Gideon Welles wrote to Acting Rear Admiral S. P. Lee in Hampton Roads that Kell had departed Halifax and was on his way to Bermuda, ultimately planning to run the blockade at Wilmington, North Carolina.[27] Lee responded by saying that measures were being taken to capture Kell and any other officers or crew members who happened to be with him.[28] Despite these efforts, Kell did exactly what Welles said he would do, entering Wilmington on the blockade runner *Flamingo* and passing directly under the guns of a Union man-of-war.[29]

James Bulloch successfully built or bought several other ships for the Confederacy. After the war he remained in Liverpool and went into the cotton business with his half-brother, Irvine S. Bulloch, midshipman on the *Alabama*. He wrote *The Secret Service of the Confederate States in Europe* in 1883, an authoritative two-volume work. In 1901, James Bulloch died, just a few months before his nephew, Theodore Roosevelt, became president of the United States.

A review of the muster rolls of both ships indicates that a disproportionate number of officers and crew members died within a few years of the battle. The lure of the sea brought with it a difficult, and too often short, life. Many of those who died an early death succumbed to diseases brought on by the life style and rigors of sea life in the 1860s. Tuberculosis, consumption, kidney disease, syphilis . . . all took their toll. But not all would die from disease. George Townley Fullam, whose meticulous logs provided historians with much of what is known about the *Alabama*'s cruise, died in 1879 when his ship went down.

As might be expected, controversies swirled around the two ships for months after the battle. Semmes and several of his officers charged that the *Kearsarge* refused to render aid, causing the needless deaths of several crewmen. However, this is an unlikely scenario, considering that only two of the *Kearsarge*'s boats were seaworthy immediately following the battle. It was Winslow who implored the *Deerhound* to assist, and the fact that more than half of those rescued were picked up by the *Kearsarge* indicates that Winslow and his men did, indeed, try to assist the men of the *Alabama*.

Uncharacteristically, Semmes also complained that the *Kearsarge* had not fought fairly, having covered her sides with chain. While this was not a common practice in the 1860s, it was not unheard of, and Winslow was under no obligation to tell Semmes about it. In a letter to the *New York Times*, Winslow explained his use of chain as a means of protecting the engines when there was no coal in the upper part of the bunkers, such as would have been the case at the time of the battle. He said that the planking was added to prevent dirt from collecting on the chains.[30]

Semmes's lack of grace on this issue even made James Bulloch uncomfortable. Bulloch would write: "Captain Winslow was quite right in doing whatever he could to increase the defensive power of his ship, and he was not bound to inform his adversary that he had encased her most vulnerable parts with chain cables. It has never been considered an unworthy ruse for a commander, whether afloat or ashore, to disguise his strength and to entice a weaker opponent within his reach."[31]

A few weeks after the battle, the *New York Times* took a similar position, admiringly calling Winslow's use of chains " . . . a bit of Yankee invention, as neat, simple, and effective as could well be thought of, upon short notice."[32] The *Times* also stated that " . . . if Semmes did not do the same, it only shows that Winslow was the best [*sic*] sailor of the two."[33]

The *Richmond Dispatch*, however, predictably took a different view. In a colorful editorial, the *Dispatch* noted, in reference to the use of chains by the *Kearsarge*: "Had such a foul advantage been taken over one knight by another in the days of chivalry, the perpetrator would have had his spurs hacked off by the common hangman, his arms reversed, his name stricken from the roll of honor, and his carcass stretched by the neck, between sun and earth, until the birds of the air had torn his eyes from their sockets."[34]

Nor is it even clear that Semmes was actually taken by surprise by the chain. The port admiral at Cherbourg stated that a French officer, seeing the armor while visiting the *Kearsarge*, reported it on his return to shore and even went so far as to advise Semmes not to fight, although Semmes denied this.[35] Arthur Sinclair, Semmes's fourth lieutenant, confirmed that the information had been given to Semmes and argued that Semmes could have done the same thing had he so chosen, since there was plenty of extra anchor chain on board the *Alabama*.[36] Sinclair would be shunned by Semmes and the men of the *Alabama* forever after for making such an accusation.

The matter should have been put to rest by a letter to the *London Times* shortly after the battle. However, controversies characteristically die a long, lingering death, and this was no exception. The letter was written by T. A. Blakely, the English gunmaker who had built the Blakely rifled gun on the *Alabama*. While the purpose of Blakely's letter was more to compare the Blakely on the *Alabama* with the Dahlgrens on the *Kearsarge*, Blakely touched on the anchor chain plating controversy near the end of his letter. Offering one of the few sensible arguments concerning the anchor chain, Blakely said, "The *Alabama* had not one steel shot or shell on board. Any gun she had, even the little 32-pounders, could have fired steel shot through the *Kearsarge*'s armor; no gun on earth could throw iron shell through it."[37] Few seemed interested in logic, however, and the argument raged on for months.

Semmes also accused Winslow of firing on the *Alabama* after she had surrendered. Winslow freely admitted that the *Kearsarge* had fired shots. However, he noted that there was a great deal of confusion over whether or not the *Alabama* had, in fact, quit the fight. Winslow countercharged that the crew of the *Alabama* had merely taken down their battle flag, which was white with a union jack and blue stars in the corner, torn off the colored portion, and run the white banner back up as their sign of surrender. Winslow said the *Kearsarge*'s crew was unsure of the *Alabama*'s surrender, as a result.[38]

Winslow also mentioned the two shots fired from the *Alabama*'s port battery after her colors had been struck. Those shots were confirmed by others who also confirmed that the *Kearsarge* had returned the fire.[39] Winslow chose not to make much of this, however, saying that such things often happened in battle and that he bore no ill will toward those who had fired the shots.

At the time of the battle it was apparent that the *Alabama*'s powder had deteriorated. While Lieutenant Joseph Wilson was held prisoner on the *Kearsarge* he said he saw wounds in the engine room that would have sunk the Union ship if the shot had penetrated properly.[40] Wilson's contention is supported by the unexploded shell lodged in the *Kearsarge*'s sternpost. What would have caused this deterioration?

Some have offered that exposure to the salt air for two years took its toll on the *Alabama*'s powder. This however, is not plausible when one considers that the *Kearsarge* was at sea for a similar amount of time, yet experienced no such deterioration. The explanation, then, must lie in something peculiar to the *Alabama*; something the *Kearsarge* did not experience.

That peculiarity may lie in the condensation system on the *Alabama*. James Bulloch said that Chief Engineer Miles Freeman told him that the *Alabama* often condensed more water than the cooling tanks could hold. Although Freeman never said why, it can be presumed that the unreliability of the condensers prompted the crew to condense extra water in the event the condensers failed. If that were the case, the boiling water and steam mixture would have been sent directly to the holding tanks, bypassing the cooling tank. These holding tanks were immediately adjacent to the magazines, and the steam that was carried over would have raised the humidity levels in the magazines to the point where the powder could have become damp.[41] This is the most likely explanation for the poor performance of the *Alabama*'s powder, both in the battle and in her target practice on the *Rockingham*.

Several of the *Alabama*'s prisoners throughout her cruise complained of poor treatment at the hands of the rebels. The complaints were so numerous that the solicitor for the United States Navy, John A. Bolles, conducted an inquiry after the war. He found that the accusations were groundless.[42]

Perhaps one of the greatest controversies surrounding the battle was the involvement of the *Deerhound*. Several Union officers and crewmen accused the *Deerhound* of being a tender to the *Alabama*, a charge that they said was supported by prisoners from the rebel ship. This charge was never proven.

Winslow contended that the *Deerhound,* whether a tender or not, was obligated to turn over the rescued crew members, including Semmes, as prisoners of war. This debate raged for months after the battle. The *New York Evening Post* demanded that the survivors be delivered as prisoners, saying that if one were to ignore the humane act of saving them from drowning, the Deerhound was in " . . . contravention of the law of nations."[43] Predictably, the *New York Times* agreed, rationalizing that the *Kearsarge* could have picked up all the survivors had the *Deerhound* not interfered, which would have made all the survivors prisoners of war.[44]

Three days later the *Times* appeared to have changed directions and now called for cooler heads, saying that the United States must stay within the law when dealing with England or anyone else. The *Times* agreed that Semmes should have been turned over had the *Deerhound* been one of the Queen's ships, but because she was privately owned there was no such obligation.[45]

A few weeks later the *Times* again argued against those who demanded the return of the survivors. The newspaper's editors had ridiculed the British a few months earlier, saying that the typical Englishman believed the earth to be square, because "he'd journeyed fifty miles and found no sign of its being circular."[46] Now, however, the editors had backpedaled and called for support for the British position. "It may have been a dishonorable thing for Semmes to escape," they wrote. "It may have been a rascally trick for Lancaster, under the circumstances, to assist him; but the British government is not responsible for the conduct of either of them. It is all one to Lord Russell, whether he got ashore by skill or treachery, so long as no employee of the government had any hand in the matter. And even if a government officer had aided him, we feel quite satisfied that Earl Russell would have no legal right to hand him over to us without his consent. An escaped prisoner of war is, no matter how he escapes, an escaped prisoner of war and nothing more . . ."[47]

Lord Russell, responding to his critics, wrote that "It appears to me that the owner of the *Deerhound*, of the Royal Yacht Squadron, performed only a common duty of humanity in saving from the waves the captain and several of the crew of the *Alabama*. They would have otherwise, in all probability, been drowned, and thus would never have been in the situation of prisoners of war. It does not appear to me to be any part of the duty of a neutral to assist in making prisoners of war for one of the belligerents."[48]

Lancaster also defended his actions, saying, "I was not aware then, and I am not aware now, that the men whom I saved were, or ever had been, Captain Winslow's prisoners." He went on to say that an English ship is English territory, and that he was no more bound to turn the men over than would be someone who owned property to which a crew member could swim to gain his freedom.

As for Winslow's request that the *Deerhound* assist, Lancaster argued that the plea for help was not accompanied by any stipulations that those rescued should be turned over. If it had been, he stated, he would have declined the task. "I should have deemed it dishonorable, that is, inconsistent with my notions of honor, to lend my yacht and crew for the purpose of rescuing those brave men from drowning, only to hand them over to their enemies for imprisonment, ill treatment, and perhaps execution," he argued.[49]

The editors of the *New York Times* did still another aboutface and editorialized against Lancaster's explanation. "If there had ever been any danger of Ill treatment," they said, "if the Libby Prison had been in Washington instead of Richmond, and the massacre of Fort Pillow had been committed by our troops instead of by the companions in arms of Captain Semmes, there might have been a shadow of an excuse for such a display of 'honor' as this. But the words are nonsense."[50] The *Times* agreed that Lancaster had done right by rescuing the crew but had been wrong to take advantage of Winslow's confidence.

Whatever the position, the arguments were moot. The men rescued by the *Deerhound* had already been allowed to depart, and none of the newspapers calling for their return saw fit to address the fact that they were no longer in the possession of the British, and therefore, could not have been turned over even if Lord Russell had chosen to do so.

Even the Navy Department would not let the matter rest, and in October, four full months after the battle had taken place, Assistant Secretary of the Navy G. V. Fox wrote to Major General Benjamin Butler that all officers and crew of the *Alabama* should be considered prisoners for the purposes of exchange. Fox estimated that the *Alabama* had carried at least 150 men and officers into the battle, and because they had either been paroled or released, Butler, as commissioner of exchange, should insist on getting 15 officers and 130 men released in return.[51]

On June 21, 1864, Confederate Commissioner to England J. M. Mason penned a letter of thanks to Lancaster for his rescue of the *Alabama*'s men.[52] Six days later Lancaster sent a lengthy letter of his own to the *London Daily News*, giving his account of the rescue and defending his actions. Lancaster reiterated that Winslow's request for assistance was not accompanied by any stipulation that those rescued would be turned over as prisoners. Lancaster also said that he would not have participated in the rescue if such had been the case, and he stated once more that he had always been brought up to believe that an English ship is English territory, making the *Deerhound* as much a place of refuge as if the men had been able to swim to shore. Near the end of his letter Lancaster noted that he would also have rescued the men of the *Kearsarge* if they had needed help, trying to refute the contention that he was a tender to the *Alabama*.[53]

On March 4, however, Lancaster received another letter. The letter was from Jefferson Davis, Confederate president. Davis's letter thanked Lancaster for his assistance, but perhaps more importantly, it included a certified copy of a Resolution of Thanks passed by the Congress of the Confederate States of America.[54]

Following the battle many saw fit to question Semmes's decision to fight. In addition to the rationale already discussed, Semmes may have fought out of hubris. He had been hearing for two years that the *Alabama* was good at burning merchant ships but seemed to avoid a fair fight with a legitimate warship. Notwithstanding the *Alabama*'s true mission, this still had to affect Semmes's pride. He may have thought that he and his crew would be immortalized if he could sink the *Kearsarge*. At the very least, he had to feel that his reputation for courage had been impugned, and could be resurrected only with a convincing victory over a ship such as the *Kearsarge*.

Whatever Semmes's reasons were, he was supported by John Slidell, Confederate commissioner to France. Two days after the battle he sent a note to Semmes saying, " . . . I desire to say that your course in going to meet the Kearsarge commands my most unqualified admiration." Referring to those who now criticized Semmes for his decision to fight, Slidell added, "It may perhaps seem to you that this declaration is uncalled for; but I am induced to make it because I learn that too many of our Confederates in Paris entertain and express a different opinion, although I have no doubt that had the combat resulted in the capture of the enemy they would have been the loudest in extolling, not only your courage, but your gallantry and judgment."[55]

After the war, relations between the United States and Britain remained strained. The United States continued to insist that England must be held accountable for the damages caused by the British-built Confederate ships. Disputes over Canadian fisheries only added to the problem. Finally on May 8, 1871, England and the United States signed the Treaty of Washington as a means of settling the differences. For the first time, England officially expressed regret over her participation in the construction of the ships.

One provision of this treaty was the arbitration of what would become known as the *Alabama* claims. In 1872 a tribunal consisting of representatives of the United States, England, Brazil, Switzerland, and Italy met in Geneva to hear claims involving 11 Confederate cruisers: the *Alabama, Shenandoah, Florida, Georgia, Tallahassee, Retribution, Sallie, Chickamauga, Boston, Sumter,* and *Nashville*. Claims totaling more than $19 million were filed, with $6,547,609 of this attributed to the *Alabama*. After hearing the evidence, the tribunal threw out claims against all but the *Alabama, Florida*, and *Shenandoah*, saying that England was not responsible for the others.[56] In a unanimous decision the tribunal ruled that England was directly responsible for losses caused by these three ships, however, and awarded the United States damages in the amount of $15,500,000 in gold.

In November 1925, the last living survivor of the battle would take his final breath. Ironically, that survivor was Arthur Sinclair, the *Alabama* officer who had fallen into disfavor with his shipmates for criticizing Semmes. Although they ignored him in the years following the battle, he outlived them all.

One important link to the *Alabama* remained. Lairds' Shipyard, which had built the rebel cruiser, continued making ships until finally closing in 1993.

The *Alabama* rested in her watery grave for more than 120 years, until the French navy mine hunter *Circe* discovered her in 1984, some two hundred feet below the surface. Four years later a joint expedition was agreed to by the French and American governments. On June 29, 1994, the *Alabama*'s Blakely gun was recovered, still loaded and ready to fire.

Considering the history of these two great ships it is only proper that their names lived on even though both had sunk. The name of the *Alabama* was affixed to a ship once more in 1898 with the launching of the USS *Alabama*, a battleship given the official number of BB 8. This *Alabama* sailed for nearly 26 years before the navy scrapped her on March 19, 1924. In 1942, with World War II raging, the *Alabama* once again sailed the world's oceans as a battleship (BB 60). Active throughout the war, she was decommissioned in 1947 and donated in 1964 for public display in a battleship park in Mobile, Alabama, the home of Raphael Semmes.

The *Kearsarge* also lived on in the form of a battleship launched in 1898. Known as Battleship Number 5, she served as the flagship of the North Atlantic Squadron and the European Squadron, sailing with the Great White Fleet. Before her decommissioning she would serve as both a training ship and a crane ship. In 1946 a third *Kearsarge* was born, this time as an aircraft carrier (CV 33, later CVA 33). Later converted to an antisubmarine warfare support carrier (CVS 33) she saw action in Korea and Vietnam. She became known to television viewers around the world as the recovery ship for astronauts Walter Schirra and Gordon Cooper. Today the name of the *Kearsarge* roams the seas as an amphibious assault ship (LHD 3) which was launched in March 1992.

The two ships were evenly matched in armament, crew size, and even ship size and speed, an unusual scenario rarely seen. Both had outstanding service records. Both were captained by dedicated naval officers. Both were manned by crews who lived hard and fought hard. It is only fitting that both are linked together in our memories.

Appendix A

Ships Captured or Detained by the *Alabama*

The following Union vessels were captured by the *Alabama* during her two-year voyage. Values shown are those determined by the boarding officer of the *Alabama* and may differ from values submitted by owners in the Alabama Claims.

No.	Date	Vessel Name, Type	Captain	From/To	Cargo	Value, $	Disposition
1	September 5, 1862	*Ocmulgee*, Whaling Ship	Abraham Osborn	Martha's Vineyard/Cruising	Whale Oil	50,000	Burned
2	September 7, 1862	*Starlight*, Merchant Schooner	Samuel H. Doane	Boston/Flores, via Fayal	Mail	4,000	Burned
3	September 8, 1862	*Ocean Rover*, Whaling Bark	James M. Clark	New London/Cruising	Whale Oil	70,000	Burned
4	September 9, 1862	*Alert*, Whaling Bark	Charles E. Church	New Bedford/Indian Ocean	Provisions	20,000	Burned
5	September 9, 1862	*Weather Gauge*, Whaling Schooner	Samuel C. Small	Provincetown/Cruising	None	10,000	Burned
6	September 13, 1862	*Altamaha*, Whaling Brig	Rufus Gray	New Bedford, MA/Cruising	None	3,000	Burned
7	September 14, 1862	*Benjamin Tucker*, Whaling Brig	William Childs	New Bedford/Cruising	Whale Oil	18,000	Burned
8	September 16, 1862	*Courser*, Whaling Schooner	Silas S. Young	Provincetown/Cruising	Whale Oil	7,000	Burned
9	September 17, 1862	*Virginia*, Whaling Bark	Shadrach R. Tilton	New Bedford/Cruising	None	25,000	Burned
10	September 18, 1862	*Elisha Dunbar*, Whaling Bark	David R. Gifford	New Bedford/Cruising	Whale Oil	25,000	Burned
11	October 3, 1862	*Brilliant*, Ship	George Hagar	New York/London	Grain	164,000	Burned
12	October 3, 1862	*Emily Farnham*, Ship	N. P. Simes	Portsmouth, NH/Liverpool	Flour and grain	Not valued	Released
13	October 7, 1862	*Wave Crest*, Bark	John E. Harmon	New York/Cardiff	Flour and grain	44,000	Burned
14	October 7, 1862	*Dunkirk*, Brigantine	Samuel B. Johnson	New York/Lisbon	Grain	25,000	Burned
15	October 9, 1862	*Tonawanda*, Ship	Theodore Julius	Philadelphia/Liverpool	Wheat	80,000	Ransomed
16	October 11, 1862	*Manchester*, Ship	John Landerskin	New York/Liverpool	Grain, cotton	164,000	Burned

273

Captured Union Vessels *(cont.)*

No.	Date	Vessel Name, Type	Captain	From/To	Cargo	Value, $	Disposition
17	October 15, 1862	*Lamplighter*, Bark	O. V. Harding	New York/Gibraltar	Tobacco	117,600	Burned
18	October 23, 1862	*Lafayette*, Ship	Alfred T. Small	New Haven/Belfast	Wheat and corn	100,337	Burned
19	October 26, 1862	*Crenshaw*, Schooner	William Nelson	New York/Glasgow	Flour and grain	33,869	Burned
20	October 28, 1862	*Lauretta*, Bark	Marshall M. Wells	Boston/Gibraltar, via New York	Herring, flour, pipe staves, nails	32,880	Burned
21	October 29, 1862	*Baron de Castine*, Brigantine	John Saunders	Bangor, ME/Cardenas, Cuba	Lumber	6,000	Ransomed
22	November 2, 1862	*Levi Starbuck*, Whaling Ship	Thomas Mellen	New Bedford/Pacific Ocean cruise	Whalebone and provisions	25,000	Burned
23	November 8, 1862	*Thomas B. Wales*, Ship	Edgar Lincoln	Boston/Boston, via Calcutta	Linseed oil, saltpeter, jute	245,625	Burned
24	November 21, 1862	*Clara L. Sparks*, Whaling Schooner	Unknown	Provincetown/Cruising	Whale oil	Not valued	Released
25	November 30, 1862	*Parker Cook*, Bark	Thomas M. Fulton	Boston/Aux Cayes, Santo Domingo	Provisions	10,000	Burned
26	December 5, 1862	*Union*, Schooner	Joseph H. Young	Baltimore/Port Maria, Jamaica	General	1,500	Ransomed
27	December 7, 1862	*Ariel*, Mail Steamer	Albert J. Jones	New York/Aspinwall	Assorted cargo	261,000	Ransomed
28	January 11, 1863	USS *Hatteras*, Steam Gunboat	Homer C. Blake	Galveston/In port	None	160,000	Sunk in battle
29	January 26, 1863	*Golden Rule*, Bark	Peter H. Whiteberry	New York/Aspinwall	Food products, medicine, ship rigging	112,000	Burned
30	January 27, 1863	*Chastelaine*, Brig	James Warren	Boston/Cienfuegos, via Guadeloupe, West Indies	In ballast	10,000	Burned
31	February 3, 1863	*Palmetto*, Schooner	Oren H. Leland	New York/Puerto Rico	Lumber and provisions	18,430	Burned

#	Date	Ship	Captain	Route	Cargo	Value	Disposition
32	February 21, 1863	Golden Eagle, Ship	Edward A. Swift	New Bedford/Cork, via Chinchas	Guano	61,000	Burned
33	February 21, 1863	Olive Jane, Bark	Robert Kallock	Boston/New York via Bordeaux	Liquors, canned meats	43,208	Burned
34	February 27, 1863	Washington, Ship	Joseph G. White	New York/Cork via Calleo	Guano	50,000	Ransomed
35	March 1, 1863	Bethiah Thayer, Ship	Thomas Mitchell Cartney	Rockland, ME/Cork via Callao	Guano	40,000	Ransomed
36	March 2, 1863	John A. Parks, Ship	John S. Cooper	Hallowell, ME/Montevideo via New York	Lumber	66,157	Burned
37	March 15, 1863	Punjaub, Ship	Lewis F. Miller	Boston/London via Calcutta	Guano	50,000	Ransomed
38	March 23, 1863	Morning Star, Ship	Unknown	Boston/London via Calcutta	General	61,750	Ransomed
39	March 23, 1863	Kingfisher, Whaling Schooner	Thomas F. Lambert	New Bedford/Cruising	Whale oil	2,400	Burned
40	March 25, 1863	Nora, Ship	Charles E. Adams	Boston/Calcutta via London	Salt	76,636	Burned
41	March 25, 1863	Charles Hill, Ship	Franklin Percival	Boston/Montevideo via Liverpool	Salt	28,450	Burned
42	April 4, 1863	Louisa Hatch, Ship	William Grant	Rockland, ME/East Indies via Cardiff	Coal	38,315	Burned
43	April 15, 1863	Lafayette, Whaling Bark	William Lewis	New Bedford/Cruising	Whale oil	20,908	Burned
44	April 15, 1863	Kate Cory, Whaling Brig	Stephen Flanders	Westport/Cruising	Whale oil	10,568	Burned
45	April 24, 1863	Nye, Whaling Bark	Joseph B. Baker	New Bedford/Cruising	Whale oil, whalebone	31,127	Burned
46	April 26, 1863	Dorcas Prince, Ship	Frank B. Melcher	New York/Shanghai	Coal	44,108	Burned
47	May 3, 1863	Union Jack, Bark	Charles P. Weaver	New York/Shanghai	General	77,000	Burned
48	May 3, 1863	Sea Lark, Ship	W. F. Peck	Boston/San Francisco	General	550,000	Burned
49	May 25, 1863	S. Gildersleeve, Ship	John McCallum	New York/Calcutta via Sunderland	Coal	62,783	Burned
50	May 25, 1863	Justina, Bark	Charles Miller	Baltimore/Rio de Janeiro	In ballast	7,000	Ransomed
51	May 29, 1863	Jabez Snow, Ship	George W. Guin	Buckport, ME/Montevideo via Cardiff	Coal	72,781	Burned

Captured Union Vessels *(cont.)*

No.	Date	Vessel Name, Type	Captain	From/To	Cargo	Value, $	Disposition
52	June 2, 1863	*Amazonian*, Bark	Winslow Loveland	Boston/Montevideo via New York	Candles, soap	97,665	Burned
53	June 5, 1863	*Talisman*, Clipper Ship	D. H. Howard	New York/Shanghai	Coal	139,195	Burned
54	June 20, 1863	*Conrad*, Bark	William H. Salsbury	Philadelphia/New York via Buenos Aires	Wool	100,936	Converted to *Tuscaloosa*, Confederate cruiser
55	July 2, 1863	*Anna F. Schmidt*, Ship	Henry B. Twombly	Boston/San Francisco via St. Thomas	General	350,000	Burned
56	July 6, 1863	*Express*, Ship	William S. Frost	Portsmouth, NH/Antwerp via Valparaiso	Guano	121,300	Burned
57	August 5, 1863	*Sea Bride*, Bark	Charles F. White	Boston/Cape Town via New York	Cloth and notions	16,940	Sold
58	August 9, 1863	*Martha Wenzell*, Bark	Unknown	Boston/Falmouth, England via Akyab	Rice	Not valued	Released (captured in territorial waters)
59	November 6, 1863	*Amanda*, Bark	Isaiah Larrabee	Bangor, ME/Queenstown via Manila	Sugar and hemp	104,442	Burned
60	November 10, 1863	*Winged Racer*, Clipper Ship	George Cumming	New York/New York via Manila	Sugar and hemp	150,000	Burned
61	November 11, 1863	*Contest*, Clipper Ship	Frederick George Lucas	New York/New York via Yokohama	Japanese curios, tea, silk	122,815	Burned
62	December 24, 1863	*Texan Star (aka Martaban)*, Bark	Samuel B. Pike	Galveston/Singapore	Rice	97,628	Burned
63	December 26, 1863	*Sonora*, Clipper Ship	Lawrence W. Brown	Newburyport, MA/Akyab via Singapore	In ballast	46,545	Burned
64	December 26, 1863	*Highlander*, Clipper Ship	Jabez H. Snow	Boston/Akyab via Singapore	In ballast	75,965	Burned

No.	Date	Vessel	Origin/Destination	Cargo		Disposition
65	January 14, 1864	Emma Jane, Ship	Bath, ME/Moulmein, Burma	In ballast	40,000	Burned
66	April 23, 1864	Rockingham, Ship	Portsmouth, NH/Cork via Calleo	Guano	97,878	Burned
67	April 27, 1864	Tycoon, Bark	New York/San Francisco	Assorted cargo	390,000	Burned

In addition to the above Union ships seized, the *Alabama* investigated 236 ships hauling neutral cargo. Those ships follow, with their names where they are known. All were permitted to proceed.

No.	Date	Vessel/Country
1	August 30, 1862	French brig
2	August 31, 1862	Portuguese brig
3	September 2, 1862	French bark *La Foi*
4	September 6, 1862	French bark *Senegambia*
5	September 8, 1862	Portuguese brigantine
6	September 9, 1862	Portuguese whaling brig
7	September 10, 1862	Danish bark *Overman*
8	September 10, 1862	English ship
9	September 12, 1862	Portuguese bark
10	September 13, 1862	Spanish bark
11	September 18, 1862	French brig
12	September 29, 1862	French bark
13	October 4, 1862	Prussian bark
14	October 5, 1862	French bark
15	October 5, 1862	Oldenham brig (German)
16	October 9, 1862	English brig *Ann Williams*
17	October 10, 1862	Mecklenburg ship *Johanna Hepler*
18	October 13, 1862	Spanish ship
19	October 14, 1862	Danish ship *Judith*
20	October 14, 1862	French schooner
21	October 14, 1862	English ship
22	October 17, 1862	English ship
23	October 20, 1862	English bark
24	October 20, 1862	Dutch brig
25	October 21, 1862	English bark *Heron*
26	October 23, 1862	English brig
27	October 24, 1862	English brig
28	October 29, 1862	Dutch bark
29	November 1, 1862	English bark
30	November 1, 1862	French bark
31	November 6, 1862	French bark
32	November 11, 1862	English brig
33	November 11, 1862	English bark *Princess Royal*
34	November 15, 1862	Spanish ship
35	November 29, 1862	English bark *Barbados*
36	November 30, 1862	Spanish schooner *Neuveaux*
37	December 1, 1862	Spanish brig
38	December 1, 1862	Dutch galliot
39	December 1, 1862	Spanish bark
40	December 2, 1862	Spanish schooner
41	December 3, 1862	Spanish brig
42	December 3, 1862	English brig
43	December 3, 1862	Oldenburg bark
44	December 3, 1862	French bark *Feu Sacre*
45	December 4, 1862	Spanish bark
46	December 8, 1862	Dutch bark
47	December 9, 1862	English schooner
48	December 9, 1862	German brig
49	January 17, 1863	English brig
50	January 27, 1863	Spanish brig
51	January 30, 1863	Spanish schooner

Ships investigated *(cont.)*

No.	Date	Vessel/Country
52	February 2, 1863	English brig *Ida Abbott*
53	February 2, 1863	Hamburg bark
54	February 6, 1863	Spanish brig
55	February 11, 1863	English schooner *Hero*
56	February 13, 1863	English schooner
57	February 22, 1863	English bark
58	February 22, 1863	Dutch bark
59	February 22, 1863	English bark
60	February 23, 1863	English ship *Prince of Wales*
61	February 23, 1863	English ship *Charles Lambert*
62	February 23, 1863	English ship
63	February 23, 1863	French bark *Gil Blas*
64	February 24, 1863	French bark
65	February 24, 1863	Portuguese brig *Oporto*
66	February 25, 1863	Dutch bark
67	February 25, 1863	English brig *Cedar*
68	February 26, 1863	English four-master *Sarah Sands*
69	February 26, 1863	English bark
70	February 26, 1863	Hamburg bark
71	February 26, 1863	English ship
72	February 26, 1863	French ship
73	February 26, 1863	English brig
74	February 27, 1863	Portuguese bark
75	February 27, 1863	English ship *Henry*
76	February 27, 1863	English ship *Glendover*
77	February 28, 1863	English ship *Schomburg*
78	February 28, 1863	English bark *Three Bells*
79	February 28, 1863	French ship *Alphonse Cezard*
80	March 1, 1863	English bark *William Edward*
81	March 1, 1863	Maltese bark *Nile*
82	March 2, 1863	English bark *Miss Nightingale*
83	March 6, 1863	Spanish brig
84	March 7, 1863	English brig *Eleanor*
85	March 8, 1863	Norwegian bark
86	March 8, 1863	English schooner
87	March 8, 1863	English bark
88	March 16, 1863	English ship *Hermione*
89	March 21, 1863	Dutch ship
90	March 22, 1863	English bark
91	March 24, 1863	Spanish ship
92	March 24, 1863	English ship
93	March 25, 1863	English bark *Pizarro*
94	March 25, 1863	English brig *Isabella*
95	March 25, 1863	Sardinian bark
96	March 28, 1863	English bark *Chili*
97	March 30, 1863	English bark *Sinope*
98	April 3, 1863	French ship *Mathilde*
99	April 5, 1863	English bark
100	April 6, 1863	Brazilian schooner
101	April 29, 1863	Hanoverian brig *Elsie*
102	May 1, 1863	English brig *Hound*
103	May 1, 1863	Austrian brig
104	May 1, 1863	English brig
105	May 1, 1863	English hermaphrodite brig
106	May 4, 1863	Spanish brig
107	May 4, 1863	Uruguayan brig
108	May 5, 1863	Spanish brig
109	May 8, 1863	Norwegian brig
110	May 9, 1863	English brig
111	May 10, 1863	Danish bark
112	May 11, 1863	Spanish brig
113	May 21, 1863	Hamburg brig
114	May 23, 1863	English ship *Virginia*
115	May 24, 1863	Dutch ship
116	May 25, 1863	Dutch bark *Arnheim*
117	May 27, 1863	Dutch bark
118	May 28, 1863	French ship

No.	Date	Ship
119	May 28, 1863	English ship *Lady Octavia*
120	June 3, 1863	English hermaphrodite brig *Widna*
121	June 6, 1863	English ship *St. Leonard*
122	June 8, 1863	Hanoverian brig
123	June 13, 1863	English bark
124	June 16, 1863	English bark *G Azzopadi*
125	June 16, 1863	French bark
126	June 16, 1863	English bark
127	June 17, 1863	English ship *Queen of Beauty*
128	June 18, 1863	Norwegian brig *Iduma*
129	June 19, 1863	Bremen bark *Brema*
130	June 21, 1863	English ship *Mary Kendall*
131	June 25, 1863	Spanish bark
132	June 26, 1863	French ship
133	June 28, 1863	English ship *Vernon*
134	June 29, 1863	English ship
135	June 29, 1863	English bark *Asshur*
136	July 1, 1863	English bark *Medora*
137	July 2, 1863	English ship *Thorndeer*
138	July 2, 1863	English frigate *Diomede*
139	July 22, 1863	English ship *Star of Erin*
140	July 26, 1863	Dutch ship
141	July 26, 1863	English ship *Lillian*
142	July 26, 1863	English ship *Havelock*
143	July 27, 1863	English schooner *Rover*
144	August 9, 1863	English bark
145	August 15, 1863	English bark *Saxon*
146	August 17, 1863	English ship *Broughton Hall*
147	August 18, 1863	English ship *Camperdown*
148	August 19, 1863	English bark *Durban*
149	August 21, 1863	Dutch bark
150	August 22, 1863	English ship *Sarawak*
151	August 23, 1863	Dutch bark *Maria Elizabeth*
152	August 24, 1863	Dutch bark *Minister Van Hall*
153	August 27, 1863	African schooner *Flower of Yarrow*
154	September 2, 1863	English ship *Punjaub*
155	September 3, 1863	English bark *Isle O'May*
156	September 7, 1863	English ship
157	September 8, 1863	English ship
158	September 8, 1863	English ship
159	September 8, 1863	English ship
160	September 8, 1863	English bark
161	September 9, 1863	English bark
162	September 9, 1863	English ship *Cameronian*
163	September 11, 1863	English bark *Flora*
164	September 25, 1863	English ship
165	October 3, 1863	English steamer *Mona*
166	October 26, 1863	English ship *Alma*
167	October 29, 1863	Dutch ship *Anna*
168	October 31, 1863	English ship *Jubilee*
169	October 31, 1863	Dutch bark *Jacob and Cornelia*
170	October 31, 1863	English ship *Tamana*
171	October 31, 1863	English ship *Moneta*
172	November 2, 1863	English ship *Janet Mitchell*
173	November 4, 1863	French ship *Jules Cezard*
174	November 4, 1863	Dutch bark *Frans and Elise*
175	November 6, 1863	English ship *Burmah*
176	November 8, 1863	Dutch bark *Java Whistle*
177	November 19, 1863	English ship *Avalanche*
178	November 20, 1863	Siamese bark *Amy Douglas*
179	November 20, 1863	French bark *Aloinir*
180	November 21, 1863	Norwegian bark
181	November 22, 1863	English ship
182	November 23. 1863	English ship *Maiden Queen*

Ships investigated *(cont.)*

No.	Date	Vessel/Country
183	November 23, 1863	English bark *Roy O'More*
184	December 21, 1863	Dutch bark
185	December 25, 1863	English bark *Gallant Neill*
186	December 25, 1863	French ship *Puget*
187	December 26, 1863	Bremen ship *Ottone*
188	December 30, 1863	English ship *Thomas Blythe*
189	January 4, 1864	English ship *Glennalice*
190	January 5, 1864	French ship
191	January 7, 1864	English bark *Lady Harriet*
192	January 14, 1864	English bark
193	January 16, 1864	French ship
194	January 17, 1864	English ship
195	January 17, 1864	English bark
196	January 17, 1864	English bark
197	January 18, 1864	Portuguese bark *Alexandra and Herculano*
198	January 19, 1864	English ship *Ally*
199	February 25, 1864	English ship *Caspatrick*
200	March 7, 1864	English ship
201	March 9, 1864	English ship
202	March 9, 1864	French ship
203	March 9, 1864	Dutch bark *Van der Palau*
204	March 11, 1864	Dutch ship
205	March 13, 1864	English ship *Scottish Chief*
206	March 13, 1864	Hamburg bark *Orion*
207	March 18, 1864	Spanish bark *Manilla*
208	March 20, 1864	English ship *Sardinia*
209	March 20, 1864	English schooner
210	March 20, 1864	Dutch ship
211	April 17, 1864	Italian bark *Carlo*
212	April 17, 1864	French ship *Formose*
213	April 18, 1864	Hamburg bark *Alster*
214	April 23, 1864	English ship *Robert McKensie*
215	April 24, 1864	English ship *Kent*
216	April 25, 1864	English bark *Bertha Martha*
217	April 26, 1864	English bark *La Flor del Plata*
218	May 10, 1864	Hamburg brig *Margarite*
219	May 15, 1864	Portuguese brig
220	May 15, 1864	Spanish brig *Tores Eliza*
221	May 19, 1864	French bark *Mere de Famille*
222	May 20, 1864	English ship
223	May 21, 1864	English ship
224	May 23, 1864	English bark *Cymbeline*
225	May 24, 1864	English schooner *Maria Louisa*
226	May 26, 1864	French ship
227	May 28, 1864	English barkentine
228	May 31, 1864	Dutch bark
229	May 31, 1864	English brig
230	June 4, 1864	Hamburg brig *Julie Caroline*
231	June 5, 1864	Bremen brig *Koenigsmunde*
232	June 5, 1864	English brig *Bengaine*
233	June 5, 1864	Hanoverian brig
234	June 8, 1864	Spanish ship *Iberica*
235	June 9, 1864	Italian barkentine *Raffaeline*
236	June 9, 1864	Dutch bark

Summary:

Sunk in battle	1
Sold	1
Burned	52
Released	239
Ransomed	9
Converted to Confederate ship	1
Total	303

Value of ships burned	$4,613,914
Value of ships bonded	562,250
	$5,176,164

Appendix B

Officers and Crew of the *Alabama*

Officers and Crew of the CSS *Alabama* on June 19, 1864

Names in **bold print** are members of the original *Alabama* crew. Ranks are those in effect at the time of the battle with the *Kearsarge*. Individual's battle conclusion shown in parentheses.

Raphael Semmes, Captain (wounded, rescued)
John McIntosh Kell, 1st Lieutenant (rescued)
Richard Armstrong, 2nd Lieutenant (wounded, rescued)
Joseph D. Wilson, 3rd Lieutenant (captured)
Arthur Sinclair, 4th Lieutenant (rescued)
Irvine S. Bulloch, Master (rescued)
James Evans, Master's Mate (rescued)
George T. Fullam, Master's Mate (rescued)
Max von Meulnier, Master's Mate (rescued)
Julius Schroeder, Master's Mate (rescued)
E. Anderson Maffitt, Midshipman (rescued)
E. Maffitt Anderson, Midshipman (rescued)
Francis L. Galt, Surgeon/Acting Paymaster (captured)
David H. Llewellyn, Asst. Surgeon (drowned)
Miles Freeman, Chief Engineer (captured)
William P. Brooks, 2nd Asst. Engineer (rescued)
Matthew O'Brien, 3rd Asst. Engineer (rescued)

281

John M. Pundt, 3rd Asst. Engineer (captured)
William Robertson, 3rd Asst. Engineer (missing)
Beckett K. Howell, Marine Lieutenant (rescued)
Benjamin P. McCaskey, Boatswain (captured)
Thomas C. Cuddy, Gunner (rescued)
William Breedlove Smith, Captain's Clerk (rescued)
William Robinson, Carpenter (drowned)
Henry Allcot, Sailmaker (rescued)
James G. Dent, Quartermaster (rescued)
W. F. Forestall, Quartermaster (captured)
Brent Johnson, Quartermaster (wounded, rescued)
James Brosnan, Chief Boatswain's Mate (wounded, rescued)
Peter Hughes, Boatswain's Mate (wounded, captured)
James Clements, Yeoman (captured)
George Freemantle, Captain's Coxswain (rescued)
William Wilson, Coxswain (captured)
William McGinley, Coxswain (wounded, captured)
James Broderick, Coxswain (captured)
William Burns, Quarter Gunner (captured)
Charles Seymour, Quarter Gunner (rescued)
William Crawford, Gunner's Mate (rescued)
George Addison, Carpenter's Mate (missing)
Frederick Myers, Carpenter's Mate (missing)
Edward Rawse, Master-at-Arms (missing)
William Purdy, Sailing Master's Mate (captured)
Robert Wright, Captain of the Maintop (wounded, captured)
William Morgan, Captain of the Foretop (wounded, captured)
Charles Steeson, Captain of the Foretop (rescued)
Fred Columbia, Captain of the Hold (captured)
James Higgs, Captain of the Hold (captured)
Henry Eustachia, Captain of the Head (captured)
Joseph Connor, Captain of the After Guard (rescued)
Charles Godwin, Captain of the After Guard (rescued)
Abram Norhoek, Ship's Corporal (missing)
Frederick Johns, Paymaster's Steward (missing)
A. G. Bartelli, Captain's Steward (drowned)
Richard Parkinson, Wardroom Steward (captured)
Henry Tucker, Wardroom Cook (captured)
Owen Duffy, First Class Fireman (rescued)
Frank Curran, First Class Fireman (captured)
Andrew Shilland, Fireman (missing)
James Mair, Fireman (killed)
John Harrigan, Fireman (captured)
Patrick Bradley, Fireman (captured)

Pete Lanerty, Fireman (captured)
Thomas Potter, Fireman (captured)
Thomas Murphy, Fireman (rescued)
James Foxton, Fireman (rescued)
Martin King, Fireman (wounded, rescued)
James Mason, Fireman (wounded, rescued)
Thomas Winter, Fireman (wounded, captured)
Peter Duncan, Fireman (killed)
Malcom McFarland, Fireman (wounded, rescued)
Samuel Williams, Fireman (wounded, captured)
Christian Pust, Coal Heaver (killed)
James Maguire, Coal Heaver (captured)
John Benson, Coal Heaver (captured)
Joseph Pearson, Coal Trimmer (captured)
John Riley, Coal Trimmer (captured)
William Levins, Coal Trimmer (rescued)
James Welsh, Coal Trimmer (rescued)
R. B. Hobbs, Seaman (captured)
George Appleby, Seaman (killed)
Thomas McMillan, Seaman (rescued)
Michael Mars, Seaman (rescued)
John Caren, Seaman (wounded, captured)
John Roberts, Seaman (killed)
Samuel Henry, Seaman (captured)
William Hearn, Seaman (rescued)
John Neil, Seaman (wounded, captured)
Henry Yates, Seaman (captured)
William Robinson, Seaman (rescued)
Michael Shields, Seaman (captured)
William Clark, Seaman (captured)
David Thurston, Seaman (captured)
David Leggett, Seaman (captured)
Walter Van Ness, Seaman (drowned)
Henry Fisher, Seaman (missing)
James Hart, Seaman (killed)
John Williams, Seaman (missing)
Edward Burrell, Seaman (captured)
Juan Ochoa, Seaman (captured)
Jacob Verber, Seaman (wounded, captured)
Ralph Masters, Ordinary Seaman (rescued)
George Egerton, Ordinary Seaman (rescued)
Edgar Fripp, Ordinary Seaman (captured)
John Emery, Ordinary Seaman (captured)
Frank Townshend, Ordinary Seaman (wounded, rescued)

William Miller, Ordinary Seaman (captured)
David Williams, Ordinary Seaman (wounded, captured)
William Bradford, Ordinary Seaman (missing)
Philip Wharton, Ordinary Seaman (rescued)
John Russell, Ordinary Seaman (captured)
John Smith, Ordinary Seaman (captured)
Henry Angel, Ordinary Seaman (rescued)
John Mehan, Ordinary Seaman (rescued)
Richard Evans, Ordinary Seaman (captured)
John Welham, Ordinary Seaman (drowned)
Andrew Pfeiffer, Ordinary Seaman (rescued)
Thomas Kehoe, Ordinary Seaman (rescued)
George Conroy, Ordinary Seaman (captured)
Thomas Watson, Ordinary Seaman (captured)
Robert Devine, Ordinary Seaman (wounded, captured)
Karl Pajorva, Ordinary Seaman (killed)
James King II, Ordinary Seaman (mortally wounded)
Charles Colson, Ordinary Seaman (missing)
John Jonson, Ordinary Seaman (captured)
John Buckley, Ordinary Seaman (missing)
Henry McCoy, Ordinary Seaman (captured)
Richard Longshaw, Ordinary Seaman (rescued)
George Yeoman, Ordinary Seaman (wounded, rescued)
Martin Midich, Ordinary Seaman (captured)
Charles Olson, Ordinary Seaman (killed)
Henry Godson, Ordinary Seaman (captured)
Louis Dupois, Ordinary Seaman (rescued)
William McClellan, Ordinary Seaman (rescued)
William Jones, Ordinary Seaman (missing)
George Percy, Ordinary Seaman (captured)
Fred Lennon, Ordinary Seaman (rescued)
John Adams, Landsman (missing)
Thomas Brandon, Landsman (captured)
Thomas White, Landsman (missing)
Henry Higgins, Landsman (captured)
Nicholas Adams, Landsman (captured)
David H. White, Wardroom Boy (missing)
Maurice Bright, Boy (rescued)
John Wilson, Boy (captured)
Thomas L. Parker, Boy (captured)

Officers on hand, June 19, 1864	25
Crew members on hand, June 19, 1864	<u>120</u>
Total in battle with *Kearsarge*	145

Others Who Served on the *Alabama*

These crew members served on the *Alabama* but were not present at the time of the battle with the *Kearsarge*. Names in **bold print** are members of the original *Alabama* crew. Ranks are those in effect at the time of their departure from the *Alabama*.

John Low, 4th Lieutenant (transferred to *Tuscaloosa*)
Simeon Cummings, 3rd Asst. Engineer (accidentally killed)
William Sinclair, Midshipman (transferred to *Tuscaloosa*)
James W. S. King, Quartermaster (deserted)
William King, Quartermaster (deserted)
Adolphus Marmelstein, Quartermaster (transferred to *Tuscaloosa*)
Thomas Weir, Quartermaster (deserted)
George Horwood, Chief Boatswain's Mate (discharged)
James Williams, Captain of the Foretop (deserted)
James Smith, Captain of the Forecastle (deserted)
Clarence Yonge, Paymaster (deserted, court-martialed)
Michael Kinshlea, Fireman (discharged as invalid)
John Jack, Fireman (deserted)
John Latham, Fireman (deserted)
James McFadden, Fireman (discharged)
David Roach (Roche), Fireman (deserted)
John Allen, Seaman (deserted)
Samuel Brewer, Seaman (transferred to *Tuscaloosa*)
Sam Brown, Seaman (transferred to *Tuscaloosa*)
Charles Coles, Seaman (deserted)
John Doyle, Seaman (deserted)
John Duggan, Seaman (transferred to *Tuscaloosa*)
George Forrest, Seaman (dishonorably discharged)
John Hughes, Seaman (deserted)
Edwin Jones, Seaman (transferred to *Tuscaloosa*)
Henry Legris, Seaman (transferred to *Tuscaloosa*)
James Martin, Seaman (discharged as invalid)
Joseph Minor, Seaman (transferred to *Tuscaloosa*)
James Raleigh, Seaman (deserted)
William Rinton, Seaman (transferred to *Tuscaloosa*)
Robert Williams, Seaman (transferred to *Tuscaloosa*)
Thomas Williams, Ordinary Seaman (transferred to *Tuscaloosa*)
James Adams, Ordinary Seaman (court-martialed, discharged)
Thomas Allman, Ordinary Seaman (transferred to *Tuscaloosa*)
Edward Fitzmaurice, Ordinary Seaman (discharged as invalid)
George Getzinger, Ordinary Seaman (discharged as invalid)
Albert Gilman, Ordinary Seaman (deserted)
William Halford, Ordinary Seaman (deserted)

Richard Hambly, Ordinary Seaman (deserted)
Peter Henney, Ordinary Seaman (deserted)
Albert Hyer, Ordinary Seaman (deserted)
Peter Jackson, Ordinary Seaman (deserted)
Thomas James, Ordinary Seaman (deserted)
John McAlee, Ordinary Seaman (deserted)
Frank Mahany, Ordinary Seaman (deserted)
Nicholas Maling, Ordinary Seaman (deserted)
Valentine Mesner, Ordinary Seaman (deserted)
John Miller, Ordinary Seaman (deserted)
Martin Molk, Ordinary Seaman (transferred to *Tuscaloosa*)
Alfred Morris, Ordinary Seaman (deserted)
Joseph Neal, Ordinary Seaman (deserted)
William Nordstrom, Ordinary Seaman (deserted)
Robert Owens, Ordinary Seaman (transferred to *Tuscaloosa*)
William Price, Ordinary Seaman (discharged as invalid)
Richard Ray, Ordinary Seaman (deserted)
George Ross, Ordinary Seaman (deserted)
Henry Saunders, Ordinary Seaman (deserted)
Gustave Schwalbe, Ordinary Seaman (deserted)
George Thomas, Ordinary Seaman (deserted)
Samuel Valens, Ordinary Seaman (deserted)
John Vial, Ordinary Seaman (deserted)
James Wallace, Ordinary Seaman (deserted)
Thomas Walsh, Ordinary Seaman (deserted)
John Williams, Ordinary Seaman (deserted)
Robert Egan, Boy (deserted)
John Grady, Boy (deserted)
Henry Cosgrove, Boy (deserted)
James Wilson, Boy (deserted)

Total who served on the *Alabama* for any length of time = 213

Appendix C

Officers and Crew of the *Kearsarge*

Officers and Crew of the USS *Kearsarge* on June 19, 1864

Names in **bold print** are members of the original *Kearsarge* crew. Ranks are those in effect at the time of the battle with the *Alabama*. Individual battle conclusion shown in parentheses.

John Winslow, Captain
James S. Thornton, Lt. Commander
David H. Sumner, Acting Master
Eben Stoddard, Acting Master
James R. Wheeler, Acting Master
Ezra Bartlett, Acting Master's Mate
Charles Danforth, Acting Master's Mate
Edward E. Preble, Lieutenant
John M. Browne, Surgeon
William Cushman, Chief Engineer
William Badlam, 2nd Asst. Engineer
Sidney L. Smith, 2nd Asst. Engineer
Frederick L. Miller, 3rd Asst. Engineer
Henry McConnell, 3rd Asst. Engineer
James C. Walton, Boatswain
Seth Hartwell, Captain's Clerk
Franklin A. Graham, Gunner

Carsten DeWit, Yeoman
Joseph Adams Smith, Asst. Paymaster
William Gurney, Quartermaster
Charles Butts, Quartermaster
William Smith, Quartermaster (Medal of Honor)
James Saunders, Quartermaster ((Medal of Honor)
William Poole, Quartermaster (Medal of Honor)
William Bond, Boatswain's Mate (Medal of Honor)
Thomas Perry, Boatswain's Mate (Medal of Honor)
John Hayes, Coxswain (Medal of Honor)
William Morgan, Coxswain
Charles A. Read, Coxswain (Medal of Honor)
James Wilson, Coxswain
George Russell, Armorer
John Dempsey, Quarter Gunner (wounded)
Andrew Rowley, Quarter Gunner
Hugh McPherson, Gunner's Mate
Jason N. Watrus, Master at Arms
Joshua Carey, Sailmaker's Mate
Mark Ham, Carpenter's Mate (Medal of Honor)
John Bickford, Captain of the Top (Medal of Honor)
James H. Lee, Captain of the Top (Medal of Honor)
Robert Strahan, Captain of the Maintop (Medal of Honor)
James Haley, Captain of the Forecastle (Medal of Honor)
William Ellis, Captain of the Hold
Henry Cook, Captain of the After Guard
Francis Viannah, Captain of the After Guard
Michael Ahern, Paymaster's Steward (Medal of Honor)
Edward Williams, Captain's Steward
George A. Tittle, Surgeon's Steward
William Y. Evans, Nurse
George Williams, Captain's Cook
Charles B. Fisher, Officers' Cook
Timothy Hurley, Ship's Cook
Daniel B. Sargent, Paymaster's Clerk
Charles T. Young, Orderly Sergeant, USMC
Henry Hobson, Corporal, USMC
Austin Quinby, Corporal, USMC
Patrick Flood, Private, USMC
John Batchelder, Private, USMC
Roscoe D. Dolley, Private, USMC (wounded)
James Kerrigan, Private, USMC
John McAllen, Private, USMC
George Raymond, Private, USMC

Isaac Thornton, Private, USMC
James Tucker, Private, USMC
Benjamin Blaisdell, 1st Class Fireman
Joel Blaisdell, 1st Class Fireman
William Donnelly, 1st Class Fireman
Joseph Dugan, 1st Class Fireman
John Dwyer, 1st Class Fireman
Henry Jamison, 1st Class Fireman
True Priest, 1st Class Fireman
George Remick, 1st Class Fireman
Joel L. Sanborn , 1st Class Fireman
William Smith, 1st Class Fireman
Jere Young, 1st Class Fireman
Patrick O'Connor, 2nd Class Fireman
John Ordion, 2nd Class Fireman
Thomas Salmon, 2nd Class Fireman
James W. Sheffield, 2nd Class Fireman
John Stackpole, 2nd Class Fireman
William Stanley, 2nd Class Fireman
George Smart, 2nd Class Fireman
Stephen Smith, 2nd Class Fireman
Clement Antoine, Coal Heaver
Sylvanus Brackett, Coal Heaver
Jean Briset, Coal Heaver
Benjamin Buttons, Coal Heaver
John F. Dugan, Coal Heaver
Lyman H. Hartford, Coal Heaver
Adoniram K. Littlefield, Coal Heaver
Timothy Lynch, Coal Heaver
Thomas Marsh, Coal Heaver
Charles Poole, Coal Heaver
John Pope, Coal Heaver
Lyman P. Spinney, Coal Heaver
John W. Sanborn, Coal Heaver
William Wainwright, Coal Heaver
John W. Young, Coal Heaver
Thomas Alloway, Seaman
James Bradley, Seaman
Timothy Canty, Seaman
Michael Conroy, Seaman
Benedict Drury, Seaman
George English, Seaman
William Giles, Seaman
George Harrison, Seaman (Medal of Honor)

Jeremiah Horrigan, Seaman
Augustus Johnson, Seaman
Charles Jones, Seaman
Peter Ludy, Seaman
James Magee, Seaman
Charles Moore, Seaman (Medal of Honor)
Levi W. Nye, Seaman
Joachim Pease, Seaman (Medal of Honor)
William O'Halloran, Seaman
George E. Read, Seaman (Medal of Honor)
John Shields, Seaman
William Turner, Seaman
Edward Wallace, Seaman
Philip Weeks, Seaman
Edward Wilt, Seaman
George Andrew, Ordinary Seaman
John Barrows, Ordinary Seaman
John Boyle, Ordinary Seaman
John E. Bradley, Ordinary Seaman
Thomas Buckley, Ordinary Seaman
Joshua Collins, Ordinary Seaman
Lawrence Crowley, Ordinary Seaman
William Gowin, Ordinary Seaman (mortally wounded)
George Kinne, Ordinary Seaman
James McBeth, Ordinary Seaman (wounded)
Charles Mattison, Ordinary Seaman
James Morey, Ordinary Seaman
Zaran Phillips, Ordinary Seaman
John C. Woodbury, Ordinary Seaman
George A. Whipple, Ordinary Seaman
William Alsdorf, Landsman
George Bailey, Landsman
George Baker, Landsman
William Barnes, Landsman
Jacob Barth, Landsman
William Bastine, Landsman
Jonathan Brier, Landsman
William Chappel, Landsman
Daniel Charles, Landsman
Jose Dabney, Landsman
Benjamin Davis, Landsman
James Devine, Landsman
William Fisher, Landsman
Vanburn Francois, Landsman

James Hayes, Landsman
James Henson, Landsman
Charles Hill, Landsman
Martin Hoyt, Landsman
Nathan Ives, Landsman
John H. McCarthy, Landsman
Dennis McCarty, Landsman
Patrick McKeever, Landsman
Charles Redding, Landsman
William M. Smith, Landsman
John Sonius, 1st Class Boy
James O. Stone, 1st Class Boy
Manuel Jose Gallardo, 2nd Class Boy

Officers on hand, June 19, 1864   18
Crew members on hand, June 19, 1864   <u>145</u>
Total in battle with *Alabama*   163

Others Who Served on the *Kearsarge*

These crew members served on the *Kearsarge* but were not present at the time of the battle with the *Alabama*. Names in **bold print** are members of the original *Kearsarge* crew. Ranks are those in effect at the time of their departure from the *Kearsarge*.

Charles Pickering, Commander (relieved of command)
Thomas C. Harris, Lieutenant (transferred to *Chippewa*)
James Whitaker, 1st Asst. Engineer (detached)
William H. Yeaton, Acting Master's Mate (absent due to illness)
Christian Smith, Quartermaster (deserted)
Henry Adams, Officers' Steward (deserted)
Sabine DeSanto, Officers' steward (died at sea)
Archibald McClaymont, Officers' Steward (deserted)
Robert T. Scott, Wardroom Steward (deserted)
Charles Muzzey, Captain's Clerk (returned to United States)
Peter Mulhall, Corporal, USMC (in hospital before start of cruise)
James Golden, Captain's Clerk (returned to United States)
Norman Kelly, Captain of the Top (deserted)
John Chase, 1st Class Fireman (returned to United States)
John Lambert, 2nd Class Fireman (returned to United States)
Clement Boener, Coal Heaver (died at sea)
Richard Vincent, Coal Heaver (deserted)
Heinrich Meinsen, Coal Heaver (deserted)
James Carroll, Seaman (returned to United States)

Andrew Tupic, Seaman (in hospital before start of cruise)
Thomas Burns, Seaman (deserted)
Edward Gilson, Seaman (returned to United States)
John Murphy, Seaman (returned to United States)
Frank Wilson, Seaman (deserted)
William Bell, Ordinary Seaman (deserted)
James Burns, Ordinary Seaman (returned home to Ireland)
William Cameron, Ordinary Seaman (deserted)
William Cummings, Ordinary Seaman (deserted)
Thomas Igo, Ordinary Seaman (deserted)
Jose Iguacio, Ordinary Seaman (deserted)
Thomas Jones, Ordinary Seaman (deserted)
Alexander Joseph, Ordinary Seaman (deserted)
Daniel Lahie, Ordinary Seaman (deserted)
Matthew McNally, Ordinary Seaman (deserted)
Antonio Rousserz, Ordinary Seaman (deserted)
William Spencer, Ordinary Seaman (deserted)
James Taylor, Ordinary Seaman (deserted)
John Thompson, Ordinary Seaman (deserted)
Edward (Tibbetts) Sampson, Ordinary Seaman (killed by shark)
Fred Antoine, Landsman (deserted)
William Clark, Landsman (deserted)
John Coalter, Landsman (deserted)
Mark Emery, Landsman (died at sea)
John Kelly, Landsman (deserted)
Thomas Melvin, Landsman (deserted)
John Netto, Landsman (deserted)
Martin Roach, Landsman (deserted)
Edward Roland, Landsman (deserted)
John Wood, Ordinary Seaman (deserted)
Charles Brown, Supernumerary (deserted)
Robert Jones, Supernumerary (deserted)
Hugh Murphy, Supernumerary (deserted)
Thomas Turner, Supernumerary (deserted)
Henry Wards, Supernumerary (discharged)
Richard Benson, Rank Unknown (never mustered in)
Thomas Blake, Rank Unknown (deserted)
Charles Blees, Rank Unknown (deserted)
William Brown, Rank Unknown (deserted)
Daniel Clark, Rank Unknown (deserted)
J. W. Griffin, Rank Unknown (deserted)
W. Langton, Rank Unknown (no information available)
Manuel Lewis, Rank Unknown (sent home)
William Locke, Rank Unknown (deserted)

Charles Maguire, Rank Unknown (deserted)
James Mellus, Rank Unknown (deserted)
Robert Motley, Rank Unknown (deserted)
Jacob Pike, Rank Unknown (sent home)
G. T. Quanstrom, Rank Unknown (no information available)
Charles Roney, Rank Unknown (no information available)
Martin T. Simpson, Rank Unknown (no information available)
David M. Smith, Rank Unknown (no information available)
P. E. Stevens, Rank Unknown (transferred to USS *Ino*)
Thomas Sullivan, Rank Unknown (no information available)
Charles Tirnan, Rank Unknown (sent home)
Francis Trude, Rank Unknown (deserted)
H. H. Van Dyke, Rank Unknown (sent home)
Charles White, Rank Unknown (deserted)
John Wilson, Rank Unknown (deserted)

Total who served on the *Kearsarge* for any length of time = 241
(NOTE: This does not include the "Queenstown Stowaways")

NOTES

INTRODUCTION

1. *New York Times*, September 29, 1861.
2. Ibid., June 5, 1861.
3. Edward Boykin, *Ghost Ship of the Confederacy* (New York: Funk and Wagnalls, 1957), 78–79.
4. James D. Bulloch, *Secret Service of the Confederate States in Europe* (London: Richard Bentley and Son, 1883), vol. 1, 23.

CHAPTER ONE

1. *Official Records of the Union and Confederate Navies in the War of the Rebellion*, ser. 2, vol. 2, 64–65 (hereinafter cited as *ORN*).
2. Charles Grayson Summersell, *CSS "Alabama": Builder, Captain, and Plans* (University, Alabama: University of Alabama Press, 1985), 9–12.
3. Ibid., 4.
4. J. Thomas Scharf, *History of the Confederate States Navy* (New York: Rogers and Sherwood, 1887), 783.
5. James D. Bulloch, *Secret Service of the Confederate States in Europe* (London: Richard Bentley and Son, 1883), vol. 1, 48.
6. *New York Times*, May 28, 1861.
7. Ibid.
8. Charles Grayson Summersell, *CSS "Alabama": Builder, Captain, and Plans* (University, Alabama: University of Alabama Press, 1985), 9–12.
9. Ibid.
10. *London Economist*, as quoted in *New York Times*, May 14, 1861.
11. *London Shipping Gazette*, April 29, 1861.
12. *Manchester Guardian*, April 30, 1861.
13. James D. Bulloch, *Secret Service of the Confederate States in Europe* (London: Richard Bentley and Son, 1883), vol. 1, 48.
14. Print No. 48027/24070, Library of Congress, Washington, D.C.

15. J. Thomas Scharf, *History of the Confederate States Navy* (New York: Rogers and Sherwood, 1887), 784.

16. Lawrence H. Officer, *Between the Dollar-Sterling Gold Points* (Cambridge: Cambridge University Press, 1996), 55.

17. Charles Grayson Summersell, *CSS "Alabama": Builder, Captain, and Plans* (University, Alabama: University of Alabama Press, 1985), 108.

18. Ibid., 111.

19. James D. Bulloch, *Secret Service of the Confederate States in Europe* (London: Richard Bentley and Son, 1883), vol. 1, 64.

20. Edward Boykin, *Ghost Ship of the Confederacy* (New York: Funk and Wagnalls, 1957), 82.

Chapter Two

1. *ORN,* ser. 2, vol. 1, 118–19.

2. Navy Dependents' Pension Files, National Archives, Washington, D.C., M-1279, pension applied for by Mary Pickering, May 14, 1888, Certificate No. 3860.

3. *Portsmouth Chronicle,* November 8, 1861.

4. Henry S. Hobson, *The Famous Cruise of the "Kearsarge"* (Bonds Village, Massachusetts: the author, 1894), 107–9.

5. Gideon Welles to William L. Hudson, January 24, 1862, Reel 67, Letters Sent, National Archives, Washington, D.C.

6. *Portsmouth Chronicle,* January 25, 1862.

7. *Kearsarge* log, January 28–February 3, 1862.

8. Ibid., February 5, 1862.

9. Henry S. Hobson, *The Famous Cruise of the "Kearsarge"* (Bonds Village, Massachusetts: the author, 1894), 8.

10. Ibid., 109.

11. *ORN,* ser. 1, vol. 1, 284.

12. *Kearsarge* log, February 5–7, 1862.

13. Ibid., February 10–11, 1862.

14. Ibid., February 16–19, 1862.

15. Ibid.

16. Ibid., February 22–26, 1862.

17. *Kearsarge* muster rolls, February 25, 1862, National Archives, Washington, D.C.

18. Henry S. Hobson, *The Famous Cruise of the "Kearsarge"* (Bonds Village, Massachusetts: the author, 1894) 12–13.

19. *ORN,* ser. 1, vol. 1, 310–17, 665, 687; *Official Records of the Union and Confederate Armies in the War of the Rebellion,* ser. 2, vol. 3, 473–75 (hereinafter cited as *OR*).

20. *ORN,* ser. 1, vol. 1, 310, 670–80.

21. Ezra Bartlett Diary, March 11–13, 1862, Library of Congress, Washington, D.C.

Chapter Three

1. Charles Grayson Summersell, *CSS "Alabama": Builder, Captain, and Plans* (University, Alabama: University of Alabama Press, 1985), 7.

2. James D. Bulloch, *Secret Service of the Confederate States in Europe* (London: Richard Bentley and Son, 1883), vol. 1, 127–49.

3. Ibid., 150.

4. J. Thomas Scharf, *History of the Confederate States Navy* (New York: Rogers and Sherwood, 1887), 785–86.

5. L. Thomas, Attorney-General to A. C. Sands, Esq., U.S. Marshal in Cincinnati, *OR,* ser. 2, vol. 2, 261.

6. Raphael Semmes, *Memoirs of Service Afloat During the War Between the States* (Baltimore: Kelly, Piet and Company, 1869), 351–52.

7. *ORN,* ser. 1, vol. 1, 771.

8. James D. Bulloch, *Secret Service of the Confederate States in Europe* (London: Richard Bentley and Son, 1883), vol. 1, 235.

9. *ORN,* ser. 2, vol. 2, 205–15.

10. Edward Boykin, *Ghost Ship of the Confederacy* (New York: Funk and Wagnalls, 1957), 160.

11. Ibid., 81.

12. Letter, James Bulloch to Stephen Mallory, April 11, 1862. *ORN,* ser. 2, vol. 2, 183–84.

13. Edward Boykin, *Ghost Ship of the Confederacy* (New York: Funk and Wagnalls, 1957), 82.

14. Charles Grayson Summersell, *CSS "Alabama": Builder, Captain, and Plans* (University, Alabama: University of Alabama Press, 1985), 13.

15. James D. Bulloch, *Secret Service of the Confederate States in Europe* (London: Richard Bentley and Son, 1883), vol. 1, 231.

16. *Spy Reports on the "290,"* May 18, 1862, CSS *Alabama* Digital Collection, University of Alabama.

17. Ibid., June 20, 1862.

18. Ibid., June 27, 1862.

19. Edward Boykin, *Ghost Ship of the Confederacy* (New York: Funk and Wagnalls, 1957), 170.

20. John McIntosh Kell, *Recollections of a Naval Life* (Washington, D.C.: The Neale Company, 1900), 180–84.

21. Charles Grayson Summersell, *CSS "Alabama": Builder, Captain, and Plans* (University, Alabama: University of Alabama Press, 1985), 12.

22. William Passmore, *Affidavit of William Passmore of Birkenhead,* July 21, 1862, CSS *Alabama* Digital Collection, University of Alabama.

23. *Spy Reports on the "290,"* July 15, 1862, CSS *Alabama* Digital Collection, University of Alabama.

24. Ibid., July 14, 1862.

25. Edward Boykin, *Ghost Ship of the Confederacy* (New York: Funk and Wagnalls, 1957), 170.

26. Ibid., 170–71.

27. Charles Grayson Summersell, *CSS "Alabama": Builder, Captain, and Plans* (University, Alabama: University of Alabama Press, 1985), 13–14.

28. James D. Bulloch, *Secret Service of the Confederate States in Europe* (London: Richard Bentley and Son, 1883), vol. 1, 263.

29. Raphael Semmes to J. H. North, June 8, 1862. *ORN,* ser. 1, vol. 1, 771–72.

30. James D. Bulloch to C. R. Yonge, July 28, 1862. *ORN,* ser. 1, vol. 1, 773.

31. James D. Bulloch to M. J. Butcher, July 30, 1862. *ORN,* ser. 1, vol. 1, 773–74.

32. James D. Bulloch, *Secret Service of the Confederate States in Europe* (London: Richard Bentley and Son, 1883), vol. 1, 239–42.

33. T. A. Cravens, Official Report, *ORN,* ser. 1, vol. 1, 414.

34. James D. Bulloch, *Secret Service of the Confederate States in Europe* (London: Richard Bentley and Son, 1883), vol. 1, 242.

35. *Alabama* log, August 1–5, 1862.

CHAPTER FOUR

1. *Kearsarge* log, April 5, 1862.

2. Ibid., April 6, 1862.

3. Ibid., May 13, 1862.

4. Ibid., May 30, 1862.

5. Henry S. Hobson, *The Famous Cruise of the "Kearsarge"* (Bonds Village, Massachusetts: the author, 1894), 17–18.

6. Ibid., 18–19.

7. Diary of Charles B. Fisher, June 10–15, 1862, U.S. Army Military History Institute.

8. *Kearsarge* log, June 15–23, 1862.

9. Diary of Charles B. Fisher, June 28–30, 1862, U.S. Army Military History Institute.

10. Charles Grayson Summersell, *CSS "Alabama": Builder, Captain, and Plans* (University, Alabama: University of Alabama Press, 1985), 28.

11. *Alabama* log, August 20–22, 1862.

12. Edward Boykin, *Ghost Ship of the Confederacy* (New York: Funk and Wagnalls, 1957), 180.

13. Sinclair, Arthur. *Two Years on the "Alabama"* (Boston: Lee and Shepard, 1896), 15.

14. Ibid., 16.

15. Ibid., 18.

16. Edward Boykin, *Ghost Ship of the Confederacy* (New York: Funk and Wagnalls, 1957), 181.

17. Arthur Sinclair. *Two Years on the "Alabama"* (Boston: Lee and Shepard, 1896), 300–301.

18. Ibid.

19. Charles Grayson Summersell, *CSS "Alabama": Builder, Captain, and Plans* (University, Alabama: University of Alabama Press, 1985), 28.

20. Ibid., 27.

21. Norman C. Delaney, *John McIntosh Kell of the Raider "Alabama"* (University, Alabama: University of Alabama Press, 1973), 131.

22. *ORN,* ser. 1, vol. 3, 677.

23. Charles Grayson Summersell, *CSS "Alabama": Builder, Captain, and Plans* (University, Alabama: University of Alabama Press, 1985), 29–32.

Chapter Five

1. Charles Grayson Summersell, *CSS "Alabama": Builder, Captain, and Plans* (University, Alabama: University of Alabama Press, 1985), 23.

2. Edward Boykin, *Ghost Ship of the Confederacy* (New York: Funk and Wagnalls, 1957), 189–90; George Townley Fullam, *The Journal of George Townley Fullam* (University, Alabama: University of Alabama Press, 1973), 16–17.

3. George Townley Fullam, *The Journal of George Townley Fullam* (University, Alabama: University of Alabama Press, 1973), 16.

4. Charles Grayson, *CSS "Alabama": Builder, Captain, and Plans* (University, Alabama: University of Alabama Press, 1985), 24.

5. Raphael Semmes, *Memoirs of Service Afloat during the War Between the States* (Baltimore: Kelly, Piet, and Company, 1869), 566.

6. Edward Boykin, *Ghost Ship of the Confederacy* (New York: Funk and Wagnalls, 1957), 191.

7. *Harper's Weekly,* October 22, 1862.

8. George Townley Fullam, *The Journal of George Townley Fullam* (University, Alabama: University of Alabama Press, 1973), 17.

9. Edward Boykin, *Ghost Ship of the Confederacy* (New York: Funk and Wagnalls, 1957), 193.

10. *ORN,* ser. 1, vol. 2, 735.

11. George Townley Fullam, *The Journal of George Townley Fullam* (University, Alabama: University of Alabama Press, 1973), 18–19.

12. Edward Boykin, *Ghost Ship of the Confederacy* (New York: Funk and Wagnalls, 1957), 192.

13. Ibid., 198–99; George Townley Fullam, *The Journal of George Townley Fullam* (University, Alabama: University of Alabama Press, 1973), 18.

14. Edward Boykin, *Ghost Ship of the Confederacy* (New York: Funk and Wagnalls, 1957), 198–99.

15. *New York Sunday World*, April 19, 1891.

16. George Townley Fullam, *The Journal of George Townley Fullam* (University, Alabama: University of Alabama Press, 1973), 22.

17. Ibid., 22–23; Edward Boykin, *Ghost Ship of the Confederacy* (New York: Funk and Wagnalls, 1957), 200.

18. George Townley Fullam, *The Journal of George Townley Fullam* (University, Alabama: University of Alabama Press, 1973), 24.

19. Ibid.

20. Edward Maffitt Anderson to his father, November 18, 1862. William Stanley Poole Papers, University of Alabama.

21. Edward Boykin, *Ghost Ship of the Confederacy* (New York: Funk and Wagnalls, 1957), 203.

22. *Kearsarge* log, March 26, 1862.

23. Ibid., July 13, 1862; Henry S. Hobson, *The Famous Cruise of the "Kearsarge"* (Bonds Village, Massachusetts, the author, 1894), 146.

24. *Kearsarge* log, July 20, 1862.

25. Ibid., July 28, 1862.

26. Ibid., August 6, 1862; *ORN,* ser. 1, vol. 1, 570.

27. *Kearsarge* log, August 6–19, 1862.

28. Ibid., August 19, 1862.

29. Ibid., August 25, 1862.

30. *ORN,* ser. 1, vol. 7, 583–84.

31. *Kearsarge* log, September 14–15, 1862.

32. *ORN,* ser. 1, vol. 3, 677–78.

33. Edward Boykin, *Ghost Ship of the Confederacy* (New York: Funk and Wagnalls, 1957), 206.

Chapter Six

1. Arthur Sinclair, *Two Years on the "Alabama"* (Boston: Lee and Shepard, 1896), 39.

2. Charles Grayson Summersell, *CSS "Alabama": Builder, Captain, and Plans* (University, Alabama: University of Alabama Press, 1985), 35.

3. Arthur Sinclair, *Two Years on the "Alabama"* (Boston: Lee and Shepard, 1896), 235.

4. Edward Boykin, *Ghost Ship of the Confederacy* (New York: Funk and Wagnalls, 1957), 215.

5. George Townley Fullam, *The Journal of George Townley Fullam* (University, Alabama: University of Alabama Press, 1985), 28–29.

6. Ibid., 30.

7. New York Chamber of Commerce, *Proceedings of the Chamber of Commerce of the State of New York on the Burning of the Ship "Brilliant", by the Pirate "Alabama"* (New York: J. W. Amerman, Printer, 1862).

8. Edward Boykin, *Ghost Ship of the Confederacy* (New York: Funk and Wagnalls, 1957), 218–19.

9. *Alabama* log, October 7, 1862.

10. Raphael Semmes, *The Cruise of the "Alabama" and the "Sumter",* reprinted in the CSS *Alabama* Digital Collection, University of Alabama.

11. Ibid.

12. *ORN,* ser. 1, vol.1, 794.

13. *New York Herald*, October 5, 1862.

14. Edward Boykin, *Ghost Ship of the Confederacy* (New York: Funk and Wagnalls, 1957), 227.

15. Raphael Semmes, *The Cruise of the "Alabama" and the "Sumter"*, reprinted in the CSS *Alabama* Digital Collection, University of Alabama.

16. Arthur Sinclair, *Two Years on the "Alabama"* (Boston: Lee and Shepard, 1896), 44.

17. Edward Boykin, *Ghost Ship of the Confederacy* (New York: Funk and Wagnalls, 1957), 227; Raphael Semmes, *The Cruise of the "Alabama" and the "Sumter"*, reprinted in the CSS *Alabama* Digital Collection, University of Alabama.

18. George Townley Fullam, *The Journal of George Townley Fullam* (University, Alabama: University of Alabama Press, 1985), 39.

19. Edward Boykin, *Ghost Ship of the Confederacy* (New York: Funk and Wagnalls, 1957), 233.

20. George Townley Fullam, *The Journal of George Townley Fullam* (University, Alabama: University of Alabama Press, 1985), 43–44.

21. Ibid, 45; *Alabama* log, October 30, 1862.

22. *ORN,* ser. 1, vol. 3, 677–78.

23. Henry S. Hobson, *The Famous Cruise of the "Kearsarge"* (Bonds Village, Massachusetts, the author, 1894), 26–27.

24. Edward Boykin, *Ghost Ship of the Confederacy* (New York: Funk and Wagnalls, 1957), 188.

25. Henry S. Hobson, *The Famous Cruise of the "Kearsarge"* (Bonds Village, Massachusetts, the author, 1894), 27–28.

26. *Kearsarge* log, October 8, 1862.

27. Arthur Sinclair, *Two Years on the "Alabama"* (Boston: Lee and Shepard, 1896), 192.

28. *ORN,* ser. 1, vol. 1, 509–10.

29. *Kearsarge* log, October 16, 1862.

30. Ibid., October 23, 1862, October 30, 1862.

31. Gideon Welles, *The Diary of Gideon Welles* (Boston and New York: Houghton Mifflin Company, 1911), vol. 1, 175.

CHAPTER SEVEN

1. *ORN,* ser. 1, vol. 3, 678.

2. *Alabama* log, November 8, 1862.

3. Edward Boykin, *Ghost Ship of the Confederacy* (New York: Funk and Wagnalls, 1957), 238.

4. George Townley Fullam, *The Journal of George Townley Fullam* (University, Alabama: University of Alabama Press, 1985), 49.

5. Arthur Sinclair, *Two Years on the "Alabama"* (Boston: Lee and Shepard, 1896), 48.

6. George Townley Fullam, *The Journal of George Townley Fullam* (University, Alabama: University of Alabama Press, 1985), 49.

7. Raphael Semmes, *Memoirs of Service Afloat during the War Between the States.* (Baltimore: Kelly, Piet and Company, 1869), 511–13.

8. George Townley Fullam, *The Journal of George Townley Fullam* (University, Alabama: University of Alabama Press, 1985), 53.

9. Edward Boykin, *Ghost Ship of the Confederacy* (New York: Funk and Wagnalls, 1957), 238.

10. *Report of Commander Ronckendorf*, CSS *Alabama* Digital Collection, University of Alabama.

11. Edward Boykin, *Ghost Ship of the Confederacy* (New York: Funk and Wagnalls, 1957), 245.

12. George Townley Fullam, *The Journal of George Townley Fullam* (University, Alabama: University of Alabama Press, 1985), 56–57.

13. Ibid., 57.

14. Edward Boykin, *Ghost Ship of the Confederacy* (New York: Funk and Wagnalls, 1957), 247.

15. *ORN,* ser. 1, vol. 1, 781–82.

16. *Frank Leslie's Illustrated Newspaper*, January 10, 1863.

17. *Harper's Weekly*, January 10, 1863.

18. Edward Boykin, *Ghost Ship of the Confederacy* (New York: Funk and Wagnalls, 1957), 251–54.
19. Raphael Semmes, *Journal of Commander Semmes*, December 8, 1862, CSS *Alabama* Digital Collection, University of Alabama.
20. Ibid., December 9, 1862.
21. Edward Boykin, *Ghost Ship of the Confederacy* (New York: Funk and Wagnalls, 1957), 259.
22. *ORN,* ser. 1, vol. 1, 816.
23. *Kearsarge* log, November 4, 1862.
24. Ibid., November 5–28, 1862.
25. *ORN,* ser. 1, vol. 8, 266–67.
26. *ORN,* ser. 1, vol. 1, 545.
27. *New York Times*, November 18, 1862.
28. Ibid, November 21, 1862.
29. *ORN,* ser. 1, vol. 1, 576.
30. Gideon Welles, *The Diary of Gideon Welles* (Boston and New York: Houghton Mifflin Company, 1911), vol. 1, 207.

CHAPTER EIGHT

1. *ORN,* ser. 1, vol. 1, 816.
2. John Hope Franklin, "The Emancipation Proclamation: An Act of Justice," in *Prologue: Quarterly of the National Archives*, Washington, D.C., Summer 1993, vol. 25, No. 2.
3. George Townley Fullam, *The Journal of George Townley Fullam* (University, Alabama: University of Alabama Press, 1985), 69–70.
4. Norman C. Delaney, *John McIntosh Kell of the Raider "Alabama"* (University, Alabama: University of Alabama Press, 1973), 70.
5. Edward Boykin, *Ghost Ship of the Confederacy* (New York: Funk and Wagnalls, 1957), 264.
6. *OR*, ser. 1, vol. 15, 647.
7. Homer Blake to Gideon Welles, January 21, 1863, Library of Congress, Washington, D.C.
8. Raphael Semmes, *Memoirs of Service Afloat during the War Between the States* (Baltimore: Kelly, Piet and Company, 1869), 543.
9. *Alabama* log, January 11, 1863.
10. Edward Boykin, *Ghost Ship of the Confederacy* (New York: Funk and Wagnalls, 1957), 265.
11. Ibid., 266–67.
12. *New York Times*, February 17, 1863.
13. Ibid., January 29, 1863.
14. Arthur Sinclair, *Two Years on the "Alabama"* (Boston: Lee and Shepard, 1896), 73.
15. Edward Boykin, *Ghost Ship of the Confederacy* (New York: Funk and Wagnalls, 1957), 268–70.
16. Subject file of the Confederate Navy, M-1091, Reel 7, Washington, D.C.: National Archives, Washington, D.C.
17. John McIntosh Kell, *Recollections of a Naval Life* (Washington, D.C.: The Neale Company, 1900), 209.
18. Edward Boykin, *Ghost Ship of the Confederacy* (New York: Funk and Wagnalls, 1957), 271.
19. Norman C. Delaney, *John McIntosh Kell of the Raider "Alabama"* (University, Alabama: University of Alabama Press, 1973), 145.
20. Arthur Sinclair, *Two Years on the "Alabama"* (Boston: Lee and Shepard, 1896), 79.
21. George Townley Fullam, *The Journal of George Townley Fullam* (University, Alabama: University of Alabama Press, 1985), 81.
22. Arthur Sinclair, *Two Years on the "Alabama"* (Boston: Lee and Shepard, 1896), 78.
23. *Alabama* log, January 26, 1863.

24. George Townley Fullam, *The Journal of George Townley Fullam* (University, Alabama: University of Alabama Press, 1985), 86.

25. Arthur Sinclair, *Two Years on the "Alabama"* (Boston: Lee and Shepard, 1896), 85.

26. Edward Boykin, *Ghost Ship of the Confederacy* (New York: Funk and Wagnalls, 1957), 282–83.

27. *ORN,* ser. 1, vol. 3, 679.

28. George Townley Fullam, *The Journal of George Townley Fullam* (University, Alabama: University of Alabama Press, 1985), 90.

29. *New York Times*, January 1, 1863.

30. Bern Anderson, *By Sea and by River* (New York: Alfred A. Knopf, 1962),192.

31. *New York Times*, February 28, 1863.

CHAPTER NINE

1. Edward Boykin, *Ghost Ship of the Confederacy* (New York: Funk and Wagnalls, 1957), 287.

2. George Townley Fullam. *The Journal of George Townley Fullam* (University, Alabama: University of Alabama Press, 1985), 95.

3. Ibid., 97.

4. Ibid., 98.

5. Edward Boykin, *Ghost Ship of the Confederacy* (New York: Funk and Wagnalls, 1957), 289.

6. George Townley Fullam, *The Journal of George Townley Fullam* (University, Alabama: University of Alabama Press, 1985), 101.

7. Ibid., 102.

8. Edward Boykin, *Ghost Ship of the Confederacy* (New York: Funk and Wagnalls, 1957), 290.

9. George Townley Fullam, *The Journal of George Townley Fullam* (University, Alabama: University of Alabama Press, 1985), 104.

10. Edward Boykin, *Ghost Ship of the Confederacy* (New York: Funk and Wagnalls, 1957), 291.

11. Ibid., 292.

12. George Townley Fullam, *The Journal of George Townley Fullam* (University, Alabama: University of Alabama Press, 1985), 104–5.

13. Arthur Sinclair, *Two Years on the "Alabama"* (Boston: Lee and Shepard, 1896), 107–9.

14. George Townley Fullam, *The Journal of George Townley Fullam* (University, Alabama: University of Alabama Press, 1985), 107.

15. Arthur Sinclair, *Two Years on the "Alabama"* (Boston: Lee and Shepard, 1896), 110.

16. Edward Boykin, *Ghost Ship of the Confederacy* (New York: Funk and Wagnalls, 1957), 295.

17. *Times* (London), March 14, 1863.

18. *Kearsarge* log, March 20–26, 1863.

19. Ibid., March 29, 1863

20. Gideon Welles, *The Diary of Gideon Welles* (Boston and New York: Houghton Mifflin Company, 1911), vol. 1, 251, March 31, 1863.

21. Henry S. Hobson, *The Famous Cruise of the "Kearsarge"* (Bonds Village, Massachusetts, the author, 1894), 148.

22. Ibid., 150.

23. Clarence Edward Macartney, *Mr. Lincoln's Admirals* (New York: Funk and Wagnalls, 1956), 223.

24. Ivan Musicant, *Divided Waters* (New York: Harper Collins, 1995), 349.

25. Clarence Edward Macartney, *Mr. Lincoln's Admirals* (New York: Funk and Wagnalls, 1956), 222.

26. *New York Times*, April 12, 1863.

27. *Kearsarge* log, April 23, 1863.

28. Henry S. Hobson, *The Famous Cruise of the "Kearsarge"* (Bonds Village, Massachusetts, the author, 1894), 115.

29. *New York Times*, April 22, 1863.

Chapter Ten

1. Edward Boykin, *Ghost Ship of the Confederacy* (New York: Funk and Wagnalls, 1957), 96.
2. George Townley Fullam, *The Journal of George Townley Fullam* (University, Alabama: University of Alabama Press, 1985), 110–11.
3. Edward Boykin, *Ghost Ship of the Confederacy* (New York: Funk and Wagnalls, 1957), 298.
4. George Townley Fullam, *The Journal of George Townley Fullam* (University, Alabama: University of Alabama Press, 1985), 112.
5. Ibid., 113.
6. Ibid., 115.
7. Ibid., 118.
8. Edward Boykin, *Ghost Ship of the Confederacy* (New York: Funk and Wagnalls, 1957), 301.
9. *Alabama Claims,* Record Group 39.2.3, National Archives, Washington, D.C.
10. George Townley Fullam, *The Journal of George Townley Fullam* (University, Alabama: University of Alabama Press, 1985), 121.
11. Ibid., 122.
12. Arthur Sinclair, *Two Years on the "Alabama"* (Boston: Lee and Shepard, 1896), 133.
13. Edward Boykin, *Ghost Ship of the Confederacy* (New York: Funk and Wagnalls, 1957), 302.
14. Arthur Sinclair, *Two Years on the "Alabama"* (Boston: Lee and Shepard, 1896), 134.
15. George Townley Fullam, *The Journal of George Townley Fullam* (University, Alabama: University of Alabama Press, 1985), 124.
16. *Kearsarge* log, May 26, 1863.
17. *ORN,* ser. 1, vol. 2, 269–70.
18. *ORN,* ser. 1, vol. 20, 595.
19. *Kearsarge* log, June 29, 1863.

Chapter Eleven

1. Arthur Sinclair, *Two Years on the "Alabama"* (Boston: Lee and Shepard, 1896), 81.
2. George Townley Fullam, *The Journal of George Townley Fullam* (University, Alabama: University of Alabama Press, 1985), 125.
3. *ORN,* ser. 1, vol. 3, 680.
4. Edward Boykin, *Ghost Ship of the Confederacy* (New York: Funk and Wagnalls, 1957), 304.
5. *Alabama* log, July 22, 1863.
6. George Townley Fullam, *The Journal of George Townley Fullam* (University, Alabama: University of Alabama Press, 1985), 128–29.
7. Charles Grayson Summersell, *CSS "Alabama": Builder, Captain, and Plans* (University, Alabama: University of Alabama Press, 1985), 31.
8. *ORN,* ser. 1, vol. 3, 758.
9. George Townley Fullam, *The Journal of George Townley Fullam* (University, Alabama: University of Alabama Press, 1985), 129.
10. George Townley Fullam, *The Journal of George Townley Fullam* (University, Alabama: University of Alabama Press, 1985), 132.
11. *Cape Argus*, August 6, 1863.
12. Edward Boykin, *Ghost Ship of the Confederacy* (New York: Funk and Wagnalls, 1957), 308.
13. Ibid., 313.
14. George Townley Fullam, *The Journal of George Townley Fullam* (University, Alabama: University of Alabama Press, 1985), 137.
15. Norman C. Delaney, *John McIntosh Kell of the Raider "Alabama"* (University, Alabama: University of Alabama Press, 1973), 151.

16. *ORN*, ser. 1, vol. 2, 760–61, 765–67.

17. Ibid., 680–81.

18. George Townley Fullam, *The Journal of George Townley Fullam* (University, Alabama: University of Alabama Press, 1985), 141.

19. Ibid., 142.

20. Edward Boykin, *Ghost Ship of the Confederacy* (New York: Funk and Wagnalls, 1957), 314.

21. *Kearsarge* log, July 17–18, 1863.

22. Henry S. Hobson, *The Famous Cruise of the "Kearsarge"* (Bonds Village, Massachusetts, the author, 1894), 40.

23. *New York Times*, August 4, 1863.

24. *Kearsarge* log, August 18–19, 1863.

25. Ibid., August 20–26, 1863.

Chapter Twelve

1. George Townley Fullam, *The Journal of George Townley Fullam* (University, Alabama: University of Alabama Press, 1985), 143–44.

2. Ibid., 144–45.

3. Edward Boykin, *Ghost Ship of the Confederacy* (New York: Funk and Wagnalls, 1957), 319.

4. Ibid.

5. George Townley Fullam, *The Journal of George Townley Fullam* (University, Alabama: University of Alabama Press, 1985), 146.

6. Norman C. Delaney, *John McIntosh Kell of the Raider "Alabama"* (University, Alabama: University of Alabama Press, 1973), 152.

7. Arthur Sinclair, *Two Years on the "Alabama"* (Boston: Lee and Shepard, 1896), 111.

8. Ibid., 141.

9. *ORN*, ser. 1, vol. 3, 680.

10. George Townley Fullam, *The Journal of George Townley Fullam* (University, Alabama: University of Alabama Press, 1985), 147.

11. Ibid.

12. Ibid., 148.

13. *ORN*, ser. 1, vol. 2, 449.

14. *Kearsarge* log, September 14–15, 1863.

15. *ORN*, ser. 1, vol. 2, 458.

16. *Kearsarge* log, September 26, 1863.

17. Zaran Philips pension application, Certificate No. 3163, National Archives, Washington, D.C.

18. Henry S. Hobson, *The Famous Cruise of the "Kearsarge"* (Bonds Village, Massachusetts, the author, 1894), 143.

19. *ORN*, ser. 1, vol. 2, 473.

20. *London News*, September 4, 1863.

Chapter Thirteen

1. *ORN*, ser. 1, vol. 2, 473–74, 494–502.

2. George Townley Fullam, *The Journal of George Townley Fullam* (University, Alabama: University of Alabama Press, 1985), 150–51.

3. Ibid., 152.

4. *ORN*, ser. 1, vol. 3, 680–81.

5. George Townley Fullam, *The Journal of George Townley Fullam* (University, Alabama: University of Alabama Press, 1985), 154–55.

6. Arthur Sinclair, *Two Years on the "Alabama"* (Boston: Lee and Shepard, 1896), 184–85.

7. Edward Boykin, *Ghost Ship of the Confederacy* (New York: Funk and Wagnalls, 1957), 324–25.

8. Ibid.

9. Ibid., 326.

10. Arthur Sinclair, *Two Years on the "Alabama"* (Boston: Lee and Shepard, 1896), 186–87.

11. George Townley Fullam, *The Journal of George Townley Fullam* (University, Alabama: University of Alabama Press, 1985), 157.

12. *ORN,* ser. 1, vol. 2, 562.

13. *Alabama* muster roll, Confederate subject file, National Archives, Washington, D.C.

14. George Townley Fullam, *The Journal of George Townley Fullam* (University, Alabama: University of Alabama Press, 1985), 161.

15. *ORN,* ser. 1, vol. 3, 681.

16. Edward Boykin, *Ghost Ship of the Confederacy* (New York: Funk and Wagnalls, 1957), 328–30.

17. George Townley Fullam, *The Journal of George Townley Fullam* (University, Alabama: University of Alabama Press, 1985), 162.

18. Edward Boykin, *Ghost Ship of the Confederacy* (New York: Funk and Wagnalls, 1957), 330.

19. Ibid.

20. George Townley Fullam, *The Journal of George Townley Fullam* (University, Alabama: University of Alabama Press, 1985), 166.

21. Edward Boykin, *Ghost Ship of the Confederacy* (New York: Funk and Wagnalls, 1957), 333.

22. George Townley Fullam, *The Journal of George Townley Fullam* (University, Alabama: University of Alabama Press, 1985), 168.

23. Ibid., 170.

24. Arthur Sinclair, *Two Years on the "Alabama"* (Boston: Lee and Shepard, 1896), 221–22.

25. OR, ser. 1, vol. 26, part 1, 546.

26. *ORN,* ser. 1, vol. 2, 564–65.

27. Ibid., 565.

28. Ibid., 564.

29. Ibid., 498–99.

30. Henry S. Hobson, *The Famous Cruise of the "Kearsarge"* (Bonds Village, Massachusetts, the author, 1894), 345.

31. *ORN,* ser. 1, vol. 2, 564.

32. Ibid., 567.

33. Ibid., 566–67.

34. *Kearsarge* log, December 7–23, 1863.

35. *ORN,* ser. 1, vol. 2, 566.

CHAPTER FOURTEEN

1. George Townley Fullam, *The Journal of George Townley Fullam* (University, Alabama: University of Alabama Press, 1985), 173–74.

2. Edward Boykin, *Ghost Ship of the Confederacy* (New York: Funk and Wagnalls, 1957), 337.

3. Arthur Sinclair, *Two Years on the "Alabama"* (Boston: Lee and Shepard, 1896), 96.

4. *Times of India,* January 23, 1864.

5. Arthur Sinclair, *Two Years on the "Alabama"* (Boston: Lee and Shepard, 1896), 238.

6. George Townley Fullam, *The Journal of George Townley Fullam* (University, Alabama: University of Alabama Press, 1985), 177–78.

7. *Kearsarge* log, January 2, 1864.

8. *ORN,* ser. 1, vol. 2, 583.
9. Ibid., 663–64.
10. Ibid., 589.
11. *Kearsarge* log, January 1–19, 1864.
12. *ORN,* ser. 1, vol. 2, 596–97.
13. Ibid., 597.
14. Ibid, 597–98.
15. Ibid., 598.
16. Henry S. Hobson, *The Famous Cruise of the "Kearsarge"* (Bonds Village, Massachusetts, the author, 1894), 51.
17. Ibid., 144.
18. *ORN,* ser. 1, vol. 2, 606–8.
19. *Kearsarge* log, February 21–24, 1864.

CHAPTER FIFTEEN

1. *ORN,* ser. 1, vol. 3, 681.
2. Ibid.
3. George Townley Fullam, *The Journal of George Townley Fullam* (University, Alabama: University of Alabama Press, 1985), 179.
4. *ORN,* ser. 1, vol. 3, 681.
5. Edward Boykin, *Ghost Ship of the Confederacy* (New York: Funk and Wagnalls, 1957), 340.
6. Ibid.
7. Charles Grayson Summersell, *CSS "Alabama": Builder, Captain, and Plans* (University, Alabama: University of Alabama Press, 1985), 70.
8. *Cape Argus,* March 22, 1864.
9. George Townley Fullam, *The Journal of George Townley Fullam* (University, Alabama: University of Alabama Press, 1985), 181.
10. Edward Boykin, *Ghost Ship of the Confederacy* (New York: Funk and Wagnalls, 1957), 341–42.
11. *Alabama* muster roll, Confederate Subject File, National Archives, Washington, D.C.
12. Charles Grayson Summersell, *CSS "Alabama": Builder, Captain, and Plans* (University, Alabama: University of Alabama Press, 1985), 71.
13. *ORN,* ser. 1, vol. 2, 624.
14. *Kearsarge* log, March 15–26, 1864.
15. Henry S. Hobson, *The Famous Cruise of the "Kearsarge"* (Bonds Village, Massachusetts, the author, 1894), 53.
16. *Kearsarge* log, April 14–16, 1864.
17. Ibid., April 17, 1864.
18. Ibid., April 18–25, 1864.
19. Henry S. Hobson, *The Famous Cruise of the "Kearsarge"* (Bonds Village, Massachusetts, the author, 1894), 54–55.

CHAPTER SIXTEEN

1. George Townley Fullam, *The Journal of George Townley Fullam* (University, Alabama: University of Alabama Press, 1985), 186.
2. *ORN,* ser. 1, vol. 3, 681.
3. George Townley Fullam, *The Journal of George Townley Fullam* (University, Alabama: University of Alabama Press, 1985), 189.
4. Edward Boykin, *Ghost Ship of the Confederacy* (New York: Funk and Wagnalls, 1957), 342–43.

5. Ibid., 343.

6. *ORN,* ser. 1, vol. 3, 651.

7. Ibid, 652.

8. *Kearsarge* log, May 6–7, 1864.

9. Henry S. Hobson, *The Famous Cruise of the "Kearsarge"* (Bonds Village, Massachusetts, the author, 1894), 61.

10. Clarence Edward Macartney, *Mr. Lincoln's Admirals* (New York: Funk and Wagnalls, 1956), 224.

11. Alfred Iverson Branham, *Interview with Captain John McIntosh Kell, Executive Officer of the "Alabama,"* CSS *Alabama* Digital Collection, University of Alabama.

12. Edward Boykin, *Ghost Ship of the Confederacy* (New York: Funk and Wagnalls, 1957), 348.

13. *ORN,* ser. 1, vol. 3, 651.

14. Ibid., 648.

15. Ibid., 651.

16. Arthur Sinclair, *Two Years on the "Alabama"* (Boston: Lee and Shepard, 1896), 87–88.

17. Edward Boykin, *Ghost Ship of the Confederacy* (New York: Funk and Wagnalls, 1957), 352.

18. Charles Grayson Summersell, *CSS "Alabama": Builder, Captain, and Plans* (University, Alabama: University of Alabama Press, 1985), 33.

19. Arthur Sinclair, *Two Years on the "Alabama"* (Boston: Lee and Shepard, 1896), 259–60.

20. Ibid., 262.

21. *ORN,* ser. 1, vol. 3, 57.

22. Ivan Musicant, *Divided Waters* (New York: Harper Collins, 1995), 350–51.

23. Arthur Sinclair, *Two Years on the "Alabama"* (Boston: Lee and Shepard, 1896), 260.

24. Ibid.

25. Edward Boykin, *Ghost Ship of the Confederacy* (New York: Funk and Wagnalls, 1957), 354–55.

26. Arthur Sinclair, *Two Years on the "Alabama"* (Boston: Lee and Shepard, 1896), 263.

Chapter Seventeen

1. Edward Boykin, *Ghost Ship of the Confederacy* (New York: Funk and Wagnalls, 1957), 356.

2. Ibid., 357–58.

3. *New York Times,* July 9, 1864.

4. Henry S. Hobson, *The Famous Cruise of the "Kearsarge"* (Bonds Village, Massachusetts, the author, 1894), 132.

5. *ORN,* ser. 1, vol. 1, 62.

6. James D. Bulloch, *Secret Service of the Confederate States in Europe* (London: Richard Bentley and Son, 1883), vol. 1, 278.

7. Norman C. Delaney, *John McIntosh Kell of the Raider "Alabama"* (University, Alabama: University of Alabama Press, 1973), 164.

8. *ORN,* ser. 1, vol. 3, 79.

9. Arthur Sinclair, *Two Years on the "Alabama"* (Boston: Lee and Shepard, 1896), 186.

10. Edward Boykin, *Ghost Ship of the Confederacy* (New York: Funk and Wagnalls, 1957), 362.

11. Raphael Semmes, *Memoirs of Service Afloat during the War Between the States.* (Baltimore: Kelly, Piet and Company, 1869), 756.

12. Edward Boykin, *Ghost Ship of the Confederacy* (New York: Funk and Wagnalls, 1957), 358.

13. Ibid., 363.

14. Ibid.

15. Henry S. Hobson, *The Famous Cruise of the "Kearsarge"* (Bonds Village, Massachusetts, the author, 1894), 64.

16. Ibid., 114–15.

17. *ORN,* ser. 1, vol. 3, 63.

18. Norman C. Delaney, *John McIntosh Kell of the Raider Alabama* (University, Alabama: University of Alabama Press, 1973), 165.

19. Edward Boykin, *Ghost Ship of the Confederacy* (New York: Funk and Wagnalls, 1957), 366.

20. John McKintosh Kell, *Recollections of a Naval Life* (Washington, D.C.: The Neale Company, 1900), 247.

21. Henry S. Hobson, *The Famous Cruise of the "Kearsarge"* (Bonds Village, Massachusetts, the author, 1894), 71.

22. Clarence Edward Macartney, *Mr. Lincoln's Admirals* (New York: Funk and Wagnalls, 1956), 234.

23. *ORN,* ser. 1, vol. 3, 60.

24. Henry S. Hobson, *The Famous Cruise of the "Kearsarge"* (Bonds Village, Massachusetts, the author, 1894), 114–15.

25. Edward Boykin, *Ghost Ship of the Confederacy* (New York: Funk and Wagnalls, 1957), 364.

26. Henry S. Hobson, *The Famous Cruise of the "Kearsarge"* (Bonds Village, Massachusetts, the author, 1894), 115.

27. Arthur Sinclair, *Two Years on the "Alabama"* (Boston: Lee and Shepard, 1896), 259.

28. Henry S. Hobson, *The Famous Cruise of the "Kearsarge"* (Bonds Village, Massachusetts, the author, 1894), 113.

29. Ibid., 73.

30. Edward Boykin, *Ghost Ship of the Confederacy* (New York: Funk and Wagnalls, 1957), 367.

31. *ORN,* ser. 1, vol. 3, 61.

32. Edward Boykin, *Ghost Ship of the Confederacy* (New York: Funk and Wagnalls, 1957), 368.

33. Ibid., 369.

34. Henry S. Hobson, *The Famous Cruise of the "Kearsarge"* (Bonds Village, Massachusetts, the author, 1894), 116–17.

35. Norman C. Delaney, *John McIntosh Kell of the Raider "Alabama"* (University, Alabama: University of Alabama Press, 1973), 165.

Chapter Eighteen

1. *ORN,* ser. 1, vol. 3, 74–75.

2. Alfred Iverson Branham, *Interview with Captain John McIntosh Kell, Executive Officer of the "Alabama,"* CSS *Alabama* Digital Collection, University of Alabama.

3. Edward Boykin, *Ghost Ship of the Confederacy* (New York: Funk and Wagnalls, 1957), 372.

4. Alfred Iverson Branham, *Interview with Captain John McIntosh Kell, Executive Officer of the "Alabama,"* CSS *Alabama* Digital Collection, University of Alabama.

5. Edward Boykin, *Ghost Ship of the Confederacy* (New York: Funk and Wagnalls, 1957), 376.

6. *London News,* June 21, 1864.

7. *ORN,* ser. 1, vol. 3, 653.

8. Ibid.

9. Henry S. Hobson, *The Famous Cruise of the "Kearsarge"* (Bonds Village, Massachusetts, the author, 1894), 137.

10. Ibid., 138–39.

11. *New York Herald,* July 14, 1864.

12. Henry S. Hobson, *The Famous Cruise of the "Kearsarge"* (Bonds Village, Massachusetts, the author, 1894), 137.

13. *Boston Journal,* February 11, 1894.

14. Edward Boykin, *Ghost Ship of the Confederacy* (New York: Funk and Wagnalls, 1957), 377.

15. Ibid, 378.
16. Clarence Edward Macartney, *Mr. Lincoln's Admirals* (New York: Funk and Wagnalls, 1956), 233.
17. *ORN,* ser. 1, vol. 3, 59.
18. Ibid., 78.
19. James Magee, *The Story of the Battle between the Steam Sloop-of-War "Kearsarge" and the Rebel Cruiser "Alabama,"* CSS *Alabama* Digital Collection, University of Alabama.
20. Ibid.
21. *ORN,* ser. 1, vol. 3, 77.
22. James Magee, *The Story of the Battle between the Steam Sloop-of-War "Kearsarge" and the Rebel Cruiser "Alabama,"* CSS *Alabama* Digital Collection, University of Alabama.
23. Alfred Iverson Branham, *Interview with Captain John McIntosh Kell, Executive Officer of the "Alabama,"* CSS *Alabama* Digital Collection, University of Alabama.

Epilogue

1. *New York Times,* July 6, 1864.
2. *London Star,* June 22, 1864.
3. *New York Times,* July 11, 1864.
4. *Manchester Examiner,* July 22, 1864.
5. *OR,* ser. 1, vol. 42, part 3, 274.
6. *ORN,* ser. 1, vol. 3, 70.
7. Clarence Edward Macartney, *Mr. Lincoln's Admirals* (New York: Funk and Wagnalls, 1956), 23.
8. *ORN,* ser. 1, vol. 3, 65.
9. Ibid., 67–68.
10. Ibid., 70.
11. Ibid., 73–74.
12. Ibid., 74–75.
13. Ibid., 64–65.
14. Arthur Sinclair, *Two Years on the "Alabama"* (Boston: Lee and Shepard, 1896), 19.
15. *New York Times,* July 18, 1864.
16. Henry S. Hobson, *The Famous Cruise of the "Kearsarge"* (Bonds Village, Massachusetts, the author, 1894), 88.
17. Ibid.,165–67.
18. *OR,* ser. 1, vol. 38, 65.
19. *New York Times,* July 9, 1864.
20. Ibid., July 14, 1864.
21. Henry S. Hobson, *The Famous Cruise of the "Kearsarge"* (Bonds Village, Massachusetts, the author, 1894), 379.
22. *New York Times,* August 10, 1864.
23. *ORN,* ser. 1, vol. 12, 181.
24. Ibid., 183.
25. *OR,* ser. 1, vol. 46, part 1, 998.
26. Edward Boykin, *Ghost Ship of the Confederacy* (New York: Funk and Wagnalls, 1957), 238.
27. *ORN,* ser. 1, vol. 10, 307.
28. Ibid., 316.
29. Alfred Iverson Branham, *Interview with Captain John McIntosh Kell, Executive Officer of the "Alabama,"* CSS *Alabama* Digital Collection, University of Alabama.
30. *New York Times,* July 9, 1864.

31. James D. Bulloch, *Secret Service of the Confederate States in Europe* (London: Richard Bentley and Son, 1883), vol. 1, 287.

32. *New York Times*, July 9, 1864.

33. Ibid.

34. *Richmond Dispatch*, July 13, 1864.

35. Arthur Sinclair, *Two Years on the "Alabama"* (Boston: Lee and Shepard, 1896), 261.

36. Edward Boykin, *Ghost Ship of the Confederacy* (New York: Funk and Wagnalls, 1957), 354.

37. *Times* (London), June 22, 1864.

38. *New York Times*, July 9, 1864.

39. James D. Bulloch, *Secret Service of the Confederate States in Europe* (London: Richard Bentley and Son, 1883), vol. 1, 282.

40. Arthur Sinclair, *Two Years on the "Alabama"* (Boston: Lee and Shepard, 1896), 259.

41. James D. Bulloch, *Secret Service of the Confederate States in Europe* (London: Richard Bentley and Son, 1883), vol. 1, 287.

42. George Townley Fullam, *The Journal of George Townley Fullam* (University, Alabama: University of Alabama Press, 1985), 46.

43. *New York Evening Post*, July 7, 1864.

44. *New York Times*, July 6, 1864.

45. Ibid., July 9, 1864.

46. Ibid., December 31, 1864.

47. Ibid., August 1, 1864.

48. James D. Bulloch, *Secret Service of the Confederate States in Europe* (London: Richard Bentley and Son, 1883), vol. 1, 291.

49. *New York Times*, July 12, 1864.

50. Ibid.

51. *OR,* ser. 2, vol. 7, 1033.

52. *ORN,* ser. 1, vol. 3, 656.

53. Ibid., 665–67.

54. Ibid., 668.

55. Ibid., 654.

56. J. Thomas Scharf, *History of the Confederate States Navy* (New York: Rogers and Sherwood, 1887), vol. 2, 782–83.

BIBLIOGRAPHY

Anderson, Bern. *By Sea and by River*. New York: Alfred A. Knopf, 1962.

Anderson, Midshipman Edward Maffitt. Letter to his father, Edward Clifford Anderson, November 18, 1862. William Stanley Hoole Papers, William Stanley Hoole Special Collections Library, University of Alabama.

Beaman, Charles C., Jr. *Deposition of Clarence Yonge, Paymaster of the "Alabama."* From "The National and Private 'Alabama Claims' and their 'Final and Amicable Settlement.'" Washington: W. H. Moore, 1871. CSS *Alabama* Digital Collection, University of Alabama.

Boatner, Mark M. III. *The Civil War Dictionary*. New York: Vintage Books, 1991.

Boykin, Edward. *Ghost Ship of the Confederacy*. New York: Funk and Wagnalls, 1957.

Bradford, Gamaliel. *Confederate Portraits*. Freeport, New York: Books for Libraries Press, 1914.

Bradlee, Francis B. C. "The *Kearsarge-Alabama* Battle: The Story as Told to the Writer by James Magee of Marblehead, Seaman on the *Kearsarge*." Reprinted from the *Historical Collections of the Essex Institute*, Volume 57, 1921. CSS *Alabama* Digital Collection, University of Alabama.

Bradlow, Edna, and Frank Bradlow. *Here Comes the "Alabama."* Cape Town, South Africa: A. A. Balkema, 1958.

Branham, Alfred Iverson. *Interview with Captain John McIntosh Kell, Executive Officer of the "Alabama."* CSS *Alabama* Digital Collection, University of Alabama.

Bulloch, James D. *Secret Service of the Confederate States in Europe*, Volume 1. London: Richard Bentley and Son, 1883.

Copy Contract for the Building of the Confederate States Steamship "Alabama." Liverpool, 1961. William Stanley Hoole Papers, William Stanley Hoole Special Collections Library, University of Alabama.

Davis, Jefferson. *The Rise and Fall of the Confederate Government*, Volume 2. Richmond: Barrett and Massie, Inc., date unknown.

Delaney, Norman C. *Ghost Ship: The Confederate Raider "Alabama."* Middletown, Connecticut: Southfarm Press, 1989.

———. *John McIntosh Kell of the Raider "Alabama."* University, Alabama: University of Alabama Press, 1973.

Edge, Frederick Milnes. *The "Alabama" and the "Kearsarge." An Account of the Naval Engagement in the British Channel on Sunday, June 19th, 1864, from Information Furnished to the Writer by the Wounded and Paroled Prisoners of the "Alabama" and the Officers of the "Kearsarge," and Citizens of London.* London, W. Ridgway, 1861.

Ellicott, John M. *The Life of John Ancrum Winslow.* New York and London: G. P. Putnam's Sons, 1902.

Franklin, John Hope. "The Emancipation Proclamation: An Act of Justice," in *Prologue: Quarterly of the National Archives*, Summer 1993, vol. 25, no. 2.

Fullam, George Townley. *Our Cruise on the Confederate States' War Steamer "Alabama."* London: A. Schulze, 1863(?).

———. *The Journal of George Townley Fullam.* University, Alabama: University of Alabama Press, 1973.

Haywood, P. D. *The Cruise of the "Alabama"—by One of the Crew.* Boston: Houghton, 1882.

Hobson, Henry S. *The Famous Cruise of the "Kearsarge."* Bonds Village, Massachusetts: the author, 1894.

Jessup, John E., Editor. *Encyclopedia of the American Military*, Volume 1. New York: Charles Scribner's Sons, 1994.

Kell, John McIntosh. *Recollections of a Naval Life.* Washington, D.C.: The Neale Company, 1900.

London News, September 4, 1863, June 21, 1864.

London Shipping Gazette, April 29, 1861.

London Star, June 22, 1864.

Times (London), April 29–30, 1861, March 14, 1863, June 22, 1864.

Low, John. *The Logs of the CSS "Alabama" and CSS "Tuscaloosa."* University, Alabama: Confederate Publishing Company, 1972.

Lowrey, Grosvenor Porter. *English Neutrality: Is the "Alabama" a British Pirate?* New York: A. D. F. Randolph, 1863.

Macartney, Edward Clarence. *Mr. Lincoln's Admirals.* New York: Funk and Wagnalls, 1956.

Magee, James. *The Story of the Battle between the Steam Sloop-of-War "Kearsarge" and the Rebel Cruiser "Alabama."* Salem, Massachusetts: Observer Steam Book and Printing Rooms, 1873.

Manchester Examiner, July 22, 1864.

Manchester Guardian, April 30, 1861.

Maynard, Douglas. "Union Efforts to Prevent the Escape of the *Alabama*," *Mississippi Valley Historical Review*, June 1954.

McMillan, Malcom Cook. *The "Alabama" Confederate Raider.* University, Alabama: University of Alabama Press, 1963.

Mitchell, Lt. Col. Joseph B. *The Badge of Gallantry.* New York: The Macmillan Company, 1968.

Mooney, James L., Editor. *Dictionary of American Naval Fighting Ships.* Washington, D.C.: Navy Department, Office of the Chief of Naval Operations, Naval History Division.

Musicant, Ivan. *Divided Waters.* New York: Harper Collins, 1995.

National Archives. *Abstracts of Service Records of Naval Officers, 1798–1893,* M-330.

———. *Alabama Claims, The.* Record Group 39.2.3.

———. *"Alabama" Crew and Payroll.* Record Group 109.12.

———. *Letters Sent by the Secretary of the Navy to Officers, 1798–1868.* M-149, Reel 67.

———. *Log of the USS "Kearsarge," 1862–1864.* Record Group 24.

———. *Muster Rolls of the USS "Kearsarge," 1862–1864.* Record Group 24.

———. *Navy Dependents' Pension Files.* M-1279.

New York Chamber of Commerce. *Proceedings of the Chamber of Commerce of the State of New York, on the Burning of the Ship "Brilliant."* New York: J. W. Amerman, Printer, 1862.

New York Evening Post, July 7, 1864.

New York Herald, October 5, 1862.

New York Times, May 14–15, 28, June 5, September 29, 1861; November 3, 5, 18, 21, 1862; January 1, February 28, April 12, 22, August 4, 1863; July 6–14, 18, August 1, 10, October 7, December 26, 31, 1864.

Officer, Lawrence H. *Between the Dollar-Sterling Gold Points.* Cambridge: Cambridge University Press, 1996.

Official Records of the Union and Confederate Armies in the War of the Rebellion, 128 vols. Washington, D.C.: U.S. Government Printing Office, 1890–1901.

Official Records of the Union and Confederate Navies in the War of the Rebellion, 30 vols. Washington, D.C.: U.S. Government Printing Office, 1894–1922.

Passmore, William. *Affidavit of William Passmore of Birkenhead, July 21, 1862.* CSS *Alabama* Digital Collection, University of Alabama.

Poolman, Kenneth. *The "Alabama" Incident.* London: W. Kimber, 1958.

Porter, David Dixon. *Naval History of the Civil War.* New York: The Sherman Publishing Company, 1881.

Portsmouth Chronicle, November 8, 1861, January 25, 1862, July 13, 1864.

Roberts, Walter Adolphe. *Semmes of the "Alabama."* Indianapolis and New York: The Bobbs-Merrill Company, 1938.

Robinson, Charles M. *Shark of the Confederacy.* Annapolis: Naval Institute Press, 1995.

Scharf, J. Thomas. *History of the Confederate States Navy.* New York: Rogers and Sherwood, 1887.

Semmes, Raphael. *Captain Raphael Semmes and the CSS "Alabama."* Washington, D.C.: The Naval Historical Foundation, 1968.

———. *The Confederate Raider "Alabama."* Bloomington, Indiana: Indiana University Press, 1962.

———. *The Cruise of the "Alabama" and the "Sumter."* London: Saunders, Otley and Company, 1864.

———. *Journal of Captain Semmes.* Rare book collection, William Stanley Hoole Special Collections Library, University of Alabama.

———. *Memoirs of Service Afloat During the War Between the States.* Baltimore: Kelly, Piet and Company, 1869.

———. Report of Captain Semmes, Commanding C.S.S. *Alabama*, of Cruise and Captures Made by that Vessel from September 19 to December 22, 1863. CSS *Alabama* Digital Collection, University of Alabama.

Sinclair, Arthur. *Two Years on the "Alabama."* Boston: Lee and Shepard, 1896.

Smith, Joseph Adams. *An Address Delivered before the Union League of Philadelphia.* Philadelphia: J. B. Lippincott, 1906.

Summersell, Charles Grayson. *CSS "Alabama": Builder, Captain, and Plans.* University, Alabama: University of Alabama Press, 1985.

Symonds, Craig L. *Historical Atlas of the U.S. Navy.* Annapolis: Naval Institute Press, 1995.

Times of India, The (Bombay), January 23, 1864.

University of Alabama. *Spy Reports of the "290."* CSS *Alabama* Digital Collection, University of Alabama.

————. *Ransom Bond of the U.S. Ship "Bethia Thayer," Captured by the C.S.S. "Alabama," March 1, 1863.* CSS *Alabama* Digital Collection, University of Alabama.

Wallace, Willard Mosher. *The Raiders.* Boston: Little Brown and Co., 1970.

Welles, Gideon. *The Diary of Gideon Welles,* Volume 1. Boston and New York: Houghton Mifflin Company, 1911.

INDEX

First names are listed when known.

A

Adams, Charles E., 116, 275
Adams, Charles Francis: protests *Enrica*'s construction, 27–28; threatens to return to United States, 29; told to use own judgment regarding protests, 70; gets stowaway explanation from Winslow, 183; discusses stowaways with Welles, 184; demands damage payments, 199
Adams, Henry, 291
Adams, James, 107, 285
Adams, John, 151, 188, 284
Adams, John Quincy, 23
Adams, Nicholas, 199, 284
Addison, George, 282
Admiralty Court, Confederate States of America: Semmes names, 78; condemns prize, 110, 115, 119, 136–37, 201; spares prize, 93, 111, 160
Ahern, Michael, 182, 204, 256, 288
Alabama Claims, 138, 269
Algeciras, 18, 38, 65
Allcot, Henry, 186, 241, 282
Allen, John, 69, 177, 285
Allman, Thomas, 139–40, 285
Alloway, Thomas, 193, 289
Alsdorf, William, 192, 290
Anderson, Edward C., 21
Anderson, Edward Maffitt, 56, 232, 281
Andrew, George, 36, 59–61, 290
Angel, Henry, 163, 284
Angra de Heroismo, 41, 81, 125, 141, 155, 157

A

Antoine, Clement, 289
Antoine, Fred, 292
Appleby, George, 256, 283
Armstrong, Richard F.: boards prize, 49, 53, 69, 78, 94–95; ordered to discard liquor from prize, 53; questions changing *Alabama*'s route, 68; sits on court-martial, 72; calms passengers of *Ariel,* 94–95; fires gun to halt escaping prize, 174; relays order to open fire on *Kearsarge,* 229; lodges shell in *Kearsarge*'s sternpost, 233; rescued, 241; member of crew, 281
Articles of War, 45, 52, 185, 196
Ayres, Edward, 202, 277
Azores (Azore Islands): *Sumter* cruises in, 11; *Kearsarge* can't reach, 14; *Agrippina* ordered to, 30; *Enrica* sails for, 31–33; area searched for *Alabama*, 65; prisoners put ashore, 68; *Kearsarge* to, 80, 97, 142, 154; *Alabama* reported to be in area, 98; Pickering reports to, 122

B

Badlam, William H., 9, 243, 287
Bailey, George, 290
Baker, George, 205, 290
Baker, Joseph B., 120, 275
Baldwin, Charles H., 161
Banks, Nathaniel P., 102
Barnes, William, 193, 290
Barron, Samuel, 211, 216
Barrows, John, 290

Bartelli, A. G.: captain's steward, 48; alerts Semmes to mutiny, 87; retrieves sword knot for Armstrong, 94; misses out on feast, 110; witnesses meeting between Semmes and convicts, 118; watches Semmes write threatening letter, 134; screens visitors for Semmes, 149; enjoys *Punjaub*'s captain's discomfort, 160; summons Kell, 214; prepares for victory celebration, 218; waxes Semmes's mustache, 225; retrieves Semmes papers, 238–39; stays on board as ship sinks, 239–40; confirmed drowned, 256; member of crew, 282

Barth, Jacob, 290

Bartlett, Ezra, 226, 287

Bastine, William, 290

Batchelder, John G., 288

Bell, Commodore H. H., 102

Bell, William, 192, 292

Benson, John, 116, 283

Benson, Richard, 292

Bermuda, 21, 98, 262

Bickford, John, 256, 288

Bizot, Monsieur ———, 176

Black Sophie's bordello, 151

Blaisdell, Benjamin H., 289

Blaisdell, Joel, 289

Blake, Homer C., 102–6, 274

Blake, Thomas, 192, 292

Blakely gun, 227, 229–30, 233, 264, 270

Blakely, T. A., 264

Blees, Charles, 192, 292

Boener, Clement, 158, 291

Bolles, John A., 261–62, 265

Bond, George, 31–33

Bond, William, 256, 288

Bonfils, Ad., 217

Boston, 63, 108, 115, 123, 144, 178, 257, 259–60, 273–76

Boston Towing Company, 259

Boulogne, 195, 202, 204–5

Boyle, John, 290

Brackett, Sylvanus, 289

Bradford, William, 146, 283

Bradley, James, 289

Bradley, John E., 290

Bradley, Patrick, 282

Brandon, Thomas, 163, 188, 284

Brazil, 15, 117, 119, 179, 259

Brest, 166, 168, 181–83, 189–90, 193, 203

Brewer, Samuel, 85, 139, 285

Brier, Jonathan, 192, 290

Bright, Maurice, 119, 241, 284

Briset, Jean, 192, 289

British Foreign Enlistment Act: presents challenge to shipbuilders, 1; highlights of, 4; ruled not violated with *Oreto*'s construction, 22; Bulloch tries to avoid violating, 4, 5, 26, 30; Union accuses violation of, 27–28; conflict avoided, 30; press believes easy to prove violation of, 111–12; Semmes fears violation of, 141; ignored by Semmes, 152, 210; Winslow violates, 180–82; US Consul tries to comply with, 192; British want accountability to, 204

Broderick, James, 146, 282

Broderick, Richard, 28–29

Brogan, Richard, 28

Brooks, William P., 96, 241, 281

Brosnan, James, 282

Brown, Charles, 292

Brown, Lawrence W., 179, 276

Brown, Sam, 139, 285

Brown, William, 192, 292

Browne, John M.: performs amputation, 19–20; suggests ill crew members be sent home, 36, 63; sits on court-martial, 61; begs Winslow to stop liberties, 157; tries to save crew members, 157–58; examines crew member of *Florida*, 167; treats weather-related illnesses, 184; goes to Brussels with Winslow, 206; asks for place to treat casualties, 217; pronounces *Alabama* crew member dead, 242; meets counterpart from *Alabama*, 257; member of crew, 287

Buckley, John, 199, 284

Buckley, Thomas, 63, 290

Bulloch, Irvine S., 140, 146–47, 262, 281

Bulloch, James D.: travels to England to arrange for ships, 1–5; contracts for construction of *Alabama*, 5–7; supervises construction of *290*, 8; returns to Savannah, 21; receives orders and commission, 21–22; asks for command of *290*, 22; offers *Oreto* to North, 22; relinquishes command of *290*, 23; offers *290* to Semmes, 24; loses command, 25; changes name of *290*, 25; disagreement with builders, 26; concerned about spies, 26; selects captain, 27; identified as Southern Commissioner, 29; moves *Enrica*, 29–30; gives instructions to McQueen and Yonge, 30–31; *Enrica* to be outfitted as ship of war, 32; rendezvous with *Agrippina*, 33–34; presents Semmes to Butcher, 40; calms Portuguese officials, 41; pays *Alabama*'s crew, 43; watches *Alabama* sail away, 43–44; purchases ships in name of emperor of China, 113; half brother appointed master, 140; postwar life, 262; defends Winslow, 263; *Alabama* powder explanation, 265

Burden, H. J., 79

Burns, James, 36, 292

Burns, Thomas, 203, 292
Burns, William, 85, 282
Burrell, Edward, 202, 283
Butcher, Matthew J.: temporary captain for *Enrica*, 26–27; comments included in testimony, 29; helps arrange payment for *Enrica*, 30; ordered to outfit *Enrica* as ship of war, 32; evades *Tuscarora*, 33; uses alias to avoid detection, 33–34; awaits arrival of *Bahama*, 39; meets Semmes, 40
Butler, General Benjamin, 268
Buttons, Benjamin, 289
Butts, Charles, 288

C

Cadiz: *Kearsarge* recoals, 15–16; site of Confederate States of America officials' arrest, 18; *Kearsarge* in, 15, 35, 97, 121, 142, 191, 193; *Kearsarge* refuses poor merchandise in, 191
Calais, 195, 202–3, 207, 212
Cameron, William, 292
Canty, Timothy, 193, 289
Cape of Good Hope, 141, 197
Cape Town, 148, 150–51, 153, 165, 198–99, 218, 276
Cardiff, 117, 273, 275
Caren, John, 283
Carey, Joshua, 288
Carroll, James, 142–43, 292
Cartney, Thomas Mitchell, 114, 275
Chamber of Commerce, New York State, 70, 79, 98
Chappell, William, 290
Charles, Daniel, 290
Chase, John M., 37, 291
Cherbourg: *Georgia* sails from, 193; *Kearsarge* sails to, 194, 213–14; *Alabama* enters, 210; Semmes justifies entry into, 210; *Alabama*'s arrival known, 211, 215; *Alabama*'s entry into ruled illegal, 216; *Alabama*'s ransom bonds taken ashore, 217; *Deerhound* arrives, 218; battle site, 224–37, 254, 258; *Alabama* leaves port, 225–26; *Kearsarge* leaves, 226; burial site for *Kearsarge* crew member, 256; *Kearsarge* remains in port, 258; placed on sword inscription, 261; port admiral quoted, 264
Childs, William, 55, 273
China, Emperor of, 113
China Tea Company, 121–22
Church, Charles E., 54, 273
Clark, James M., 53–54, 273
Clark, William (*Alabama* seaman), 70, 283
Clark, William W. (*Kearsarge* landsman), 121, 292

Clarke, Daniel, 111, 292
Cleary, John C., 105
Clements, James, 78, 282
Coalter, John, 11, 292
Cohen, David, 94
Coles, Charles, 116, 285
Collins, Joshua, 192, 290
Colson, Charles, 284
Columbia, Fred, 146, 282
Conde, Moussion de, 86–87, 89
Connor, Joseph, 282
Conroy, George, 163, 284
Conroy, Michael, 289
Consul, British, 41, 116, 156
Consul, United States (American), 98, 102, 123, 136, 150, 161, 173, 191, 216
Cook, Henry, 288
Cooper, Gordon, 270
Cooper, John S., 115, 275
Cork, Ireland, 180, 275, 277
Cosgrove, Henry, 177, 286
Craven, T. Augustus: files complaint about naval policy, 33; plots strategy with Pickering, 65; searches for *Alabama*, 65–66, 80; tells Pickering no Confederate States of America ships in area, 121
Crawford, William, 282
Crowley, Lawrence, 290
Cuba, 92, 153, 261
Cuddy, Thomas C., 186, 282
Cumming, George, 172–73, 276
Cummings, Simeon W., 146–48, 158, 285
Cummings, William, 292
Curran, Frank, 282
Currie, M. R. and Company, 178
Cushman, William H.: becomes chief engineer of *Kearsarge*, 9; supervises and tests engines, 10; attempts to sign recruits, 10; struggles to keep engines operating, 12–13, 81; prepares *Kearsarge* to go to Cherbourg, 213; member of crew, 287
Customs Board, 28, 29

D

Dabney, Jose, 290
Dahlgren gun, 11, 227, 233–35, 264
Danforth, Charles A., 287
Davis, Benjamin, 290
Davis, Jefferson, 3, 24, 255, 268
Davis, Mrs. Jefferson, 68
Dayton, William Jr., 219, 243
Dayton, William Sr.: orders Winslow to return stowaways, 181; reiterates attack warning to Winslow, 191; allows Winslow to add to crew, 191–93; initiates diplomatic action, 211; alerts

Winslow of *Alabama*'s location, 213; discusses three-mile limit, 219; tells Winslow to hold prisoners, 243–44
DeLong James 17, 18
deMattos, W. N., 116
Dempsey, John W., 59, 61, 63, 233, 255, 257, 288
Dent, James G., 282
DeSanto, Sabine, 18, 19, 291
Devine, James O., 290
Devine, Robert, 177, 284
DeWit, Carsten B., 288
Doane, Samuel H., 53, 273
Dolley, Roscoe D., 288
Dominica/Dominican Republic, 86, 108
Donnelly, William, 289
Dover, 194, 203–4, 207, 212, 214, 258
Doyle, John, 177, 285
Drury, Benedict, 63, 289
Dudley, Thomas H., 27–29
Duffy, Owen, 282
Dugan, John F., 289
Dugan, Joseph, 289
Duggan, John, 139, 285
Duncan, Peter, 256, 283
Dupois, Louis, 85, 284
Dupouy, Augustin, 210, 216, 219, 243
Dwyer, John, 289

E

Edwards, S. Price, 30
Egan, Robert, 119–20, 286
Egerton, George, 241, 283
Eggleston, Ebenezer, 16
Ellis, William, 288
Elmstone, Thomas, 153–54
Emancipation Proclamation, 101–2
Emery, John, 283
Emery, Mark W., 157–58, 292
English Channel, 203, 207, 209, 228, 255
English, George, 193, 289
Equator, 175, 188, 208
Eustachia, Henry, 282
Evans, James: questions burning of prize, 50; boards prize, 69, 117, 133, 149, 170; ability to identify ships, 116; helps relocate gun, 165; member of crew, 281
Evans, Richard, 163, 284
Evans, William Y., 288

F

Fairchild, George H., 85, 261
Fairchild, Mrs. George H., 85, 261
Farragut, David, 2, 123, 256
Fawcett, Preston and Company, 6

Fayal, Azores, 30, 80, 156, 273
Fernando de Noronha, 117, 119
Fisher, Charles B., 38, 288
Fisher, Henry, 283
Fisher, William, 290
Fisler, Lorenzo F., 137–38
Fitzmaurice, Edward, 285
Fitzsimmons, Edward, 92
Flanders, Stephen, 119, 275
Flood, Patrick, 288
Flushing, 211, 213
Forrest, George: arrested and court-martialed, 71–73; incites mutiny, 87–89; dismissed from *Alabama*, 92, member of crew, 285
Forrestall, William, 282
Forsyth, Charles G., 150
Fort Warren, 18, 257
Fox, G. V., 268
Foxton, James, 283
France/French, 176, 211, 216
Francois, Vanburn, 193, 291
Fraser, Trenholm and Company, 4, 30
Freeman, Miles J.: repairs *Alabama*'s engines, 96; pallbearer for Simeon Cummings, 147; can't keep engines running, 235; held as prisoner, 244, 257; explanation of *Alabama*'s powder, 265; member of crew, 281
Freemantle, George, 94, 236, 238, 257, 282
Fripp, Edgar, 283
Frost, William S., 145–46, 276
Fullam, George Townley: boards prize, 46–47, 49, 55, 71, 86, 110, 114, 116–17, 119, 137, 139, 141, 144, 149, 160, 170–72, 175, 177, 197, 201, 209; warned of Union ship in area, 114; warned of *Alabama*'s presence, 117; fools captains of prizes, 119; releases English vessel, 141; pallbearer for Simeon Cummings, 147; brings Low from *Tuscaloosa,* 148; faces wrath of prize's captain, 160–61; notes rainbow in log, 164; suggests relocating gun, 165; writes of missed opportunities, 199; notes problems with shells, 201; concerned about lack of wind, 208; records ships stopped by *Alabama*, 209; requests help from *Kearsarge,* 236–37; indicates heavy casualties, 237, 256; death of, 262; member of crew, 281
Fulton, Thomas M., 92, 274

G

Gallardo, Manuel Jose, 291
Galt, Francis: sits on court-martial, 72; gains assistant, 73; appointed paymaster, 107; goes ashore to arrange for provisions, 118; prepares list for boarders, 133; tends to wounded, 257; member of crew, 281

Galveston, 102, 105, 274, 276
Gerrish, Edward A., 201, 277
Getzinger, George, 119, 285
Gibraltar: *Sumter* anchors in, 14, 59; *Kearsarge* enters, 16–17, 82, 142–43; *Sumter* trapped by *Tuscarora,* 23–24; *Kearsarge* stalks *Mary Scaife* around, 62–63; *Kearsarge* stocks up at, 65; destination of prize, 274
Gifford, David R., 57, 273
Giles, William, 289
Gilman, Albert, 107, 146, 285
Gilson, Edward, 63, 292
Glasgow, 98, 274
Glisson, O. S., 134–35
Godson, Henry, 85, 189, 196, 284
Godwin, Charles, 241, 282
Golden, James, 63, 291
Gowin, William, 38, 232–33, 255–56, 290
Grady, John, 177, 286
Graham, Franklin, 288
Graham, Walter, 150–51, 161
Granger, Robert and Company, 154
Grant, William, 117, 275
Gray, Rufus, 55, 273
Great Britain, 70, 100
Great White Fleet, 270
Griffin, J. W., 292
Guin, George W., 137, 275
Gulf of Mexico, 11, 179
Gurney, William, 288

H

Hagar, George: captain of *Brilliant,* 69–70, 273; complains of treatment in newspapers, 78; informs Welles of *Alabama*'s possible destination, 81; certifies sketch of *Brilliant*'s capture, 249
Haley, James, 256, 288
Halford, William, 73, 107, 285
Halleck, General H. W., 260
Halliday, Fox and Company, 171
Ham Fat. *See* Williams, George
Ham, Mark G., 126, 256, 288
Hambly, Richard, 163, 177, 286
Hanscom, Isaiah, 8
Harding, O. V., 76, 274
Harding, Sir John, 29
Harmon, John E., 71, 273
Harrigan, John, 282
Harris, Thomas C., 35, 61, 113, 123, 291
Harrison, George, 256, 290
Hart, James, 163, 256, 283
Hartford, Lyman H., 289
Hartwell, Seth, 287
Hayes, James F., 291

Hayes, John, 256, 288
Healy, William, 105
Hearn, William, 283
Henney, Peter, 136, 286
Henry, Samuel, 283
Henson, James, 291
Hewitt, Captain ———, 217
Higgins, Henry, 177, 188, 284
Higgs, James, 109, 282
Hill, Charles, 291
Hobbs, Russell B., 151, 283
Hobson, Henry, 288
Holland. *See* Netherlands
Horrigan, Jeremiah, 290
Horta: Pickering mistakes sidewheeler for *Alabama,* 80–81; *Kearsarge* anchors in, 80, 122, 126; *Kearsarge* departs, 141; *Kearsarge* takes *Juno* to, 154–56; *Kearsarge* crew members die, 157–58
Horwood, George, 111, 285
Hottentots, 153
House of Commons, 125, 157
Howard, D. H., 137, 276
Howell, Beckett K., 68, 72, 165, 282
Hoyt, Martin, 291
Hughes, John, 116, 285
Hughes, Peter, 282
Hull, F. S., 4
Hurley, Timothy, 288
Hyer, Albert, 116, 175, 177, 286

I

Igo, Thomas W., 292
Iguacio, Jose, 193, 292
Indian Ocean, 164, 273
Ives, Nathan, 291

J

Jack, John, 285
Jackson, Peter, 116, 286
Jamaica, 96, 106, 108
James River Squadron, 261
James, Thomas, 151, 286
Jamison, Henry, 63, 289
Johns, Frederick M., 108, 282
Johnson, Andrew, 261–62
Johnson, Augustus, 290
Johnson, Brent, 152, 282
Johnson, Samuel B., 71, 273
Johnston, General Joseph, 261
Jones, Albert J., 94, 274
Jones, Charles, 290
Jones, Edwin, 139, 285
Jones, Evan P., 218–19, 242
Jones, Lewis T., 182

Jones, Robert, 292
Jones, Thomas, 82, 292
Jones, William, 107, 275, 284
Jonson, John, 284
Jordan, Francis C., 185–86, 277
Joseph, Alexander, 193, 292
Julius, Theodore, 73–75, 273

K

Kallock, Robert, 110
Kane, Patrick, 105
Kehoe, Thomas, 163, 284
Kell, John McIntosh: goes to London with
    Semmes, 24; boards blockade runner, 24;
    tours *Alabama* with Semmes, 44–45;
    addresses crew's frustration, 47; selects ship
    to be chased, 48; ordered to redirect chase,
    49; orders liquor thrown off prize, 53;
    describes exhilaration of watching prize burn,
    55; brings first crewman from prize to
    Semmes, 56; posts assignments, 67; sits on
    court-martial, 72; reviews list of gunboats
    from newspaper, 74; named associate justice
    of Admiralty Court, 78; values prizes, 85, 133,
    145; quells mutiny, 87–89; observes whaler
    crew, 90; pushes crew to overtake prize, 93–
    94; communicates with *Hatteras*, 103–4;
    renews acquaintance with captain of *Hatteras*,
    106; writes of crew celebration, 107;
    dispatches boarding party, 110, 116; sum-
    mons surgeon for injured *Mary Kendall* crew
    member, 140; communicates with *Diomede*,
    145; leads funeral service, 147–48; daughter
    dies, 163; admires *Contest*, 173; rigs caisson
    for underwater work, 176; deals with
    phosphorescence, 187; man overboard, 189;
    directs target practice, 201; discusses
    possible battle, 214–15; pronounces *Alabama*
    ready to fight, 221; receives French naval
    officer, 224; directed to open fire, 228–30;
    directs crew member to clean gore from deck,
    230, 232; changes firing strategy, 232; orders
    Alabama to run for shore, 234–35; passes
    order for surrender, 235–36; abandons ship,
    239–40; checks on Semmes's condition, 242;
    arrives safely in England, 245; returns to
    Confederacy, 262; crew list, 281
Kelly, John, 180, 292
Kelly, Norman J., 291
Kelway, Robert, 245
Ker and Company, 171
Kerrigan, James, 288
King, James (ordinary seaman on *Kearsarge*),
    177, 256, 284
King, James W. S. (quartermaster on *Kearsarge*),
    136, 285

King, Martin, 283
King, William, 285
Kingston, 95–96, 106, 108
Kinshlea, Michael, 92, 285

L

La Carraca, Spain, 37, 111
Lahie, Daniel, 82, 292
Laird, John and Sons: contracts with Bulloch to
    build *Alabama*, 4–7; rename *290*, 25;
    disagreement with Bulloch, 26; prepare *Enrica*
    for sea trial, 26–27, 30–31; builds in name of
    emperor of China, 113; sister ships of
    Alabama, 151, 219; ceases operating, 270
Laird, John Jr., 5, 29, 31
Laird, John Sr., 5, 7, 31
Laird, William, 5
Lambert, John J., 291
Lambert, Thomas F., 115, 118, 275
Lancaster, Catherine, 222
Lancaster, John: owner of *Deerhound*, 218;
    arrives in Cherbourg, 221; discusses watching
    battle, 221–22; follows *Alabama* out of harbor,
    226; orders captain to take survivors to
    England, 242; defends actions, 266–68;
    receives thanks, 268
Landerskin, John, 74, 273
Lanerty, Peter, 283
Langton, W. T., 292
Larrabee, Isaiah, 170–71, 173, 276
Latham, John, 107, 285
Lee, James H., 256, 288
Lee, Rear Admiral S. P., 81, 262
Leggett, David, 71, 283
Legris, Henry, 139, 285
Leland, Oren H., 109, 274
Lennon, Fred, 199, 284
Levins, William, 283
Lewis, Manuel, 36, 292
Lewis, William, 119
Liais, Edouard, 183, 211
Lincoln, Abraham, 101–2, 122–24, 259
Lincoln, Edgar, 84–85, 274
Lincoln, Mrs. Edgar, 85
Littlefield, Adoniram K., 289
Liverpool, 4, 32, 33, 69–70, 97–98, 104, 125,
    151, 157, 192, 201, 217, 273, 275
Llewellyn, David H.: takes over as surgeon,
    107; treats injured crew member from *Mary
    Kendall*, 140; tries to help Cummings, 147;
    treats wife of neutral captain, 152; examines
    new crew members, 163; treats wounded,
    235; death of, 240; member of crew, 281
Locke, William, 293
Loete, Captain ———, 153

London, 24, 70, 116, 139, 153, 171, 191, 203–5, 212, 273, 275
Longshaw, Robert, 202, 284
Loveland, Winslow, 137, 276
Low, John: serves on *Fingal*, 21; appointed as master, 22; boards prize, 46–47, 53, 57, 73, 94; named associate justice of Admiralty Court, 78; assigned to *Tuscaloosa*, 139–40; meets with Semmes, 148; member of crew, 285
Lucas, Frederick George, 173–74, 276
Luderitz Bay, Namibia, 152–53
Ludy, Peter, 193, 290
Lynch, Timothy, 289

M

Madeira, 82, 97, 143
Maffitt, Eugene Anderson, 240, 281
Maffitt, John, 166, 168
Magee, James, 290
Magruder, J. Bankhead, 179
Maguire, Charles, 37, 293
Maguire, James, 107, 283
Maguire, Matthew, 26–28
Mahany, Frank, 151, 177, 286
Mail Steamship Company, 2
Mair, James, 256, 282
Maling, Nicholas, 151, 162, 286
Mallory, Stephen R.: photo, 128; sends Bulloch to acquire ships, 2–3; agrees to give Bulloch command, 21–22; orders Bulloch back to England, 21–22; puts Semmes in command of *290*, 25
Manila, 171, 276
Marmelstein, Adolphus F., 139, 285
Mars, Michael: rescues man overboard, 189; publicly praised by Semmes, 196; clears gore from deck, 230, 232; protects Semmes's papers, 238, 240, 257; rescued, 241; member of crew, 283
Marsh, Thomas, 289
Marshall, C. H., 98
Martin, James, 285
Martin, Joseph, 85
Mason, J. M., 268
Mason, James, 283
Masters, Ralph, 283
Mattison, Charles, 192, 290
Mattock, Edward, 105
Maury, William Lewis, 135
McAlee, John, 107, 286
McAllen, John, 288
McBeth, James, 192, 233, 255, 290
McCallum, John, 136, 275
McCarthy, John H., 205, 291

McCarty, Dennis, 291
McCaskey, Benjamin, 85, 165, 186, 244, 257, 282
McClaymont, Archibald, 291
McClellan, William, 116, 284
McConnell, Henry L., 287
McCoy, Henry, 199, 284
McDougall, David, 164–65, 170, 173
McFadden, James, 111, 285
McFarland, Malcolm, 283
McGinley, William, 282
McGowan, Edward, 105
McKeever, Patrick, 291
McMillan, Thomas, 283
McNally, Matthew, 292
McPherson, Hugh, 288
McQueen, Alexander: ordered to meet *Enrica*, 30–31, 34; brags about affiliation with *Alabama*, 86–87, 89; observes capture of *Clara L. Sparks*, 90–91; sells *Alabama*'s coal, 117
Mehan, John, 163, 283
Meinsen, Heinrich, 193, 291
Melcher, Frank B., 120, 275
Melcher, Mrs. Frank B., 120
Mellen, Thomas, 84, 274
Mellus, James W., 111, 293
Melvin, Thomas, 292
Mesner, Valentine, 107, 286
Miditch, Martin, 78, 284
Miller, Charles, 136, 275
Miller, Frederick L., 287
Miller, John, 141, 286
Miller, Lewis F., 159–60, 275
Miller, William, 284
Miller, William C. and Sons, 4
Minister of the Marine and the Colonies, 216
Minor, Joseph F., 116, 139, 285
Mitchell, Flag Officer John K., 261
Mobile, Alabama, 123, 261–62, 270
Molk, Martin, 91, 139, 286
Montevideo, 275–76
Moore, Charles, 256, 290
Morey, James, 290
Morgan, William S., 76, 282, 288
Morris, Alfred, 79, 151, 286
Morse, Freeman H., 191–92
Motley, Robert, 63, 100, 293
Mulhall, Peter, 11, 291
Murphy, Hugh, 292
Murphy, John, 63, 292
Murphy, Thomas, 241, 283
Muzzey, Charles O., 125, 291
Myers, Frederick, 116, 282
Myers, Henry, 18

N

Napoleon, 199
Napoleon III, 210
Naval Academy, United States, 68
Navy, Provisional, 261
Navy, United States, 44, 83, 261
Neal, Joseph, 85, 107, 286
Neil, John, 283
Nelson, Horatio Lord, 182
Nelson, William, 78, 274
Netherlands, 171, 211, 216
Netto, John, 191, 292
New Bedford, Massachusetts, 57, 84, 273–75
New Orleans, 24, 44, 123, 147
New York City, 71, 79, 86, 108, 109, 111, 114, 137, 273–77
Nordstrom, William, 116, 146, 286
Norhoek, Abram, 56, 282
North Atlantic Blockading Squadron, 81, 270
North, James H., 21–23, 25
Nye, Levi, 290

O

O'Brien, Matthew, 96, 147, 173, 281
O'Connor, Patrick, 289
O'Halloran, William, 290
Ochoa, Juan, 85, 283
Olson, Charles, 116, 256, 284
Ordion, John, 289
Osborn, Abraham, 50–52, 273
Owens, Robert, 119, 139, 286

P

Pajorva, Karl, 256, 284
Palmerston, Lord, 113
Parker, Thomas L., 119–20, 284
Parkinson, Richard, 87, 282
Partridge, S. H., 103, 105
Passmore, William, 28–29
Pearson, George, 9
Pearson, Joseph, 283
Pease, Joachim, 15, 256, 290
Peck, W. F., 133, 275
Percival, Franklin, 116, 275
Percy, George, 141, 284
Perry, Matthew C., 123
Perry, Thomas, 256, 288
Person, Samuel J., 255
Pfeiffer, Andrew, 163, 284
Philadelphia, 139, 273, 276
Phillips, Zaran, 167, 183, 290
Pickering, Charles W.: assigned to *Kearsarge*, 9; evaluates crew, 10; commissions *Kearsarge*, 10; original orders revised, 11; guides *Kearsarge* through storm, 12–14; changes destination, 14; orders drills, 16–17, 64; locates *Sumter*, 17; sends ill crew members home, 36, 63; offers reward for missing crewmen, 37; forbids card playing, 58–59; court-martial, 61; searches for *Mary Scaife*, 62–63; abolishes grog rations, 63–64; begins search for *Alabama*, 65–66; orders chase of sidewheeler, 80–81; mistaken for captain of *Alabama*, 82; ignores Welles's orders, 97; replaced by Welles, 99; allows liberty, 112; confronts Spanish dock superintendents, 120–21; chases ship from China Tea Company, 121–22; meets Winslow, 123; leaves *Kearsarge*, 124–25; Winslow compared to, 142; failed to send in muster role, 257; ignored after battle, 260; commander of *Kearsarge,* 291
Pike, Jacob, 36, 293
Pike, Samuel B., 177–78, 276
Poole, Charles A., 289
Poole, William, 256, 288
Pope, John, 192, 289
Port Royal, Jamaica, 106, 125
Porter, David, 2, 75, 123
Portsmouth Navy Yard, 8, 260
Portsmouth, New Hampshire, 273, 276–77
Potter, Thomas, 107, 283
Praya Bay, Azores, 30, 31, 33
Preble, Edward E., 287
Preble, George, 214
Price, William, 286
Priest, True, 289
Provincetown, Massachusetts, 273–74
Prussian Navy, 152, 218
Pundt, John M., 147, 244, 257, 282
Purdy, William, 282
Pust, Christian, 256, 283
Putnam, James O., 190–92
Pyrrho, Sebastiao Jose Basilo, 118, 120

Q

Quanstrom, G. T., 293
Queenstown (stowaways): stowaways come on board, 180–83; Winslow ordered to return stowaways, 191–92; Winslow hopes British forget, 204; one of stowaways awarded Medal of Honor, 256; ship list, 276
Quinby, Austin, 288

R

Raleigh, James, 85, 285
Rawse, Edward, 282
Ray, Richard, 151, 162, 286
Raymond, George A., 289
Read, Charles A., 256, 288

Read, George E., 256, 290
Redding, Charles, 291
Remick, George W., 289
Riley, John, 175, 283
Rinton, William, 105, 139, 285
Rio de Janeiro, 141, 275
Roach (Roche), David, 107, 285
Roach, Martin, 204, 292
Roberts, John, 235, 256, 283
Roberts, William, 240
Robertson, William, 96, 282
Robinson, William (carpenter on *Alabama*), 86, 115, 176, 242, 282
Robinson, William (seaman on *Alabama*), 91, 241, 283
Rockland, Maine, 114, 117, 275
Roland, Edward, 292
Roney, Charles, 293
Roncador Reef, 259
Ronckendorff, William, 89–90
Roosevelt, Theodore, 262
Ross, George, 286
Rousserz, Antonio, 193, 292
Rowley, Andrew, 288
Royal Navy, 148, 150, 261
Royal Yacht Squadron, 218, 226, 267
Russell, George H., 288
Russell, John, 151, 284
Russell, Lord: orders inspection of *Enrica*, 27–28; recommends seizure of *290*, 29; captain of neutral ship afraid to offend, 137; *Deerhound* controversy, 266–68

S

St. Domingo/Santo Domingo, 92, 108
Salmon, Thomas, 289
Salsbury, William H., 139, 276
Sampson, Edward H. *See* Tibbetts, Edward
Sanborn, Joel, 289
Sanborn, John W., 289
Sands, B. F., 113
San Francisco, 275–77
Sargent, Daniel B., 58, 288
Sartori, Lewis C., 95
Saunders, Henry, 146, 286
Saunders, James, 256, 288
Saunders, John, 79, 274
Schirra, Walter, 270
Schroeder, Julius, 152, 165, 218, 281
Schwalbe, Gustave, 107, 286
Scott, Robert T., 63, 291
Semmes, Anne Elizabeth (Mrs. Raphael), 48
Semmes, Anne Elizabeth (Semmes's daughter), 48
Semmes, Catherine Middleton, 48
Semmes, Electra Louise, 48

Semmes, Oliver John, 48
Semmes, Raphael Jr., 48
Semmes, Raphael Sr.: photo, 127, 250; discussed by American consul, 17–18; captain of *Sumter*, 23; background information on, 23–24; receives orders to command new vessel, 25; sails for Liverpool, 28; arrives too late to command *Enrica*, 30; tries to meet *Enrica*, 33; pays off *Sumter* crew, 35; arrives at rendezvous, 40; confrontation with Portuguese officials, 41; takes command of *Alabama*, 42–44; attorney for Kell, 44; first chase and boarding, 46; ignores complaints, 47; misses family, 48; captures and burns first ship, 49–52; captures additional Union ships, 53–57, 69–79, 84–85, 90–96, 108–11, 114–20, 133–34, 136–41, 144–46, 149–50, 159, 170–74, 177–79, 185–86, 200–202; orders gun drills, 56, 96, 165, 201, 208, 210; described to crew of *Kearsarge*, 58; identified as captain of *Alabama*, 65; considers relocating, 67–68; courts-martial, 71–73, 92, 107, 152, 175, 188; uncovers smuggling, 72; signs ex-slave onto crew, 73; discovers list of Union gunboats in captured newspaper, 74; sails into hurricane, 75–77; taunts New York Chamber of Commerce, 79; uses name of Union ship as alias, 55, 77, 84, 108, 110, 114, 141, 160, 164, 166, 170, 175, 188, 197, 200, 209; stops ship infected by yellow fever, 86; puts down mutiny, 87–89; records comments about crew, 97, 148, 163; gathers intelligence from captured newspapers, 99, 175; responds to Emancipation Proclamation, 101–2; battles *Hatteras*, 102–6; fights fire in spirit room, 108–9; orders no liquor brought back from prizes, 110; accuses captain of tender of selling *Alabama's* coal, 117; meets with convicts, 118; punishes powder monkey, 119–20; signs affidavit to protect governor, 120; wedding anniversary, 133; threatens Department of Bahia, 134; taunts *Mohican*, 134–35; meets *Georgia*, 135; refuses to leave Bahia, 135–36; releases former United States vessel, 138–39; converts *Conrad*, 139–40; supports Fullam decision, 141; encounters *Diomede*, 145; Simeon Cummings funeral, 146–48; meets with *Tuscaloosa*, 148; charged with illegal capture, 149–50; concerned about *Vanderbilt*, 150–51, 161, 163; meets with other commanders, 151; skirts Foreign Enlistment Act, 151–52, 181, 199, 210; sells prize, 153–54, 198; recognizes captain of *Punjaub*, 159–60; meets with crimp, 162–63; celebrates birthday at sea, 164; concerned about *Wyoming*, 164–66, 172, 176;

has concerns about *Alabama*'s condition, 173, 179, 186, 199, 211; passes out cigars from prize, 175; orders *Alabama* in for repairs, 176; personally boards prize, 177–78; reminds crew of battle with *Hatteras*, 185, 228; shows strain of cruise, 186; orders soundings in phosphorescent water, 187–88; praises Mars, 196; allows crew to celebrate St. Patrick's day, 197; prepares brief to recover *Tuscaloosa*, 198; learns Confederacy is losing war, 209; disguises *Alabama*, 209; justifies docking in Cherbourg, 210–11; asks to be relieved of duty, 211; observes approach of *Kearsarge*, 214; discusses plan to fight *Kearsarge*, 214–16; challenges Winslow, 216; removes valuables from *Alabama*, 217; prepares for battle, 217–18, 220–21; directs battle, 223–37; wounded, 234; dispatches boat to request aid, 236; asks Mars to care for papers, 238, discards sword, 239; abandons ship, 239; rescued, 240–42, 248; arrives in Southampton, 245; criticized by newspapers, 254–55; decision to fight questioned and defended, 258, 268–69; refuses new command, 260; *Deerhound* controversy, 260, 266–68; receives sword from Royal Navy, 261; post-battle life, 260–62, 270; controversy over *Kearsarge* chain, 263–64; commander of *Alabama*, 281

Semmes, Samuel Spencer, 48
Seward, William, 122
Seymour, Charles, 282
Shanghai, 137, 275–76
Sheffield, James W., 289
Sherman, General William Tecumseh, 260
Shields, John, 193, 290
Shields, Michael, 85, 283
Shilland, Andrew, 282
Ships
  Africa
    Flower of Yarrow, 279
  China
    Kwantung, 151
    Peking, 122
    Sea King, 122
  Confederate States of America 290 (*See also* Ships, Confederate States of America, *Enrica, Alabama, Barcelona*): name assignment, 7; Bulloch supervises construction of, 8; similar in size to *Kearsarge*, 8; confusion about command, 22–23; Semmes appointed to, 25; launched, 25; name changed, 25; spy reports, 28–29; impoundment ordered, 29; discussed in newspaper, 52; Chamber of Commerce discusses, 70;

frustrates Welles, 83; crew's response to Emancipation Proclamation, 101–2
Agrippina: purchased as tender for *Enrica*, 30; rendezvous with *Enrica*, 33–34; helps outfit *Enrica*, 39–42; Bulloch and Semmes arrive at, 39–40; meets *Alabama*, 80, 84–86, 96, 106; tender to *Alabama*, 86–87; present at capture of *Clara L. Sparks*, 90–91; crew members transfer to *Alabama*, 91; Semmes tries to meet, 117; Winslow tries to trap, 183
Alabama (*See also* Ships, United States, *Alabama*; Ships, Confederate States of America, 290, *Enrica, Barcelona*): photo, 129, 131, 247–49; Yonge assigned to, 31; christened, 42; crew recruited, 43; puts to sea, 43–44; crew assembled for first time, 45; first chase, 46; captures prize, 49–57, 69–79, 84–85, 90–96, 108–11, 114–20, 133–34, 136–41, 144–46, 149–50, 159, 170–74, 177–79, 185–86, 200–202 ; uses alias, 55, 77, 84, 108, 110, 114, 141, 160, 164, 166, 170, 175, 188, 197, 200, 209; flies foreign flag, 54–55, 75, 93, 160–61, 173, 188, 197–98, 201; uses prize for target practice, 56, 201; object of Union naval search, 65–66; relocates to better area, 67–68; courts-martial, 71–73, 92, 107, 152, 175, 188; enters hurricane, 75–77; abandons plan to enter New York harbor, 79–80; Welles dispatches photos of, 81; *Kearsarge* mistaken for, 82; Welles frustrated by, 83, 122; meets *Agrippina*, 80, 84–86, 96, 106; forced to flee after affiliation revealed, 86–87; mutiny, 87–89; escapes from Union ship, 89–90; in need of repairs, 96, 173, 176, 186, 197, 199, 208; rumored to be in Azores, 98; subject of newspaper articles, 98–99; battle with *Hatteras*, 102–6; docks in Jamaica, 106; fire in spirit room, 108–9; Welles hears of battle with *Hatteras*, 112; admission of construction in England, 121; Winslow wants to encounter, 124; construction and consequence debated in House of Commons, 125; charged with illegal capture, 134, 149–50; meets *Georgia*, 135; outfits *Tuscaloosa*, 140; anchors in South Africa, 146; fatal accident to crew member, 146–48; meets *Tuscaloosa*, 148; takes on stowaways, 151–52; arrives at Luderitz Bay, 152–53; *Kearsarge* prepares for chase of, 154; mistaken for Union ship, 160–61; adds crew members

through services of crimp, 162–63; fights
storms, 164, 196–98; scares Union ships
into port, 165, 177, 199–200; becalmed,
175, 188; feeling effects of cruise, 179,
186, 199, 200, 208, 211; encounters
phosphorescent water, 187–88; man
overboard, 189; possible attack on
Kearsarge, 192; *Kearsarge* mistaken for,
194; crew celebrates St. Patrick's Day,
197; location revealed to Winslow in
newspapers, 207; stops last ships, 209;
adopts disguise, 209; enters Cherbourg,
209–11; *Kearsarge* sails to encounter,
213–14; compared with *Kearsarge*, 215;
entry declared illegal, 216; prepares for
battle, 217–18, 221; Confederate States
of America officers try to join crew, 218;
sister ship of *Deerhound*, 219, 221;
presence in Cherbourg protested, 219;
onlookers try to see, 220; battle with
Kearsarge, 223–37; battle map, 231;
sinks, 237–40; crew rescued, 238–43;
accused of having *Deerhound* as tender,
244–45; newspapers disparage, 254–55;
controversies, 255, 260–69; praised by
Jefferson Davis, 255; casualties, 256–57;
value of prizes estimated, 258; powder
compared to *Kearsarge*'s, 265; *Alabama*
claims, 269; wreck discovered, 270;
name given to succeeding ships, 270; list
of ships stopped, 273–80; crew list, 281–
86
Annie Childs, 22, 23
Barcelona, 33 (See also Ships, Confederate
States of America, *290, Enrica, Alabama*)
Bermuda, 28
Boston, 269
Castor, 135–36
Chickamauga, 269
Enrica (See also Ships, Confederate States
of America, *Alabama, 290, Barcelona*):
new name assigned, 25; trial voyage, 26–
27; object of spies, 26–28; reported as
Confederate States of America warship,
27–29; avoids impoundment, 29–30, 33;
sails for Azores, 31–34; challenged by
Rising Sun, 33–34; meets *Agrippina*, 34;
outfitted, 39–42, 81; Bulloch and
Semmes arrive, 39–40; rechristened, 42
Fingal, 21
Flamingo, 262
Florida (See also Ships, Confederate States
of America, *Oreto*): renamed, 4; in dry
dock, 166; watched by *Kearsarge*, 166–
69, 181–84, 189–91; crew fights with

Kearsarge crew, 167–68, 183; possible
attack on *Kearsarge*, 190–92; escapes,
193; possible spy from, 194–95; recalled
by Winslow, 203, 212–13; Winslow learns
location of, 207; success of, 255;
rammed, 259; *Alabama* claims, 269
Georgia: meets *Alabama,* 135; thought to be
Union vessel, 160–61; *Kearsarge*
searches for and monitors, 168–69, 179,
181, 183; *Agrippina* carrying supplies for,
183; possible attack on *Kearsarge,* 190–
92; ordered to leave port, 193–94;
Winslow learns whereabouts via
newspaper, 207; evades *Kearsarge*, 213–
14; *Alabama* claims, 269
Lord Clyde, 143
Melita, 24
Merrimac(k), 258
Nashville, 269
Oreto (See also Ships, Confederate States
of America, *Florida*): first ship contracted
for by Bulloch, 4; Bulloch to command,
22; offered to North 23; identified as sister
ship to *Enrica* 27; launch infuriates
Dudley, 27; United States consul reports
on, 98
Rappahannock: possible attack on *Kearsarge,*
190–92; watched by *Kearsarge,* 195, 202–
3, 206–7, 212–13; faces impoundment,
203; Winslow reads of location in newspapers, 207; *Kearsarge* crew member
punished for actions while watching, 257
Retribution, 269
Sallie, 269
Savannah, 68
Shenandoah, 269
Sumter: photo, 250; cruises Azores, 11;
anchors at Gibraltar, 14; Pickering finds,
17; paymaster captured, 18; trapped by
Tuscarora, 23–25; officers reassigned,
27; officers meet to go to *Enrica*, 33; crew
paid off, 35; found abandoned by
Kearsarge, 38; Kell's former ship, 44;
Alabama sets standard for, 45; Semmes
recalls, 50, 86; deserter notes hatred of
Semmes, 58–61; former crew member
killed by shark, 59–61; Armstrong served
on, 68; watched by *Kearsarge*, 62–63, 86;
deserter discovered on prize, 71;
observed by *Chippewa*, 82, 97; escapes,
112; renamed, 113; former foe of USS
Ino, 114; reunion of former officers, 135;
prizes sold, 153; Winslow recalls, 213;
former crew mates in battle, 242; sinks,
258; *Alabama* claims, 269

Tallahassee, 269
Tuscaloosa (See also Ships, United States, Conrad): gets new name, 140; meets with Alabama, 148; waits for Alabama, 150; wool sold, 152–54, 198; seized by British, 198; officers rejoin Alabama, 218; returned to original owners, 258; ship list, 276
Denmark
Judith, 75, 277
Overman, 55, 277
England
Ally, 280
Alma, 279
Ann Williams, 277
Asshur, 141, 279
Avalanche, 175, 279
Bahama, 33, 39–43
Barbados, 277
Bengairne, 280
Bertha Martha, 201, 280
Broughton Hall, 152, 279
Burmah, 170, 279
Cairngorm, 52
Cameronian, 279
Camperdown, 279
Caspatrick, 188, 280
Cedar, 278
Challenger, 139
Charles Lambert, 278
Chili, 116–17, 278
Cymbeline, 280
Deerhound: photo, 249; arrives in Cherbourg, 218–19; sister ship of Alabama, 219, 221; Lancasters on board, 221; follows Alabama out of harbor, 226; stops to watch battle, 227; notes poor quality of Alabama's powder smoke, 233; directed to rescue survivors, 240; takes survivors to England, 242–43, 245, 257; accused of being Alabama's tender, 244–45; newspapers criticize, 255; number of survivors rescued, 257; mentioned by General Sherman, 260; controversy regarding actions, 260, 263, 266–68
Diomede, 145, 279
Durban, 279
Eleanor, 278
Excellent, 245
Flora, 160–61, 279
G. Azzopadi, 138–39, 279
Gallant Neill, 178, 280
Gibraltar, 113, 142
Glendover, 278
Glennalice, 185, 280

Good Luck, 62
Greyhound, 106
Havelock, 146, 279
Henry, 111, 278
Hercules, 31–32
Hermione, 278
Hero, 80–81, 278
Heron, 77, 277
Hornet, 217
Hound, 278
Ida Abbott, 108, 278
Isabella, 278
Isle O'May, 160, 279
Janet Mitchell, 170, 279
Jason, 106
Jubilee, 279
Juno, 154–57
Kent, 201, 280
La Flor del Plata, 201, 280
Lady Harriet, 185, 280
Lady Jocelyn, 149
Lady Octavia, 137, 279
Lillian, 146, 279
Maiden Queen, 279
Maria Louisa, 280
Mary Kendall, 140–41, 279
Mary Scaife, 62–63
Medora, 141, 279
Miss Nightingale, 115, 278
Mona, 164, 170, 279
Moneta, 279
Narcissus, 151
Petrel, 103
Pizarro, 278
Prince of Wales, 278
Princess Royal, 86, 277
Punjaub, 115, 159–60, 279. See also Ships, United States, Punjaub
Queen of Beauty, 139, 279
Racehorse, 77
Reindeer, 106
Robert McKensie, 201, 280
Rover, 146, 279
Roy O'More, 280
Sarah Sands, 278
Sarawak, 279
Sardinia, 198, 280
Saxon, 152, 279
Schomburg, 278
Scottish Chief, 197, 280
Scourge, 209
Sinope, 278
Smoker, 143
Spitfire, 103
Star of Erin, 146, 279
St. Leonard, 279

Tamana, 279
Tasmania, 142
Terrible, 28
Thomas Blythe, 280
Thorndeer, 145, 279
Three Bells, 278
Valorous, 150
Vernon, 141, 279
Virginia, 278 (*See also* Ships, United States, *Virginia*)
Vixen, 103
Widna, 137, 279
William Edward, 114, 278
France
  Aloinir, 175, 279
  Alphonse Cezard, 278
  Annette, 203–4, 207
  Circe, 270
  Fata, 89
  Feu Sacre, 277
  Formose, 200, 280
  Gil Blas, 278
  Jules Cezard, 170, 279
  La Couronne, 224–25, 227
  La Foi, 46–47, 277
  L'Invincible, 188
  Mathilde, 278
  Mere de Famille, 280
  Napoleon, 225, 243
  Puget, 178, 280
  Senegambia, 52, 277
Germany
  Alster, 200, 280
  Brema, 279
  Elsie, 278
  Helen, 154
  Johanna Hepler, 277
  Julie Caroline, 209, 280
  Koenigsmunde, 280
  Margarite, 280
  Orion, 197, 280
  Ottone, 280
Ireland
  Petrel (pilot boat), 182
Italy
  Carlo, 200, 280
  Raffaeline, 209, 280
Malta
  Nile, 114, 278
Netherlands (Holland)
  Anna, 165, 279
  Arnheim, 278
  Frans and Elise, 170, 279
  Jacob and Cornelia, 279
  Java Whistle, 171, 279

  Maria Elizabeth, 279
  Minister Van Hall, 279
  Van der Palau, 196, 280
Norway
  Iduma, 279
Portugal
  Alexandra and Herculano, 280
  Oporto, 278
Siam
  Amy Douglas, 175, 279
Spain
  Iberica, 280
  Manila, 197, 280
  Neuveaux, 277
  Tores Eliza, 280
United States (Union)
  Alabama, 65–66. *See also* Ships, United States, *Alabama*
  Albany, 44
  Alert, 54, 273
  Altamaha, 55–56, 273
  Amanda, 170–71, 173, 276
  Amazonian, 137, 276
  Anna F. Schmidt, 144–46, 276
  Ariel, photo 131, 93–96, 100, 139, 274
  Bainbridge, 108
  Baron de Castine, 79, 274
  Benton, 123
  Bienville, 3
  Benjamin Tucker, 55–56, 273
  Bethiah Thayer, 114, 275
  Brilliant, photo, 249, 69–70, 78, 81, 273
  Brooklyn, 102, 106
  Cayuga, 106
  Charles Hill, 116, 275
  Chastelaine, 108, 274
  Chippewa: joins *Kearsarge* in watching *Sumter*, 82, 97–98; meets *Kearsarge* in Cadiz, 98; lets *Sumter* escape, 112–13; lieutenant commander of *Kearsarge* takes command, 113
  Cimmaron, 65
  Clara L. Sparks, 91, 274
  Conrad, 139–40, 153, 174, 276. *See also* Ships, Confederate States of America, *Tuscaloosa*
  Contest, 173–74, 178, 276
  Courser, 56, 273
  Crenshaw, 78, 274
  Dacotah: assigned to hunt for *Alabama*, 65; used as alias by *Alabama*, 110, 141, 164, 197, 200; captain complains of weakness in blockade, 113; accused of stopping British steamer, 170
  Dorcas Prince, 120, 133–34, 275

Dunkirk, 71, 273
E. R. Sawyer, 54
Eddystone, 82
Elisha Dunbar, 57, 67, 68, 84, 273
Emily Farnham, 69–70, 81, 273
Emma Jane, 185–86, 197, 277
Express, 145–46, 171, 276
Golden Eagle, 110, 114, 275
Golden Rule, 108, 274
Hampden, 90
Hartford, 123, 126
Hatteras: photo, 131, battle with Alabama, 102–5, 125, 274; wounded tended to, 105–6; crew friendly with *Alabama*'s crew, 107; Welles hears of sinking, 112; recalled, 185, 228, 236, 240, 254,
Highlander, 179, 276
Ino, 37, 114
Iroquois, 55, 108, 110
Iosco, 260
Jabez Snow, 137, 179, 275
John A. Parks, 115, 275
Joseph Hale, 138
Justina, 136, 275
Karnack, 27
Kate Cory, 119–20, 133–34, 275
Kearsarge: photo, 130, 132, 246–47, 250–53; under construction, 8–9; commissioned, 10; puts to sea, 11; violent storm, 12–14, 203; hits land for first time, 14; moves to Cadiz, 15, 35, 97, 142; gun drills, 16, 143, 205; locates *Sumter,* 17; death on board, 18–19, 59–61, 157–58; amputation performed, 19–20; brawl on board, 35, 63; releases ill crew members, 36–37, 63; goes to La Caracca for repairs, 36–37; finds *Sumter* abandoned, 38; crew member killed by shark, 59–61; court-martial, 61, 205; cruises for *Mary Scaife,* 62–63; begins hunt for *Alabama,* 65–66; engine damage, 80–81, 125, 141–42; mistaken for *Alabama,* 82; in dry dock, 97–99, 111, 113, 120–21, 203–4, 211–12; allows *Sumter* to escape, 112; lieutenant commander transfers to *Chippewa,* 113; chases ship from China Tea Company, 121–22; Winslow reports to, 123; change of command, 124–25; chases potential blockade runner, 125; places anchor chain on sides, 126; collides with another ship, 142; crew checks for contraband on neutral ship, 143; chases *Juno* with anchor dragging, 154–57; searches for and monitors *Florida,* 166–69, 181–84, 189–91; crew

fights with crew of *Florida,* 167–68, 183; searches for and monitors *Georgia,* 168–69, 179, 181, 183; takes on stowaways, 180–81; returns stowaways, 182–83; possible attack by Confederate States of America ships, 190–92, 202, 217; recruits new crew members for possible attack, 191–93; loses *Florida,* 193; spy arrives from *Florida,* 194–95; enters Cherbourg, 194, 213–14; observes *Rappahannock,* 195, 202–3, 206–7, 212–13; runs aground, 205–6, 211–12; rumored to be returning to Cherbourg, 210; answers taunts of *Rappahannock*'s crew, 213; learns *Alabama* has arrived in Cherbourg, 213–14; challenged by Semmes, 214–16; prepares for battle, 217; news of impending battle spreads, 218; agrees to fight beyond three-mile limit, 219; Semmes expresses intention to sink or capture, 220; battle, 223–37; battle map, 231; rescue efforts, 238–42, 257; returns to Cherbourg, 243–45; newspapers praise, 254–55; casualties, 255–56; *Deerhound* controversy, 255, 260, 266–69; Medal of Honor recipients, 256; damage report, 258; returns to Boston, 258–59; sinks on Roncador Reef, 259; *Deerhound* controversy, 260, 263, 266–68; chain controversy, 263–64; criticized by Semmes, 263–65; powder compared to *Alabama*'s, 265; name given to succeeding ships, 270; crew list, 287–93
Kingfisher, 115–16, 118, 275
Lafayette No. 1, 77–79, 119, 274
Lafayette No. 2, 119–20, 133–34, 275
Lamplighter, 76, 274
Lauretta, 79, 274
Levi Starbuck, 84, 274
Louisa Hatch, 117–19, 275
Manchester, 74, 81, 273
Martaban (aka *Texan Star*), 177–78, 276
Martha Wenzell, 150, 161, 276
Mohican, 134–35
Monitor, 258
Monongahela, 260
Morning Star, 115, 275
Nora, 116, 275
North American, 3
Nye, 120, 133–34, 275
Ocean Rover, 53–54, 273
Ocmulgee, 50–52, 273
Octorora, 65
Olive Jane, 110, 114, 275
Oraville, 36

Palmetto, 109, 274

Parker Cook, 92–93, 274

Pembroke, 165

Punjaub, 275. *See also* Ships, England, *Punjaub*

Release, 38, 63

Rising Sun, 33, 39

Rockingham: captured by *Alabama*, 200–201; used for target practice, 201; crew members join *Alabama*, 202; target practice recalled, 208, 215, 258, 265; prisoners taken to Cherbourg, 210; crew accuses *Deerhound* of being tender to *Alabama*, 244–45; ship list, 277

S. Gildersleeve, 136, 275

St. Lawrence, 65

St. Louis, 65, 192, 214, 244, 258

San Jacinto, 65, 81, 89–91, 108

Santiago de Cuba, 65

Santee, 148

Sciota, 106

Sea Bride: captured, 149–50; capture said to be illegal, 150; sold and renamed, 152–54; sinks, 154; wool sold, 198; ship list, 276

Sea Lark, 133–34, 145, 275

Somers, 23

Sonoma, 65

Sonora, 178–79, 276

Speedwell, 37

Starlight, 53–54, 273

Talisman, 137–38, 276

Texan Star (aka *Martaban*), 177–78, 276

Thomas B. Wales, 84–85, 115, 261, 274

Ticonderoga, 84, 114, 160, 258

Tioga, 65

Tonawanda, 72–74, 239, 273

Tuscarora: blockades *Sumter*, 17, 23; surgeon assists in amputation, 19–20; forces *Enrica* off route, 33; meets with *Kearsarge*, 38, 80; former crew member discusses Semmes, 58; joins in hunt for *Alabama*, 65–66, 80; commander tells Pickering of lack of Confederate States of America ships in area, 121

Tycoon, 201–2, 210, 277

Union, 92–93, 274

Union Jack, 133–34, 275

Vanderbilt: joins hunt for *Alabama*, 65; carries replacement for Pickering, 99; Semmes warned of presence, 150–51; Semmes concerned about, 161, 163

Virginia, 57, 68, 69, 273. *See also* Ships, England, *Virginia*

Wachusett, 65, 259

Wave Crest, 71, 273

Washington, 111, 275

Weather Gauge, 54–56, 273

Winged Racer, 172–73, 175, 276

Winona, 124

Wyoming: threat to *Alabama*, 164–65; lost crew members in battle with Japanese ship, 165; prepares to intercept *Alabama*, 170; *Alabama* on watch for, 172; learns of *Alabama*'s location, 173; Semmes fears confrontation with, 176; inadvertently followed by *Alabama*, 177

Simes, N. P., 69, 273

Simon's Bay, 150, 161, 162, 198

Simpson, Martin T., 38, 293

Sinclair, Arthur Jr.: given task of winding chronometers, 51, 137; gives instructions on firing a prize, 51; glad for lull in activity, 67, 186; sits on court-martial, 72; sets up feast on prize, 110; accuses McQueen of selling *Alabama*'s coal, 117; relative assigned to Conrad, 139; promoted to lieutenant, 140; present at Cummings's fatal accident, 146–47; meets Semmes on deck, 225; accuses *Kearsarge* of failing to help survivors, 241; disagrees with Semmes's decision to fight, 258; says Semmes knew of *Kearsarge*'s chain protection, 264; shunned by crew, 264; final survivor of *Alabama* crew, 270; on crew list, 281

Sinclair, George, 218, 220

Sinclair, Hamilton and Company, 30

Sinclair, William: boards prize, 71, 94–95; transfers to *Tuscaloosa*, 139; returns to Cherbourg, 218; father meets with Semmes, 220; member of crew, 285

Singapore, 176–77, 179, 185, 276

Slidell, John, 211, 269

Small, Alfred, 78, 274

Small, Samuel, 54, 273

Smart, Martin T., 289

Smith, Christian, 111, 291

Smith, David M., 293

Smith, Goldwin, 168

Smith, James, 177, 285

Smith, John, 163, 284

Smith, Joseph Adams, 191, 206, 288

Smith, Leon, 102

Smith, Sidney L., 287

Smith, Stephen, 289

Smith, William (first class fireman, *Kearsarge*), 289

Smith, William (quartermaster, *Kearsarge*), 256, 288

Smith, William M. (landsman, *Kearsarge*), 291

Smith, William Breedlove (captain's clerk, *Alabama*): introduces Semmes, 42; helps recruit *Alabama*'s crew, 43; sits on court-martial, 72; suggests relocating gun, 165; serves as ship librarian, 186; member of crew, 282
Snow, Jabez H., 179, 276
Sonius, John M., 291
Spencer, William C., 121, 292
Spinney. Lyman P., 289
Sprague, Horatio, 62
Stackpole, John T., 289
Stanley, William, 289
Stanton, Edwin, 260
Steeson, Charles, 85, 282
Steptewick, Christopher, 105
Stevens, P. E., 37, 293
Stevens, Samuel and Company, 178
Stoddard, Eben, 59, 61, 287
Stone, James O., 291
Strahan, Robert, 36, 256, 288
Sullivan, Thomas, 293
Sumner, David H., 61, 257, 287
Sunda Strait, 170, 172
Swift, Edward A., 110, 275

T

Taylor, James, 292
Taylor, John (captain of *Juno*), 155–57
Terceira: *Agrippina* ordered to, 30; *Enrica* enters harbor, 33; *Kearsarge* and *Tuscarora* enter, 80–81; *Kearsarge* catches up with *Juno*, 155; *Kearsarge* returns to, 155
Tessier, Captain, 41
Thomas, George, 141, 286
Thomas, R. C., 94
Thompson, John, 180, 292
Thorndyke, Frederick, 138–39
Thornton, Isaac, 289
Thornton, James S.: replaces T. C. Harris, 124; provides idea to drape chain, 126; buys provisions for crew, 154; orders gunners to fire at fleeing ship, 155; defies port official in Queenstown, 180; prepares *Kearsarge* to sail, 206; encourages gunners, 230, 234; refuses to accept sword of surrender, 242; post-battle career, 260; member of crew, 287
Thouvenel, M. Edouard Antoine, 3
Thurston, David, 69, 283
Tibbetts, Edward (aka Sampson, Edward), 59–61, 292
Tilton, Shadrach, 57, 69, 273
Tirnan, Charles, 142–43, 293
Tittle, George A., 19–20, 288
Townshend, Frank, 175, 283

Trent Affair, 89
Trude, Francis M., 142, 293
Tucker, Henry, 282
Tucker, James, 289
Tunstall, Thomas, 18
Tupic, Andrew, 11, 292
Turner, Thomas, 292
Turner, William, 290
Twombly, Henry B., 144, 146, 276

U

Ushant, France, 189–91

V

Valens, Samuel, 151, 162, 286
Van Dyke, Henry, 36, 293
Van Ness, Walter, 78, 283
Vanderbilt, Cornelius, 96
Veal, Jean, 110
Verber, Jacob, 110, 283
Vessels. *See* Ships
Vial, John, 286
Viannah, Francis, 61, 288
Vincent, Richard, 11, 291
von Meulnier, Maximilian, 152, 165, 175, 218, 281

W

Wainwright, William, 289
Wales,Thomas B. Jr., 115
Wales,Thomas B. Sr., 115
Walker, Baldwin W., 150
Wallace, Edward, 290
Wallace, James, 119, 146, 286
Walpole, Sir Robert, 62
Walsh, Thomas, 92, 107, 286
Walton, James C., 35, 213, 287
Wards, Henry, 292
Warren, James, 108, 274
Washington, D.C., 68, 81, 113, 261, 267
Washington, Treaty of, 269
Watrus, Jason, 288
Watson, Thomas, 177, 284
Weaver, Charles, 133, 275
Webb, J. W., 136
Webster, Daniel, 123
Weeks, Phillip, 193, 290
Weir, Thomas, 151, 285
Welham, John, 163, 284
Welles, Gideon: photo, 128; orders gunboat construction, 8; assigns Pickering to *Kearsarge*, 9; authorizes crew expansion 10; revises orders, 11; commits fourteen ships to finding *Alabama*, 65; businesses lose confidence in, 74–75, 126; sends photos of *Alabama* to North Atlantic Blockading

Squadron, 81; diary entries, 83, 100, 122; reprimands Ronckendorff, 90; revises Pickering's orders, 97; sends Pickering's replacement, 99, 123–24; hears of *Hatteras* sinking, 112; pressured by Lincoln, 122; unpopular with *Kearsarge* crew, 124–25; learns ships changing flags to avoid *Alabama*, 165; orders Winslow to file report, 184; additional guns requested by Winslow, 192; endorses Winslow's plan, 192–93; fears attack on *Kearsarge*, 202; complains about Semmes discarding sword, 239; battle report prepared for, 243; hears of prisoner release, 244; praises and rebukes Winslow, 257; holds up Winslow's promotion, 259

Wells, Marshall, 79, 274

Welsh, James, 151, 241, 283

Wharton, Philip, 151, 284

Wheeler, James R.: melee while in charge, 35–36; sits on court-martial, 61; asked to identify strange flag, 121–22; orders chase, 190; sent to recruit new crew members, 193; placed on *Annette*, 203; member of crew, 287

Whipple, George, 58–59, 241–42, 290

Whitaker, James W., 9, 291

White, Charles, 149–50, 276, 293

White, David, 73, 239–40, 256, 284

White, John, 105

White, Joseph G., 111, 275

White, Thomas, 163, 188, 284

Whiteberry, Peter, 108, 274

Wilkes, Charles, 112

Williams, David, 69, 284

Williams, Edward, 15, 288

Williams, George, 15, 63, 288

Williams, James, 85, 177, 285

Williams, John (seaman on *Alabama*), 283

Williams, John (ordinary seaman on *Alabama*), 286

Williams, John (from *Mary Kendall*), 141

Williams, John (from *Anna F. Schmidt*), 146

Williams, Robert P., 139, 285

Williams, Samuel, 283

Williams, Thomas, 139, 285

Wilson, Frank, 121, 292

Wilson, H., 150

Wilson, James (boy on *Alabama*), 141, 286

Wilson, James (coxswain on *Kearsarge*), 288

Wilson, John (boy on *Alabama*), 163, 284

Wilson, John (crewman on *Kearsarge*), 293

Wilson, Joseph D.: boards prize, 53, 57; places value on prize, 57; meets with governor in Cape Town, 149; expresses concern about battle, 220; asks if he can keep guitar, 221; orders guns to fire on *Kearsarge*, 229; unable to continue command, 230–32; held prisoner, 242, 244; exchanged, 257; notes *Alabama*'s poor powder performance, 265; member of crew, 281

Wilson, Thomas, 136

Wilson, William, 141, 282

Wilt, Edward, 290

Winslow, Catherine Amelia, 123

Winslow, John A.: photo, 127, 250; reports to *Kearsarge*, 123–24; preaches sermon, 125; learns of blockade runners, 141–43; orders *Kearsarge* into port, 142; first experience with crew on liberty, 142; sends out first boarding party, 143; chases and catches *Juno*, 154–56; conducts funeral service, 157; searches for and monitors *Florida*, 166–69, 184, 189–91; threatens to arm crew on liberty, 168; searches for *Georgia*, 168–69, 179; orders *Kearsarge* to sea in storm, 179–80; illegal addition to crew in his absence, 180–81; ordered to return stowaways, 181; explains stowaway incident, 182–83; stowaway report requested, 184; orders *Kearsarge* to Ushant, 189; learns of possible attack on *Kearsarge*, 190–92, 217; extends crew enlistments, 191; recruits new crew members, 191–92; asks permission to add guns, 192; notifies Washington of *Florida*'s escape, 193; ordered out of port, 194, 204; stymied by crew's access to liquor, 195; suspicious of approaching vessels, 202; hires *Annette* to watch *Rappahannock*, 203; orders drills, 203, 205; prepares to capture *Rappahannock*, 206–7, 212; uses newspapers to locate raiders, 207; announces to crew that *Alabama* is in Cherbourg, 213–14; challenged by Semmes, 215–16; discusses battle strategy, 217, 219–20; directed to extend three-mile limit, 219; directs battle, 224–37; sends rescue boats, 237; greets arriving prisoners, 241; watches *Deerhound* run for England, 243; releases prisoners, 243–44; files initial report, 243; defends decision to release prisoners, 244; hears reports of British sailors on *Alabama*, 244–45; reports to Welles, 257; returns to Boston, 258–59; accepts prisoners from *Florida*, 259; postwar career, 259–60; criticized and defended, 259–60, 263–64; *Deerhound* controversy, 260, 263, 266–68; chain controversy, 263–64; defends self, 264–65; commander of *Kearsarge*, 287

Winter, Thomas, 283

Wodehouse, P. E., 148–50, 198

Wood, John, 292
Woodbury, John, 290
Woodruff and Beach, 9–10
Wright, Robert, 282

Y

Yates, Henry, 283
Yeaton, William H., 193, 291
Yeoman, George, 91, 284
Yokohama, 276
Yonge, Clarence R., 30, 31, 43, 107, 285
Young, Charles T., 288
Young, Jere, 289
Young, John W., 289
Young, Joseph H., 92, 274
Young, Silas S., 273

Also by the Author

ESCAPE FROM LIBBY PRISON
by James Gindlesperger

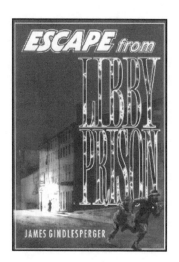

On February 9, 1864, 109 Union officers escaped from the notorious Libby Prison in Richmond by means of a tunnel, dug with only minimal tools. This escape was one of the most dramatic in military history and hastened the transfer of Union prisoners to facilities deeper in the South.

Escape from Libby Prison tells the exciting story of the escape, as well as the escapees' unsuccessful earlier attempts. It also dramatizes the brutal conditions that prisoners on both sides were required to endure. Written with meticulous attention to detail, this story will be of interest to the casual reader and the student of the Civil War alike.

—*Award Winner*—
1996 George Washington Honor Medal for Excellence from the Freedoms Foundation at Valley Forge, Pennsylvania.

Featured in a Discovery Channel documentary and requisitioned by Warner Brothers for possible movie production based on the book.

➢ "James Gindlesperger explains how 109 Union officers dug their way out of the former warehouse in which they had been confined under unspeakably filthy and vermin-ridden conditions that had already driven some captives mad."
—*AB Bookman Weekly Special Military Issue*

➢ "The book should appeal to readers who enjoy stories of men rising to overcome impossible odds, and is accurate enough to keep the interest of the more ardent Civil War buffs." —*Robert Burnham*

James Gindlesperger, a chemical engineer and longtime student of the Civil War, is active in historical, civic, and heritage organizations. He is also the author of *Seed Corn of the Confederacy* and a member of Johnstown Area Heritage Association, American Society of Safety Engineers, National Safety Council, and other organizations. He has won a number of awards, and is a director of several civic organizations.

 ISBN 0-942597-91-5 $24.95
LC 95-43550
6" x 9" HC, 272 pp., Bib

Also by the Author

SEED CORN OF THE CONFEDERACY
The Virginia Military Institute at New Market
by James Gindlesperger

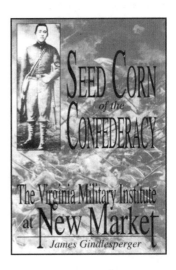

In May 1864 the Union and Confederate armies met in battle at New Market, Virginia, a crossroads town deep in the Shenandoah Valley.

The battle was similar to many others, with one notable exception: The corps of cadets from the Virginia Military Institute was among the regiments on the field that fateful day. Confederate President Jefferson Davis affectionately referred to those boys, as young as 15, as the "Seed Corn of the Confederacy." With only a few individual exceptions they had never been in battle. By day's end they had stepped into the pages of history. Their gallantry gained the respect of veteran soldiers on both sides. Their day culminated with the capture of a Union battery. The victory had a price, however. Ten of their number would die at New Market; more than fifty others would be wounded.

Award-winning author James Gindlesperger conveys the story of the Battle of New Market from the perspective of the VMI (Virginia Military Institute) Cadets.

> ➤ A group of very young, inexperienced military cadets whom Confederate President Jefferson Davis referred to as the "Seed Corn of the Confederacy" gained the respect of veteran soldiers on both sides and walked into the pages of history all in one day.

> ➤ "tells the familiar tale of the New Market Campaign from a fresh perspective. Grounded in historical research, *Seed Corn of the Confederacy* is an informed page turner." —*The Civil War News*

James Gindlesperger has received wide acclaim for his earlier work, *Escape from Libby Prison*. Active in historical, civic, and heritage organizations, he is a chemical engineer and long-time student of the War.

ISBN 1-57249-056-X $24.95
LC 97-6747
6" x 9" HC, 220 pp., 17 phs., 6 maps, Bib, Index

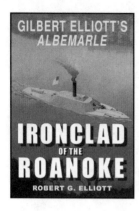

IRONCLAD OF THE ROANOKE
Gilbert Elliott's *Albemarle*

by Robert G. Elliott

Almost every student of Confederate naval history has heard of the ironclad *Albemarle*. She was successful in combat with the Union Navy in several offensive and defensive actions in the waters of North Carolina, but wartime politics prevented her from forcing the Federals to leave Albemarle Sound, North Carolina.

The author has combined research in archival and personal papers to write a comprehensive picture of Confederate naval technology. The politics, the wartime construction industry, and the strategy and tactics of the Confederate Navy are all shown here through the construction and life of the ironclad ram *Albemarle*.

➢ "The record provided by this book on the origin, design, combat career and final fate of the C.S.S. *Albemarle* is as complete as one could ask for. It gives a clear and detailed account of the ship's service in the Confederate Navy, and is likely to become the standard source."—*Warship International*

ISBN 1-57249-162-0 $19.95
LC 94-11747
6" x 9" PB, 386 pp., 42 phs., Bib, Index

CONFEDERATE PHOENIX
The CSS *Virginia*

by R. Thomas Campbell and Alan B. Flanders

In March of 1862, the CSS *Virginia* of the Confederate States Navy destroyed two of the most formidable warships in the U.S. Navy. Suddenly, with this event, every wooden warship in every navy in the world became totally obsolete. Conceived in the fertile minds of such men as John L. Porter, Stephen R. Mallory, and John M. Brooke, and constructed from the sunken and charred remains of the USS *Merrimack*, the *Virginia* in one afternoon changed the course of naval warfare forever.

➢ In one afternoon the CSS *Virginia* changed the course of naval warfare forever.
➢ A fascinating and unparalleled account of her design, construction, commitment to battle, and final destruction.
➢ Constructed from the sunken and charred remains of the USS *Merrimack*.
➢ The heart-stopping two-day Battle of Hampton Roads.

ISBN 1-57249-201-5 $34.95
LC 2001035329
6" x 9" HC, 288 pp., 96 phs., 3 maps, Bib, Index